THE WAKEFIELD PAGEANTS
IN THE
TOWNELEY CYCLE

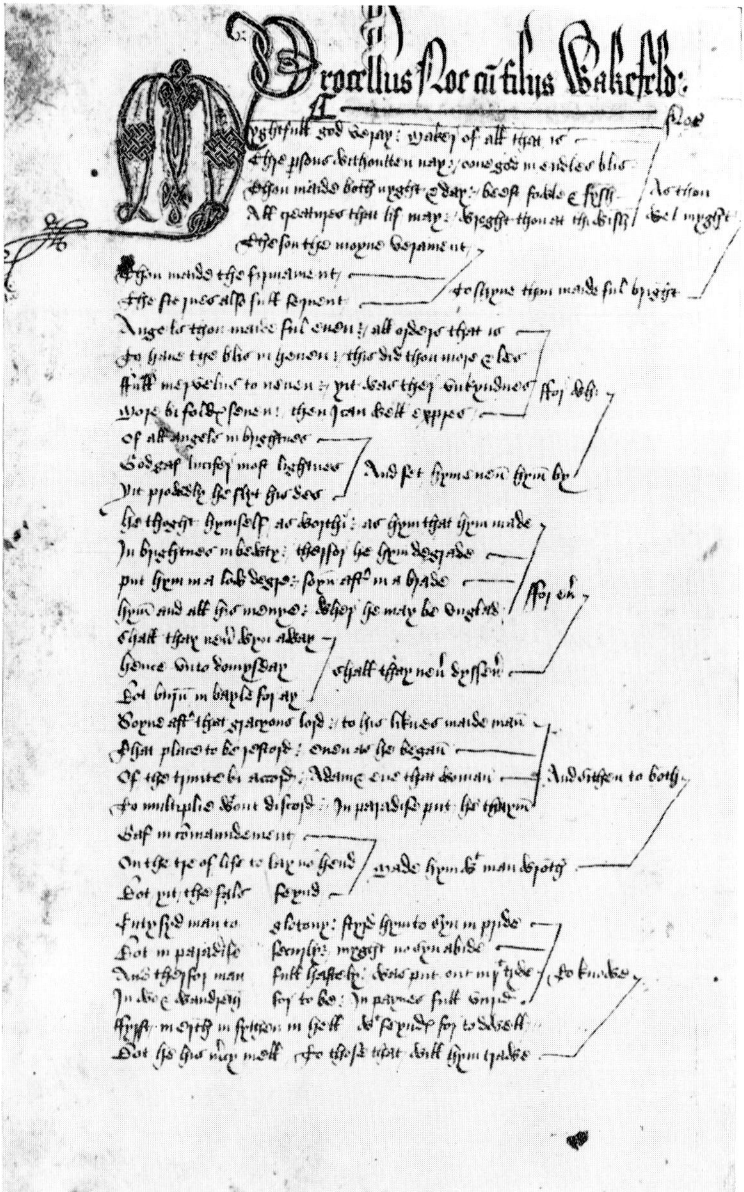

Processus Noe cum filiis. Wakefeld.

Noe

Myghtfull god veray, maker of all that is,
Thre persons withoutten nay, oone god in endles blis,
Thou maide both nyght and day, beest, fowle, and fysh,
All creatures that lif may wroght thou at thi wish,
As thou wel myght;
The son, the moyne, verament,
Thou maide the firmament,
The sternes also full feruent,
To shyne thou maide ful bright.

Angels thou maide ful euen, all orders that is,
To haue the blis in heuen: this did thou more and les,
Full mervelus to neuen; yit was ther vnkyndnes
More bi foldys seuen then I can well expres;
For why?
Of all angels in brightnes
God gaf lucifer most lightnes,
Yit prowdly he flyt his des,
And set hym euen hym by.

He thoght hymself as worthi as hym that hym made,
In brightnes, in bewty; therfor he hym degrade,
Put hym in a low degre soyn after, in a brade,
Hym and all his menye, wher he may be vnglad
For euer.
Shall thay neuer wyn away
Hence vnto domysday,
Bot burn in bale for ay;
Shall thay neuer dysseuer.

Soyne after, that gracyous lord to his liknes maide man,
That place to be restord, euen as he began,
Of the trinite bi accord, Adam and Eue that woman,
To multiplie without discord, in paradise put he thaym,
And sithen to both
Gaf in commaundement
On the tre of life to lay no hend;
Bot yit the fals feynd
Made hym with man wroth,

Entysyd man to glotony, styrd him to syn in pride;
Bot in paradise, securly, myght no syn abide,
And therfor man full hastely was put out, in that tyde,
In wo and wandreth for to be, in paynes full vnrid
To knowe,
Fyrst in erth, and sythen in hell
With feyndys for to dwell,
Bot he his mercy mell
To those that will hym trawe.

PROCESSUS NOE f. 7b.

OLD AND MIDDLE ENGLISH TEXTS

GENERAL EDITOR: G. L. BROOK

THE

WAKEFIELD PAGEANTS

IN THE TOWNELEY CYCLE

EDITED BY

A. C. CAWLEY

MANCHESTER UNIVERSITY PRESS

© 1958
Published by the University of Manchester at
THE UNIVERSITY PRESS
316–324 Oxford Road, Manchester, M13 9NR

First published 1958
Reprinted 1963, 1968, 1971

ISBN 0 7190 0119 6

Printed in Great Britain by Butler & Tanner Ltd, Frome and London

To
WINIFRED
AND
JOHN

PREFACE

This is an edition of the six complete pageants which together form the major part of the Wakefield Group in the Towneley cycle. Although they were probably written by the same playwright and are certainly among the best pageants written for the religious stage in medieval England, they have not been edited as a group before; and two of them (*Magnus Herodes* and the *Coliphizacio*) have not been reprinted since 1897, except by the Early English Text Society in its reprints of the *Towneley Plays*, which it first published in that year. Further, every edition of a Towneley pageant published since 1897 has been based on the EETS. text, without reference to the manuscript itself (Huntington Library MS. HM 1). The text of the present edition, however, is newly transcribed from photographs of the manuscript, and this has resulted in several improved readings.

A lot of scholarly work has been done on the Towneley cycle during the half-century which has gone by since the publication of the first EETS. edition. The Introduction and Notes to the present edition are therefore indebted to many earlier students of the medieval drama. It is hoped that this critical apparatus, together with the Glossary (the first full glossary published for any medieval English pageants), will make possible a better understanding of the Wakefield Group in the Towneley cycle.

In its original form this edition was approved as a thesis for the Ph.D. degree of London University in 1953; and I am glad to have an opportunity now of thanking Professor George Kane and Mr. John Crow, who were my examiners on that occasion, for their painstaking scrutiny of my work and their valuable suggestions for its improvement. It would be difficult to mention everyone who has been indulgent enough to answer my enquiries during the past eight years or more. But I cannot do less than record my indebtedness to the following: Professor Harold Orton, who has guided me through many a philological maze and has been constantly kind and encouraging; Professor R. M. Wilson, whose patience in reading through this book in manuscript was equalled only by the care he gave to criticizing it in a constructive manner; Professor A. Hugh Smith, who long ago was largely responsible for my becoming interested in medieval literature, and who more recently has helped me with 'Goodybower'; Professor G. N. Garmonsway, whose scholarship and friendship I value highly; Dr. P. P. Townend of the Department of Textile Industries at Leeds University, who explained to me some of the allusions to spinning and weaving in the

Wakefield pageants; Mr. T. L. Jones, Secretary of the Manchester University Press, who has kept an expert eye on such things as layout and format; and Professor G. L. Brook who, as General Editor of the series to which this book belongs, has done a lot of indispensable work on it behind the scenes. My thanks are also due to the Council of the Yorkshire Archaeological Society for their courtesy in allowing me to consult the Wakefield Manor Court Rolls in their safe-keeping; and to the authorities of the Huntington Library, San Marino, California, who readily gave me permission to publish my transcript of the Wakefield pageants in Huntington Library MS. HM 1.

Finally, I have great pleasure in thanking the Leeds Philosophical and Literary Society for its generous gift which helped to make possible the publication of this work.

A. C. C.

CONTENTS

ABBREVIATIONS

AB.	*Beiblatt zur Anglia*
EDD.	*The English Dialect Dictionary*
EDS.	English Dialect Society
EETS.	Early English Text Society edition of *The Towneley Plays*
EETS. OS. ES.	Early English Text Society, Original Series, Extra Series
ES.	*Englische Studien*
JEGP.	*Journal of English and Germanic Philology*
LMS.	*London Mediaeval Studies*
LSE.	*Leeds Studies in English and Kindred Langauges*
MED.	*Middle English Dictionary* (Michigan)
MLN.	*Modern Language Notes*
MLR.	*Modern Language Review*
MP.	*Modern Philology*
NED.	*The Oxford (New) English Dictionary*
PMLA.	*Publications of the Modern Language Association of America*
PQ.	*Philological Quàrterly*
RES.	*Review of English Studies*
SP.	*Studies in Philology*
Spec.	*Speculum*
STS.	Scottish Text Society
TLS.	*Times Literary Supplement*
Tolkien	J. R. R. Tolkien's *A Middle English Vocabulary*, designed for use with K. Sisam's *Fourteenth Century Verse and Prose*
YAJ.	*Yorkshire Archaeological Journal*
YAS. RS.	Yorkshire Archaeological Society, Record Series

INTRODUCTION

THE MANUSCRIPT

MS. HM 1 in the Huntington Library, California, is a parchment folio of 132 leaves, 12 inches by 8¼ inches. It contains 32 pageants,[1] some of them incomplete, on biblical subjects ranging from the Creation to the Last Judgment. There are 28 leaves missing at different places in the manuscript: these include the first gathering of eight leaves (the whole of signature A), which may have contained the banns of the cycle; the other missing leaves must have provided space not only for the lost portions of some of the incomplete pageants (e.g. Play I, four leaves of which are missing), but also for three or four pageants now entirely lost. All the pageants from I to XXXI were evidently written by the same scribe at some time during the third quarter of the fifteenth century,[2] but the incomplete Play XXXII (*Suspencio Iude*) has been added in an early sixteenth-century hand.[3]

History of the Manuscript

The pageants in Huntington Library MS. HM 1 are usually known as the 'Towneley plays' or 'Towneley cycle' because the manuscript was long in the possession of the Towneley family of Towneley Hall near Burnley, Lancashire. Professor Wann has shown that the manuscript has the press-mark of one part of the Towneley family library, and that this press-mark probably goes back to the time of the antiquarian and collector Christopher Towneley (1604–74).[4] He also suggests that the Lancashire personal names written on two leaves of the manuscript in an early seventeenth-century hand may be the names of former owners.[5] How and when the manuscript, which in all probability was written at Wakefield, found its way into Lancashire

[1] The pageants in this edition are numbered 1 to 6, but their numerical positions in the cycle as a whole are II, III, XII, XIII, XVI, and XXI respectively. The other pageants in Huntington MS. HM 1 are numbered with large roman numerals, according to their position in the cycle. See the first note to Play 1.

[2] L. Wann (*PMLA*. xliii. 141) dates the manuscript 'about 1450'. S. de Ricci and W. J. Wilson (*Census of Medieval and Renaissance Manuscripts in the United States and Canada*, i. 37) date it '*ca*. 1460'. E. K. Chambers (*English Literature at the Close of the Middle Ages*, p. 34) suggests that the handwriting 'may be as late as 1485'.

[3] Wann, op. cit., 141. Wann's description of the manuscript is supplemented, and one or two details of it are corrected, by M. G. Frampton in *PMLA*. l. 631–60 and in *AB*. xiviii. 366.

[4] Wann, op. cit., 139.

[5] *Thomas Hargraues* (f. 73b), *Thomas Hargraues of Burnley* and *James blake bovorn* (f. 90a).

is a problem which remains unsolved. But the early date of the Lancashire names, which are not those of the Towneley family, makes it hazardous to attribute the ownership of the manuscript by the Towneleys to the marriage of one of them to a Wakefield person at a still earlier period.[1] If it could be definitely established that the manuscript is identical with the official register of the Corpus Christi play which was in use at Wakefield in 1554 and 1576,[2] there would not be many years to account for between the latest known date of its presence at Wakefield and the earliest known date of its appearance in Lancashire.

The manuscript changed hands several times during the nineteenth century after it was first sold by the Towneley family in 1814.[3] Finally, on 8 February 1922, it was bought from Sir Edward Coates by Mr. Henry E. Huntington, who placed it in the Huntington Library, California.

Evidence that the Manuscript is a Register

There is evidence that the manuscript of the Towneley plays is a 'register', i.e. an official text of the cycle, copied from 'originals' of the individual pageants belonging to the various craft-guilds. In the first place it can be shown that the manuscript is a copy; there are many errors in the text which must be due to a copyist. It can also be shown that on at least one occasion the copyist was closely following the layout of his original.[4] Consequently, the palaeographical details distinguishing one pageant from another in the manuscript—variations in the size of capital letters, in the manner of writing the stage directions, etc.—may suggest that the copyist was faithfully reproducing the peculiarities of independent source manuscripts.[5] In other words, the manuscript has the appearance of being a compilation made by copying individual texts of the different pageants; and this is consistent with its being a register.

Again, we know that the manuscript was in the hands of someone responsible for the staging of one of the pageants after the Reformation, for the words *corectyd & not playd* have been written in a later hand in the margin of Play XIX, f. 66a.[6] This marginal comment refers

---

[1] E.g. J. W. Walker's suggestion in *Wakefield, Its History and People*, i. 156, that the manuscript may have come into the possession of the Towneley family through the grandchildren of Roger Nowell, the founder in 1478 of the Nowell Chantry in Wakefield Parish Church, who married a granddaughter of John Towneley.

[2] See Appendix I, pp. 124 ff.

[3] For details of ownership see Wann, op. cit., 139; also de Ricci and Wilson, op. cit.

[4] See note to 1. 271-2.   [5] See Frampton, *PMLA*. l. 646 ff.

[6] First pointed out by J. P. Collier, *The History of English Dramatic Poetry* (London, 1831), ii. 151, 197-8.

to lines 193–200, which have been struck through. The reason for the cancellation of these lines is that they mention the sacrament of baptism and [v]j *othere*—a popish doctrine in the eyes of the Reformers.[1] There are other alterations in the manuscript which show that it was once examined by someone particularly interested in those parts open to objection on religious grounds. Thus in 4.553 the word *lady* (used of the Virgin Mary) is crossed through, and above it is written *lord* in a later hand. In 5.263 the words *a pope* have been largely erased, and there is a cross under the first of these offending words. Lines 328–33 in Play XXVI, which support the doctrine of transubstantiation, are crossed through in red ink.[2] Further, the whole of f. 20*b* has been carefully erased. This erasure, as well as some of the lacunae in the manuscript, may also be due to the removal of objectionable doctrine.

The corrections described above are reminiscent of the more numerous alterations made in the York register in 1568,[3] when the York City Council agreed 'that the book therof shold be perused and otherwise amendyd before it were playd',[4] in anticipation of the criticism or censure of the puritanical Archbishop Grindal. At Chester also, where the Whitsun play had been attacked by Archbishop Grindal, the Mayor and Council tried in 1575 to make the text of the play acceptable to the authorities by agreeing that 'the plaies comonly called the Whitson plaies at Midsummer next comynge shalbe sett furth & plaied . . . with such corrections & amendment as shalbe thought convenient by the said maior [Sir John Savage]'.[5] It seems reasonable to infer that the corrections in the manuscript of the Towneley plays were likewise made by a municipal authority in an effort to counter Reformist objections.[6] This inference, if considered together with the evidence that the manuscript was copied from individual texts of the different pageants, would suggest that the manuscript was an official register compiled for, and used by, the municipal authorities of the town at which the cycle was acted.

[1] The *v* of *vj* has been erased. See Article 25 of the Anglican Articles of Religion.

[2] Towneley XXVI corresponds to York XXXVIII, but the cancelled lines are not found in the York play.

[3] L. Toulmin Smith, *York Plays* (Oxford, 1885), pp. xv–xvi. Chambers (*English Literature at the Close of the Middle Ages*, p. 28) believes that these alterations date from 1579.

[4] A. Raine, *York Civic Records*, vi, YAS. RS. 112, p. 135.

[5] R. H. Morris, *Chester in the Plantagenet and Tudor Reigns* (Chester, 1893), p. 319; see also F. M. Salter, 'The Banns of the Chester Plays', *RES*. xv. 448 and *Mediaeval Drama in Chester* (University of Toronto Press, 1955), p. 51.

[6] For a possible connexion between these corrections in the manuscript of the Towneley plays and the objections levelled against the Wakefield Corpus Christi play in 1576 by the Ecclesiastical Commissioners, see Appendix I, p. 126.

Associations with Wakefield and its Craft-guilds

(a) *The Name 'Wakefeld'.*[1] The name *Wakefeld* is written in red as a part of the titles of Plays I and III respectively:

> *In dei nomine Amen Assit principio Sancta Maria meo Wakefeld* (f. 1a).
> *Processus Noe cum filiis Wakefeld* (f. 7b).

It is clear that these names were written by the rubricator who supplied the titles of the pageants, and that neither is a later addition. But it is not certain what they signify. One scholar has pointed out that the appearance of the name on only two of the pageants, and these not in consecutive order, may 'establish a presumption that the others were not connected with Wakefield'.[2] But it has also been suggested that the title of Play I refers to the manuscript as a whole, and is not meant as the title of Play I only.[3] This suggestion has much to recommend it. The scribe is asking the Blessed Virgin Mary to be favourable to the beginning of his labour,[4] and his words *In dei nomine Amen* are the formula used at the beginning of any solemn undertaking, whether it be the compilation of a 'register', the drawing up of a will or the building of the Ark, for Noah uses a similar formula when he says (2. 251–2):

> *In nomine patris, et filii,*
> *Et spiritus sancti. Amen.*

(b) *Local Allusions.* Apart from the name *Wakefeld*, there are local allusions in certain of the pageants which connect them with Wakefield or its neighbourhood. These include:

(i) *Bery me in Gudeboure at the quarell hede* (1.367). This is certainly a reference to Goodybower in Wakefield, where there was once a stone quarry.[5]

(ii) *ayll of Hely* (3.244). *Hely*, which is doubtless a place-name, may be Healey in the West Riding, between Ossett and Horbury.[6]

(iii) *the crokyd thorne* (4.403) and *Horbery shrogys* (4.455).[7]

(iv) *Watlyn strete* (XXX.126).[8] This allusion to Watling Street

---

[1] For the meaning of *Wakefeld* as the 'field where the wake or annual festival was held' see E. Ekwall, *The Concise Oxford Dictionary of English Place-Names*, s.v., and A. H. Smith, *English Place-Name Elements* (Cambridge, 1956), ii. 234. But there seems to be no evidence for associating the craft-plays of Wakefield with either of the two annual fairs held there at Midsummer and All Saints.   [2] Wann, op. cit., 151–2.

[3] Chambers, *English Literature at the Close of the Middle Ages*, p. 34.

[4] Cf. the copyist's marginal note on the Passion play in the thirteenth-century Benediktbeuern manuscript: 'Sancta Maria virgo assit nostro principio. Amen' (Karl Young, *The Drama of the Medieval Church*, i. 518, note 3).

[5] See note to 1.367.   [6] See note to 3.244.   [7] See notes to 4.403 and 4.554.

[8] J. Hewitt, *The History and Topography of the Parish of Wakefield* (Wakefield, 1864), p. 258: 'The great Roman road, "Watling Street" . . . crossed Wakefield Parish. Remains of this are supposed to be in existence at Potovens, and in that neighbourhood.'

occurs in one of 42 nine-line stanzas inserted into a pageant which is otherwise substantially the same as York XLVIII.

Although these local allusions are confined to certain of the pageants belonging to the Wakefield Group in the Towneley cycle, it will be seen that the homogeneity of the pageants and parts of pageants written in the Wakefield nine-line stanza[1] allows us to infer that *all* of them have associations with the Wakefield area. This means that not only Play 2 (superscribed *Wakefeld*), Plays 1, 3 and 4 (with local allusions), but also 5 and 6 (in which no local allusions have so far been discovered) are probably associated with Wakefield. Similarly, not only Play XXX (with a local allusion) but all the other pageants with revisions in the nine-line stanza may, we suppose, have Wakefield connexions, viz. XX, XXII, XXIII, XXIV, XXVII and XXIX.

(c) *Names of Crafts.* Of the pageants directly or indirectly associated with Wakefield, three have the names of crafts written on them in a sixteenth-century hand in black ink. One of these is Play I (superscribed *Wakefeld*), which has *Barker* written in the right margin, just below the title on f. 1a. The other two are Play II, inscribed *Glover pac . . .* (f. 3a),[2] and XXVII, which has *fysher pagent* written below the title (f. 107b). In addition, two other pageants bear the names of crafts in a sixteenth-century hand in black ink: Play VIII, on which *Litsters pagonn* and *lyster play* are written (f. 21a), and XXXII, inscribed *Lysters pag . . .* (f. 131b).[3]

In *Glover pac . . .* the second word is incomplete because the margins have been trimmed in binding. It is therefore possible that other names of crafts, which were once written in the margin, have disappeared altogether. Even so it is difficult to explain why, if the manuscript contains an official text of the Wakefield Corpus Christi cycle, the names of the performing crafts were not written on all the pageants when the manuscript was first compiled (as they are, for example, in the register of the York plays).

Concerning the craft-names found in the manuscript it may be noted that there are two references in tax returns to the Barkers or Tanners of Wakefield. From these references it appears that they had long been one of the more prosperous trades of Wakefield. In 1247 only thirty-four persons in the town were liable to the Subsidy Tax, and nine of these were tanners, with an aggregate capital of 103s. 6d.[4]

---

[1] For discussion of the homogeneity of the Wakefield Group see pp. xvii ff. below.

[2] See p. 1, footnote.

[3] The last of these is pointed out by Frampton, *PMLA.* l. 649. As Professor Frampton observes, 'by the time this play was entered [in the early sixteenth century], the Dyers had ceased to sponsor Play VIII'.

[4] W. Brown, *Yorkshire Lay Subsidy, 25 Edward I*, YAS. RS. 16, pp. 113–15.

Again, the poll-tax returns of 1379 include sums paid by three tanners of Wakefield.[1]

The Fishers included the fishmongers of Wakefield: in the Wakefield Burgess Court Roll for 1554 the word *fesshers*[2] evidently refers to retailers of fish. The prosperity of at least one Wakefield fishmonger, John Smyth, is attested by his will (1551), from which we learn the details of the land and property he owned.[3]

Altogether, the names of the crafts written in a sixteenth-century hand in the manuscript of the Towneley plays are reminiscent of Leland's description of Wakefield (1535–43): 'Wakefeld apon Calder ys a very quik market toune, and meately large; wel servid of flesch and fische both from the se and by ryvers, wherof dyvers be theraboute at hande. . . . It standith now al by clothyng.'[4] It is possible, then, that the names in the manuscript are those of some of the more prosperous crafts which took part in producing pageants when an effort was made at Wakefield (as at Lincoln)[5] during the reign of Queen Mary to revive the plays of the old religion.[6]

To sum up: there is internal evidence that the Huntington manuscript contains the official text of a Corpus Christi cycle, which was used by a municipal authority. There is also internal evidence for identifying this authority as that of Wakefield. If the title of Play I, in which the name *Wakefeld* appears, refers to the whole manuscript, the localization of the cycle is not in any doubt. If it refers to Play I only, there are still no fewer than fourteen pageants (Play I together with the thirteen pageants written or revised in the nine-line stanza) which are connected, directly or indirectly, with Wakefield and its neighbourhood. Of the five pageants bearing the names of crafts in the manuscript, one (Play I) also has the name *Wakefeld*, and two (Plays II and XXVII) are associated with Wakefield. But it will be noticed that the craft-names, like the place-name, do not occur only in

---

[1] *YAJ.* vi. 150–2.

[2] *Miscellanea*, ii, YAS. RS. 74, pp. 20–2. In Burton's 1415 list of the York pageants *Fysshmongers* is written as a gloss above *Pessoners* who, with the *Mariners*, acted the pageant of Noah and his wife (Smith, *York Plays*, p. xx); but the York register ascribes the same pageant (Play IX) to the *Fysshers and Marynars*.

[3] G. D. Lumb, *Testamenta Leodiensia*, Thoresby Soc. 19, p. 285.

[4] L. Toulmin Smith, *The Itinerary of John Leland* (London, 1910), v. 38.

[5] See A. F. Leach, 'Some English Plays and Players, 1220–1548', *Furnivall Miscellany* (Oxford, 1901), p. 227.

[6] See Appendix I, p. 125. Of the four crafts to whom pageants are ascribed in the Huntington manuscript, two have the same biblical episodes to perform as the corresponding crafts in other towns: thus the York Barkers also performed the Creation, and both the York and Beverley Glovers acted the murder of Abel. It might therefore seem that York and Beverley have somehow influenced the equation of pageants and crafts in the Huntington manuscript. But against this, it should be noticed that Towneley VIII is assigned to the Litsters, while York XI (which is substantially the same pageant) belongs to the Hosiers.

pageants belonging to the Wakefield Group. In other words, the associations with Wakefield and with craft-guilds are not confined to the Wakefield Group but are found in other pageants of the cycle.

In spite of the difficulties, it is not straining credence too far to believe that the whole cycle was probably connected with Wakefield and its crafts. Nevertheless, it was an act of courage on the part of M. H. Peacock[1] to maintain this connexion nearly thirty years before the publication of the Wakefield Burgess Court Rolls for 1554 and 1556, which provided the first external evidence that Wakefield had crafts performing a Corpus Christi play.[2] Even now it must be remembered that these Rolls belong to the middle of the sixteenth century, so that it remains to be proved that Wakefield had crafts prosperous enough by the middle of the fifteenth century—the Huntington manuscript may be as early as 1450—to support a cycle of more than thirty pageants. Unfortunately, there is scarcely enough evidence to prove or disprove the capacity of the Wakefield crafts to do this. But what evidence there is at least encourages us to believe that the guilds of Wakefield were prosperous enough by the second half of the fifteenth century to 'bring forth' the cycle preserved in the Huntington manuscript.[3]

THE WAKEFIELD GROUP

The six complete pageants included in what is known as the Wakefield Group in the Towneley cycle[4] occupy the following folios of the manuscript: Play 1 (*Mactacio Abel*), 3a–7a; 2 (*Processus Noe cum filiis*), 7b–12b; 3 (*Pagina pastorum*), 32b–38a; 4 (*Alia eorundem*), 38a–46b;[5] 5 (*Magnus Herodes*), 55a–60a; 6 (*Coliphizacio*), 73b–78b. There is cumulative evidence that all these pageants, with the possible exception of parts of the *Mactacio Abel*, are by one and the

---

[1] Peacock first put forward the claims of Wakefield to be considered as the home of the Towneley plays in 1900, when his article in *YAJ*. xv. 94–103 was published. His last contribution on the same subject was a letter in *TLS*., 7 June 1928, 431. He was even more successful in demolishing the claims of Whalley or Widkirk (Woodkirk) to be considered as the place of presentation. This he does so effectively in *Anglia*, xxiv. 509–24 that it is unnecessary to reconsider the evidence for connecting either of these places with the Towneley plays.

[2] See Appendix I, p. 124.

[3] For example, towards the middle of the fifteenth century a start was made on rebuilding the Parish Church, which by about 1470 was completely transformed into the Perpendicular style. Again, three chantries were founded in the Parish Church during the last decades of the fifteenth century; see Walker, *Wakefield, Its History and People*, i. 186 ff. For the progress of Wakefield in the fifteenth century see H. Heaton, *The Yorkshire Woollen and Worsted Industries* (Oxford, 1920), pp. 77–8.

[4] See F. W. Cady, *JEGP*. xi. 244–62; M. Carey, *The Wakefield Group in the Towneley Cycle*, pp. 237 ff.

[5] The two Shepherds' Plays are now usually known as the *Prima Pastorum* and *Secunda Pastorum* respectively, and they are referred to as such in this edition.

W.P.—B

same dramatist, often referred to as the 'Wakefield Master', who lived in Wakefield or its neighbourhood. Certainly, the dialect of the pageants is appropriate to the Wakefield area,[1] and there are allusions to Wakefield or its environs in at least four of them.[2]

The most impressive single feature suggestive of common authorship is the regular use in five of these pageants of a nine-line stanza to which no exact parallel has been found outside the Towneley cycle.[3] But several stanzas of the same type occur in other pageants of the cycle, viz. in Play XX, stanzas 1–5; XXII, stanzas 5–27; XXIII, stanza 57; XXIV, stanzas 1–5, 56–9; XXVII, stanza 4; XXIX, stanzas 57–8; XXX, stanzas 16–48, 68–76.[4] These stanzas, which look like the work of the same dramatist, are usually included in the Wakefield Group. Within the Group the 'Wakefield stanza' is adapted to many different moods, but is especially effective in rapid monologue and in quick conversational exchange. It is skilfully handled in all the complete Wakefield pageants, and yet there are signs of a growing mastery of technique, which reaches its full strength in the *Secunda Pastorum*.[5]

All the pageants and parts of pageants in the nine-line stanza are further distinguished by a highly original use of colloquial idiom. Nowhere except in the Wakefield Group is there an Uxor who could long for *a measse of wedows coyll* (2.389) or a shepherd who could say to his companions (3.208–10):

> Syrs, let vs cryb furst, for oone thyng or oder,
> That thise wordys be purst, and let vs go foder
> Oure mompyns.

The language of the Wakefield pageants, no less than the metre, is handled—sometimes rough-handled—with a lighthearted mastery.[6]

Apart from this linguistic vitality common to all the members of the Wakefield Group, there are distinct verbal parallels of an unconventional kind which help to link them together. These verbal similarities include the following:

3.58	Sich wryers and wragers.
XXX. 143	Of Wraggers and wrears.[7]
3.64–5	He will make it as prowde . . .
	With a hede lyke a clowde.

---

[1] See p. xxxi below.   [2] See p. xiv above.   [3] See Appendix II, p. 127.
[4] For these and all other references to parts of pageants in the nine-line stanza see EETS.
[5] See Appendix II, p. 128.
[6] For the use of language in the Wakefield Group see p. xxvii below.
[7] Cf. 'Wreieres and wrobberes', *Havelok* 39; see G. V. Smithers, *Archivum Linguisticum*, vi. 74–7.

XXX. 262–3 She can make it full prowde . . .
              Hir hede as hy as a clowde.

3.206–7   Thou has euer bene curst syn we met togeder.
              Now in fayth, if I durst, ye ar euen my broder.
6.379–80   Well had thou thi name, for thou was euer curst.
              Sir, I myght say the same to you, if I durst.

3.271   Godys forbot thou spart.
XXX. 254   Goddys forbot thou sparte.[1]

3.321   That betokyns yond starne.
4.654   That betokyns yond starne.

3.459   Hayll, the worthyst of all.
5.71   Hayll, the worthyest of all.

3.467   Hayll, lytyll tyn mop.
4.724   Hayll, lytyll tyne mop.

3.468   Hayll! Bot oone drop of grace at my nede.
5.265–6   thou shall haue a drope
              Of my good grace.

3.470   Of oure crede thou art crop.
4.725   Of oure crede thou art crop.

3.471,5   This ball . . .
              To play the withall.
4.734–5   I bryng the bot a ball:
              Haue and play the withall.

4.526   Outt, thefys, fro my wonys.
5.229   Outt, thefys, fro my wonys.

6.136–7   Illa-hayll was thou borne . . . or to-morne.
XXX. 606–7 Illa haill were ye borne . . . or to morne.

6.139   Now wols-hede and outhorne on the be tane.
XXX. 605   Blaw, wolfys-hede and oute-horne.

Several of these verbal parallels occur, it will be seen, in Plays 3 and 4, which are also linked by a close similarity in structure. Further, Play 4 contains what appears to be an allusion to the main comic incident of Play 3. For Mak's mention of Gybon Waller and of John Horne who *made all the garray* (4.564) may very well hark back to John Horne of the *Prima Pastorum* and his quarrel with Gyb over an imaginary flock of sheep.

---

[1] Cf. 'God shilde that ye spare' in *Shipman's Tale* (*Cant. Tales*, VII. 286).

To the above features shared by the members of the Wakefield Group must be added a lively use of gesture and action,[1] an outspoken criticism of contemporary abuses, a bold rehandling of secular material for comic purposes, and an unusual skill in characterization. Thus the attack on the oppressive practices of the *gentlery-men* and their hirelings in the Shepherds' Plays is paralleled by the attack on tyranny in the *Magnus Herodes* and by the bitter satire on corrupt ecclesiastical lawyers in the *Coliphizacio*. An enterprising use of non-biblical materials for comedy is found not only in the part played by the termagant Uxor of popular tradition (Play 2), but in the folk-tale of the madmen of Gotham (Play 3) and of the trick to conceal the stolen sheep (Play 4), as well as in the identification of the Buffeting with the ancient game of Hot Cockles (Play 6). Again, the characterization of non-biblical persons like Uxor, Mak, and Gyll is obviously vitalized by a shrewd observation of human beings and their behaviour. But this is no less true of a biblical character like Herod, who is distinguished by a vitality and psychological truth which could not have sprung from purely literary sources. The ranting Herod of medieval tradition is recreated as a contemporary magnate. He graciously offers *grith* to the barons who will pay him homage. In his imagination the three kings of the Epiphany are planning an alliance with Christ which may result in his own downfall: he lives in a world of intrigue and counter-intrigue, of ruthless means and bloody ends. His rodomontade is a reflex of his overweening ambition; his fear, greed and anger find their natural outlet in verbal violence and abuse.

One man, possessed of remarkable gifts, seems to have chosen to dramatize some of the most critical happenings in man's spiritual history: the first murder, the Deluge, the Nativity, the Massacre of the Innocents, the Buffeting. The legends which had grown up round these events, leavened by his own imagination, gave him opportunities for a humorous and realistic treatment of the scriptural narrative and for a wide survey of the society of his day. But his lively exploitation of non-biblical materials never once makes him lose sight of the rebellion of sinful man against God, which is one of the basic themes of the Christian interpretation of history and therefore of the Corpus Christi cycle.

Mactacio Abel

The authorship of the *Mactacio Abel* presents a special problem. Most scholars are of the opinion that it is an old play which has undergone thorough revision, and that some of this revision is the work of

---

[1] See p. xxvii below.

the Wakefield Master.[1] The bewildering variety of metrical forms in this pageant points to revision.[2] The favourite stanza of the Wakefield playwright is used near the end of the pageant (450–62), and the concluding verses have nearly the same structure.[3] But apart from this brief appearance of the Wakefield stanza, 'the extraordinary boldness of the play, and the character of its humour, make it difficult to dissociate it from the work of the author of the Shepherds' Plays'.[4]

However, there is no general agreement about the extent of the Wakefield author's contributions. Several attempts have been made to separate his work from the older pageant he is supposed to have revised; but none of them is convincing. If we hold that all the regular couplets in the *Mactacio Abel*, in which the serious action is developed, belonged to the older pageant,[5] we are bound to deprive the Wakefield playwright of what seems to be some of his most characteristic work— for example, the realistic picture in lines 182 ff. of Cain tithing *wrang, and of the warst*. Or, if we distinguish between the Garcio of the stanzas at the beginning of the pageant and the Garcio of the irregular couplets near the end, and try to maintain that only the first of these is subtle enough to be the work of the Wakefield Master,[6] we begin to wonder whether the Garcio of the irregular couplets (418 ff.) really is less subtly drawn. For Garcio's mocking asides are cleverly interpolated into Cain's bogus proclamation of pardon, and must have been even more amusing on the stage than they are to read. They are certainly worthy of the Wakefield author's comic talent, and could very well be his work.

Whatever his exact contribution to the *Mactacio Abel* may have been, it is not surprising that he was attracted by the story of Cain. For Cain was not only the first murderer but the founder of the earthly city,[7] and so the beginner of the struggle between the city of man and the city of God which the Wakefield playwright has dramatized so powerfully in pageants like the *Magnus Herodes* and *Coliphizacio*.

INFLUENCES ON THE WAKEFIELD PAGEANTS

Although the raw materials of the Wakefield pageants are as variegated as life itself, it is clear that the Christian tradition is the dominant influence on these pageants.

---

[1] One dissentient opinion is that of E. K. Chambers, *English Literature at the Close of the Middle Ages*, p. 41.   [2] See Appendix II, p. 129.   [3] See note to 1.463–70.
[4] A. W. Pollard's Introduction to EETS., p. xxii.
[5] A view put forward by M. C. Lyle, *The Original Identity of the York and Towneley Cycles*, p. 95. Cf. Cady (*JEGP*. xi. 259–60), who believes that the older pageant was written in stanzas.
[6] The opinion of M. G. Frampton, *PMLA*. lii. 900.
[7] St. Augustine, *De Civitate Dei*, xv. 1 ff.

The Towneley cycle, like every other Corpus Christi cycle, is firmly based on the Vulgate and on the patristic interpretation of scriptural history; together these give unity of meaning to the whole cycle and admit it to full membership of the Christian arts in the Middle Ages. Further, in several pageants can be seen the influence of the Christian liturgy: for example, the liturgical Christmas plays in Latin have helped to determine certain features of the Shepherds' and Herod pageants in the Towneley cycle, just as in the other English cycles.[1]

Sometimes, however, there are verbal similarities between the Towneley pageants and the corresponding pageants in other cycles which are striking enough to suggest not merely their descent from a remote liturgical play in Latin, but some kind of vernacular connexion between them. It is possible to account for these similarities by supposing that one English cycle has borrowed from another, or even that both are derived from the same parent cycle.[2] But such similarities may also be due on occasion to the use by different playwrights of the same vernacular source. Thus the English *Northern Passion* has left its mark on both the *Coliphizacio* and the corresponding pageant (Play XXIX) in the York Cycle.[3] Again, the English religious lyric is known to have influenced the Shepherds' Plays in all the cycles.[4] Another general influence is that of the vernacular sermon, to which may be due 'similarities [between sermons and plays] in the actual handling of the matter, the details of certain characters and topics, the very texture and language'.[5] The close connexion which evidently existed between the dramatic cycles and other kinds of religious

---

[1] See F. W. Cady, *PMLA*. xxiv. 419–69; M. H. Marshall, *PMLA*. lvi. 962–91. A bolder claim is made by E. M. Clark (*Orate Fratres*, xvi. 69–79), who maintains that the liturgy not only influenced individual pageants of the Towneley cycle but determined the structure of the cycle as a whole.

[2] Both these explanations have been offered to account for the verbal and structural similarities between pageants of the Towneley cycle and those of the York cycle. Thus Towneley VIII, XVIII, XXV, XXVI and XXX, which are substantially the same as York XI, XXII, XXXVII, XXXVIII and XLVIII respectively, are generally believed to have been borrowed from York. M. C. Lyle (*The Original Identity of the York and Towneley Cycles*) argues in favour of a parent cycle for York and Towneley, and her hypothesis is supported by Hardin Craig, *English Religious Drama of the Middle Ages*, pp. 214 ff. But her lists of resemblances between the pageants of the Wakefield Group and the corresponding York pageants are not impressive enough to suggest more than a loose and indefinable vernacular connexion between them; see Lyle, op. cit., 63, 73, 87, 93.

[3] Lyle, op. cit., 18–19.   [4] See note to 3.458 ff.

[5] G. R. Owst, *Literature and Pulpit in Medieval England*, p. 485. This is an extreme view of the influence of the vernacular sermon on English religious drama. We can agree with Professor Owst's opinion that in the sermon is found that 'free dramatic interpretation of human life and conduct' (op. cit., 491) which also distinguishes the vernacular drama at its best, without necessarily agreeing with him that the sermon was the only, or even the main, source of the dramatist's inspiration.

literature in the vernacular reminds us that 'the plays are not isolated phenomena springing from a Latin Bible, Latin Apocrypha, etc., detached from English literature, but that the dramatists, like the lyric poets, drew from the common store of English tradition'.[1]

The apocryphal writings and the legends which grew up round the biblical narrative are an integral part of the Christian tradition in the Middle Ages. The influence of the New Testament apocrypha on the Wakefield Group is slight, and seems to be confined to the *Magnus Herodes* and *Coliphizacio*.[2] But the medieval legends concerning Cain and the ancient story of Uxor's truculence have an important part to play in the *Mactacio Abel* and *Processus Noe*.[3]

Next in importance to the influence of the Christian tradition and the legends it attracted to itself is that of popular material such as proverbs, folk-tales and folk-drama. The pageants of the Wakefield Group are rich in proverbs. The rustic trots out a homely English proverb (1.436):

> ill-spon weft ay comes foule out.

The 'man of astate' quotes a well-known Latin proverb (6.143–4):

> *Et omnis qui tacet*
> *Hic consentire videtur.*

There are indeed so many proverbs used in these pageants that an attempt has actually been made to determine the extent of the Wakefield author's work on the basis of the proverbial content of any given pageant.[4] A traditional tale of the men of Gotham and the story of Moll and her pitcher of milk contribute to the comedy of the *Prima Pastorum*,[5] while a folk-tale of a sheep-stealer and the trick to conceal his theft is the main comic episode of the *Secunda Pastorum*.[6]

The influence of folk-drama is harder to determine. But the Christian liturgy and liturgical drama, and so inevitably the Corpus Christi cycles derived from them, all seem to have absorbed the pre-Christian ritual pattern of conflict between good and evil, of the death and victorious resurrection of the royal hero-god, which is preserved in fragmentary form in folk-drama, and especially in the mummers' plays.[7] Given this identity of basic pattern, it is reasonable to suppose that medieval folk-drama coalesced with and made an impression on

---

[1] F. A. Foster, *The Northern Passion*, EETS. OS. 147, p. 101.

[2] See notes to 5.244, 6.82–6, 91–2, 103.

[3] See notes to 1.192 ff., 324, and 2.300 ff.

[4] B. J. Whiting, *Proverbs in the Earlier English Drama* (Cambridge, Mass., 1938), p. 22.

[5] See notes to 3.101 ff., 153–60.   [6] See note to 4.190 ff.

[7] All the mummers' plays of St. George, for example, have as their central theme a symbolic death and resurrection. But these plays, it should be remembered, are represented by late and often very corrupt texts.

the Corpus Christi cycles.[1] In particular, it is likely that some of the comic elements in the Corpus Christi pageants show the influence of medieval folk-drama or festival.[2] Thus the parody of the Nativity in the *Secunda Pastorum* is comparable with the burlesque ceremonies enacted on the Feast of Fools,[3] when the folk spirit of revelry found untrammelled expression. There is an important difference between them, it is true, since in the Feast of Fools an irreverent comic use was made of sacred ritual, while in the *Secunda Pastorum* the comedy is subservient to the sacred theme it so closely parallels. Nevertheless, it is plain that the spirit of nonsense has infected the Wakefield playwright, who wrote his pageants for Corpus Christi day, just as it did the subdeacons who played the fool on the feast of the Circumcision. Nor is there anything unique about the juxtaposition of religion and comedy in the Corpus Christi pageants; the comic scenes in the Wakefield pageants are of a piece with the marginal babewyns of the Gorleston Psalter,[4] the mitred fox preaching to a congregation of hens on a misericord at Boston, and the monkey's funeral (with a cock reading the service) in the nave windows of York Minster. In fact, the 'mixing of the story of the redemption with horse-play and farce . . . is seen to be the natural expression of medieval life and thought'.[5]

In this summary review of the more important influences at work on the Wakefield Group it is unnecessary to mention more than a few of the details of contemporary life which have found their way into the pageants. Local topography and place-names, disputes over rights of common, economic grievances, aristocratic and plebeian dishes, digs at corrupt churchmen, tyrannophobia, music, spinning, night-spells, cock-fighting, skittles—these are some of the endless ramifications of medieval life and thought and superstition in the Wakefield pageants.[6] The essential meaning of all these diverse elements, pagan, secular, and divine, is to be found in their author's fusion of them into a Christian pattern.

Finally, it should be remembered that the Wakefield plays are both guild pageants and Corpus Christi pageants. As guild pageants they were written for, and acted by, master craftsmen organized in societies

---

[1] See R. J. E. Tiddy, *The Mummers' Play* (Oxford, 1923), pp. 90 ff.; E. K. Chambers, *The English Folk-Play* (Oxford, 1933), pp. 160 ff.; E. O. James, *Christian Myth and Ritual* (London, 1933), pp. 268–9; two articles by John Speirs in *Scrutiny*, xviii. 86–117, 246–65; Arthur Brown, 'Folklore Elements in the Medieval Drama', *Folk-Lore*, lxiii. 65–78.

[2] See notes to 1.37, 438, 5.98–9.

[3] E. K. Chambers, *The Mediaeval Stage*, i. 274 ff.

[4] Joan Evans, *English Art 1307–1461* (Oxford, 1949), pp. 39–40.

[5] F. M. Tisdel, *JEGP*. v. 340.

[6] See notes to 1.367, 3.244, 4.455; 3.101 ff.; 4.33; 3.211 ff.; 6.46; 5.80 ff.; 3.414, 4.657; 2.364; 3.292–5, 4.265–8; 6.354–5, 408.

which achieved a union of secular and religious activities no less remarkable than that to be found in the Wakefield Group.[1] As Corpus Christi pageants they were written for, and acted on, the annual festival commemorating the Mass and celebrating the Real Presence of Christ in the Blessed Sacrament. The Corpus Christi play was, indeed, a grand occasional piece; and, in keeping with the occasion, it took the form of an elaborate dramatic presentation of 'every phase of the Christian story as a commentary on the daily ritual of the Mass'.[2]

THE STAGING OF THE PAGEANTS

There are grounds for believing that the Wakefield Corpus Christi pageants, like those of York and Chester, were acted processionally. The evidence is provided by the Wakefield Burgess Court 'paynes' for 1556,[3] some of which are strongly reminiscent of the Mayor's 'Proclamacio ludi corporis cristi' at York (1415).[4] Thus at York every player must 'be redy in his pagiaunt at convenyant tyme, that is to say, at the mydhowre betwix iiij[th] and v[th] of the cloke in the mornynge', and likewise at Wakefield every player is enjoined to 'be redy in his pagyaunt at setled tyme before 5 of ye clocke in ye mornynge'. Again, the York injunction that 'men yat bryngs furth pacentes yat yai play at the places yat is assigned yerfore and nowere elles' recalls the 'payne' imposed at Wakefield that the 'players playe where setled and no where els'. Although not as explicit as its York counterpart, the Wakefield 'payne' almost certainly refers to the different 'stations' at which the pageants were acted in turn.

Apart from this external evidence for processional presentation, the pageants themselves give some idea of the manner in which they were 'brought forth'. To begin with, there are no convincing indications that the Wakefield pageants were acted indoors. References to *flett* 'floor' (2.223), *dowore* 'door' (4.362), and *wonys* 'dwelling' (4.526, 5.169, etc.) must be taken very literally before they can be used as evidence of indoor presentation.[5] There are more reliable indications that the pageants were acted on a stage which represented more than one locality, so that the action could go forward without the actors

---

[1] C. Dawson (*Religion and the Rise of Western Culture*, London, 1950, p. 207) says of the medieval trade-guild: 'The gild chantry, the provision of prayers and masses for deceased brethren, and the performance of pageants and mystery plays on the great feasts were no less functions of the gild than the common banquet, the regulation of work and wages, the giving of assistance to fellow gild-men in sickness or misfortune and the right to participate in the government of the city.'

[2] James, op. cit., 264.   [3] See Appendix I, p. 124.   [4] See Smith, *York Plays*, p. xxxiv.

[5] As they are by Walker, *Wakefield, Its History and People*, i. 150–1.

having to leave the stage.[1] It will be noticed that much of the action
in the Wakefield pageants is divided between two groups of people
who are supposed to be in different localities. By grouping the actors
at opposite ends of the stage it would be possible for an actor to go
from one locality to another without doing more than cross the stage.
In the *Processus Noe*, for example, there is constant coming and going
between the Ark and the hill where Uxor does her spinning. Appro-
priately enough, it is Uxor who remains seated and Noah who does
the running about, and the Latin stage direction before line 190 in
the *Processus Noe* calls our attention to this: *Tunc perget ad vxorem.*
Similarly, in the *Secunda Pastorum* a lot of the action alternates
between the open fields,[2] where the shepherds meet, and Mak's
cottage. Here also the two localities were probably represented by
different parts of the stage, so that movement from one to the other
would simply mean crossing the stage. The grouping and movement
of the actors make the same sort of pattern in the *Magnus Herodes*
and *Coliphizacio*. Here the great men remain in one place, and their
subordinates come and go as required.[3]

The normal stage could be extended in at least two different ways—
by the use of the street or ground-level and of a balcony or upper stage.
Both of these devices seem to have been used in the *Mactacio Abel*.
If Cain's plough horses and oxen were real animals, they must have
made their entrance on an open space close by the stage.[4] Again, there
is reason to believe that God spoke to Cain from a balcony representing
heaven.[5]

Descriptive details in the text no doubt often took the place of
scenery: Uxor sits *on this hill* (2.337), Gyb walks *ouer the corne* (3.83),
Coll says he will *abyde on a balk, or sytt on a stone* (4.49), and the
Angel's radiance lights up the wood (4.650). On the other hand, a
large-scale model of a ship, or a pageant-wagon with the super-
structure of a ship, would have provided a strong scenic attraction for
the *Processus Noe*.[6]

It appears that animals were sometimes used, as well as properties
of various kinds. Eight animals pull Cain's plough, and Slawpase of

[1] This method of simultaneous staging was used in liturgical performances; see Allardyce
Nicoll, *The Development of the Theatre* (London, 1937), p. 65.

[2] See note to 4.49.

[3] See stage directions before 5.276 and 6.343. In view of the pattern of grouping and movement described above, stage directions like 'Enter' and 'Exit' should be interpreted as meaning
'Comes forward' and 'Withdraws', without necessarily implying that the actors leave the
stage.

[4] Cf. the Digby play of the *Conversion of St. Paul*, EETS. ES. 70, p. 32. We know that
this play was acted on a pageant-wagon, and that the wagon was placed on a site open enough
for Saul to ride 'forth with hys seruantes abowt the place, [&] owt of the pl[ace]'.

[5] See note to 1.297.

[6] As it did for the Hull Noah play; see note to 2.271–2.

the *Prima Pastorum* comes in leading a horse. In the *Prima Pastorum* the properties used probably included a *mayll* (224), a *skayll* (249), and a *panyere* (281). But it is not always certain whether the things referred to in the text were real or make-believe. It is difficult to tell what attempt, if any, was made to represent the embarkation of Noah's *catall* (2.326). Again, it seems likely that the shepherds' meal in the *Prima Pastorum* was mostly make-believe.[1]

There are a few indications of costume. Thus Noah takes off his *gowne* and works in his *cote* (2.262). Mak makes his first appearance *in clamide se super togam vestitus*, and comic use is made of his 'chlamys'.[2] It is known that care was taken over the costumes in the guild pageants: we learn from the records of the Coventry Smiths' Company that distinctive costumes were worn by the actors taking the parts of Herod, Annas and Caiaphas, and the torturers. We can imagine the Wakefield Annas and Caiaphas, like their counterparts at Coventry, wearing 'myttyrs' and 'a byschops taberd of scarlet', and the torturers dressed in 'jakketts of blake bokeram'.[3]

No-one can read the Wakefield pageants without realizing that the spoken words are continually being reinforced by expressions, gestures, and movements. Thus in the *Processus Noe* the activities of Noah and his wife embrace carpentry, spinning, and brawling as well as the repeated sounding of the flood waters with a plumb-line and the release of the raven and doves. These are their main activities. But some of the minor details of their movements are no less effective, whether it is Noah removing his gown in preparation for his ship-wrighting, or Uxor taking over the tiller from her husband (2.435). On occasion, however, the very absence of action can be striking and significant. In the *Coliphizacio* the contrast between Christ and his tormentors is heightened not only by Christ's silence but by his immobility in the presence of Caiaphas, with his violent words and movements, and of the torturers, who buffet Christ and drive him along like an animal. A playwright who knows when to set his characters in motion and when to immobilize them is an experienced man of the theatre. Such a playwright was the Wakefield Master, who had learned how to hold the attention of his audience, 'nunc silentes, nunc cachinnantes', through a long summer's day.

THE WAKEFIELD PLAYWRIGHT'S USE OF LANGUAGE

The Wakefield playwright draws on a varied vocabulary of English, Scandinavian, and Romance words. It must have taxed his ingenuity to the utmost to find thirteen rhyme-words for each of his nine-line

---

[1] See *Spec.* xxx. 215.   [2] See note to stage direction before 4.190.
[3] *Two Coventry Corpus Christi Plays*, EETS. ES. 87, pp. 86, 88.

stanzas. But he has managed it by pressing into service all the different sounds, forms, and words of his North Midland dialect,[1] in which Northern and Midland,[2] English and Scandinavian,[3] elements existed side by side.

He has a superb command of ludicrous diction and of the language of violence and abuse. He is equally at home in the verbal worlds of the foul-mouthed Cain and the smooth-tongued Annas. He finds the right words to express moods of anger and indignation, pathos and tenderness. Not once does his 'Middle English', or his handling of it, let him down.

He is especially fond of producing comic effects by using words figuratively, as when Noah yells *ram-skyt* (2.217) at his wife, or when Uxor longs for *a measse of wedows coyll* (2.389). His shepherds make comic-figurative play with the everyday words of a shepherd's life: *mangere* (3.201) in the sense of 'board, table', *cryb* (3.208) meaning 'eat', *purst* and *foder* (3.209). Again, the contemptuous use of *barke* by Caiaphas, when he curses the man who first made him a priest and taught him *On bookys for to barke* (6.308), tells us as much about Caiaphas and his attitude to his clerkly profession as a single word can be expected to do.

He is always exploiting the ambiguities of words for comic purposes. We find him punning on words,[4] or juggling with the incongruous meanings of words like *croyne*[5] and *knaue* (4.554). The word *knaue* can mean not only 'boy' but 'low-born person, rascal', so that when the Second Shepherd asks Mak, *Is youre chyld a knaue?*, his question has an edge to it. Mak assumes it to be maliciously meant, for he replies with dignity (4.555–6):

> Any lord myght hym haue,
> This chyld, to his son.

We also find him making comic use of the Southern dialect.[6] It is a welcome change to find a Northerner enjoying himself at the expense of the Southerner's linguistic habits, and so reversing the situation found in the *Reeve's Tale*.

His verbal humour is not always of an obvious kind. The humour of the First Shepherd's phrase *boyte of oure bayll* (3.247), to describe the *Good holsom ayll* he is about to drink, depends upon our realizing that this phrase is a dignified alliterative formula used elsewhere of

[1] See p. xxxi below.

[2] For the Wakefield author's use of doublets in rhyme, in which he exploits to the full the resources of his mixed dialect, see M. Trusler, *SP*. xxxiii. 25 ff.

[3] See A. Rynell, *The Rivalry of Scandinavian and Native Synonyms in Middle English*, pp. 154 ff., 294 ff.

[4] E.g. 6.351.   [5] See note to 4.476.   [6] See Appendix IV, p. 131.

God or Christ.[1] When Herod's messenger pompously announces that his master's realms extend *From Egyp to Mantua, vnto Kemptowne* (5.47), we may not be able to identify *Kemptowne*[2] with any certainty, but we can safely guess that bathos is intended. Sometimes an idiomatic phrase is given a humorous twist which may escape the reader in a hurry. Thus when the Second Shepherd in the *Prima Pastorum* wishes his oppressors *good mendyng With a short endyng* (3.78–9), he is playing a spiteful variation on the saying 'to mend or end'. He does not suggest the mending and ending as alternatives, but wants the *good mendyng* to be followed by a *short endyng*.

In contrast to this comic use of words, the language of violence and abuse leaps out of the verses of both the *Magnus Herodes* and the *Coliphizacio*. Herod's language is indeed the man himself: it is impossible to separate this wrathful, fear-ridden tyrant from his spluttering maledictions. The same is true of Caiaphas in the *Coliphizacio*. But this pageant is also distinguished by its use of legal language. Annas and Caiaphas have been refashioned by the Wakefield playwright as a pair of corrupt ecclesiastical lawyers of his own day. It is appropriate therefore that they should display an easy command of legal jargon.

The humorous and colloquial elements in the diction of the Wakefield author are so much in evidence that it is easy to over-stress them, and to lose sight of both his serious purpose and the serious language he often uses to express it. In the *Processus Noe*, for example, the speeches expressing God's anger and Noah's contrition, which are gravely worded in traditional poetic language, have an essential contribution to make to the meaning of the Noah legend.[3] There is nothing commonplace about the spiritual meaning of this legend; and there is nothing plebeian about poetic phrases like *Beytter of bayll* (2.311) or words like *all-weldand* (2.494) and *anoynt*.[4] Again, in the Shepherds' Plays the tenderness of the adoration scene is achieved by a blend of affectionate colloquial idiom and dignified figurative language (4.724–7):

> Hayll, lytyll tyne mop!
> Of oure crede thou art crop;
> I wold drynk on thy cop,
> Lytyll day-starne.

In the *Magnus Herodes* the Second Woman pleads for her baby in words which are universal in their simplicity and spontaneity (5.350–1)

[1] E.g. in 2.311, XXIII.380.   [2] See note to 5.47.
[3] The traditional interpretation of the story of the Flood—the cleansing of the soul preparatory to its salvation through Christ and His Church—is preserved in the Baptismal Service.   [4] See note to 2.127.

> Mercy, lord, I cry!
> It is myn awne dere son.

In fact, the Wakefield dramatist may be a master of racy, colloquial idiom, but he is not trying to be racy and colloquial all the time. What he is doing is to juxtapose and harmonize the comic and serious elements that all together make up his Christian interpretation of life. He is a distinguished dramatist because he finds the right words and the right rhythms to express many different moods—tender, gloomy, and reflective as well as 'sharp, stinging, defiant'.[1] So far from being a crude gag in his mouth,[2] his language is an integral part of his vision and achievement.

THE AUTHOR

Although the pageants of the Wakefield Group may be confidently assigned to a single playwright of Wakefield, nothing is known about his identity. An attempt has been made to identify him with Gilbert Pilkington, the alleged author of the *Turnament of Totenham*.[3] But while there is no good evidence for assigning the authorship of either the *Turnament* or the Wakefield pageants to Gilbert Pilkington, it can be shown that they have certain features in common, including a similar stanza-form.[4] And even if it cannot be proved that the *Turnament* is by the author of the Wakefield Group, at least it is possible that one work has influenced the other.

The Wakefield playwright was no doubt a cleric or a man with clerical training, judging by his use of Latin and his biblical knowledge. We are at liberty to guess that he was a subdeacon[5] or a chantry priest,[6] but there is little or no evidence on which to base such guesses. All that we can be fairly sure of is that he was neither a friar[7] nor a Lollard.[8]

We may learn something of the man's personality from the pageants attributed to him. His sympathy for the underdog, his sharpness of eye and tongue, his sense of humour, broad, hilarious, and sometimes deliberately brutal—all these qualities force themselves on our attention. He is a man of many moods, amused and indignant, harsh and tender in turn. He has lived an uncloistered life in which people, books,

[1] H. W. Wells, *PMLA.* xxxviii. 517.

[2] See A. P. Rossiter, *English Drama from Early Times to the Elizabethans* (London, 1950), p. 75.

[3] See O. Cargill, *PMLA.* xli. 810–31. Much of Cargill's evidence is undermined by F. A. Foster, *PMLA.* xliii. 124–36. Her reply to Cargill is reinforced by Carey, *The Wakefield Group in the Towneley Cycle*, pp. 230 ff., by Frampton in *PMLA.* xlvii. 622–35 and Trusler in *SP.* xxxiii. 26. [4] See Appendix II, p. 127, note 5; also note to 4.67.

[5] See note to 4.100. [6] See Walker, *Wakefield, Its History and People*, i. 153.

[7] See notes to 3.286, 389–90. [8] The devil Tutivillus is a *master lollar* (XXX.213).

and music have all played a part; his knowledge of men and their nature ranges from king to peasant; he is artist enough to make good use of the most unpromising materials—crabbed legal language, blanket-tossing, and Hot Cockles. Above all, he is an artist for whom life has meaning—a religious meaning. His drama is part and parcel of the great Christian drama which gives shape and purpose to human life, opposing harmony to conflict and love to hatred, but without minimizing the conflict or pretending that the hatred does not exist.

DATE

Date of the Wakefield Author's contributions to the Cycle

The available evidence favours a date during the first half of the fifteenth century for the Wakefield author's work. The use of the musical term 'crotchet'[1] in the *Secunda Pastorum* and the reference to tennis[2] in the same pageant suggest a period not earlier than *c.* 1400. Certain sound-changes, established by rhyme, support a date later than the fourteenth century for the Wakefield Group as a whole.[3] There are grounds for believing that the Wakefield playwright was influenced by the 'York realist', whose work has been dated after 1415.[4] Some of the allusions to costume in Plays 2, 5, and XXX seem to point to a date not earlier than *c.* 1420.[5] Again, the manuscript containing the Wakefield pageants may itself be not much later than *c.* 1450.

While the weight of the evidence is therefore in favour of the years 1400–50, there is no strong evidence for preferring one particular decade to another. The pageants of the Wakefield Group were possibly written at different times during several decades. But it is doubtful whether the chronological sequence of these pageants can be determined at all accurately on the strength of the metrical differences between them,[6] and there is certainly no way of measuring metrical progress in terms of years and decades.

DIALECT

The phonology and, to a lesser degree, the accidence of the Wakefield pageants are characterized by a combination of Northern and Midland elements such as we might expect to find in a North Midland dialect. Some of the Midland spellings are scribal, e.g. the occasional substitution of *o* for *a* to represent the sounds derived from OE. *ā* and

---

[1] See note to 4.658.   [2] See note to 4.736.   [3] See Appendix III, p. 130.
[4] See Frampton, *PMLA*. liii. 86–117.
[5] Frampton, *PMLA*. l. 632 ff. See also notes to 2.224 and 5.357.
[6] See Appendix II, p. 128.

ā(w), as in *sory* 2.211, rhyming with *wary, Mary, tary* and in *knowe* 3.161, rhyming with *lawe, sawe, thrawe*. But the Midland rounded development of OE. *ā* and of *a* before *ld* is also proved original by rhymes, as in *wo* 2.116, rhyming with *fordo, floo* and in *old, cold* 2.60, rhyming with *mold*.[1] Another Midland development established by rhyme is the raising of ME. *-ong* to [ung] in *emong* 2.400, rhyming with *yong, tong, long* (OE. *lungen*).[2]

The gen. sg. of nouns normally ends in *-(y)s*, as in the Midland dialects, but the Northern uninflected form is also found: *woman avyse* 4.342 (cf. *wamans kne* 4.608), *Cryst curs* 6.395 (cf. *Crystys curs* 4.147).

The 3 pers. pron. fem. is consistently the Midland form *she* within the line; Northern *sho*, as a rhyme-word, has been replaced by *she* in 4.235 and by *so* in 4.239. The plural personal pronouns are regularly the Northern combination *thay, thare, thaym* (variously spelt), the last of which is found in rhyme in 2.31 and 5.424.

The verbal inflexions are for the most part typically Northern both within the line and in rhyme.[3] Of the few Midland inflexions which occur, those within the line may be scribal: *byrkyn* infin. 5.63, 108, *doyst* 6.132, *doth* 6.183.[4] But at least two Midland verb endings are confirmed by rhymes: *-en* in (*ye*) *liffen* 1.448 and the pres. part. ending *-yng* in *comyng* 3.30, *lyfyng* 5.12. It can also be shown that certain majority forms of the verb 'to be', attested by rhymes, are Midland rather than Northern, viz. *art, is*,[5] *ar(e)* (Northern *ert, es, er(e)*).[6] Some minority forms of this verb which appear in rhyme are also non-Northern: *bene* infin. 3.353, *wore*, 3.352, 4.510, 6.120, *be* pp. 2.192.

Although there has evidently been considerable scribal dilution of the Northern features of the author's language, the Midland elements proved original by rhymes are strong enough to suggest for the dialect of the Wakefield Group a locality somewhat south of the northern

---

[1] In the Wakefield pageants edited here the *o* spellings for OE. *ā*, ON. *á* predominate within the line, and those attested by rhymes outnumber *a* by a little more than 4 to 1. This calculation is based on the editor's own examination of rhyme-words containing OE. *ā*, ON. *á*; cf. J. P. Oakden, *Alliterative Poetry in Middle English: The Dialectal and Metrical Survey*, p. 21, where it is stated that '*The Towneley Plays* have *ā:ǭ::2:3*'.

[2] For this North-Midland sound-change see Oakden, op. cit., 78–9.

[3] Thus the 1 sg. pres. and all persons of the plural follow Northern usage by having the ending *-(e)* when the subject is a pers. pron. which immediately precedes or follows its verb (e.g. *drowne* 4.132, *teyn* 5.115), but otherwise *-es, -ys, -s(e)*, e.g. *tyes* 1.46, *mars* 3.93, *swynkys* 4.154, *seys* 5.61, *bese* 5.506; cf. *haue, has* (see Glossary s. Hafe).

[4] Cf. MS. *makethe*, changed from *mase the* 3.434 (note). For Mak's deliberate use of Southern verbal forms in imitation of Southern speech see Appendix IV, p. 131.

[5] Midland *is*, which has replaced Northern *es* in 1.229, 2.10, is proved original by rhyme in 1.244, 332, 2.1, 3.262, 453, 5.300.

[6] See G. Forsström, *The Verb 'To Be' in Middle English*, pp. 181 ff., for examples in the Towneley plays.

boundary of the Midland dialect area. In particular, the predominance of the Midland rounded development of OE. *ā*, ON. *á* suggests a locality south of the Ouse and Wharfe.[1] The original dialect of these pageants may thus be localized in the northernmost part of the Midland area, where both Northern and Midland sounds and forms would be used, but where Northern influence would be especially strong. Further, the regular use of characteristic Eastern sounds, e.g. the unrounded development of OE. *a* (before a nasal, unlengthened), *ў* and *ĕo*,[2] points to an Eastern part of the North Midland area. It will be seen that this localization of the original dialect of the Wakefield pageants in the North-East Midlands is consistent with, and lends support to, their association with Wakefield and its neighbourhood.[3]

---

[1] E. Ekwall (*English Studies*, xx. 147–68) finds that place-name evidence establishes the Wharfe-Ouse as the approximate *ā/ǭ* boundary in the West Riding during the later ME. period. J. A. Sheard (Philological Society Transactions, 1945, pp. 184–6) points out that the normal development of OE. *ā* in the living Wakefield dialect is to [ʊə], by way of ME. *ǭ*, but that the Northern unrounded development is still preserved in the pa.t.sg. of OE. Class I strong verbs such as [rɛːd] 'rode', [rɛːt] 'wrote'.

[2] Represented by the spellings *a*, *i/y*, and *e*, *ee/ei*, *ey* respectively. For examples in rhyme see *can* I 4.88; *hill* 2.337, *fyll* 3.197; *heuen* 1.174, *freyndly* 5.324.

[3] The Towneley plays fall within the North-East Midland dialect area as defined by Oakden, op. cit., 12, and by Moore, Meech, and Whitehall in *Middle English Dialect Characteristics and Dialect Boundaries*; see also *MED.*, *Plan and Bibliography*, pp. 8–11. M. Trusler (*SP.* xxxiii. 19) describes the dialect of the plays as 'primarily Northern, modified by Midland, specifically East Midland, and interspersed with some Southern'.

SELECT BIBLIOGRAPHY

Works are listed in alphabetical order within each section.

I. BIBLIOGRAPHICAL INFORMATION

BROWN, CARLETON, and ROBBINS, R. H. *The Index of Middle English Verse.* New York, 1943.

HENSHAW, M. 'A Survey of Studies in Medieval Drama: 1933–50' in *Progress of Medieval and Renaissance Studies in the United States and Canada.* Bulletin No. 21. University of Colorado, 1951.

RENWICK, W. L., and ORTON, HAROLD. *The Beginnings of English Literature to Skelton 1509.* 2nd ed. London, 1952.

STRATMAN, CARL. J. *Bibliography of Medieval Drama.* Berkeley and Los Angeles, 1954.

WELLS, J. E. *A Manual of the Writings in Middle English 1050–1400,* and *Supplements I–IX.* New Haven, 1916–51.

II. GENERAL STUDIES OF MEDIEVAL DRAMA

CHAMBERS, E. K. *The Mediaeval Stage,* 2 vols. Oxford, 1903.

—— 'Medieval Drama' in *English Literature at the Close of the Middle Ages.* Oxford, 1947.

CRAIG, HARDIN. *English Religious Drama of the Middle Ages.* Oxford, 1955.

GAYLEY, C. M. *Plays of Our Forefathers.* New York, 1907.

ROSSITER, A. P. *English Drama from Early Times to the Elizabethans.* London, 1950.

YOUNG, KARL. *The Drama of the Medieval Church,* 2 vols. Oxford, 1933.

III. THE TOWNELEY CYCLE

EDITIONS

ADAMS, J. Q. *Chief Pre-Shakespearean Dramas.* Boston, 1924. Plays II, III, VIII, XIII, XXVI.

AUDEN, W. H., and PEARSON, N. H. *Poets of the English Language: I. Langland to Spenser.* London, 1952. Play XIII (with emendations of text and glosses by E. Talbot Donaldson).

BRANDL, A., and ZIPPEL, O. *Mittelenglische Sprach- und Literaturproben.* 2nd ed. Berlin, 1927. Play XIII.

COLLIER, J. P. *Five Miracle Plays, or Scriptural Dramas.* London, 1836. Play XIII.

COOK, A. S. *A Literary Middle English Reader.* Boston, 1915, 1943. Play XIII.

DOUCE, F. *Juditium.* Roxburghe Club, 1822. Play XXX.

ENGLAND, G., and POLLARD, A. W. *The Towneley Plays.* EETS. ES. 71 (1897, reprinted 1907, 1925, 1952). Full cycle.

GORDON, J., and HUNTER, J. *The Towneley Mysteries.* Surtees Society, 1836. Full cycle.[1]

---

[1] The editors' names have hitherto been uncertain; but see *YAJ.* i (1870), 347, where it is stated that this work was ' Ed. by James Gordon Esq. The Preface by Joseph Hunter, F.S.A.'.

HEMINGWAY, S. B. *English Nativity Plays.* New York, 1909. Plays X, XI, XII, XIII.

KAISER, R. *Alt- und mittelenglische Anthologie.* Berlin, 1955. Play XIII, extracts from III and XXX.

MANLY, J. M. *Specimens of the Pre-Shaksperean Drama,* 2 vols. Boston, 1897. Plays III, V, VI, XIII.[1]

MARRIOTT, W. *A Collection of English Miracle-Plays or Mysteries.* Basel, 1838. Plays VIII, XIII, XXIII, XXV, XXX.

MÄTZNER, E. *Altenglische Sprachproben,* 2 vols. Berlin, 1867. Play III.

MOSSÉ, F. *Manuel de l'anglais du moyen âge: II. Moyen-anglais.* Paris, 1949. Play XIII (abridged).

POLLARD, A. W. *English Miracle Plays, Moralities, and Interludes.* 8th ed. Oxford, 1927. Play XIII (abridged).

SISAM, K. *Fourteenth Century Verse and Prose.* Oxford, 1921. Play III.

SMITH, L. TOULMIN. *York Plays.* Oxford, 1885. Parallel passages from Plays VIII, XVIII, XXV, XXVI, XXX.

ZUPITZA, Z., and SCHIPPER, J. *Alt- und mittelenglisches Übungsbuch.* 13th ed. Wien und Leipzig, 1928. Play III.

MANUSCRIPT

DE RICCI, S., and WILSON, W. J. *Census of Medieval and Renaissance Manuscripts in the United States and Canada,* 3 vols. New York, 1935–40.

WANN, L. 'A New Examination of the Manuscript of the Towneley Plays', *PMLA.* xliii (1928), 137–52.

PROVENANCE

PEACOCK, M. H. 'Towneley, Widkirk, or Wakefield Plays?', *YAJ.* xv (1900), 94–103.

—— 'The Wakefield Mysteries. The Place of Representation', *Anglia,* xxiv (1901), 509–24.

—— 'Widkirk: The Wakefield Mysteries', *Notes and Queries,* 10th series, x (1908), 128–9.

—— 'The Wakefield Mysteries', *TLS.,* No. 1207 (5 March 1925), 156, No. 1216 (7 May 1925), 316.

—— 'A Note on the Identity of the Towneley Plays with the Wakefield Mysteries', *AB.* xxxvi (1925), 111–14.

—— 'The Wakefield Mysteries', *YAJ.* xxviii (1926), 427–30.

—— 'The Wakefield Mysteries', *TLS.,* No. 1375 (7 June 1928), 431.

SKEAT, W. W. 'The Locality of "The Towneley Plays" ', *Athenaeum,* No. 3449 (2 Dec. 1893), 779.

SOURCES, ANALOGUES, AND INFLUENCES

BAUGH, A. C. 'The Mak Story', *MP.* xv (1918), 729–34.

CADY, F. W. 'The Liturgical Basis of the Towneley Mysteries', *PMLA.* xxiv (1909), 419–69.

[1] The text of play XIII (4 in this edition) includes some emendations suggested by G. L. Kittredge.

Cady, F. W. 'The Passion Group in Towneley', *MP.* x (1913), 587–600.

Cawley, A. C. 'The "Grotesque" Feast in the *Prima Pastorum*', *Spec.* xxx (1955), 213–17.

Clark, E. M. 'Liturgical Influences in the Towneley Plays', *Orate Fratres*, xvi (1941), 69–79.

Cook, A. S. 'Another Parallel to the Mak Story', *MP.* xiv (1916), 11–15.

Cosbey, R. C. 'The Mak Story and Its Folklore Analogues', *Spec.* xx (1945), 310–17.

Eaton, H. A. 'A Source for the Towneley *Prima Pastorum*', *MLN.* xiv (1899), 265–8.

Gerould, G. H. 'Moll of the *Prima Pastorum*', *MLN.* xix (1904), 225–30.

James, E. O. 'The Mystery Drama' in *Christian Myth and Ritual*. London, 1933.

Marshall, M. H. 'The Dramatic Tradition established by the Liturgical Plays', *PMLA.* lvi (1941), 962–91.

Owst, G. R. 'Sermon and Drama' in *Literature and Pulpit in Medieval England*. Cambridge, 1933.

Parrott, T. M. 'Mak and Archie Armstrang', *MLN.* lix (1944), 297–304.

Schering, K. *Die Quellen der Towneley-Plays*. Dissertation. Kiel, 1923.

Smyser, H. M., and Stroup, T. B. 'Analogues to the Mak Story', *Journal of American Folklore*, xlvii (1934), 378–81.

Speirs, John. 'The Mystery Cycle: Some Towneley Cycle Plays', *Scrutiny*, xviii (1951–2), 86–117, 246–65.

Stroup, T. B. 'Another Southern Analogue to the Mak Story', *Southern Folklore Quarterly*, iii (1939), 5–6.

Wann, L. 'The Influence of French Farce on the Towneley Cycle of Mystery Plays', *Transactions of the Wisconsin Academy of Sciences, Arts, and Letters*, xix (1918), 356–68.

Whiting, B. J. 'An Analogue to the Mak Story', *Spec.* vii (1932), 552.

Relations with the York Cycle

Cady, F. W. 'Towneley, York, and True-Coventry', *SP.* xxvi (1929), 386–400.

Davidson, C. 'Studies in the English Mystery Plays', *Transactions of the Connecticut Academy of Arts and Sciences*, ix (1892), 125–297.

Frampton, M. G. 'Towneley XX: the *Conspiracio (et Capcio)*', *PMLA.* lviii (1943), 920–37.

—— 'The *Processus Talentorum*: Towneley XXIV', *PMLA.* lix (1944), 646–54.

Frank, G. 'On the Relation between the York and Towneley Plays', *PMLA.* xliv (1929), 313–19.

Greg, W. W. 'Bibliographical and Textual Problems of the English Miracle Cycles', *The Library*, 3rd series, v (1914), 280–319.

Hohlfeld, A. R. 'Die altenglischen Kollektivmisterien', *Anglia*, xi (1889), 219–310.

Lyle, M. C. *The Original Identity of the York and Towneley Cycles*. Minneapolis, 1919.

Authorship

Cargill, O. 'The Authorship of the *Secunda Pastorum*', *PMLA.* xli (1926), 810–31.

FOSTER, F. A. 'Was Gilbert Pilkington Author of the *Secunda Pastorum?*', *PMLA.*
xliii (1928), 124–36.
FRAMPTON, M. G. 'Gilbert Pilkington Once More', *PMLA.* xlvii (1932), 622–35.

DATE

FRAMPTON, M. G. 'The Date of the Flourishing of the "Wakefield Master"'
PMLA. l (1935), 631–60.
—— 'The Date of the "Wakefield Master": Bibliographical Evidence', *PMLA.* liii
(1938), 86–117.
SMITH, J. H. 'The Date of Some Wakefield Borrowings from York', *PMLA.* liii
(1938), 595–600.
TRAVER, H. 'The Relation of Musical Terms in the Woodkirk Shepherds' Plays
to the Dates of their Composition', *MLN.* xx (1905), 1–5.

DIALECT

BANKS, W. S. *A List of Provincial Words in Use at Wakefield.* London, 1865.
BAUMANN, I. *Die Sprache der Urkunden aus Yorkshire im 15 Jahrhundert.* Anglis-
tische Forschungen, 11. Heidelberg, 1902.
FORSSTRÖM, G. *The Verb 'To Be' in Middle English: A Survey of the Forms.* Lund,
1948.
GREEN, J. H. 'Yorkshire Dialect as Spoken in the West Riding during the Fifteenth
and Nineteenth Centuries', *Transactions of the Yorkshire Dialect Society*, i,
part 2 (1899), 54–68.
MOORE, S., MEECH, S. B., and WHITEHALL, H. *Middle English Dialect Character-
istics and Dialect Boundaries.* Ann Arbor, 1935.
OAKDEN, J. P. *Alliterative Poetry in Middle English: The Dialectal and Metrical
Survey.* Manchester University Press, 1930.
RYNELL, A. *The Rivalry of Scandinavian and Native Synonyms in Middle English,
especially 'Taken' and 'Nimen'.* Lund, 1948.
TRUSLER, M. 'The Language of the Wakefield Playwright', *SP.* xxxiii (1936),
15–39.

TEXTUAL STUDIES

CLARK, E. M. 'A Restored Reading in the Towneley Purification Play', *MLN.* lvi
(1941), 358–60.
DUSTOOR, P. E. 'Some Textual Notes on the English Mystery Plays', *MLR.* xxi
(1926), 427–31.
—— 'Textual Notes on the Towneley Old Testament Plays', *ES.* lxiii (1929), 220–8.
FRAMPTON, M. G. 'The Early English Text Society Edition of the Towneley
Plays', *AB.* xlviii (1937), 330–3, 366–8, xlix (1938), 3–7.
HOLTHAUSEN, F. 'Studien zu den Towneley Plays', *ES.* lviii (1924), 161–78.
KÖKERITZ, H. 'Some Marginal Notes to the Towneley *Resurrection*', *MLN.* lxi
(1946), 529–32.
KÖLBING, E. Review of A. W. Pollard's *English Miracle Plays, Moralities, and
Interludes* (1890), *ES.* xvi (1892), 278–82.
—— 'Kleine Beiträge zur Erklärung und Textkritik vor-Shakespeare'scher
Dramen', *ES.* xxi (1895), 162–76.
MALONE, K. 'A Note on the Towneley *Secunda Pastorum*', *MLN.* xl (1925), 35–9.

ONIONS, C. T. 'Middle English *Alod, Olod*', *Medium Ævum*, i (1932), 206–8, ii (1933), 73.

OXLEY, J. E. [*sam* in the *Processus Noe* 320], *TLS.*, No. 1692 (5 July 1934), 476.

SPENCER, H. 'The Lost Lines of *Secunda Pastorum*', *MLN.* lviii (1943), 49–50.

STRUNK, W. 'Two Notes on the Towneley Second Shepherds' Play', *MLN.* xlv (1930), 151.

TRUSLER, M. 'Some Textual Notes based on Examination of the Towneley Manuscript', *PQ.* xiv (1935), 301–6.

—— 'The Language of the Wakefield Playwright', *SP.* xxxiii (1936), 18–19, note 12.

VRIEND, J. *'That all myghtys may* in the Towneley *Secunda Pastorum'*, *English Studies*, viii (1926), 185–6.

WITHINGTON, R. *'Water Fastand'*, *MLN.* l (1935), 95–6.

OTHER STUDIES

BUNZEN, A. *Ein Beitrag zur Kritik der Wakefielder Mysterien*. Dissertation. Kiel, 1903.

CADY, F. W. 'The Couplets and Quatrains in the Towneley Mystery Plays', *JEGP.* x (1911), 572–84.

—— 'The Wakefield Group in Towneley', *JEGP.* xi (1912), 244–62.

—— 'The Maker of Mak', *University of California Chronicle*, xxix (1927), 261–72.

CAREY, M. *The Wakefield Group in the Towneley Cycle*. Baltimore, 1930.

CARPENTER, N. C. 'Music in the *Secunda Pastorum*', *Spec.* xxvi (1951), 696–700.

CAWLEY, A. C. 'Iak Garcio of the *Prima Pastorum*', *MLN.* lxviii (1953), 169–72.

—— 'The Wakefield First Shepherds' Play', *Proceedings of the Leeds Philosophical Society (Literary and Historical Section)*, vii (1953), 113–22.

CHIDAMIAN, C. 'Mak and the Tossing in the Blanket', *Spec.* xxii (1947), 186–90.

HAMELIUS, P. 'The Character of Cain in the Towneley Plays', *Journal of Comparative Literature*, i (1903), 324–44.

LUKE, C. *The Rôle of the Virgin Mary in the Coventry, York, Chester, and Towneley Cycles*. Washington, D.C., 1933.

MARIE, SR. JEAN. 'The Cross in the Towneley Plays', *Traditio*, v (1947), 331–4.

MOORMAN, F. W. 'The Wakefield Miracle Plays', *Transactions of the Yorkshire Dialect Society*, i, part 7 (1906), 5–24.

SHARPE, L. 'Remarks on the Towneley Mysteries . . .', *Archaeologia*, xxvii (1838), 251–6.

SMITH, J. H. 'Another Allusion to Costume in the Work of the "Wakefield Master"', *PMLA.* lii (1937), 901–2.

THOMPSON, F. J. 'Unity in *The Second Shepherds' Tale*', *MLN.* lxiv (1949), 302–6.

WALKER, J. W. 'Gilds and Mystery Plays' in *Wakefield, Its History and People*, 2 vols. 2nd ed. Wakefield, 1939.

WATT, H. A. 'The Dramatic Unity of the *Secunda Pastorum*' in *Essays and Studies in Honor of Carleton Brown*. New York, 1940.

WILLIAMS, A. *The Characterization of Pilate in the Towneley Plays*. Michigan State College Press, 1950.

WITHINGTON, R. 'Thre Brefes to a Long', *MLN.* lviii (1943), 115–16.

—— 'Mak, Op-Signorken and Mr. Hardwick', *Notes and Queries*, cxciv (1949), 530–1.

NOTE ON THE EDITED TEXT

For the arrangement of the nine-line stanza, the use of metrical marks, and the position of speakers' names in the manuscript see the facsimile of f. 7*b* (frontispiece). Only the Latin stage directions in Plays 2 and 4 have manuscript authority; those in English are editorial. The readings and spellings of the manuscript are reproduced except for the emendations indicated in footnotes. Scribal spellings affecting the forms of rhyme-words without changing the words themselves are usually retained, and the correct forms are given in the Notes. The strokes and flourishes added to a number of final letters in the manuscript seem to have no significance and are therefore not reproduced: these include the stroke above final *m* or *n*, the curl after final *g*, *m*, *n*, the faintly drawn slanting stroke after final *d*, *f*, *t*, and the cross-stroke through the final *l* of words ending in *ll*. The abbreviations are expanded without notice. Only two of these need any comment: the abbreviation for *syr*, *sir* 'sir' (both spellings are found at different times when the word is written in full) is expanded as *syr*; again, the hook after final *d*, *f*, *g*, *k*, *t*(*t*) is expanded as *ys*, which appears more often than *is* or *es* when the ending is written in full in the manuscript. Punctuation, capitals, and word-division are modern. Stressed final *e*, derived from OF. *é*(*e*) or *ie*, OE. *-ig*, is printed with an acute accent, to distinguish it from unstressed final *e*, which is usually not pronounced.

MACTACIO ABEL

Garcio (Pikeharnes)   Cayn   Abell   Deus

Enter Garcio, Cain's servant.

Garcio. All hayll, all hayll, both blithe and glad,
For here com I, a mery lad!
Be peasse youre dyn, my master bad,
Or els the dwill you spede.
5   Wote ye not I com before?
Bot who that ianglis any more,
He must blaw my blak hoill bore,
Both behynd and before,
Till his tethe blede.
10   Felows, here I you forbede
To make nother nose ne cry;
Whoso is so hardy to do that dede,
The dwill hang hym vp to dry!

Gedlyngys, I am a full grete wat.
15   A good yoman my master hat:
Full well ye all hym ken.
Begyn he with you for to stryfe,
Certys, then mon ye neuer thryfe;
Bot I trow, bi God on life,
20   Som of you ar his men.
Bot let youre lippis couer youre ten,
Harlottys euerichon!
For if my master com, welcom hym then.
Farewell, for I am gone.   [*Exit.*

Enter Cain, driving his plough-team.

25 *Cayn.* Io furth, Greynhorne! and war oute, Gryme!
Drawes on! God gif you ill to tyme!
Ye stand as ye were fallen in swyme.

After Mactacio abel *is written* Secunda pagina *as a part of the title. In the right margin
opposite the title is written* Glover pac ... *in a sixteenth-century hand. Immediately after*
pac ... *the first stroke of a fourth letter is visible, the remaining letters having disappeared
when the margins of the MS. were trimmed in binding.*
   13 *There is an* e *superscribed by a different hand between* d *and* w *in* dwill.

What, will ye no forther, mare?
War! let me se how Down will draw;
30   Yit, shrew, yit, pull on a thraw!
What, it semys for me ye stand none aw!
I say, Donnyng, go fare!
Aha! God gif the soro and care!
Lo, now hard she what I saide;
35   Now yit art thou the warst mare
In plogh that euer I haide.

How, Pikeharnes, how! com heder belife!
          Re-enter Garcio.

Garcio. I fend, Godys forbot, that euer thou thrife!
Cayn. What, boy, shal I both hold and drife?
40   Heris thou not how I cry?
Garcio. Say, Mall and Stott, will ye not go?   [*Calls to the team.*
Lemyng, Morell, Whitehorn, io!
Now will ye not se how thay hy?
Cayn. Gog gif the sorow, boy. Want of mete it gars.
45 *Garcio.* Thare prouand, syr, forthi, I lay behynd thare ars,

And tyes them fast bi the nekys,
With many stanys in thare hekys.
f. 3b *Cayn.* That shall bi thi fals chekys!   [*Strikes him.*
Garcio. And haue agane as right!   [*Strikes back.*
50 *Cayn.* I am thi master. Wilt thou fight?
Garcio. Yai, with the same mesure and weght
That I boro will I qwite.
Cayn. We! now nothyng bot call on tyte,
That we had ployde this land.
55 *Garcio.* Harrer, Morell! io furth, hyte!
And let the plogh stand.   [*Aside.*
          Enter Abel.

Abell. God, as he both may and can,
Spede the, brother, and thi man.
Cayn. Com kis myne ars! Me list not ban;
60   As welcom standys theroute.
Thou shuld haue bide til thou were cald;
Com nar, and other drife or hald—
And kys the dwillis toute!
Go grese thi shepe vnder the toute,
65   For that is the moste lefe.

Abell. Broder, ther is none hereaboute
That wold the any grefe.

Bot, leif brother, here my sawe:
It is the custom of oure law,
70 All that wyrk as the wise
Shall worship God with sacrifice.
Oure fader vs bad, oure fader vs kend,
That oure tend shuld be brend.
Com furth, brothere, and let vs gang
75 To worship God; we dwell full lang.
Gif we hym parte of oure fee,
Corn or catall wheder it be.

And therfor, brother, let vs weynd,
And first clens vs from the feynd
80 Or we make sacrifice;
Then blis withoutten end
Get we for oure seruyce,

Of hym that is oure saulis leche.
Cayn. How! let furth youre geyse; the fox will preche.
85 How long wilt thou me appech
With thi sermonyng?
Hold thi tong, yit I say,
Euen ther the good wife strokid the hay;
Or sit downe in the dwill way,
90 With thi vayn carpyng.

Shuld I leife my plogh and all thyng,
And go with the to make offeryng?
Nay, thou fyndys me not so mad!
Go to the dwill, and say I bad!
95 What gifys God the to rose hym so?
Me gifys he noght bot soro and wo.

f. 4a *Abell.* Caym, leife this vayn carpyng,
For God giffys the all thi lifyng.
Cayn. Yit boroed I neuer a farthyng
100 Of hym—here my hand.
Abell. Brother, as elders haue vs kend,
First shuld we tend with oure hend,
And to his lofyng sithen be brend.

100 MS. hend.

Cayn. My farthyng is in the preest hand
105   Syn last tyme I offyrd.
Abell. Leif brother, let vs be walkand;
    I wold oure tend were profyrd.

    Cayn. We! wherof shuld I tend, leif brothere?
    For I am ich yere wars then othere—
110   Here my trouth, it is none othere.
    My wynnyngys ar bot meyn:
    No wonder if that I be leyn.
    Full long till hym I may me meyn,
    For bi hym that me dere boght,
115   I traw that he will leyn me noght.
Abell. Yis, all the good thou has in wone
    Of Godys grace is bot a lone.
    Cayn. Lenys he me? As com thrift apon the so!
    For he has euer yit beyn my fo;
120   For had he my freynd beyn,
    Othergatys it had beyn seyn.
    When all mens corn was fayre in feld,
    Then was myne not worth a neld.
    When I shuld saw, and wantyd seyde,
125   And of corn had full grete neyde,
    Then gaf he me none of his;
    No more will I gif hym of this.
    Hardely hold me to blame
    Bot if I serue hym of the same.
130 *Abell.* Leif brother, say not so,
    Bot let vs furth togeder go.
    Good brother, let vs weynd sone;
    No longer here, I rede, we hone.
    Cayn. Yei, yei, thou iangyls waste!
135   The dwill me spede if I haue hast,
    As long as I may lif,
    To dele my good or gif,
    Ather to God or yit to man,
    Of any good that euer I wan.
140   For had I giffen away my goode,
    Then myght I go with a ryffen hood;
    And it is better hold that I haue
    Then go from doore to doore and craue.
Abell. Brother, com furth, in Godys name;
145   I am full ferd that we get blame.

    123 MS. an eld.

Hy we fast, that we were thore.

f. 4b *Cayn.* We! ryn on, in the dwills nayme, before!
Wemay, man, I hold the mad!
Wenys thou now that I list gad
150 To gif away my warldys aght?
The dwill hym spede that me so taght!
What nede had I my trauell to lose,
To were my shoyn and ryfe my hose?

Abell. Dere brother, hit were grete wonder
155 That I and thou shuld go in sonder;
Then wold oure fader haue grete ferly.
Ar we not brether, thou and I?

Cayn. No, bot cry on, cry, whyls the thynk good!
Here my trowth, I hold the woode.
160 Wheder that he be blithe or wroth,
To dele my good is me full lothe.
I haue gone oft on softer wise
Ther I trowed som prow wold rise.
Bot well I se go must I nede;
165 Now weynd before—ill myght thou spede!—
Syn that we shall algatys go.

Abell. Leif brother, whi sais thou so?
Bot go we furth both togeder.
Blissid be God, we haue fare weder.
[They go to the place of sacrifice.

170 *Cayn.* Lay downe thi trussell apon this hill.

Abell. Forsoth, broder, so I will;
Gog of heuen take it to good.

Cayn. Thou shall tend first, if thou were wood.

Abell. God that shope both erth and heuen,
175 I pray to the thou here my steven, *[Kneels to make his offering.*
And take in thank, if thi will be,
The tend that I offre here to the;
For I gif it in good entent
To the, my Lord, that all has sent.
180 I bren it now with stedfast thoght, *[Burns his tithe.*
In worship of hym that all has wroght.

Cayn. Ryse! Let me now, syn thou has done.
Lord of heuen, thou here my boyne!
And ouer Godys forbot be to the
185 Thank or thew to kun me;
For, as browke I thise two shankys,
It is full sore myne vnthankys
The teynd that I here gif to the

Of corn or thyng that newys me.
190   Bot now begyn will I then,
Syn I must nede my tend to bren.

[Begins to count the first ten sheaves,
reserving the best for himself.

Oone shefe, oone, and this makys two;
Bot nawder of thise may I forgo.
Two, two, now this is thre:
195   Yei, this also shall leif with me,
For I will chose and best haue—
This hold I thrift—of all this thrafe.
Wemo, wemo! foure, lo, here!
Better.groved me no this yere.
200   At yere tyme I sew fayre corn,
Yit was it sich when it was shorne:
Thystyls and brerys—yei, grete plenté—
And all kyn wedys that myght be.
Foure shefys, foure, lo, this makys fyfe:
205   Deyll I fast thus, long or I thrife!
Fyfe and sex, now this is sevyn;
Bot this gettys neuer God of heuen.
Nor none of thise foure, at my myght,
Shall neuer com in Godys sight.
210   Sevyn, sevyn, now this is aght—
Abell. Cam, brother, thou art not God betaght.
Cayn. We! therfor is it that I say
I will not deyle my good away.
f. 5a   Bot had I gyffen hym this to teynd,
215   Then wold thou say he were my freynd;
Bot I thynk not, bi my hode,
To departe so lightly fro my goode.
We! aght, aght, and neyn, and ten is this:
We! this may we best mys.   *[Chooses the first tithe-sheaf.*
220   Gif hym that that ligys thore?
It goyse agans myn hart full sore.

Abell. Cam! teynd right of all bedeyn.
Cayn. We lo! xij, xv, and xvj—

[Begins counting the second ten sheaves.
Abell. Caym, thou tendys wrang, and of the warst.
225   *Cayn.* We! com nar, and hide myne een!
In the wenyand, wist ye now at last!
Or els will thou that I wynk?

213 ffor *before* I *in MS.*

Then shall I doy no wrong, me thynk.
[Finishes counting with his eyes closed.

Let me se now how it is— *[Opens his eyes.*
230 Lo, yit I hold me paide;
I teyndyd wonder well bi ges,
And so euen I laide.

Abell. Came, of God me thynke thou has no drede.
Came. Now and he get more, the dwill me spede!—
235 As mych as oone reepe—
For that cam hym full light chepe;
Not as mekill, grete ne small,
As he myght wipe his ars withall.
For that, and this that lyys here,
240 Haue cost me full dere;
Or it was shorne, and broght in stak,
Had I many a wery bak.
Therfor aske me no more of this,
For I haue giffen that my will is.
245 *Abell.* Cam, I rede thou tend right,
For drede of hym that sittys on hight.
Cayn. How that I tend, rek the neuer a deill,
Bot tend thi skabbid shepe wele;
For if thou to my teynd tent take,
250 It bese the wars for thi sake.
Thou wold I gaf hym this shefe? or this sheyfe?
Na, nawder of thise ij wil I leife.
Bot take this. Now has he two, *[Chooses the second tithe-sheaf.*
And for my saull now mot it go;
255 Bot it gos sore agans my will,
And shal he like full ill.
Abell. Cam, I reyde thou so teynd
That God of heuen be thi freynd.
Cayn. My freynd?—na, not bot if he will!
260 I did hym neuer yit bot skill.
If he be neuer so my fo,
I am avisid gif hym no mo.
Bot chaunge thi conscience, as I do myn.
Yit teynd thou not thi mesel swyne?
265 *Abell.* If thou teynd right thou mon it fynde.
Cayn. Yei, kys the dwills ars behynde!
The dwill hang the bi the nek!
How that I teynd, neuer thou rek.

Will thou not yit hold thi peasse?
270   Of this ianglyng I reyde thou seasse;
And teynd I well or tend I ill,
Bere the euen and speke bot skill.

f. 6a   Bot now, syn thou has teyndid thyne,
Now will I set fyr on myne.   [*Tries to burn his tithe.*
275   We! out, haro! help to blaw!
It will not bren for me, I traw.
Puf! this smoke dos me mych shame—   [*Blows on it.*
Now bren in the dwillys name!
A! what dwill of hell is it?
280   Almost had myne breth beyn dit;
Had I blawen oone blast more,
I had beyn choked right thore.
It stank like the dwill in hell,
That longer ther myght I not dwell.
285   *Abell.* Cam, this is not worth oone leke;
Thy tend shuld bren withoutten smeke.
Caym. Com kys the dwill right in the ars!
For the it brens bot the wars.
I wold that it were in thi throte,
290   Fyr, and shefe, and ich a sprote.

God speaks from above:

Deus. Cam, whi art thou so rebell
Agans thi brother Abell?
Thar thou nowther flyte ne chyde.
If thou tend right thou gettys thi mede;
295   And be thou sekir, if thou teynd fals,
Thou bese alowed therafter als.

Caym. Whi, who is that hob ouer the wall?
We! who was that that piped so small?
Com, go we hens, for parels all;
300   God is out of hys wit!
Com furth, Abell, and let vs weynd.
Me thynk that God is not my freynd;
On land then will I flyt.

Abell. A, Caym, brother, that is ill done.
305   *Cayn.* No, bot go we hens sone;
And if I may, I shall be

273 *The verses from here to 335 are written by mistake on f. 6a, so that f. 6a must be taken before f. 5b.*

Ther as God shall not me see.

Abell. Dere brother, I will fayre
On feld ther oure bestys ar,
310 To looke if thay be holgh or full.

Caym. Na, na, abide! We haue a craw to pull.
Hark, speke with me or thou go.
What, wenys thou to skape so?
We! na! I aght the a fowll dispyte,
315 And now is tyme that I hit qwite.

Abel. Brother, whi art thou so to me in ire?

Caym. We! theyf, whi brend thi tend so shyre,
Ther myne did bot smoked,
Right as it wold vs both haue choked?

320 *Abel.* Godys will I trow it were
That myn brened so clere;
If thyne smoked am I to wite?

Caym. We! yei! that shal thou sore abite;
With cheke-bon, or that I blyn,
325 Shal I the and thi life twyn.
[*Strikes Abel down with a jaw-bone.*
So, lig down ther and take thi rest;
Thus shall shrewes be chastysed best.

Abell. Veniance, veniance, Lord, I cry!
For I am slayn, and not gilty.   [*Dies.*
330 *Cayn.* Yei, ly ther, old shrew! ly ther, ly!
And if any of you thynk I did amys,   [*To the audience.*
I shal it amend wars then it is,
That all men may it se:
Well wars then it is,
335 Right so shall it be.

f. 5b Bot now, syn he is broght on slepe,
Into som hole fayn wold I crepe.
For ferd I qwake, and can no rede;
For be I taken, I be bot dede.
340 Here will I lig thise fourty dayes,
And I shrew hym that me fyrst rayse.

God speaks from above:

Deus. Caym, Caym!

Caym.   Who is that that callis me?

---

322 *The scribe originally wrote* I am not to wite, *but* I *and* not *are cancelled in red ink,
and* I *is inserted by the same hand after* am.

W.P.—D

I am yonder, may thou not se?
Deus. Caym, where is thi brother Abell?
345 *Caym.* What askys thou me? I trow at hell,
At hell I trow he be—
Whoso were ther then myght he se—
Or somwhere fallen on slepyng.
When was he in my kepyng?
350 *Deus.* Caym, Caym, thou was wode.
The voyce of thi brotherys blode,
That thou has slayn on fals wise,
From erth to heuen venyance cryse.
And, for thou has broght thi brother downe,
355 Here I gif the my malison.
Caym. Yei, dele aboute the, for I will none,
Or take it the when I am gone.
Syn I haue done so mekill syn
That I may not thi mercy wyn,
360 And thou thus dos me from thi grace,
I shall hyde me fro thi face.
And whereso any man may fynd me,
Let hym slo me hardely,
And whereso any man may me meyte,
365 Ayther bi sty or yit bi strete;
And hardely, when I am dede,
Bery me in Gudeboure at the quarell hede;
For, may I pas this place in quarte,
Bi all men set I not a fart.
370 *Deus.* Nay, Caym, it bese not so;
I will that no man other slo,
For he that sloys the, yong or old,
It shall be punyshid sevenfold.
Caym. No force! I wote wheder I shall:
375 In hell, I wote, mon be my stall.
It is no boyte mercy to craue,
For if I do I mon none haue.

Bot this cors I wold were hid,
For som man myght com at vngayn:
380 'Fle, fals shrew!' wold he bid,
And weyn I had my brother slayn.

Bot were Pikeharnes, my knafe, here
We shuld bery hym both in fere.

372 the *not in MS.*

How, Pykeharnes! scapethryft! how, Pikeharnes, how!
Re-enter Garcio.

385 *Garcio.* Master, master!

Cayn. Harstow, boy? Ther is a podyng in the pot.
Take the that, boy, tak þe þat!   [*Strikes him.*
Garcio. I shrew thi ball vnder thi hode,
    If thou were my syre of flesh and blode!
390 All the day to ryn and trott,
    And euer amang thou strykeand;
    Thus am I comen bofettys to fott.
Cayn. Peas, man! I did it bot to vse my hand.

f. 6b   Bot harke, boy, I haue a counsell to the to say—
395 I slogh my brother this same day;
    I pray the, good boy, and thou may,
    To ryn away with the bayn.
Garcio. We! out apon the, thefe!
    Has thou thi brother slayn?
400 *Caym.* Peasse, man, for Godys payn!

    I saide it for a skaunce.
Garcio. Yey, bot for ferde of grevance,
    Here I the forsake;
    We mon haue a mekill myschaunce
405 And the bayles vs take.

Caym. A, syr, I cry you mercy! Seasse,
    And I shall make you a releasse.
Garcio. What, wilt thou cry my peasse
    Throughout this land?

410 *Cayn.* Yey, that I gif God avow, belife.
Garcio. How will thou do, long or thou thrife?
Caym. Stand vp, my good boy, belife,
    And thaym peasse, both man and wife;
    And whoso will do after me,
415 Full slape of thrift then shal he be.
    Bot thou must be my good boy,
    And cry 'oyes, oyes, oy!'
Garcio. Browes, browes to thi boy!
    [*Cain proclaims the king's peace for himself and Pikeharnes,
    who echoes him in mocking asides addressed to the audience.*

Caym. I commaund you in the kyngys nayme,
420 *Garcio.* And in my masteres, fals Cayme,
Caym. That no man at thame fynd fawt ne blame,
Garcio. Yey, cold rost is at my masteres hame.
Caym. Nowther with hym nor with his knafe,
Garcio. What! I hope my master rafe.
425 *Caym.* For thay ar trew full manyfold.
Garcio. My master suppys no coyle bot cold.
Caym. The kyng wrytys you vntill.
Garcio. Yit ete I neuer half my fill.
Caym. The kyng will that thay be safe.
430 *Garcio.* Yey, a draght of drynke fayne wold I hayfe.
Caym. At thare awne will let tham wafe.
Garcio. My stomak is redy to receyfe.
Caym. Loke no man say to theym, on nor other—
Garcio. This same is he that slo his brother.
435 *Caym.* Byd euery man thaym luf and lowt.
Garcio. Yey, ill-spon weft ay comes foule out.
Caym. Long or thou get thi hoyse, and thou go thus aboute!

Byd euery man theym pleasse to pay.
Garcio. Yey, gif Don, thyne hors, a wisp of hay!
[Saves himself from Cain's wrath by climbing out of his reach.
440 *Caym.* We! com downe in twenty dwill way!
The dwill I þe betake;
f. 7a   For bot it were Abell, my brothere,
Yit knew I neuer thi make.
[Garcio addresses the audience:
Garcio. Now old and yong, or that ye weynd,
445 The same blissyng withoutten end,
All sam then shall ye haue,
That God of heuen my master has giffen.
Browke it well, whils that ye liffen;
He vowche it full well safe.

450 *Caym.* Com downe yit, in the dwillys way,   *[Garcio descends.*
And angre me no more!
And take yond plogh, I say,
And weynd the furth fast before;
And I shall, if I may,
455 Tech the another lore.
I warn the, lad, for ay,
Fro now furth euermore,
That thou greue me noght;

For, bi Codys sydys, if thou do,
460   I shall hang the apon this plo,
With this rope, lo, lad, lo,
By hym that me dere boght!
[Exit Garcio. Cain addresses the audience:
Now fayre well, felows all, for I must nedys weynd,
And to the dwill be thrall, warld withoutten end:
465   Ordand ther is my stall, with Sathanas the feynd.
Euer ill myght hym befall that theder me commend
This tyde.
Fare well les, and fare well more!
For now and euermore
470   I will go me to hyde.   *[Exit.*

Explicit Mactacio Abell. Sequitur Noe.

2

Noe	*Primus Filius*	*Prima Mulier*
Deus	*Secundus Filius*	*Secunda Mulier*
Vxor Noe	*Tercius Filius*	*Tercia Mulier*

Noah, alone, prays to God:

Noe. Myghtfull God veray, maker of all that is,
Thre persons withoutten nay, oone God in endles blis,
Thou maide both nyght and day, beest, fowle, and fysh;
All creatures that lif may wroght thou at thi wish,
5   As thou wel myght.
The son, the moyne, verament,
Thou maide; the firmament;
The sternes also full feruent,
To shyne thou maide ful bright.

10   Angels thou maide ful euen, all orders that is,
To haue the blis in heuen: this did thou more and les,
Full mervelus to neuen. Yit was ther vnkyndnes
More bi foldys seuen then I can well expres,
Forwhi
15   Of all angels in brightnes
God gaf Lucifer most lightnes,
Yit prowdly he flyt his des,
And set hym euen hym by.

He thoght hymself as worthi as hym that hym made,
20   In brightnes, in bewty; therfor he hym degrade,
Put hym in a low degré soyn after, in a brade,
Hym and all his menye, wher he may be vnglad
For euer.
Shall thay neuer wyn away
25   Hence vnto domysday,
Bot burn in bayle for ay;
Shall thay neuer dysseuer.

Soyne after, that gracyous Lord to his liknes maide man,
That place to be restord, euen as he began;

30 Of the Trinité bi accord, Adam, and Eue that woman,
   To multiplie without discord, in Paradise put he thaym,
   And sithen to both
   Gaf in commaundement
   On the tre of life to lay no hend.
35 Bot yit the fals feynd
   Made hym with man wroth,

   Entysyd man to glotony, styrd him to syn in pride.
   Bot in Paradise, securly, myght no syn abide;
   And therfor man full hastely was put out in þat tyde,
40 In wo and wandreth for to be, in paynes full vnrid
   To knowe:
   Fyrst in erth, and sythen in hell
   With feyndys for to dwell,
   Bot he his mercy mell
45 To those that will hym trawe.

f. 8a Oyle of mercy he hus hight, as I haue hard red,
   To euery lifyng wight that wold luf hym and dred;
   Bot now before his sight euery liffyng leyde,
   Most party day and nyght, syn in word and dede
50 Full bold:
   Som in pride, ire, and enuy,
   Som in couetous and glotyny,
   Som in sloth and lechery,
   And other wise manyfold.

55 Therfor I drede lest God on vs will take veniance,
   For syn is now alod, without any repentance.
   Sex hundreth yeris and od haue I, without distance,
   In erth, as any sod, liffyd with grete grevance
   Allway;
60 And now I wax old,
   Seke, sory, and cold;
   As muk apon mold
   I widder away.

   Bot yit will I cry for mercy and call:
65 Noe, thi seruant, am I, Lord ouer all!
   Therfor me, and my fry shal with me fall,
   Saue from velany, and bryng to thi hall
   In heuen;

42 MS. in sythen.

And kepe me from syn
70 This warld within.
Comly kyng of mankyn,
I pray the here my stevyn!

God speaks from above:

Deus. Syn I haue maide all thyng that is liffand,
Duke, emperour, and kyng, with myne awne hand,
75 For to haue thare likyng bi see and bi sand,
Euery man to my bydyng shuld be bowand
Full feruent,
That maide man sich a creatoure,
Farest of favoure;
80 Man must luf me paramoure
By reson, and repent.

Me thoght I shewed man luf when I made hym to be
All angels abuf, like to the Trynyté;
And now in grete reprufe full low ligys he,
85 In erth hymself to stuf with syn that displeasse me
Most of all.
Veniance will I take
In erth for syn sake;
My grame thus will I wake
90 Both of grete and small.

I repente full sore that euer maide I man;
Bi me he settys no store, and I am his soferan.
f. 8b I will distroy therfor both beest, man, and woman:
All shall perish, les and more. That bargan may thay ban
95 That ill has done.
In erth I se right noght
Bot syn that is vnsoght;
Of those that well has wroght
Fynd I bot a fone.

100 Therfor shall I fordo all this medill-erd
With floodys that shal flo and ryn with hidous rerd.
I haue good cause therto; for me no man is ferd.
As I say shal I do—of veniance draw my swerd,
And make end
105 Of all that beris life,
Sayf Noe and his wife,
For thay wold neuer stryfe
With me then me offend.

Hym to mekill wyn, hastly will I go
110 To Noe my seruand, or I blyn, to warn hym of his wo.
In erth I se bot syn reynand to and fro
Emang both more and myn, ichon other fo
With all thare entent.
All shall I fordo
115 With floodys that shall floo;
Wirk shall I thaym wo
That will not repent.

[*God descends and addresses Noah:*
Noe, my freend, I the commaund, from cares the to keyle,
A ship that thou ordand of nayle and bord ful wele.
120 Thou was alway well-wirkand, to me trew as stele,
To my bydyng obediand; frendship shal thou fele
To mede.
Of lennthe thi ship be
Thre hundreth cubettys, warn I the;
125 Of heght euen thirté;
Of fyfty als in brede.

Anoynt thi ship with pik and tar without and als within,
The water out to spar: this is a noble gyn.
Look no man the mar. Thre chese chambres begyn;
130 Thou must spend many a spar, this wark or thou wyn
To end fully.
Make in thi ship also
Parloures oone or two,
And houses of offyce mo
135 For beestys that ther must be.

Oone cubite on hight a wyndo shal thou make;
On the syde a doore, with slyght, beneyth shal thou take.
With the shal no man fyght, nor do the no kyn wrake.
f. 9a When all is doyne thus right, thi wife, that is thi make,
140 Take in to the;
Thi sonnes of good fame,
Sem, Iaphet, and Came,
Take in also thame,
Thare wifys also thre.

145 For all shal be fordone that lif in land, bot ye,
With floodys that from abone shal fall, and that plenté.

125 MS. thrirte.   129 MS. chefe.   143 MS. hame.

It shall begyn full sone to rayn vncessantlé,
After dayes seuen be done, and induyr dayes fourty,
Withoutten fayll.
150 Take to thi ship also
Of ich kynd beestys two,
Mayll and femayll, bot no mo,
Or thou pull vp thi sayll;

For thay may the avayll when al this thyng is wroght.
155 Stuf thi ship with vitayll, for hungre that ye perish noght.
Of beestys, foull, and catayll—for thaym haue thou in thoght—
For thaym is my counsayll that som socour be soght
In hast;
Thay must haue corn and hay
160 And oder mete alway.
Do now as I the say,
In the name of the Holy Gast.

Noe. A, benedicite! what art thou that thus
Tellys afore that shall be? Thou art full mervelus!
165 Tell me, for charité, thi name so gracius.
Deus. My name is of dignyté, and also full glorius
To knowe:
I am God most myghty,
Oone God in Trynyty,
170 Made the and ich man to be;
To luf me well thou awe.

Noe. I thank the, Lord so dere, that wold vowchsayf
Thus low to appere to a symple knafe.
Blis vs, Lord, here, for charité I hit crafe;
175 The better may we stere the ship that we shall hafe,
Certayn.
Deus. Noe, to the and to thi fry
My blyssyng graunt I;
Ye shall wax and multiply
180 And fill the erth agane,

When all thise floodys ar past, and fully gone away. [Exit Deus.
Noe. Lord, homward will I hast as fast as that I may;
My wife will I frast what she will say,
And I am agast that we get som fray
185 Betwixt vs both,

183 wife *not in* MS.

For she is full tethee,
For litill oft angré;
If any thyng wrang be,
Soyne is she wroth.

[Tunc perget ad vxorem.

f. 9b   God spede, dere wife! How fayre ye?
Vxor. Now, as euer myght I thryfe, the wars I the see.
Do tell me belife, where has thou thus long be?
To dede may we dryfe, or lif, for the,
For want.
195   When we swete or swynk,
Thou dos what thou thynk,
Yit of mete and of drynk
Haue we veray skant.

Noe. Wife, we ar hard sted with tythyngys new.
200 *Vxor.* Bot thou were worthi be cled in Stafford blew,
For thou art alway adred, be it fals or trew.
Bot God knowes I am led—and that may I rew—
Full ill;
For I dar be thi borow,
205   From euen vnto morow
Thou spekys euer of sorow;
God send the onys thi fill!

[To the women in the audience:
We women may wary all ill husbandys;
I haue oone, bi Mary that lowsyd me of my bandys!
210   If he teyn, I must tary, howsoeuer it standys,
With seymland full sory, wryngand both my handys
For drede;
Bot yit otherwhile,
What with gam and with gyle,
215   I shall smyte and smyle,
And qwite hym his mede.

Noe. We! hold thi tong, ram-skyt, or I shall the still.
Vxor. By my thryft, if thou smyte, I shal turne the vntill.
Noe. We shall assay as tyte. Haue at the, Gill !
220   Apon the bone shal it byte.   *[Strikes her.*
Vxor.   A, so! Mary, thou smytys ill!
Bot I suppose
I shal not in thi det
Flyt of this flett:

Take the ther a langett
225   To tye vp thi hose!   [*Strikes him.*

Noe. A! wilt thou so? Mary, that is myne!
Vxor. Thou shal thre for two, I swere bi Godys pyne!
Noe. And I shall qwyte the tho, in fayth, or syne.
Vxor. Out apon the, ho!
Noe.   Thou can both byte and whyne
230   With a rerd;
For all if she stryke,   [*To the audience.*
Yit fast will she skryke;
In fayth, I hold none slyke
In all medill-erd.

235   Bot I will kepe charyté, for I haue at do.
Vxor. Here shal no man tary the; I pray the go to!
Full well may we mys the, as euer haue I ro.
To spyn will I dres me.   [*Sits down to spin.*
Noe.   We! fare well, lo;
Bot, wife,
240   Pray for me beselé
To eft I com vnto the.
Vxor. Euen as thou prays for me,
As euer myght I thrife.

f. 10a *Noe.* I tary full lang fro my warke, I traw;
245   Now my gere will I fang, and thederward draw.
                    [*Goes off to his shipwrighting.*
I may full ill gang, the soth for to knaw;
Bot if God help amang, I may sit downe daw
To ken.
Now assay will I
250   How I can of wrightry,
In nomine patris, et filii,
Et spiritus sancti. Amen.

To begyn of this tree my bonys will I bend;
I traw from the Trynyté socoure will be send.
255   It fayres full fayre, thynk me, this wark to my hend;
Now blissid be he that this can amend.
Lo, here the lenght,   [*Takes measurements.*
Thre hundreth cubettys euenly;
Of breed, lo, is it fyfty;

260   The heght is euen thyrty
        Cubettys full strenght.

        Now my gowne will I cast, and wyrk in my cote;
        Make will I the mast or I flyt oone foote.
        A! my bak, I traw, will brast! This is a sory note!
265   Hit is wonder that I last, sich an old dote,
        All dold,
        To begyn sich a wark.
        My bonys ar so stark:
        No wonder if thay wark,
270   For I am full old.

        The top and the sayll both will I make;
        The helme and the castell also will I take;
        To drife ich a nayll will I not forsake.
        This gere may neuer fayll, that dar I vndertake
275   Onone.
        This is a nobull gyn:
        Thise nayles so thay ryn
        Thoro more and myn,
        Thise bordys ichon.

280   Wyndow and doore, euen as he saide;
        Thre ches chambre, thay ar well maide;
        Pyk and tar full sure therapon laide.
        This will euer endure, therof am I paide,
        Forwhy
285   It is better wroght
        Then I coude haif thoght.
        Hym that maide all of noght
        I thank oonly.
                            [*Goes to his wife, his sons and their wives.*
        Now will I hy me, and nothyng be leder,
290   My wife and my meneye to bryng euen heder.
        Tent hedir tydely, wife, and consider;
        Hens must vs fle, all sam togeder,
        In hast.
f. 10b *Vxor.* Whi, syr, what alis you?
295   Who is that asalis you?
        To fle it avalis you
        And ye be agast.

                    261 MS. streght.

Noe. Ther is garn on the reyll other, my dame.
Vxor. Tell me that ich a deyll, els get ye blame.
300 *Noe.* He that cares may keill—blissid be his name!—
He has behete, for oure seyll, to sheld vs fro shame;
And sayd
All this warld aboute
With floodys so stoute,
305 That shall ryn on a route,
Shall be ouerlaide.

He saide all shall be slayn, bot oonely we,
Oure barnes that ar bayn, and thare wifys thre.
A ship he bad me ordayn, to safe vs and oure fee;
310 Therfor with all oure mayn thank we that fre,
Beytter of bayll.
Hy vs fast, go we thedir.
Vxor. I wote neuer whedir;
I dase and I dedir
315 For ferd of that tayll.

Noe. Be not aferd. Haue done; trus sam oure gere,
That we be ther or none, without more dere.
1 Filius. It shall be done full sone. Brether, help to bere.
2 Filius. Full long shall I not hoyne to do my devere.
320 Brether, sam.
3 Filius. Without any yelp,
At my myght shall I help.
Vxor. Yit, for drede of a skelp,
Help well thi dam!

[*They cross to the Ark, and all but Uxor go on board.*
325 *Noe.* Now ar we there as we shuld be.
Do get in oure gere, oure catall and fe,
Into this vessell here, my chylder fre.
Vxor. I was neuer bard ere, as euer myght I the,
In sich an oostré as this!
330 In fath, I can not fynd
Which is before, which is behynd.
Bot shall we here be pynd,
Noe, as haue thou blis?

Noe. Dame, as it is skill, here must vs abide grace;
335 Therfor, wife, with good will com into this place.
Vxor. Sir, for Iak nor for Gill will I turne my face,
301 behete *not in MS.*

Till I haue on this hill spon a space
On my rok.
Well were he myght get me!
340 Now will I downe set me;   [*Sits down to spin.*
Yit reede I no man let me,
For drede of a knok.

         [*Noah speaks to her from the Ark:*
Noe. Behold to the heuen! The cateractes all,
Thai ar open full euen, grete and small,
345 And the planettys seuen left has thare stall.
Thise thoners and levyn downe gar fall
Full stout
f. 11a Both halles and bowers,
Castels and towres.
350 Full sharp ar thise showers
That renys aboute.

Therfor, wife, haue done; com into ship fast.
Vxor. Yei, Noe, go cloute thi shone! The better will thai last.
1 Mulier. Good moder, com in sone, for all is ouercast,
355 Both the son and the mone.
2 Mulier.   And many wynd-blast
Full sharp.
Thise floodys so thay ryn;
Therfor, moder, com in.
Vxor. In fayth, yit will I spyn;
360 All in vayn ye carp.

3 Mulier. If ye like ye may spyn, moder, in the ship.
Noe. Now is this twyys com in, dame, on my frenship.
Vxor. Wheder I lose or I wyn, in fayth, thi felowship,
Set I not at a pyn. This spyndill will I slip
365 Apon this hill
Or I styr oone fote.
Noe. Peter! I traw we dote.
Without any more note,
Com in if ye will.

370 *Vxor.* Yei, water nyghys so nere that I sit not dry;
Into ship with a byr, therfor, will I hy
For drede that I drone here.   [*Rushes into the ship.*
Noe.   Dame, securly,
It bees boght full dere ye abode so long by
Out of ship.

375 *Vxor.* I will not, for thi bydyng,
Go from doore to mydyng.
Noe. In fayth, and for youre long taryyng
Ye shal lik on the whyp.

Vxor. Spare me not, I pray the, bot euen as thou thynk;
380   Thise grete wordys shall not flay me.
Noe.   Abide, dame, and drynk,
For betyn shall thou be with this staf to thou stynk.
Ar strokys good? say me.
Vxor.   What say ye, Wat Wynk?
Noe. Speke!
Cry me mercy, I say!
385 *Vxor.* Therto say I nay.
Noe. Bot thou do, bi this day,
Thi hede shall I breke!
                [Uxor addresses the women in the audience:
Vxor. Lord, I were at ese, and hertely full hoylle,
Might I onys haue a measse of wedows coyll.
390   For thi saull, without lese, shuld I dele penny doyll;
So wold mo, no frese, that I se on this sole
Of wifys that ar here,
For the life that thay leyd,
Wold thare husbandys were dede;
395   For, as euer ete I brede,
So wold I oure syre were!
                [Noah addresses the men in the audience:
Noe. Yee men that has wifys, whyls thay ar yong,
If ye luf youre lifys, chastice thare tong.
Me thynk my hert ryfys, both levyr and long,
400   To se sich stryfys, wedmen emong.
Bot I,
f. 11b As haue I blys,
Shall chastyse this.
Vxor. Yit may ye mys,
405   Nicholl Nedy!

Noe. I shall make þe still as stone, begynnar of blunder!
I shall bete the bak and bone, and breke all in sonder.
                        [They fight.
Vxor. Out, alas, I am gone! Oute apon the, mans wonder!
Noe. Se how she can grone, and I lig vnder!
410   Bot, wife,
In this hast let vs ho,

For my bak is nere in two.
Vxor. And I am bet so blo
That I may not thryfe.

415 *1 Filius.* A! whi fare ye thus, fader and moder both?
2 Filius. Ye shuld not be so spitus, standyng in sich a woth.
3 Filius. Thise weders ar so hidus, with many a cold coth.
Noe. We will do as ye bid vs; we will no more be wroth,
      Dere barnes.
420 Now to the helme will I hent,   [*Goes to the tiller.*
    And to my ship tent.
Vxor. I se on the firmament,
    Me thynk, the seven starnes.

Noe. This is a grete flood, wife, take hede.
425 *Vxor.* So me thoght, as I stode. We ar in grete drede;
    Thise wawghes ar so wode.
Noe.   Help, God, in this nede!
    As thou art stere-man good, and best, as I rede,
    Of all,
    Thou rewle vs in this rase,
430 As thou me behete hase.
Vxor. This is a perlous case.
    Help, God, when we call!

Noe. Wife, tent the stere-tre, and I shall asay
    The depnes of the see that we bere, if I may.
435 *Vxor.* That shall I do ful wysely. Now go thi way,
    For apon this flood haue we flett many day
    With pyne.
Noe. Now the water will I fownd: [*Lowers a plummet.*
    A! it is far to the grownd.
440 This trauell I expownd
    Had I to tyne.

    Aboue all hillys bedeyn the water is rysen late
    Cubettys xv. Bot in a highter state
    It may not be, I weyn, for this well I wate:
445 This fourty dayes has rayn beyn; it will therfor abate
    Full lele.
    This water in hast
    Eft will I tast;   [*Lowers plummet again.*

                417 weders *not in MS.*

Now am I agast—
450   It is wanyd a grete dele!

Now ar the weders cest, and cateractes knyt,
    Both the most and the leest.
Vxor.   Me thynk, bi my wit,
    The son shynes in the eest. Lo, is not yond it?
    We shuld haue a good feest, were thise floodys flyt
455   So spytus.
Noe. We haue been here, all we,
    CCC dayes and fyfty.
Vxor. Yei, now wanys the see;
    Lord, well is vs!
                    [*Noah prepares to lower plummet a third time.*
f. 12a *Noe.* The thryd tyme will I prufe what depnes we bere.
Vxor. How long shall thou hufe? Lay in thy lyne there.
Noe. I may towch with my lufe the grownd evyn here.
Vxor. Then begynnys to grufe to vs mery chere.
    Bot, husband,
465   What grownd may this be?
Noe. The hyllys of Armonye.
Vxor. Now blissid be he
    That thus for vs ordand!

Noe. I see toppys of hyllys he, many at a syght;
470   Nothyng to let me, the wedir is so bright.
Vxor. Thise ar of mercy tokyns full right.
Noe. Dame, thi counsell me what fowll best myght
    And cowth
    With flight of wyng
475   Bryng, without taryyng,
    Of mercy som tokynyng,
    Ayther bi north or southe.

For this is the fyrst day of the tent moyne.
Vxor. The ravyn, durst I lay, will com agane sone.
480   As fast as thou may, cast hym furth—haue done!
                        [*Noah sends out the raven.*
    He may happyn to-day com agane or none
    With grath.
Noe. I will cast out also
    Dowfys oone or two.

461 MS. Now.   476 can *between* vs *and* ordand *in MS.*

485 Go youre way, go;   [*Sends out the doves.*
    God send you som wathe!

    Now ar thise fowles flone into seyr countré.
    Pray we fast ichon, kneland on oure kne,
    To hym that is alone, worthiest of degré,
490 That he wold send anone oure fowles som fee
    To glad vs.
Vxor. Thai may not fayll of land,
    The water is so wanand.
Noe. Thank we God all-weldand,
495 That Lord that made vs!

    It is a wonder thyng, me thynk, sothlé,
    Thai ar so long taryyng, the fowles that we
    Cast out in the mornyng.
Vxor.   Syr, it may be
    Thai tary to thay bryng.
Noe.   The ravyn is a-hungrye
500 Allway.
    He is without any reson;
    And he fynd any caryon,
    As peraventure may be fon,
    He will not away.

505 The dowfe is more gentill: her trust I vntew,
    Like vnto the turtill, for she is ay trew.
Vxor. Hence bot a litill she commys, lew, lew!
    She bryngys in her bill som novels new.
    Behald!
510 It is of an olif-tre
    A branch, thynkys me.
Noe. It is soth, perdé;
    Right so is it cald.

f. 12b Doufe, byrd full blist, fayre myght the befall!
515 Thou art trew for to trist as ston in the wall;
    Full well I it wist thou wold com to thi hall.
Vxor. A trew tokyn ist we shall be sauyd all,
    Forwhi
    The water, syn she com,
520 Of depnes plom
    Is fallen a fathom
    And more, hardely.

1 Filius. Thise floodys ar gone, fader, behold!
2 Filius. Ther is left right none, and that be ye bold.
525 *3 Filius.* As still as a stone oure ship is stold.
Noe. Apon land here anone that we were, fayn I wold.
My childer dere,
Sem, Iaphet and Cam,
With gle and with gam,
530 Com go we all sam;
We will no longer abide here.
                    [*They all leave the Ark.*
Vxor. Here haue we beyn, Noy, long enogh
With tray and with teyn, and dreed mekill wogh.
Noe. Behald on this greyn! Nowder cart ne plogh
535 Is left, as I weyn, nowder tre then bogh,
Ne other thyng,
Bot all is away;
Many castels, I say,
Grete townes of aray,
540 Flitt has this flowyng.

Vxor. Thise floodys not afright all this warld so wide
Has mevid with myght on se and bi side.
Noe. To dede ar thai dyght, prowdist of pryde,
Euerich a wyght that euer was spyde
545 With syn:
All ar thai slayn,
And put vnto payn.
Vxor. From thens agayn
May thai neuer wyn?

550 *Noe.* Wyn? No, iwis, bot he that myght hase
Wold myn of thare mys, and admytte thaym to grace.
As he in bayll is blis, I pray hym in this space,
In heven hye with his to purvaye vs a place,
That we,
555 With his santys in sight,
And his angels bright,
May com to his light.
Amen, for charité.

Explicit processus Noe.

3

PRIMA PASTORUM

f. 32b

Incipit Pagina pastorum

Primus Pastor (Gyb)	*Angelus*
Secundus Pastor (Iohn Horne)	*Maria*
Tercius Pastor (Slawpase)	*Christ-child*
Iak Garcio	

Grazing land near a town. Enter the First Shepherd

1 Pastor. Lord, what thay ar weyll that hens ar past!
For thay noght feyll theym to downe cast.
Here is mekyll vnceyll, and long has it last:
Now in hart, now in heyll, now in weytt, now in blast;
5 Now in care,
Now in comforth agane;
Now in fayre, now in rane;
Now in hart full fane,
And after full sare.

f. 33a Thus this warld, as I say, farys on ylk syde,
For after oure play com sorows vnryde;
For he that most may when he syttys in pryde,
When it comys on assay is kesten downe wyde.
This is seyn:
15 When rychest is he,
Then comys pouerté;
Horsman Iak Copé
Walkys then, I weyn.

I thank it God, hark ye what I mene:
20 For euen or for od I haue mekyll tene;
As heuy as a sod, I grete with myn eene
When I nap on my cod, for care that has bene,
And sorow.
All my shepe ar gone,
25 I am not left oone,

7 MS. is fayre . . . is rane.   15 MS. ryches.

29

The rott has theym slone;
Now beg I and borow.

My handys may I wryng and mowrnyng make,
Bot if good will spryng, the countré forsake;
30   Fermes thyk ar comyng, my purs is bot wake,
I haue nerehand nothyng to pay nor to take.
I may syng
With purs penneles,
That makys this heuynes,
35   'Wo is me this dystres!'
And has no helpyng.

Thus sett I my mynde, truly to neuen,
By my wytt to fynde to cast the warld in seuen.
My shepe haue I tynde by the moren full euen;
40   Now if hap will grynde, God from his heuen
Send grace!
To the fare will I me,
To by shepe, perdé,
And yit may I multyplé,
45   For all this hard case.

Enter the Second Shepherd, who does not see the First Shepherd.

2 *Pastor.* Bensté, bensté be vs emang,
And saue all that I se here in this thrang!
He saue you and me, ouertwhart and endlang,
That hang on a tre, I say you no wrang.
50   Cryst sane vs
From all myschefys,
From robers and thefys,
From those mens grefys
That oft ar agans vs.

f. 33b   Both bosters and bragers God kepe vs fro,
That with thare long dagers dos mekyll wo;
From all byll-hagers with colknyfys that go.
Sich wryers and wragers gose to and fro
For to crak:
60   Whoso says hym agane
Were better be slane;
Both ploghe and wane
Amendys will not make.

He will make it as prowde a lord as he were,
65   With a hede lyke a clowde, felterd his here;
He spekys on lowde with a grym bere
I wold not haue trowde, so galy in gere
As he glydys.
I wote not the better,
70   Nor wheder is gretter—
The lad or the master—
So stowtly he strydys.

If he hask me oght that he wold to his pay,
Full dere bese it boght if I say nay.
75   Bot God that all wroght, to the now I say,
Help that thay were broght to a better way
For thare sawlys;
And send theym good mendyng
With a short endyng,
80   And with the to be lendyng
When that thou callys.
                            [*Sees the First Shepherd.*
How, Gyb, goode morne! Wheder goys thou?
Thou goys ouer the corne! Gyb, I say, how!
1 Pastor. Who is that?—Iohn Horne, I make God avowe!
85   I say not in skorne, Ihon, how farys thou?
2 Pastor. Hay, ha!
Ar ye in this towne?
1 Pastor. Yey, by my crowne!
2 Pastor. I thoght by youre gowne
90   This was youre aray.

1 Pastor. I am euer elyke, wote I neuer what it gars;
Is none in this ryke, a shepard, farys wars.
2 Pastor. Poore men ar in the dyke and oft-tyme mars;
The warld is slyke; also helpars
95   Is none here.
1 Pastor. It is sayde full ryfe,
'A man may not wyfe
And also thryfe,
And all in a yere.'

100 *2 Pastor.* Fyrst must vs crepe and sythen go.
1 Pastor. I go to by shepe.
2 Pastor.   Nay, not so!
                85 Ihon, MS. thom.

f. 34a   What, dreme ye or slepe? Where shuld thay go?
         Here shall thou none kepe.
    1 Pastor.   A, good syr, ho!
         Who am I?
105   I wyll pasture my fe
         Wheresoeuer lykys me;
         Here shall thou theym se.
    2 Pastor. Not so hardy!

         Not oone shepe-tayll shall thou bryng hedyr.
110 *1 Pastor.* I shall bryng, no fayll, a hundreth togedyr.
    2 Pastor. What, art thou in ayll? Longys thou oght-whedir?
    1 Pastor. Thay shall go, saunce fayll. Go now, bell-weder!
                        [*Urges forward his imaginary sheep.*
    2 Pastor. I say, tyr!
    1 Pastor. I say, tyr, now agane!
115   I say skyp ouer the plane.
    2 Pastor. Wold thou neuer so fane,
         Tup, I say, whyr!

    1 Pastor. What, wyll thou not yit, I say, let the shepe go ?
         Whop!
    2 Pastor.   Abyde yit!
    1 Pastor.   Will thou bot so?
120   Knafe, hens I byd flytt. As good that thou do,
         Or I shall the hytt on thi pate—lo,
         Shall thou reyll!   [*Threatens to strike him.*
         I say gyf the shepe space.
    2 Pastor. Syr, a letter of youre grace!
125   Here comys Slawpase
         Fro the myln-whele.

         Enter the Third Shepherd, with a horse carrying a sack of meal.

    3 Pastor. What ado, what ado is this you betweyn?
         A good day, thou, and thou.
    1 Pastor.   Hark what I meyn
         You to say:
130   I was bowne to by store,
         Drofe my shepe me before;
         He says not oone hore
         Shall pas by this way;

         Bot, and he were wood, this way shall thay go.
135 *3 Pastor.* Yey, bot tell me, good, where ar youre shepe, lo?

2 Pastor. Now, syr, by my hode, yit se I no mo,
Not syn I here stode.
3 Pastor.   God gyf you wo
And sorow!
Ye fysh before the nett,
140   And stryfe on this flett;
Sich folys neuer I mett
Evyn or at morow.

                              [*To the audience:*
It is wonder to wyt where wytt shuld be fownde.
Here ar old knafys yit standys on this grownde:
145   These wold by thare wytt make a shyp be drownde;
He were well qwytt had sold for a pownde
Sich two.
Thay fyght and thay flyte
For that at comys not tyte;
150   It is far to byd 'hyte'
To an eg or it go.

                              [*To the other shepherds:*
f. 34b   Tytter want ye sowll then sorow, I pray!
Ye brayde of Mowll that went by the way—
Many shepe can she poll, bot oone had she ay.
155   Bot she happynyd full fowll: hyr pycher, I say,
Was broken.
'Ho, God!' she sayde;
Bot oone shepe yit she hade.
The mylk-pycher was layde;
160   The skarthis was the tokyn.

Bot syn ye ar bare of wysdom to knowe,
Take hede how I fare and lere at my lawe;
Ye nede not to care, if ye folow my sawe.
Hold ye my mare. This sek thou thrawe
165   On my bak,
Whylst I, with my hand,
Lawse the sek-band.
Com nar and by stand,
Both Gyg and Iak.

                              [*Empties the sack.*
170   Is not all shakyn owte, and no meyll is therin?
1 Pastor. Yey, that is no dowte.
3 Pastor.   So is youre wyttys thyn,
And ye look well abowte, nawther more nor myn;
                    140 MS. bett.

So gose youre wyttys owte, evyn as it com in.
Geder vp
175   And seke it agane!
2 Pastor. May we not be fane?
He has told vs full plane
Wysdom to sup.

Enter Iak Garcio.

Iak Garcio. Now God gyf you care, foles all sam!
180   Sagh I neuer none so fare bot the foles of Gotham.
Wo is hir that yow bare! Youre syre and youre dam,
Had she broght furth an hare, a shepe, or a lam,
Had bene well.
Of all the foles I can tell,
185   From heuen vnto hell,
Ye thre bere the bell;
God gyf you vnceyll!

1 Pastor. How pastures oure fee? Say me, good pen.
Garcio. Thay ar gryssed to the kne.
2 Pastor.   Fare fall the!
Garcio.   Amen.
190   If ye will ye may se; youre bestes ye ken.   [*Exit Garcio.*
1 Pastor. Sytt we downe all thre, and drynk shall we then.
3 Pastor. Yey, torde!
I am leuer ete;
What is drynk withoute mete?
195   Gett mete, gett,
And sett vs a borde;

Then may we go dyne, oure bellys to fyll.
2 Pastor. Abyde vnto syne.
3 Pastor.   Be God, syr, I nyll!
I am worthy the wyne, me thynk it good skyll.
f. 35a   My seruyse I tyne; I fare full yll
At youre mangere.
1 Pastor. Trus, go we to mete!
It is best that we trete;
I lyst not to plete
205   To stand in thi dangere.

Thou has euer bene curst syn we met togeder.
3 Pastor. Now in fayth, if I durst, ye ar euen my broder.
2 Pastor. Syrs, let vs cryb furst, for oone thyng or oder,

That thise wordys be purst, and let vs go foder
210 Oure mompyns.
Lay furth of oure store:
Lo, here browne of a bore!
1 Pastor. Set mustard afore;
Oure mete now begyns.

215 Here a foote of a cowe well sawsed, I wene,
The pestell of a sowe that powderd has bene,
Two blodyngys, I trow, a leueryng betwene;
Do gladly, syrs, now, my breder, bedene!
With more—
220 Both befe, and moton
Of an ewe that was roton
(Good mete for a gloton);
Ete of this store.

2 Pastor. I haue here in my mayll sothen and rost:
225 Euen of an ox-tayll that wold not be lost—
Ha, ha! goderhayll! I let for no cost;
A good py or we fayll: this is good for the frost
In a mornyng;
And two swyne-gronys,
230 All a hare bot the lonys.
We myster no sponys
Here at oure mangyng.

3 Pastor. Here is to recorde the leg of a goys,
With chekyns endorde, pork, partryk to roys,
235 A tart for a lorde—how thynk ye this doys?—
A calf-lyuer skorde with the veryose:
Good sawse,
This is a restorité
To make a good appeté.
240 *1 Pastor.* Yee speke all by clergé,
I here by youre clause.

Cowth ye by youre gramery reche vs a drynk,
I shuld be more mery—ye wote what I thynk.
2 Pastor. Haue good ayll of Hely! Bewar now, I wynk,
245 For and thou drynk drely, in thy poll wyll it synk.
1 Pastor. A, so!
This is boyte of oure bayll,
Good holsom ayll.   [*Drinks.*

3 Pastor. Ye hold long the skayll;
250   Now lett me go to.   [*Drinks.*

2 Pastor. I shrew those lyppys bot thou leyff me som parte.
1 Pastor. Be God, he bot syppys; begylde thou art.
f. 35*b*   Behold how he kyppys!   [*Second Shepherd snatches the cup.*
2 Pastor.   I shrew you so smart,
    And me on my hyppys, bot if I gart
255   Abate.
    Be thou wyne, be thou ayll,   [*Addresses contents of the cup.*
    Bot if my brethe fayll,
    I shall sett the on sayll;
    God send the good gayte!   [*Drinks.*

260 *3 Pastor.* Be my dam saull, Alyce, it was sadly dronken!
                            [*First Shepherd peers into the cup.*
1 Pastor. Now, as euer haue I blys, to the bothom it is sonken.
2 Pastor. Yit a botell here is—
3 Pastor.   That is well spoken;
    By my thryft, we must kys!
2 Pastor.   —that had I forgoten.
    Bot hark!
265   Whoso can best syng
    Shall haue the begynnyng.
1 Pastor. Now prays at the partyng;
    I shall sett you on warke.   [*They sing.*

    We haue done oure parte and songyn right weyll;
270   I drynk for my parte.   [*Drinks.*
2 Pastor.   Abyde, lett cop reyll!   [*Drinks.*
1 Pastor. Godys forbot thou spart, and thou drynk euery deyll.
3 Pastor. Thou has dronken a quart, therfor choke the the deyll!
1 Pastor. Thou rafys;
    And it were for a sogh
275   Ther is drynk enogh.
3 Pastor. I shrew the handys it drogh!   [*Examines empty cup.*
    Ye be both knafys.

1 Pastor. Nay, we knaues all; thus thynk me best,
    So, syr, shuld ye call.
2 Pastor.   Furth let it rest;
280   We will not brall.
1 Pastor.   Then wold I we fest,
    This mete who shall into panyere kest.

3 Pastor. Syrs, herys!
 For oure saules lett vs do
 Poore men gyf it to.
285 *1 Pastor.* Geder vp, lo, lo,
 Ye hungré begers, frerys!

2 Pastor. It draes nere nyght. Trus, go we to rest.
 I am euen redy dyght; I thynk it the best.
 3 Pastor. For ferde we be fryght, a crosse lett vs kest—
290 Cryst-crosse, benedyght eest and west—
 For drede.
  Iesus onazorus
  Crucyefixus,
  Morcus, Andreus,
295 God be oure spede!
   [*The shepherds sleep. Angelic singing is heard, and an angel*
         speaks to them from above:
Angelus. Herkyn, hyrdes! Awake! Gyf louyng ye shall;
 He is borne for youre sake, lorde perpetuall.
 He is comen to take and rawnson you all;
 Youre sorowe to slake, kyng emperiall,
300 He behestys.
 That chyld is borne
 At Bethelem this morne;
 Ye shall fynde hym beforne
 Betwix two bestys.   [*The angel withdraws.*

f. 36a *1 Pastor.* A, Godys dere Dominus! What was that sang?
 It was wonder curiose, with small noytys emang.
 I pray to God, saue vs now in this thrang!
 I am ferd, by Iesus, somwhat be wrang.
 Me thoght
310 Oone scremyd on lowde;
 I suppose it was a clowde;
 In myn erys it sowde,
 By hym that me boght!

2 Pastor. Nay, that may not be, I say you certan,
315 For he spake to vs thre as he had bene a man.
 When he lemyd on this lee, my hart shakyd than;
 An angell was he, tell you I can,
 No dowte.
 He spake of a barne:
   297 *Originally* oure, *with initial* y *inserted by a **different** hand.*

320 We must seke hym, I you warne;
     That betokyns yond starne
     That standys yonder owte.   [*Points to the sky.*

     3 Pastor. It was meruell to se, so bright as it shone;
       I wold haue trowyd, veraly, it had bene thoner-flone,
325   Bot I sagh with myn ee as I lenyd to this stone.
       It was a mery gle: sich hard I neuer none,
       I recorde,
       As he sayde in a skreme—
       Or els that I dreme—
330   We shuld go to Bedleme,
       To wyrship that lorde.

     1 Pastor. That same childe is he that prophetys of told,
       Shuld make them fre that Adam had sold.
     2 Pastor. Take tent vnto me! This is inrold
335   By the wordys of Isae: a prynce most bold
       Shall he be,
       And kyng with crowne
       Sett on Dauid trone;
       Sich was neuer none
340   Seyn with oure ee.

     3 Pastor. Also Isay says—oure faders vs told—
       That a vyrgyn shuld pas of Iesse, that wold
       Bryng furth, by grace, a floure so bold.
       That vyrgyn now has these wordys vphold,
345   As ye se.
       Trust it now we may
       He is borne this day:
       Exiet virga
       De radice Iesse.

350 *1 Pastor.* Of hym spake more: Sybyll, as I weyn,
       And Nabugodhonosor from oure faythe alyene;
       In the fornace where thay wore, thre childer, sene,
       The fourt stode before, Godys son lyke to bene.
     2 Pastor. That fygure
f. 36b Was gyffen by reualacyon
       That God wold haue a son;
       This is a good lesson
       Vs to consydure.

3 Pastor. Of hym spake Ieromy, and Moyses also,
360 Where he sagh hym by a bushe burnand, lo!
When he cam to aspy if it were so,
Vnburnyd was it truly at commyng therto—
A wonder!
1 Pastor. That was for to se
365 Hir holy vyrgynyté;
That she vnfylyd shuld be—
Thus can I ponder—

And shuld haue a chyld sich was neuer sene.
2 Pastor. Pese, man, thou art begyld! Thou shall se hym with eene—
370 Of a madyn so myld greatt meruell I mene;
Yee, and she vnfyld, a virgyn clene—
So soyne.
1 Pastor. Nothyng is inpossybyll,
Sothly, that God wyll;
375 It shal be stabyll
That God wyll haue done.

2 Pastor. Abacuc and Ely prophesyde so,
Elezabeth and Zacharé, and many other mo;
And Dauid as veraly is witnes therto,
380 Iohn Baptyste sewrly, and Daniel also.
3 Pastor. So sayng,
He is Godys son alon,
Without hym shal be none;
His sete and his trone
385 Shall euer be lastyng.

1 Pastor. Virgill in his poetré sayde in his verse,
Euen thus by grameré, as I shall reherse:
Iam noua progenies celo demittitur alto;
Iam rediet Virgo, redeunt Saturnia regna.
2 Pastor. Weme! tord! what speke ye here in myn eeres?
Tell vs no clergé! I hold you of the freres;
390 Ye preche.
It semys by youre Laton
Ye haue lerd youre Caton.
1 Pastor. Herk, syrs! ye fon.
I shall you teche:

395 He sayde from heuen a new kynde is send,
Whom a vyrgyn to neuen, oure mys to amend,

Shall conceyue full euen, thus make I an end;
f. 37a And yit more to neuen, that Saturne shall bend
　　　Vnto vs,
400 With peasse and plenté,
　　　With ryches and menee,
　　　Good luf and charyté
　　　Blendyd amanges vs.

　　　3 Pastor. And I hold it trew, for ther shuld be,
405 When that kyng commys new, peasse by land and se.
　　　2 Pastor. Now, brethere, adew! Take tent vnto me:
　　　I wold that we knew of this song so fre
　　　Of the angell;
　　　I hard by hys steuen
410 He was send downe fro heuen.
　　　1 Pastor. It is trouth that ye neuen;
　　　I hard hym well spell.

　　　2 Pastor. Now, by God that me boght, it was a mery song!
　　　I dar say that he broght foure and twenty to a long.
415 *3 Pastor.* I wold it were soght, that same, vs emong.
　　　1 Pastor. In fayth, I trow noght so many he throng
　　　On a heppe;
　　　Thay were gentyll and small,
　　　And well tonyd withall.
420 *3 Pastor.* Yee, bot I can thaym all;
　　　Now lyst I lepe.

　　　1 Pastor. Breke outt youre voce! Let se as ye yelp!
　　　3 Pastor. I may not for the pose, bot I haue help.
　　　2 Pastor. A, thy hart is in thy hose!
　　　1 Pastor.　　　　　　　　　　　Now, in payn of a skelp,
425 This sang thou not lose!
　　　3 Pastor.　　　　　　　　　Thou art an yll qwelp
　　　For angre!
　　　2 Pastor. Go to now—begyn!
　　　1 Pastor. He lyst not well ryn.
　　　3 Pastor. God lett vs neuer blyn;
430 Take at my sangre.　　　　　　[*He sings, and the others join in.*

　　　1 Pastor. Now an ende haue we doyn of oure song this tyde.
　　　2 Pastor. Fayr fall thi growne! Well has thou hyde.
　　　3 Pastor. Then furth lett vs ron; I wyll not abyde.

1 Pastor. No lyght mase the mone; that haue I asspyde.
435 Neuertheles,
    Lett vs hold oure beheste.
2 Pastor. That hold I best.
3 Pastor. Then must we go eest,
    After my ges.   [*They go to Bethlehem.*

440 *1 Pastor.* Wold God that we myght this yong bab see!
2 Pastor. Many prophetys that syght desyryd veralee,
    To haue seen that bright.
3 Pastor.   And God so hee
f. 37b Wold shew vs that wyght, we myght say, perdé,
    We had sene
445 That many sant desyryd,
    With prophetys inspyryd;
    If thay hym requyryd,
    Yit closyd ar thare eene.

2 Pastor. God graunt vs that grace!
3 Pastor.   God so do.
450 *1 Pastor.* Abyde, syrs, a space. Lo, yonder, lo!
    It commys on a rase, yond sterne vs to.
2 Pastor. It is a grete blase! Oure gate let vs go.
    Here he is!   [*They arrive at the stable.*
3 Pastor. Who shall go in before?
455 *1 Pastor.* I ne rek, by my hore.
2 Pastor. Ye ar of the old store;
    It semys you, iwys.   [*They enter the stable.*

1 Pastor. Hayll, kyng I the call! Hayll, most of myght!
    Hayll, the worthyst of all! Hayll, duke! Hayll, knyght!
460 Of greatt and small thou art Lorde by right.
    Hayll, perpetuall! Hayll, faryst wyght!
    Here I offer:
    I pray the to take,
    If thou wold, for my sake—
465 With this may thou lake—
    This lytyll spruse cofer.

2 Pastor. Hayll, lytyll tyn mop, rewarder of mede!
    Hayll! Bot oone drop of grace at my nede!
    Hayll, lytyll mylksop! Hayll, Dauid sede!

434 *A* k *written by a different hand over the long* s *of* mase.
448 *Before* closyd *an upright stroke, apparently an incomplete letter.*

470   Of oure crede thou art crop: hayll, in Godhede!
       This ball
       That thou wold resaue!
       Lytyll is that I haue;
       This wyll I vowchesaue,
475   To play the withall.

       3 Pastor. Hayll, maker of man! Hayll, swetyng!
       Hayll, so as I can! Hayll, praty mytyng!
       I cowche to the than, for fayn nere gretyng.
       Hayll, Lord! Here I ordan, now at oure metyng,
480   This botell—
       It is an old byworde,
       'It is a good bowrde
       For to drynk of a gowrde'—
       It holdys a mett potell.

485 *Maria.* He that all myghtys may, the makere of heuen,
       That is for to say, my son that I neuen,
       Rewarde you this day, as he sett all on seuen;
       He graunt you for ay his blys full euen
       Contynuyng;
f. 38a   He gyf you good grace!
       Tell furth of this case;
       He spede youre pase,
       And graunt you good endyng.

       1 Pastor. Fare well, fare Lorde, with thy moder also.
495 *2 Pastor.* We shall this recorde whereas we go.
       3 Pastor. We mon all be restorde—God graunt it be so!
       1 Pastor. Amen to that worde! Syng we therto
       On hight:
       To ioy all sam,
500   With myrth and gam,
       To the lawde of this lam
       Syng we in syght.   [*They sing.*

              Explicit Vna pagina pastorum.

4

SECUNDA PASTORUM

Incipit Alia eorundem

Primus Pastor (Coll)	*Mak*	*Angelus*
Secundus Pastor (Gyb)	*Vxor eius (Gyll)*	*Maria*
Tercius Pastor (Daw)		*Christ-child*

Open fields near a town. Enter the First Shepherd.

1 Pastor. Lord, what these weders ar cold! And I am yll happyd.
I am nerehande dold, so long haue I nappyd;
My legys thay fold, my fyngers ar chappyd.
It is not as I wold, for I am al lappyd
5   In sorow.
In stormes and tempest,
Now in the eest, now in the west,
Wo is hym has neuer rest
Mydday nor morow!

10   Bot we sely husbandys that walkys on the moore,
In fayth we ar nerehandys outt of the doore.
f. 38b   No wonder, as it standys, if we be poore,
For the tylthe of oure landys lyys falow as the floore,
As ye ken.
15   We ar so hamyd,
Fortaxed and ramyd,
We ar mayde handtamyd
With thyse gentlery-men.

Thus thay refe vs oure rest, oure Lady theym wary!
20   These men that ar lord-fest, thay cause the ploghe tary.
That men say is for the best, we fynde it contrary.
Thus ar husbandys opprest, in ponte to myscary
On lyfe;
Thus hold thay vs hunder,
25   Thus thay bryng vs in blonder;
It were greatte wonder
And euer shuld we thryfe.

10 husbandys, MS. shepardes.

43

For may he gett a paynt slefe or a broche now-on-dayes,
Wo is hym that hym grefe or onys agane says!
30   Dar noman hym reprefe, what mastry he mays;
And yit may noman lefe oone word that he says—
No letter.
He can make purveance
With boste and bragance,
35   And all is thrugh mantenance
Of men that ar gretter.

Ther shall com a swane as prowde as a po;
He must borow my wane, my ploghe also;
Then I am full fane to graunt or he go.
40   Thus lyf we in payne, anger, and wo,
By nyght and day.
He must haue if he langyd,
If I shuld forgang it;
I were better be hangyd
45   Then oones say hym nay.

It dos me good, as I walk thus by myn oone,
Of this warld for to talk in maner of mone.
To my shepe wyll I stalk, and herkyn anone,
Ther abyde on a balk, or sytt on a stone
50   Full soyne;
For I trowe, perdé,
Trew men if thay be,
We gett more compané
Or it be noyne.

Enter the Second Shepherd, who does
not see the First Shepherd.

55 2 *Pastor.* Bensté and Dominus, what may this bemeyne?
Why fares this warld thus? Oft haue we not sene.
Lord, thyse weders ar spytus, and the wyndys full kene,
f. 39a   And the frostys so hydus thay water myn eeyne—
No ly.
60   Now in dry, now in wete,
Now in snaw, now in slete,
When my shone freys to my fete
It is not all esy.

Bot as far as I ken, or yit as I go,
65   We sely wedmen dre mekyll wo:

57 wyndys, MS. weders.

We haue sorow then and then; it fallys oft so.
Sely Copyle, oure hen, both to and fro
She kakyls;
Bot begyn she to crok,
70 To groyne or to clok,
Wo is hym is oure cok,
For he is in the shakyls.

These men that ar wed haue not all thare wyll;
When they ar full hard sted, thay sygh full styll.
75 God wayte thay ar led full hard and full yll;
In bowere nor in bed thay say noght thertyll.
This tyde
My parte haue I fun,
I know my lesson:
80 Wo is hym that is bun,
For he must abyde.

Bot now late in oure lyfys—a meruell to me,
That I thynk my hart ryfys sich wonders to see;
What that destany dryfys it shuld so be—
85 Som men wyll haue two wyfys, and som men thre
In store;
Som ar wo that has any.
Bot so far can I:
Wo is hym that has many,
90 For he felys sore.
            [*Admonishes the young men in the audience:*
Bot, yong men, of wowyng, for God that you boght,
Be well war of wedyng, and thynk in youre thoght:
'Had-I-wyst' is a thyng that seruys of noght.
Mekyll styll mowrnyng has wedyng home broght,
95 And grefys,
With many a sharp showre;
For thou may cach in an owre
That shall sow the full sowre
As long as thou lyffys.

100 For, as euer rede I pystyll, I haue oone to my fere
As sharp as thystyll, as rugh as a brere;
She is browyd lyke a brystyll, with a sowre-loten chere;
f. 39b Had she oones wett hyr whystyll, she couth syng full clere

71 or *between* is *and* oure *in MS.*
93 that, MS. it.

Hyr Paternoster.

105   She is as greatt as a whall,
    She has a galon of gall;
    By hym that dyed for vs all,
    I wald I had ryn to I had lost hir!

[First Shepherd interrupts him:

  1 Pastor. God looke ouer the raw! Full defly ye stand.
110 *2 Pastor.* Yee, the dewill in thi maw, so tariand!
    Sagh thou awre of Daw?
  1 Pastor.   Yee, on a ley-land
    Hard I hym blaw. He commys here at hand,
    Not far.
    Stand styll.
  2 Pastor.   Qwhy?
115 *1 Pastor.* For he commys, hope I.
  2 Pastor. He wyll make vs both a ly
    Bot if we be war.

        Enter the Third Shepherd, a boy.

  3 Pastor. Crystys crosse me spede, and Sant Nycholas!
    Therof had I nede; it is wars then it was.
120   Whoso couthe take hede and lett the warld pas,
    It is euer in drede and brekyll as glas,
    And slythys.
    This warld fowre neuer so,
    With meruels mo and mo—
125   Now in weyll, now in wo,
    And all thyng wrythys.

    Was neuer syn Noe floode sich floodys seyn,
    Wyndys and ranys so rude, and stormes so keyn—
    Som stamerd, som stod in dowte, as I weyn.
130   Now God turne all to good! I say as I mene,
    For ponder:
    These floodys so thay drowne,
    Both in feyldys and in towne,
    And berys all downe;
135   And that is a wonder.

[Catches sight of the other shepherds.

    We that walk on the nyghtys, oure catell to kepe,
    We se sodan syghtys when othere men slepe.
    Yit me thynk my hart lyghtys; I se shrewys pepe.
    Ye ar two all-wyghtys—I wyll gyf my shepe

137 *Originally* slepys, *with* e *written above* ys *cancelled in red ink.*

140   A turne.
      Bot full yll haue I ment;
      As I walk on this bent,
      I may lyghtly repent,
      My toes if I spurne.

                                    [*Greets them:*
145   A, syr, God you saue, and master myne!
      A drynk fayn wold I haue, and somwhat to dyne.
      1 Pastor. Crystys curs, my knaue, thou art a ledyr hyne!
      2 Pastor. What, the boy lyst raue! Abyde vnto syne;
      We haue mayde it.
f. 40a Yll thryft on thy pate!
      Though the shrew cam late,
      Yit is he in state
      To dyne—if he had it.

      3 Pastor. Sich seruandys as I, that swettys and swynkys,
155   Etys oure brede full dry, and that me forthynkys.
      We ar oft weytt and wery when master-men wynkys;
      Yit commys full lately both dyners and drynkys.
      Bot nately
      Both oure dame and oure syre,
160   When we haue ryn in the myre,
      Thay can nyp at oure hyre,
      And pay vs full lately.

      Bot here my trouth, master: for the fayr that ye make,
      I shall do therafter—wyrk as I take.
165   I shall do a lytyll, syr, and emang euer lake,
      For yit lay my soper neuer on my stomake
      In feyldys.
      Wherto shuld I threpe?
      With my staf can I lepe;
170   And men say, 'Lyght chepe
      Letherly foryeldys.'

      1 Pastor. Thou were an yll lad to ryde on wowyng
      With a man that had bot lytyll of spendyng.
      2 Pastor. Peasse, boy, I bad. No more ianglyng,
175   Or I shall make the full rad, by the heuens kyng!
      With thy gawdys—
      Where ar oure shepe, boy?—we skorne.
      3 Pastor. Sir, this same day at morne
      I thaym left in the corne,
180   When thay rang lawdys.

Thay haue pasture good, thay can not go wrong.

1 Pastor. That is right. By the roode, thyse nyghtys ar long!
Yit I wold, or we yode, oone gaf vs a song.

2 Pastor. So I thoght as I stode, to myrth vs emong.

185 *3 Pastor.* I grauntt.

1 Pastor. Lett me syng the tenory.

2 Pastor. And I the tryble so hye.

3 Pastor. Then the meyne fallys to me.
Lett se how ye chauntt.   [*They sing.*

Tunc intrat Mak in clamide se super togam vestitus.

190 *Mak.* Now, Lord, for thy naymes vij, that made both moyn and
starnes
Well mo then I can neuen, thi will, Lorde, of me tharnys.

f. 40b I am all vneuen; that moves oft my harnes.
Now wold God I were in heuen, for ther wepe no barnes
So styll.

195 *1 Pastor.* Who is that pypys so poore?

Mak. Wold God ye wyst how I foore!
Lo, a man that walkys on the moore,
And has not all his wyll.

2 Pastor. Mak, where has thou gone? Tell vs tythyng.

200 *3 Pastor.* Is he commen? Then ylkon take hede to his thyng.
                         [*Et accipit clamidem ab ipso.*

Mak. What! ich be a yoman, I tell you, of the kyng,
The self and the some, sond from a greatt lordyng,
And sich.
Fy on you! Goyth hence

205   Out of my presence!
I must haue reuerence.
Why, who be ich?

1 Pastor. Why make ye it so qwaynt? Mak, ye do wrang.

2 Pastor. Bot, Mak, lyst ye saynt? I trow that ye lang.

210 *3 Pastor.* I trow the shrew can paynt, the dewyll myght hym hang!

Mak. Ich shall make complaynt, and make you all to thwang
At a worde,
And tell euyn how ye doth.

1 Pastor. Bot, Mak, is that sothe?

215   Now take outt that Sothren tothe,
And sett in a torde!

193 ther, MS. the.

2 Pastor. Mak, the dewill in youre ee! A stroke wold I leyne you.

3 Pastor. Mak, know ye not me? By God, I couthe teyn you.

  [*They threaten him, and Mak hastily becomes himself again.*

Mak. God looke you all thre! Me thoght I had sene you.

220 Ye ar a fare compané.

 1 Pastor.   Can ye now mene you?

 2 Pastor. Shrew, pepe!

  Thus late as thou goys,

  What wyll men suppos?

  And thou has an yll noys

225 Of stelyng of shepe.

Mak. And I am trew as steyll, all men waytt;

 Bot a sekenes I feyll that haldys me full haytt:

 My belly farys not weyll; it is out of astate.

3 Pastor. Seldom lyys the dewyll dede by the gate.

230 *Mak.* Therfor

  Full sore am I and yll,

  If I stande stone-styll.

  I ete not an nedyll

  Thys moneth and more.

235 *1 Pastor.* How farys thi wyff? By thi hoode, how farys she?

 Mak. Lyys walteryng—by the roode—by the fyere, lo!

f. 41a And a howse full of brude. She drynkys well, to;

  Yll spede othere good that she wyll do!

  Bot sho

240 Etys as fast as she can,

  And ilk yere that commys to man

  She bryngys furth a lakan—

  And, som yeres, two.

  Bot were I now more gracyus and rychere be far,

245 I were eten outt of howse and of harbar.

  Yit is she a fowll dowse, if ye com nar;

  Ther is none that trowse nor knowys a war

  Then ken I.

  Now wyll ye se what I profer?—

250 To gyf all in my cofer

  To-morne at next to offer

  Hyr hed-maspenny.

  218 MS. teyle, *but* le *apparently written by a different hand over original* n.

  239 MS. so.   244 now, MS. not; be far, MS. befar.

2 Pastor. I wote so forwakyd is none in this shyre;
I wold slepe, if I takyd les to my hyere.
255 *3 Pastor.* I am cold and nakyd, and wold haue a fyere.
1 Pastor. I am wery, forrakyd, and run in the myre—
Wake thou!   [*Lies down.*
2 Pastor. Nay, I wyll lyg downe by,
For I must slepe, truly.   [*Lies down beside him.*
260 *3 Pastor.* As good a mans son was I
As any of you.
                    [*Lies down, and makes Mak join them.*
Bot, Mak, com heder! Betwene shall thou lyg downe.
Mak. Then mygt I lett you bedene of that ye wold rowne,
No drede.
265   Fro my top to my too,
        Manus tuas commendo,
        Poncio Pilato;
        Cryst-crosse me spede!
                    [*Tunc surgit, pastoribus dormientibus, et dicit:*
        Now were tyme for a man that lakkys what he wold
270   To stalk preuely than vnto a fold,
        And neemly to wyrk than, and be not to bold,
        For he mygt aby the bargan, if it were told
        At the endyng.
        Now were tyme for to reyll;
275   Bot he nedys good counsell
        That fayn wold fare weyll,
        And has bot lytyll spendyng.
                    [*Casts a spell on the sleeping shepherds.*
        Bot abowte you a serkyll, as rownde as a moyn,
        To I haue done that I wyll, tyll that it be noyn,
280   That ye lyg stone-styll to that I haue doyne;
        And I shall say thertyll of good wordys a foyne:
        'On hight,
f. 41b   Ouer youre heydys, my hand I lyft.
        Outt go youre een! Fordo youre syght!'
285   Bot yit I must make better shyft
        And it be right.
                    [*The shepherds begin to snore.*
        Lord, what thay slepe hard! That may ye all here.
        Was I neuer a shepard, bot now wyll I lere.
        If the flok be skard, yit shall I nyp nere.
290   How! drawes hederward! Now mendys oure chere
        From sorow

291 MS. ffron.

A fatt shepe, I dar say,
A good flese, dar I lay.
Eft-whyte when I may,
295 Bot this will I borow.
                    [*Goes off home with the sheep.*
How, Gyll, art thou in? Gett vs som lyght.
Vxor eius. Who makys sich dyn this tyme of the nyght?
I am sett for to spyn; I hope not I myght
Ryse a penny to wyn, I shrew them on hight!
300 So farys
A huswyff that has bene
To be rasyd thus betwene.
Here may no note be sene
For sich small charys.

305 *Mak.* Good wyff, open the hek! Seys thou not what I bryng?
Vxor. I may thole the dray the snek. A, com in, my swetyng!
Mak. Yee, thou thar not rek of my long standyng.
Vxor. By the nakyd nek art thou lyke for to hyng.
Mak. Do way!
310 I am worthy my mete,
For in a strate can I gett
More then thay that swynke and swette
All the long day.
                    [*Shows her the sheep.*
Thus it fell to my lott, Gyll; I had sich grace.
315 *Vxor.* It were a fowll blott to be hanged for the case.
Mak. I haue skapyd, Ielott, oft as hard a glase.
Vxor. 'Bot so long goys the pott to the water,' men says,
'At last
Comys it home broken.'
320 *Mak.* Well knowe I the token,
Bot let it neuer be spoken!
Bot com and help fast.

I wold he were flayn; I lyst well ete.
This twelmothe was I not so fayn of oone shepe-mete.
325 *Vxor.* Com thay or he be slayn, and here the shepe blete—
Mak. Then myght I be tane. That were a cold swette!
Go spar
f. 42a The gaytt-doore.
Vxor.   Yis, Mak,
For and thay com at thy bak—
330 *Mak.* Then myght I by, for all the pak,
The dewill of the war!

Vxor. A good bowrde haue I spied, syn thou can none:
Here shall we hym hyde, to thay be gone,
In my credyll. Abyde! Lett me alone,
335   And I shall lyg besyde in chylbed, and grone.
Mak. Thou red,
And I shall say thou was lyght
Of a knaue-childe this nyght.
Vxor. Now well is me day bright
340   That euer was I bred!

This is a good gyse and a far-cast;
Yit a woman avyse helpys at the last.
I wote neuer who spyse; agane go thou fast.
Mak. Bot I com or thay ryse, els blawes a cold blast!
345   I wyll go slepe.   [*Returns to the shepherds.*
Yit slepys all this meneye;
And I shall go stalk preuely,
As it had neuer bene I
That caryed thare shepe.   ,   [*Lies down between them.*

[*The First and Second Shepherds awake; the Second
Shepherd helps the First to stand up.*

350 *1 Pastor.* **Resurrex a mortruus!** Haue hold my hand.
Iudas carnas dominus! I may not well stand;
My foytt slepys, by Iesus, and I water fastand.
I thoght that we layd vs full nere Yngland.
2 Pastor. A, ye?
355   Lord, what I haue slept weyll!
As fresh as an eyll,
As lyght I me feyll
As leyfe on a tre.

[*The Third Shepherd awakes from a nightmare.*
3 Pastor. Bensté be herein! So me qwakys,
360   My hart is outt of skyn, whatso it makys.
Who makys all this dyn? So my browes blakys,
To the dowore wyll I wyn. Harke, felows, wakys!
We were fowre—
Se ye awre of Mak now?
365 *1 Pastor.* We were vp or thou.
2 Pastor. Man, I gyf God avowe,
Yit yede he nawre.

359 me, MS. my.

3 Pastor. Me thoght he was lapt in a wolfe-skyn.

1 Pastor. So ar many hapt now, namely within.

370 *3 Pastor.* When we had long napt, me thoght with a gyn

f. 42b A fatt shepe he trapt; bot he mayde no dyn.

2 Pastor. Be styll!
Thi dreme makys the woode;
It is bot fantom, by the roode.

375 *1 Pastor.* Now God turne all to good,
If it be his wyll.

[*They rouse Mak, who pretends to have been fast asleep.*

2 Pastor. Ryse, Mak, for shame! Thou lygys right lang.

Mak. Now Crystys holy name be vs emang!
What is this? For Sant Iame, I may not well gang!

380 I trow I be the same. A! my nek has lygen wrang
Enoghe. [*They pull him up from the ground.*
Mekill thank! Syn yister-euen,
Now by Sant Stevyn,
I was flayd with a swevyn—

385 My hart out of sloghe!

I thoght Gyll began to crok and trauell full sad,
Wel-ner at the fyrst cok, of a yong lad
For to mend oure flok. Then be I neuer glad;
I haue tow on my rok more then euer I had.

390 A, my heede!
A house full of yong tharmes,
The dewill knok outt thare harnes!
Wo is hym has many barnes,
And therto lytyll brede.

395 I must go home, by youre lefe, to Gyll, as I thoght.
I pray you looke my slefe, that I steyll noght;
I am loth you to grefe, or from you take oght. [*Goes off home.*

3 Pastor. Go furth, yll myght thou chefe! Now wold I we soght,
This morne,

400 That we had all oure store.

1 Pastor. Bot I will go before;
Let vs mete.

2 Pastor. Whore?

3 Pastor. At the crokyd thorne. [*Exeunt.*

370-1, 372-4 *The speakers' names for these lines are transposed in MS.*
383 MS. strevyn.

Mak is seen standing outside the door of his cottage.

Mak. Vndo this doore! Who is here? How long shall I stand?
405 *Vxor eius.* Who makys sich a bere? Now walk in the wenyand!
Mak. A, Gyll, what chere? It is I, Mak, youre husbande.
Vxor. Then may we se here the dewill in a bande,
Syr Gyle!
Lo, he commys with a lote,
410 As he were holden in the throte.
I may not syt at my note
A handlang while.

Mak. Wyll ye here what fare she makys to gett hir a glose?
And dos noght bot lakys, and clowse hir toose.
415 *Vxor.* Why, who wanders, who wakys? Who commys, who gose?
Who brewys, who bakys? What makys me thus hose?
And than
It is rewthe to beholde—
Now in hote, now in colde,
420 Full wofull is the householde
That wantys a woman.

f. 43*a* Bot what ende has thou mayde with the hyrdys, Mak?
Mak. The last worde that thay sayde when I turnyd my bak,
Thay wold looke that thay hade thare shepe, all the pak.
425 I hope thay wyll nott be well payde when thay thare shepe lak,
Perdé!
Bot howso the gam gose,
To me thay wyll suppose,
And make a fowll noyse,
430 And cry outt apon me.

Bot thou must do as thou hyght.
Vxor.   I accorde me thertyll;
I shall swedyll hym right in my credyll.
            [*She muffles up the sheep and puts it in the cradle.*
If it were a gretter slyght, yit couthe I help tyll.
I wyll lyg downe stright. Com hap me.
Mak.   I wyll.   [*Covers her.*
435 *Vxor.* Behynde!
Com Coll and his maroo,
Thay will nyp vs full naroo.

407 se, MS. be.

Mak. Bot I may cry 'out, haroo!'
The shepe if thay fynde.

440 *Vxor.* Harken ay when thay call; thay will com onone.
Com and make redy all, and syng by thyn oone;
Syng 'lullay' thou shall, for I must grone,
And cry outt by the wall on Mary and Iohn,
For sore.
445 Syng 'lullay' on fast
When thou heris at the last;
And bot I play a fals cast,
Trust me no more.

The shepherds meet at the crooked thorn.

3 Pastor. A, Coll, goode morne! Why slepys thou nott?
450 *1 Pastor.* Alas, that euer was I borne! We haue a fowll blott—
A fat wedir haue we lorne.
3 Pastor.   Mary, Godys forbott!
2 Pastor. Who shuld do vs that skorne? That were a fowll spott.
1 Pastor. Som shrewe.
I haue soght with my dogys
455 All Horbery shrogys,
And of xv hogys
Fond I bot oone ewe.

3 Pastor. Now trow me, if ye will—by Sant Thomas of Kent,
Ayther Mak or Gyll was at that assent.
460 *1 Pastor.* Peasse, man, be still! I sagh when he went.
Thou sklanders hym yll; thou aght to repent
Goode spede.
2 Pastor. Now as euer myght I the,
If I shuld euyn here de,
465 I wold say it were he
That dyd that same dede.

3 Pastor. Go we theder, I rede, and ryn on oure feete.
Shall I neuer ete brede, the sothe to I wytt.
1 Pastor. Nor drynk in my heede, with hym tyll I mete.
f. 43b *2 Pastor.* I wyll rest in no stede tyll that I hym grete,
My brothere.
Oone I will hight:
Tyll I se hym in sight,
Shall I neuer slepe one nyght
475 Ther I do anothere.

[*As the shepherds draw near to Mak's cottage, they hear
    Gyll groaning and Mak singing a tuneless lullaby.*

3 Pastor. Will ye here how thay hak? Oure syre lyst croyne.

1 Pastor. Hard I neuer none crak so clere out of toyne.
    Call on hym.

2 Pastor.   Mak, vndo youre doore soyne!

Mak. Who is that spak, as it were noyne,

480   On loft?
        Who is that, I say?

3 Pastor. Goode felowse, were it day.

Mak. As far as ye may,   [*Opens the door.*
    Good, spekys soft,

485   Ouer a seke womans heede that is at maylleasse;
    I had leuer be dede or she had any dyseasse.

Vxor. Go to anothere stede! I may not well qweasse;
    Ich fote that ye trede goys thorow my nese
    So hee.

490 *1 Pastor.* Tell vs, Mak, if ye may,
    How fare ye, I say?

Mak. Bot ar ye in this towne to-day?
    Now how fare ye?

    Ye haue ryn in the myre, and ar weytt yit;
495   I shall make you a fyre, if ye will sytt.
    A nores wold I hyre. Thynk ye on yit?
    Well qwytt is my hyre—my dreme, this is itt—
    A seson.   [*Points to the cradle.*
    I haue barnes, if ye knew,
500   Well mo then enewe;
    Bot we must drynk as we brew,
    And that is bot reson.

    I wold ye dynyd or ye yode. Me thynk that ye swette.

2 Pastor. Nay, nawther mendys oure mode drynke nor mette.

505 *Mak.* Why, syr, alys you oght bot goode?

3 Pastor.   Yee, oure shepe þat we gett
    Ar stollyn as thay yode. Oure los is grette.

Mak. Syrs, drynkys!
    Had I bene thore,
    Som shuld haue boght it full sore.

510 *1 Pastor.* Mary, som men trowes that ye wore,
    And that vs forthynkys.

2 Pastor. Mak, som men trowys that it shuld be ye.
3 Pastor. Ayther ye or youre spouse, so say we.
Mak. Now if ye haue suspowse to Gill or to me,
515   Com and rype oure howse, and then may ye se
        Who had hir.
        If I any shepe fott,
        Ayther cow or stott—
        And Gyll, my wyfe, rose nott
520   Here syn she lade hir—

f.44a   As I am true and lele, to God here I pray
        That this be the fyrst mele that I shall ete this day.
                        [*Points to the cradle.*
1 Pastor. Mak, as haue I ceyll, avyse the, I say:
        He lernyd tymely to steyll that couth not say nay.
525 *Vxor.* I swelt!
        Outt, thefys, fro my wonys!
        Ye com to rob vs for the nonys.
Mak. Here ye not how she gronys?
        Youre hartys shuld melt.
                        [*The shepherds approach the cradle.*
530 *Vxor.* Outt, thefys, fro my barne! Negh hym not thor!
Mak. Wyst ye how she had farne, youre hartys wold be sore.
        Ye do wrang, I you warne, that thus commys before
        To a woman that has farne—bot I say no more.
Vxor. A, my medyll!
535   I pray to God so mylde,
        If euer I you begyld,
        That I ete this chylde
        That lygys in this credyll.

Mak. Peasse, woman, for Godys payn, and cry not so!
540   Thou spyllys thy brane, and makys me full wo.
2 Pastor. I trow oure shepe be slayn. What fynde ye two?
3 Pastor. All wyrk we in vayn; as well may we go.
        Bot hatters!
        I can fynde no flesh,
545   Hard nor nesh,
        Salt nor fresh—
        Bot two tome platers.

        Whik catell bot this, tame nor wylde,
        None, as haue I blys, as lowde as he smylde.
550 *Vxor.* No, so God me blys, and gyf me ioy of my chylde!
        W.P.—G

1 Pastor. We haue merkyd amys; I hold vs begyld.
2 Pastor. Syr, don.
  Syr—oure Lady hym saue!—   [*To Mak.*
  Is youre chyld a knaue?
555 *Mak.* Any lord myght hym haue,
  This chyld, to his son.

  When he wakyns he kyppys, that ioy is to se.
3 Pastor. In good tyme to hys hyppys, and in celé!
  Bot who was his gossyppys so sone redé?
560 *Mak.* So fare fall thare lyppys!
  1 Pastor.   Hark now, a le.   [*Aside.*
  Mak. So God thaym thank,
f. 44*b* Parkyn, and Gybon Waller, I say,
  And gentill Iohn Horne, in good fay—
  He made all the garray—
565 With the greatt shank.

2 Pastor. Mak, freyndys will we be, for we ar all oone.
Mak. We? Now I hald for me, for mendys gett I none.
  Fare well all thre! All glad were ye gone. [*Aside.*
3 Pastor. Fare wordys may ther be, bot luf is ther none
570 Þis yere.   [*Exeunt shepherds.*
  1 Pastor. Gaf ye the chyld any thyng?
2 Pastor. I trow not oone farthyng.
3 Pastor. Fast agane will I flyng;
  Abyde ye me there.   [*Runs back.*

575 Mak, take it to no grefe if I come to thi barne.
  Mak. Nay, thou dos me greatt reprefe, and fowll has thou farne.
  3 Pastor. The child will it not grefe, that lytyll day-starne.
  Mak, with youre leyfe, let me gyf youre barne
  Bot vj pence.
580 *Mak.* Nay, do way! He slepys.
  3 Pastor. Me thynk he pepys.
  Mak. When he wakyns he wepys.
  I pray you go hence!

      [*The First and Second Shepherds return.*
  3 Pastor. Gyf me lefe hym to kys, and lyft vp the clowtt.
             [*Takes a peep.*
585 What the dewill is this? He has a long snowte!
  1 Pastor. He is merkyd amys. We wate ill abowte.

    553 MS. lady *crossed through and* lord *written above by a later hand.*

2 Pastor. Ill-spon weft, iwys, ay commys foull owte.
Ay, so!   [*Recognizes the sheep.*
He is lyke to oure shepe!
590 *3 Pastor.* How, Gyb, may I pepe?
1 Pastor. I trow kynde will crepe
Where it may not go.

2 Pastor. This was a qwantt gawde and a far-cast:
It was a hee frawde.
3 Pastor.   Yee, syrs, wast.
595 Lett bren this bawde and bynd hir fast.
A fals skawde hang at the last;
So shall thou.
Wyll ye se how thay swedyll
His foure feytt in the medyll?
600 Sagh I neuer in a credyll
A hornyd lad or now.

f. 45a *Mak.* Peasse, byd I. What, lett be youre fare!
I am he that hym gatt, and yond woman hym bare.
1 Pastor. What dewill shall he hatt, Mak? Lo, God, Makys ayre!
605 *2 Pastor.* Lett be all that! Now God gyf hym care,
I sagh.
Vxor. A pratty child is he
As syttys on a wamans kne;
A dyllydowne, perdé,
610 To gar a man laghe.

3 Pastor. I know hym by the eere-marke; that is a good tokyn.
Mak. I tell you, syrs, hark!—hys noyse was brokyn.
Sythen told me a clerk that he was forspokyn.
1 Pastor. This is a fals wark; I wold fayn be wrokyn.
615 Gett wepyn!
Vxor. He was takyn with an elfe,
I saw it myself;
When the clok stroke twelf
Was he forshapyn.

620 *2 Pastor.* Ye two ar well feft sam in a stede.
1 Pastor. Syn thay manteyn thare theft, let do thaym to dede.
Mak. If I trespas eft, gyrd of my heede.
With you will I be left.
3 Pastor.   Syrs, do my reede:
For this trespas

617 MS. my felf.
621, 623-8 *The speakers' names for these lines are transposed in MS.*

625   We will nawther ban ne flyte,
      Fyght nor chyte,
      Bot haue done as tyte,
      And cast hym in canvas.   *[They toss Mak.*

   1 Pastor. Lord, what I am sore, in poynt for to bryst!
630   In fayth, I may no more; therfor wyll I ryst.
   2 Pastor. As a shepe of vij skore he weyd in my fyst.
     For to slepe aywhore me thynk that I lyst.
   3 Pastor. Now I pray you
     Lyg downe on this grene.
635 *1 Pastor.* On these thefys yit I mene.
   3 Pastor. Wherto shuld ye tene?
     Do as I say you.   *[They lie down and sleep.*

      Angelus cantat 'Gloria in exelsis'; postea dicat:

Angelus. Ryse, hyrd-men heynd, for now is he borne
   That shall take fro the feynd that Adam had lorne;
640 That warloo to sheynd, this nyght is he borne.
   God is made youre freynd now at this morne,
     He behestys.
     At Bedlem go se
     Ther lygys that fre
645   In a cryb full poorely,
     Betwyx two bestys.   *[The angel withdraws.*

f. 45b *1 Pastor.* This was a qwant stevyn that euer yit I hard.
     It is a meruell to neuyn, thus to be skard.
   2 Pastor. Of Godys son of heuyn he spak vpward.
650 All the wod on a leuyn me thoght that he gard
     Appere.
   3 Pastor. He spake of a barne
     In Bedlem, I you warne.
   1 Pastor. That betokyns yond starne;   *[Points to the sky.*
655 Let vs seke hym there.

   2 Pastor. Say, what was his song? Hard ye not how he crakyd it,
     Thre brefes to a long?
   3 Pastor.   Yee, Mary, he hakt it:
     Was no crochett wrong, nor nothyng that lakt it.
   1 Pastor. For to syng vs emong, right as he knakt it,
660   I can.
   2 Pastor. Let se how ye croyne!
        629 *There is no speaker's name at the beginning of this line in MS.*

Can ye bark at the mone?
3 Pastor. Hold youre tonges! Haue done!
1 Pastor. Hark after, than.   [*He sings, and the others join in.*

665 *2 Pastor.* To Bedlem he bad that we shuld gang;
I am full fard that we tary to lang.
3 Pastor. Be mery and not sad—of myrth is oure sang!
Euerlastyng glad to mede may we fang,
Withoutt noyse.
670 *1 Pastor.* Hy we theder forthy,
If we be wete and wery,
To that chyld and that lady;
We haue it not to lose.

[*Tries to sing again, but is interrupted by the Second Shepherd:*

2 Pastor. We fynde by the prophecy—let be youre dyn!—
675 Of Dauid and Isay and mo then I myn—
Thay prophecyed by clergy—that in a vyrgyn
Shuld he lyght and ly, to slokyn oure syn,
And slake it,
Oure kynde, from wo;
680 For Isay sayd so:
Ecce virgo
Concipiet a chylde that is nakyd.

3 Pastor. Full glad may we be, and abyde that day
That lufly to se, that all myghtys may.
685 Lord, well were me for ones and for ay,
Myght I knele on my kne, som word for to say
To that chylde.
Bot the angell sayd
In a cryb was he layde;
690 He was poorly arayd,
Both mener and mylde.

1 Pastor. Patryarkes that has bene, and prophetys beforne,
Thay desyryd to haue sene this chylde that is borne.
Thay ar gone full clene; that haue thay lorne.
f. 46a We shall se hym, I weyn, or it be morne,
To tokyn.
When I se hym and fele,
Then wote I full weyll

673 *There is an uncancelled long s before* lose.

It is true as steyll
700 That prophetys haue spokyn:

To so poore as we ar that he wold appere,
Fyrst fynd, and declare by his messyngere.
2 Pastor. Go we now, let vs fare; the place is vs nere.
3 Pastor. I am redy and yare; go we in fere
705 To that bright.   [*They go to Bethlehem.*
Lord, if thi wylles be—
We ar lewde all thre—
Thou grauntt vs somkyns gle
To comforth thi wight.   [*They enter the stable.*

710 *1 Pastor.* Hayll, comly and clene! Hayll, yong child!
Hayll, maker, as I meyne, of a madyn so mylde!
Thou has waryd, I weyne, the warlo so wylde:
The fals gyler of teyn, now goys he begylde.
Lo, he merys,
715 Lo, he laghys, my swetyng!
A wel fare metyng!
I haue holden my hetyng:
Haue a bob of cherys.

2 Pastor. Hayll, sufferan sauyoure, for thou has vs soght!
720 Hayll, frely foyde and floure, that all thyng has wroght!
Hayll, full of fauoure, that made all of noght!
Hayll! I kneyll and I cowre. A byrd haue I broght
To my barne.
Hayll, lytyll tyne mop!
725 Of oure crede thou art crop;
I wold drynk on thy cop,
Lytyll day-starne.

3 Pastor. Hayll, derlyng dere, full of Godhede!
I pray the be nere when that I haue nede.
730 Hayll, swete is thy chere! My hart wold blede
To se the sytt here in so poore wede,
With no pennys.
Hayll! Put furth thy dall!
I bryng the bot a ball:
735 Haue and play the withall,
And go to the tenys.

Maria. The fader of heuen, God omnypotent,
That sett all on seuen, his son has he sent.

My name couth he neuen, and lyght or he went.
740   I conceyuyd hym full euen thrugh myght, as he ment;
And now is he borne.
He kepe you fro wo!
I shall pray hym so.
Tell furth as ye go,
745   And myn on this morne.

f. 46b *1 Pastor.* Fare well, lady, so fare to beholde,
With thy childe on thi kne.
  2 Pastor.   Bot he lygys full cold.
Lord, well is me! Now we go, thou behold.
  3 Pastor. Forsothe, allredy it semys to be told
750   Full oft.
  1 Pastor. What grace we haue fun!
  2 Pastor. Com furth; now ar we won!
  3 Pastor. To syng ar we bun—
Let take on loft!   *[They go out singing.*

       Explicit pagina Pastorum.

MAGNUS HERODES

Nuncius	Primus Miles	Primus Consultus	Prima Mulier
Herodes	Secundus Miles	Secundus Consultus	Secunda Mulier
	Tercius Miles		Tercia Mulier

Enter Herod's messenger.

Nuncius. Moste myghty Mahowne meng you with myrth!
  Both of burgh and of towne, by fellys and by fyrth,
  Both kyng with crowne and barons of brith,
  That radly wyll rowne, many greatt grith
5 Shall behapp.
  Take tenderly intent
  What sondys ar sent,
  Els harmes shall ye hent,
  And lothes you to lap.

10 Herode, the heynd kyng—by grace of Mahowne—
  Of Iury, sourmontyng sternly with crowne
  On lyfe that ar lyfyng in towre and in towne,
  Gracyus you gretyng, commaundys you be bowne
  At his bydyng.
15 Luf hym with lewté;
  Drede hym, that doughty!
  He chargys you be redy
  Lowly at his lykyng.

  What man apon mold menys hym agane
20 Tytt teyn shall be told, knyght, sqwyere, or swayn;
  Be he neuer so bold, byes he that bargan
  Twelf thowsandfold more then I sayn,
  May ye trast.
  He is worthy wonderly,
25 Selcouthly sory:
  For a boy that is borne herby
  Standys he abast.

5 MS. be happ.
11 MS. Iourmontyng.

A kyng thay hym call, and that we deny;
How shuld it so fall, greatt meruell haue I;
30 Therfor ouerall shall I make a cry
That ye busk not to brall nor lyke not to ly
This tyde.
Carpys of no kyng
Bot Herode, that lordyng,
35 Or busk to youre beyldyng,
Youre heedys for to hyde.

f. 55b He is kyng of kyngys, kyndly I knowe,
Chefe lord of lordyngys, chefe leder of law.
Ther watys on his wyngys that bold bost wyll blaw;
40 Greatt dukys downe dyngys for his greatt aw
And hym lowtys;
Tuskane and Turky,
All Inde and Italy,
Cecyll and Surry
45 Drede hym and dowtys.

From Paradyse to Padwa, to Mownt Flascon,
From Egyp to Mantua, vnto Kemptowne,
From Sarceny to Susa, to Grece it abowne,
Both Normondy and Norwa lowtys to his crowne.
50 His renowne
Can no tong tell,
From heuen vnto hell;
Of hym can none spell
Bot his cosyn Mahowne.

55 He is the worthyest of all barnes that ar borne;
Fre men ar his thrall, full teynfully torne.
Begyn he to brall, many men cach skorne;
Obey must we all, or els be ye lorne
Att onys.
60 Downe dyng of youre knees,
All that hym seys;
Dysplesyd he beys,
And byrkyn many bonys.

Here he commys now, I cry, that lord I of spake!
65 Fast afore wyll I hy, radly on a rake,
And welcom hym worshipfully, laghyng with lake,
As he is most worthy, and knele for his sake

So low;
Downe deruly to fall,
70   As renk most ryall.
Hayll, the worthyest of all!
To the must I bow.   [*Kneels.*

Enter Herod, accompanied by knights and counsellors.
The messenger addresses him:

Hayll, luf lord! Lo, thi letters haue I layde;
I haue done I couth do, and peasse haue I prayd;
75   Mekyll more therto opynly dysplayd.
Bot romoure is rasyd so, that boldly thay brade
Emangys thame:
Thay carp of a kyng;
Thay seasse not sich chateryng.
80 *Herodes.* Bot I shall tame thare talkyng,
And let thame go hang thame.

Stynt, brodels, youre dyn—yei, euerychon!
I red that ye harkyn to I be gone;
f. 56a   For if I begyn, I breke ilka bone,
85   And pull fro the skyn the carcas anone—
Yei, perdé!
Sesse all this wonder,
And make vs no blonder,
For I ryfe you in sonder,
90   Be ye so hardy.

Peasse, both yong and old, at my bydyng, I red,
For I haue all in wold: in me standys lyfe and dede.
Who that is so bold, I brane hym thrugh the hede!
Speke not or I haue told what I will in this stede.
95   Ye wote nott
All that I will mefe;
Styr not bot ye haue lefe,
For if ye do, I clefe
You small as flesh to pott.

100   My myrthes ar turned to teyn, my mekenes into ire,
And all for oone, I weyn, within I fare as fyre.
May I se hym with eyn, I shall gyf hym his hyre;
Bot I do as I meyn, I were a full lewde syre
In wonys.
105   Had I that lad in hand,

98 *This line begins with a capital A, cancelled.*

As I am kyng in land,
I shuld with this steyll brand
Byrkyn all his bonys.

My name spryngys far and nere: the doughtyest, men me call,
110 That euer ran with spere, a lord and kyng ryall.
What ioy is me to here a lad to sesse my stall!
If I this crowne may bere, that boy shall by for all.
I anger:
I wote not what dewill me alys.
115 Thay teyn me so with talys
That, by Gottys dere nalys,
I wyll peasse no langer.

What dewill! me thynk I brast for anger and for teyn;
I trow thyse kyngys be past that here with me has beyn.
120 Thay promysed me full fast or now here to be seyn,
For els I shuld haue cast anothere sleght, I weyn.
I tell you,
A boy thay sayd thay soght,
With offeryng that thay broght;
125 It mefys my hart right noght
To breke his nek in two.

Bot be thay past me by, by Mahowne in heuen,
I shall, and that in hy, set all on sex and seuen.
Trow ye a kyng as I will suffre thaym to neuen
130 Any to haue mastry bot myself full euen?
Nay, leyfe!—
f. 56b The dewill me hang and draw,
If I that losell knaw,
Bot I gyf hym a blaw
135 That lyfe I shall hym reyfe.

For parels yit I wold wyst if thay were gone;
And ye therof her told, I pray you say anone;
For and thay be so bold, by God that syttys in trone,
The payn can not be told that thay shall haue ilkon,
140 For ire.
Sich panys hard neuer man tell,
For-vgly and for-fell,
That Lucyfere in hell
Thare bonys shall all to-tyre.

145 *1 Miles.* Lord, thynk not ill if I tell you how thay ar past;
    I kepe not layn, truly. Syn thay cam by you last,
    Anothere way in hy thay soght, and that full fast.
  Herodes. Why, and ar thay past me by? We! outt! for teyn I brast!
    We! fy!   [*He rushes about, and belabours the knights.*
150 Fy on the dewill! Where may I byde,
    Bot fyght for teyn and al to-chyde?
    Thefys, I say ye shuld haue spyde,
    And told when thay went by.

    Ye ar knyghtys to trast! Nay, losels ye ar, and thefys!
155 I wote I. yelde my gast, so sore my hart it grefys.
  2 Miles. What nede you be abast? Ther ar no greatt myschefys
    For these maters to gnast.
  3 Miles.   Why put ye sich reprefys
    Withoutt cause?
    Thus shuld ye not thrett vs,
160 Vngaynly to bete vs;
    Ye shuld not rehett vs
    Withoutt othere sawes.

  Herod. Fy, losels and lyars! lurdans ilkon!
    Tratoures and well wars! knafys, bot knyghtys none!
165 Had ye bene woth youre eres, thus had thay not gone;
    Gett I those land-lépars, I breke ilka bone.
    Fyrst vengeance
    Shall I se on thare bonys;
    If ye byde in these wonys,
170 I shall dyng you with stonys—
    Yei, dìtizance doutance!

    I wote not where I may sytt for anger and for teyn;
    We haue not done all yit, if it be as I weyn.
    Fy! dewill! now how is it? As long as I haue eyn,
175 I thynk not for to flytt, bot kyng I will be seyn
    For euer.
    Bot stand I to quart,
    I tell you my hart:
    I shall gar thayni start,
180 Or els trust me neuer.

f. 57a *1 Miles.* Syr, thay went sodanly or any man wyst,
    Els had mett we—yei, perdy!—and may ye tryst.
      177 *I is evidently intended here, but the MS. letter is shaped more like long* r.

2 Miles. So bold nor so hardy agans oure lyst
    Was none of that company durst mete me with fyst
185 For ferd.
    3 Miles. Ill durst thay abyde,
    Bot ran thame to hyde;
    Might I thaym haue spyde,
    I had made thaym a berd.

190 What couth we more do to saue youre honoure?
    1 Miles. We were redy therto, and shal be ilk howre.
    Herod. Now syn it is so, ye shall haue fauoure,
    Go where ye wyll go, by towne and by towre.
    Goys hens!   *[Exeunt knights.*
195 I haue maters to mell
    With my preuey counsell.
    Clerkys, ye bere the bell;   *[To his counsellors.*
    Ye must me encense.

    Oone spake in myne eere a wonderfull talkyng,
200 And sayde a madyn shuld bere anothere to be kyng.
    Syrs, I pray you inquere in all wrytyng,
    In Vyrgyll, in Homere, and all other thyng
    Bot legende.
    Sekys poecé-tayllys,
205 Lefe pystyls and grales;
    Mes, matyns noght avalys—
    All these I defende.
                [The counsellors consult their books.
    I pray you tell heyndly now what ye fynde.
    1 Consultus. Truly, syr, prophecy it is not blynd.
210 We rede thus by Isay: He shal be so kynde
    That a madyn, sothely, which neuer synde,
    Shall hym bere:
    Virgo concipiet,
    Natumque pariet.
215 'Emanuell' is hete,
    His name for to lere:

    'God is with vs,' that is for to say.
    2 Consultus. And othere says thus, tryst me ye may:
    Of Bedlem a gracyus lord shall spray,
220 That of Iury myghtyus kyng shal be ay,
    Lord myghty;
    And hym shall honoure

Both kyng and emperoure.
Herodes. Why, and shuld I to hym cowre?
225 Nay, ther thou lyys lyghtly!

Fy! the dewill the spede, and me, bot I drynk onys!
This has thou done indede to anger me for the nonys;
f. 57b And thou, knafe, thou thy mede shall haue, by Cokys dere bonys!
Thou can not half thi crede. Outt, thefys, fro my wonys!
230 Fy, knafys!
Fy, dottypols, with youre bookys—
Go kast thaym in the brookys!
With sich wylys and crokys
My wytt away rafys.

235 Hard I neuer sich a trant that a knafe so sleght
Shuld com lyke a sant and refe me my right.
Nay, he shall on-slant; I shall kyll hym downe stryght.
War! I say, lett me pant. Now thynk I to fyght
For anger.
240 My guttys will outt thryng
Bot I this lad hyng;
Withoutt I haue a vengyng,
I may lyf no langer.

Shuld a carll in a kafe bot of oone yere age
245 Thus make me to rafe?
1 Consultus.   Syr, peasse this outrage!
Away let ye wafe all sich langage.
Youre worship to safe, is he oght bot a page
Of a yere?
We two shall hym teyn
250 With oure wyttys betweyn,
That, if ye do as I meyn,
He shall dy on a spere.

2 Consultus. For drede that he reyn, do as we red:
Thrugoutt Bedlem and ilk othere stede
255 Make knyghtys ordeyn, and put vnto dede
All knaue-chyldren of two yerys brede
And within;
This chyld may ye spyll
Thus at youre awne will.
260 *Herodes.* Now thou says heretyll
A right nobyll gyn.

If I lyf in land good lyfe, as I hope,
This dar I the warand—to make the a pope.
O, my hart is rysand now in a glope!
265 For this nobyll tythand thou shall haue a drope
Of my good grace:
Markys, rentys, and powndys,
Greatt castels and groundys;
Thrugh all sees and soundys
270 I gyf the the chace.

Now wyll I procede and take veniance.
All the flowre of knyghthede call to legeance,
Bewshere, I the byd; it may the avance.   [*To Nuncius.*
Nuncius. Lord, I shall me spede and bryng, perchaunce,
275 To thy syght.   [*Goes off to summon the knights.*
f. 58a Hark, knyghtys, I you bryng
Here new tythyng:
Vnto Herode kyng
Hast with all youre myght,

280 In all the hast that ye may, in armowre full bright;
In youre best aray looke that ye be dight.
1 Miles. Why shuld we fray?
2 Miles.   This is not all right.
3 Miles. Syrs, withoutten delay I drede that we fight.
Nuncius. I pray you,
285 As fast as ye may
Com to hym this day.
1 Miles. What, in oure best aray?
Nuncius. Yei, syrs, I say you.

2 Miles. Somwhat is in hand, whateuer it meyn.
290 *3 Miles.* Tarry not for to stand, ther or we haue beyn.
                    [*They go to Herod.*
Nuncius. Kyng Herode all-weldand, well be ye seyn!
Youre knyghtys ar comand in armoure full sheyn
At youre wyll.
1 Miles. Hayll, dughtyest of all!
295 We ar comen at youre call
For to do what we shall,
Youre lust to fullfyll.

263 *The words* a pope *are largely erased, but* a *and the* e *of* pope *are still plainly visible.*
There is a cross under a.
269 MS. sandys.

Herod. Welcom, lordyngys, iwys, both greatt and small!
The cause now is this that I send for you all:
300   A lad, a knafe, borne is that shuld be kyng ryall;
Bot I kyll hym and his, I wote I brast my gall.
Therfor, syrs,
Veniance shall ye take
All for that lad sake;
305   And men I shall you make,
Where ye com aywhere, syrs.

To Bedlem loke ye go, and all the coste aboute;
All knaue-chyldren ye slo—and, lordys, ye shal be stoute—
Of yeres if thay be two and within. Of all that rowte,
310   On lyfe lyefe none of tho that lygys in swedyll-clowte,
I red you.
Spare no kyns bloode,
Lett all ryn on floode;
If women wax woode,
315   I warn you, syrs, to spede you.

Hens now go youre way, that ye were thore!
2 Miles. I wote we make a fray, bot I wyll go before.
3 Miles. A! thynk, syrs, I say; I mon whett lyke a bore.
1 Miles. Sett me before, ay good enogh for a skore.
320   Hayll, heyndly!
We shall for youre sake
Make a dulfull lake.
Herodes. Now if ye me well wrake,
Ye shall fynd me freyndly.
                              [*The knights withdraw.*
325 *2 Miles.* Go ye now tyll oure noytt, and handyll thaym weyll.
3 Miles. I shall pay thaym on the cote, begyn I to reyll.
        First Woman comes forward with her child.
f. 58b *1 Miles.* Hark, felose! ye dote. Yonder commys vnceyll;
I hold here a grote she lykys me not weyll
Be we parte.
330   Dame, thynk it not yll,   [*To First Woman.*
Thy knafe if I kyll.
    1 Mulier. What, thefe, agans my wyll?
Lord, kepe hym in qwarte!   [*Tries to escape.*

    1 Miles. Abyde now, abyde; no farther thou gose.
335 *1 Mulier.* Peasse, thefe! Shall I chyde and make here a nose?

1 Miles. I shall reyfe the thy pryde; kyll we these boyse!
1 Mulier. Tyd may betyde, kepe well thy nose,
  Fals thefe!
  Haue on loft on thy hode!
340 *1 Miles.* What, hoore, art thou woode?   [*Kills her child.*
  1 Mulier. Outt, alas, my chyldys bloode!
  Outt, for reprefe!

  Alas for shame and syn! Alas that I was borne!
  Of wepyng who may blyn, to se hir chylde forlorne?
345 My comforth and my kyn, my son thus al to-torne!
  Veniance for this syn I cry, both euyn and morne.
  2 Miles. Well done!
  Com hedyr, thou old stry: [*To Second Woman.*
  That lad of thyne shall dy.
350 *2 Mulier.* Mercy, lord, I cry!
  It is myn awne dere son.

  2 Miles. No mercy thou mefe; it mendys the not, Mawd.
  2 Mulier. Then thi skalp shall I clefe! Lyst thou be clawd?
  Lefe, lefe, now bylefe!
  2 Miles.   Peasse, byd I, bawd!
355 *2 Mulier.* Fy, fy, for reprefe! Fy, full of frawde—
  No man!
  Haue at thy tabard,
  Harlot and holard:
  Thou shall not be sparde!
360 I cry and I ban!
                          [*He kills her child.*
  Outt! morder-man, I say, strang tratoure and thefe!
  Out, alas, and waloway! my chyld that was me lefe!
  My luf, my blood, my play, that neuer dyd man grefe!
  Alas, alas, this day! I wold my hart shuld clefe
365 In sonder!
  Veniance I cry and call
  On Herode and his knyghtys all:
  Veniance, Lord, apon thaym fall,
  And mekyll warldys wonder!

370 *3 Miles.* This is well-wroght gere that euer may be.
  Comys hederward here! Ye nede not to fle. [*To Third Woman.*
  3 Mulier. Wyll ye do any dere to my chyld and me?
W.P.—H

  3 Miles. He shall dy, I the swere; his hart-blood shall thou se.
  3 Mulier. God forbede!
375 Thefe, thou shedys my chyldys blood!   [*He kills her child.*
  Out, I cry! I go nere wood!
  Alas, my hart is all on flood,
  To se my chyld thus blede.

f. 59a By God, thou shall aby this dede that thou has done.
380 *3 Miles.* I red the not, stry, by son and by moyn.
  3 Mulier. Haue at the, say I! Take the ther a foyn!
  Out on the, I cry! Haue at thi groyn
  Anothere!
  This kepe I in store.
385 *3 Miles.* Peasse now, no more!
  3 Mulier. I cry and I rore,
  Out on the, mans mordere!

  Alas, my bab, myn innocent, my fleshly get! For sorow
  That God me derly sent, of bales who may me borow?
390 Thy body is all to-rent! I cry, both euen and morow,
  Veniance for thi blod thus spent: 'out!' I cry, and 'horow!'
  1 Miles. Go lightly!
  Gett out of thise wonys,
  Ye trattys, all at onys,
395 Or by Cokys dere bonys
  I make you go wyghtly!   [*Exeunt women.*

  Thay ar flayd now, I wote; thay will not abyde.
  2 Miles. Lett vs ryn fote-hote—now wold I we hyde—
  And tell of this lott, how we haue betyde.
400 *3 Miles.* Thou can do thi note; that haue I aspyde.
  Go furth now,
  Tell thou Herode oure tayll.
  For all oure avayll,
  I tell you, saunce fayll
405 He wyll vs alow.

  1 Miles. I am best of you all, and euer has bene;
  The deuyll haue my saull bot I be fyrst sene!
  It syttys me to call my lord, as I wene.
  2 Miles. What nedys the to brall? Be not so kene
410 In this anger;
  I shall say thou dyd best—
  Saue myself, as I gest.   [*Aside.*

1 Miles. We! that is most honest.
3 Miles. Go, tary no langer.

[*They go to Herod.*

415 *1 Miles.* Hayll, Herode, oure kyng. Full glad may ye be;
Good tythyng we bryng. Harkyn now to me:
We haue mayde rydyng thrughoutt Iuré.
Well wyt ye oone thyng, that morderd haue we
Many thowsandys.
420 *2 Miles.* I held thaym full hote,
I payd them on the cote;
Thare dammys, I wote,
Neuer byndys them in bandys.

3 Miles. Had ye sene how I fard when I cam emang them!
425 Ther was none that I spard, bot lade on and dang them.
f. 59b I am worthy a rewarde. Where I was emangys them,
I stud and I stard; no pyté to hang them
Had I.
Herodes. Now by myghty Mahowne,
430 That is good of renowne,
If I bere this crowne
Ye shall haue a lady

Ilkon to hym layd, and wed at his wyll.
1 Miles. So haue ye lang sayde—do somwhat thertyll!   [*Aside.*
435 *2 Miles.* And I was neuer flayde, for good ne for yll.
3 Miles. Ye myght hold you well payde oure lust to fulfyll,
Thus thynk me,
With tresure vntold,
If it lyke that ye wold
440 Both syluer and gold
To gyf vs greatt plenté.

Herodes. As I am kyng crownde, I thynk it good right;
Ther goys none on grownde that has sich a wyght.
A hundreth thowsand pownde is good wage for a knyght;
445 Of pennys good and rownde, now may ye go light
With store;
And ye knyghtys of oures
Shall haue castels and towres,
Both to you and to youres,
450 For now and euermore.

1 Miles. Was neuer none borne by downes ne by dalys,
Nor yit vs before, that had sich avalys.

2 *Miles*. We haue castels and corne, mych gold in oure malys.
3 *Miles*. It wyll neuer be worne, withoutt any talys.
455   Hayll, heyndly!
Hayll, lord! Hayll, kyng!
We ar furth foundyng.   [*Exeunt*.
Herod. Now Mahowne he you bryng
Where he is lord freyndly!

460   Now in peasse may I stand—I thank the, Mahowne!—
And gyf of my lande that longys to my crowne.
                                   [*To the audience*:
Draw therfor nerehande, both of burgh and of towne:
Markys, ilkon, a thowsande, when I am bowne,
Shall ye haue.
465   I shal be full fayn
To gyf that I sayn;
Wate when I com agayn,
And then may ye craue.

I sett by no good, now my hart is at easse,
470   That I shed so mekyll blode. Pes, all my ryches!
For to se this flode from the fote to the nese
Mefys nothyng my mode—I lagh that I whese!
A, Mahowne,
So light is my saull
475   That all of sugar is my gall!
I may do what I shall,
And bere vp my crowne.

f. 60a   I was castyn in care, so frightly afrayd;
Bot I thar not dyspare, for low is he layd
480   That I most dred are, so haue I hym flayd;
And els wonder ware—and so many strayd
In the strete—
That oone shuld be harmeles,
And skape away hafles,
485   Where so many chyldes
Thare balys can not bete.

A hundreth thowsand, I watt, and fourty ar slayn,
And four thowsand. Therat me aght to be fayn;
Sich a morder on a flat shall neuer be agayn.
490   Had I had bot oone bat at that lurdan
So yong,

It shuld haue bene spokyn
How I had me wrokyn,
Were I dede and rotyn,
495 With many a tong.

Thus shall I tech knauys ensampyll to take,
In thare wyttys that rauys, sich mastré to make.
All wantones wafys—no langage ye crak!
No sufferan you sauys; youre nekkys shall I shak
500 In sonder.
No kyng ye on call
Bot on Herode the ryall,
Or els many oone shall
Apon youre bodys wonder.

505 For if I here it spokyn when I com agayn,
Youre branys bese brokyn; therfor be ye bayn.
Nothyng bese vnlokyn; it shal be so playn.
Begyn I to rokyn, I thynk all dysdayn
For-daunche.
510 Syrs, this is my counsell:
Bese not to cruell.
Bot adew!—to the deuyll!
I can no more Franch.   [*Exit.*

Explicit Magnus Herodes.

508 MS. rekyn.

COLIPHIZACIO

Primus Tortor   Cayphas   Iesus
Secundus Tortor   Anna   Froward

*Enter the First and Second Torturers, driving
Jesus before them.*

1 Tortor. Do io furth, io! and trott on apase!
To Anna will we go and Syr Cayphas.
Witt thou well: of thaym two gettys thou no grace,
Bot euerlastyng wo, for trespast thou has
5   So mekill.
Thi mys is more
Then euer gettys thou grace fore;
Thou has beyn aywhore
Full fals and full fekyll.

10 *2 Tortor.* It is wonder to dre, thus to be gangyng.
We haue had for the mekill hart-stangyng;
Bot at last shall we be out of hart-langyng,
Be thou haue had ij or thre hetys worth a hangyng.
No wonder!
15   Sich wyles can thou make,
Gar the people farsake
Oure lawes, and thyne take;
Thus art thou broght in blonder.

1 Tortor. Thou can not say agaynt, if thou be trew.
20   Som men holdys the sant, and that shall thou rew;
Fare wordys can thou paynt, and lege lawes new.
2 Tortor. Now be ye ataynt, for we will persew
On this mater.
Many wordys has thou saide
25   Of which we ar not well payde;
As good that thou had
Halden still thi clater.

1 Tortor. It is better syt still then rise vp and fall.
Thou has long had thi will, and made many brall;

4 MS. trespas.   8 beyn *written above line by a different hand.*

30 At the last wold thou spill and fordo vs all,
 If we dyd neuer yll.
 2 Tortor. I trow not he shall
 Indure it;
 For if other men ruse hym,
 We shall accuse hym.
35 Hisself shall not excuse hym,
 To you I insure it,

 With no legeance.
 1 Tortor. Fayn wold he wynk,
 Els falys his covntenance; I say as I thynk.
 2 Tortor. He has done vs greuance; therfor shall he drynk.
f. 74a Haue he mekill myschaunsce that has gart vs swynke
 In walkyng,
 That vnneth may I more.
 1 Tortor. Peas, man, we ar thore!
 I shall walk in before,
45 And tell of his talkyng.
 [*They come to where Caiaphas and Annas are sitting.*
 Haill, syrs, as ye sytt, so worthi in wonys!
 Whi spyrd ye not yit how we haue farne this onys?
 2 Tortor. Sir, we wold fayn ye witt all wery ar oure bonys;
 We haue had a fytt right yll for the nonys,
50 So tarid.
 Cayphas. Say, were ye oght adred?
 Were ye oght wrang led,
 Or in any strate sted?
 Syrs, who was myscaryd?

55 *Anna.* Say, were ye oght in dowte for fawte of light,
 As ye wached therowte?
 1 Tortor. Sir, as I am true knyght,
 Of my dame sen I sowked had I neuer sich a nyght;
 Myn een were not lowked togeder right
 Sen morowe;
60 Bot yit I thynk it well sett,
 Sen we with this tratoure met.
 Sir, this is he that forfett, [*Pointing at Jesus.*
 And done so mekill sorow.

 Cayphas. Can ye hym oght apeche? Had he any ferys?
65 *2 Tortor.* He has bene for to preche full many long yeris,
 48 ye *not in MS.*

And the people he teche a new law.

1 Tortor.   Syrs, heris!
As far as his witt reche, many oone he lerys.
When we toke hym,
We faunde hym in a yerde;
70   Bot when I drew out my swerde,
His dyscypyls wex ferde,
And soyn thay forsoke hym.

2 Tortor. Sir, I hard hym say he cowthe dystroew oure tempyll so
        gay,
And sithen beld a new on the thrid day.
75 *Cayphas.* How myght that be trew? It toke more aray!
The masons I knewe that hewed it, I say,
So wyse,
That hewed ilka stone.
1 Tortor. A, good syr, let hym oone.
80   He lyes for the quetstone—
I gyf hym the pryce!

2 Tortor. The halt rynes, the blynd sees thrugh his fals wyles;
Thus he gettys many fees of thym he begyles.
f. 74b *1 Tortor.* He rases men that dees—thay seke hym be myles—
85   And euer thrugh his soceres oure sabate-day defyles
Euermore, syr.
2 Tortor. This is his vse and his custom:
To heyll the defe and the dom,
Wheresoeuer he com;
90   I tell you before, syr.

1 Tortor. Men call hym a kyng and Godys son of heuen;
He wold fayn downe bryng oure lawes bi his steuen.
2 Tortor. Yit is ther anothere thyng that I hard hym neuen:
He settys not a fle-wyng bi Syr Cesar full euen;
95   He says thus.
Sir, this same is he
That excusyd with his sotelté
A woman in avowtré,
Full well may ye trust vs.

100 *1 Tortor.* Sir, Lazare can he rase—that men may persaue—
When he had lyne iiij dayes ded in his graue.
All men hym prase, both master and knaue,

82 wyles, MS. lyes.   91 kyng, MS. prophete.

Such wychcraft he mase.
2 *Tortor.*   If he abowte waue
Any langere,
105 His warkys may we ban;
For he has turned many man
Sen the tyme he began,
And done vs great hangere.

1 Tortor. He will not leyfe yit, thof he be culpabyll;
110 Men call hym a prophete, a lord full renabyll.
Sir Cayphas, bi my wytt, he shuld be dampnabill;
Bot wold ye two, as ye sytt, make it ferme and stabyll
Togeder?
For ye two, as I traw,
115 May defende all oure law;
That mayde vs to you draw,
And bryng this losell heder.

2 *Tortor.* Sir, I can tell you before, as myght I be maryd,
If he reyne any more oure lawes ar myscaryd.
120 *1 Tortor.* Sir, opposed if he wore, he shuld be fon waryd;
That is well seyn thore where he has long tarid
And walkyd.
He is sowre-lottyn:
Ther is somwhat forgottyn;
125 I shall thryng out the rottyn
Be we haue all talkyd.

Cayphas. Now fare myght you fall for youre talkyng!
For, certys, I myself shall make examynyng.
Harstow, harlott, of all? Of care may thou syng!   [*To Jesus.*
f. 75a How durst thou the call aythere emperoure or kyng?
I do fy the!
What the dwill doyst thou here?
Thi dedys will do the dere.
Com nar and rowne in myn eeyr,
135 Or I shall ascry the.

Illa-hayll was thou borne! Harke, says he oght agane?
Thou shall onys or to-morne to speke be full fayne.
This is a great skorne and a fals trane;
Now wols-hede and outhorne on the be tane,
140 Vile fature!
Oone worde myght thou speke ethe,

Yit myght it do the som letht;
Et omnis qui tacet
Hic consentire videtur.

145 Speke on oone word, right in the dwyllys name!
Where was thi syre at bord when he met with thi dame?
What, nawder bowted ne spurd, and a lord of name?
Speke on in a torde, the dwill gif the shame,
Sir Sybré!
150 Perdé, if thou were a kyng,
Yit myght thou be ridyng.
Fy on the, fundlyng!
Thou lyfys bot bi brybré.

Lad, I am a prelate, a lord in degré:
155 Syttys in myn astate, as thou may se,
Knyghtys on me to wate in dyuerse degré.
I myght thole the abate, and knele on thi kne
In my present.
As euer syng I mes,
160 Whoso kepis the law, I gess,
He gettys more by purches
Then bi his fre rent.

The dwill gif the shame that euer I knew the!
Nather blynde ne lame will none persew the.
165 Therfor I shall the name—that euer shall rew the—
Kyng Copyn in oure game; thus shall I indew the
For a fatur.
Say, dar thou not speke for ferde?
I shrew hym the lerd!
170 Weme! the dwillys durt in thi berd,
Vyle fals tratur!

Though thi lyppis be stokyn, yit myght thou say 'mom.'
Great wordys has thou spokyn; then was thou not dom.
Be it hole worde or brokyn; com owt with som,
175 Els on the I shal be wrokyn or thi ded com
All outt.
f. 75*b* Aythere has thou no wytt,
Or els ar thyn eres dytt.
Why, bot herd thou not yit?
180 So, I cry and I showte!

Anna. A, syr, be not yll payde though he not answere;
   He is inwardly flayde, not right in his gere.
Cayphas. No, bot the wordys he has saide doth my hart great dere.
Anna. Sir, yit may ye be dayde.
Cayphas.   Nay, whils I lif, nere!
185 *Anna.* Sir, amese you.
Cayphas. Now fowll myght hym befall!
Anna. Sir, ye ar vexed at all,
   And perauentur he shall
   Hereafter pleas you.

190   We may bi oure law examyn hym fyrst.
Cayphas. Bot I gif hym a blaw my hart will brist.
Anna. Abyde to ye his purpose knaw.
Cayphas.   Nay, bot I shall out-thrist
   Both his een on a raw.
Anna.   Syr, ye will not, I tryst,
   Be so vengeabyll;
195 Bot let me oppose hym.
Cayphas. I pray you—and sloes hym!
Anna. Sir, we may not lose hym,
   Bot we were dampnabill.

Cayphas. He has adyld his ded; a kyng he hym calde.
200   War! let me gyrd of his hede!
Anna.   I hope not ye wold;
   Bot, syr, do my red, youre worship to hald.
Cayphas. Shall I neuer ete bred to that he be stald
   In the stokys.
Anna. Sir, speke soft and styll;
205 Let vs do as the law will.
Cayphas. Nay, I myself shall hym kyll,
   And murder with knokys.

Anna. Sir, thynk ye that ye ar a man of holy kyrk;
   Ye shuld be oure techere, mekenes to wyrk.
210 *Cayphas.* Yei, bot all is out of har, and that shall he yrk.
Anna. All soft may men go far; oure lawes ar not myrk,
   I weyn.
   Youre wordys ar bustus;
   Et hoc nos volumus,
215   *Quod de iure possumus.*
   Ye wote what I meyn—

It is best that we trete hym with farenes.
Cayphas.   We, nay!
f. 76a *Anna.* And so myght we gett hym som word for to say.
Cayphas. War! let me bett hym!
Anna.   Syr, do away!
220   For if ye thus thrett hym, he spekys not this day.
Bot herys:
Wold ye sesse and abyde,
I shuld take hym on syde,
And inquere of his pryde
225   How he oure folke lerys.

Cayphas. He has renyd ouer lang with his fals lyys,
And done mekyll wrang—Sir Cesar he defyes;
Therfor shall I hym hang or I vpryse.
Anna. Sir, the law will not he gang on no kyn wyse
230   Vndemyd.
Bot fyrst wold I here
What he wold answere;
Bot he dyd any dere,
Why shuld he be flemyd?

235   And therfor examynyng fyrst will I make,
Sen that he callys hym a kyng.
Cayphas.   Bot he that forsake,
I shall gyf hym a wryng that his nek shall crak.
Anna. Syr, ye may not hym dyng; no word yit he spake
That I wyst.
240   Hark, felow, com nar!   [*To Jesus.*
Wyll thou neuer be war?
I haue meruell thou dar
Thus do thyn awne lyst.

Bot I shall do as the law wyll, if the people ruse the.
245   Say, dyd thou oght this yll? Can thou oght excuse the?
Why standys thou so styll when men thus accuse the?
For to hyng on a hyll, hark how thay ruse the
To dam.
Say, art thou Godys son of heuen,
250   As thou art wonte for to neuen?
Iesus. So thou says by thy steuen,
And right so I am;

For after this shall thou se when that I do com downe
In brightnes on he, in clowdys from abone.
255 *Cayphas.* A, ill myght the feete be that broght the to towne!
Thou art worthy to de. Say, thefe, where is thi crowne?
Anna. Abyde, syr!
Let vs lawfully redres.
Cayphas. We nede no wytnes;
260 Hysself says expres.
Whi shuld I not chyde, syr?

Anna. Was ther neuer man so wyk bot he myght amende
When it com to the pryk, right as youreself kend.
f. 76b *Cayphas.* Nay, syr, bot I shall hym styk euen with myn awne hend;
265 For if he rene and be whyk, we ar at an end,
All sam.
Therfor, whils I am in this brethe,
Let me put hym to deth.
Anna. *Sed nobis non licet*
270 *Interficere quemquam.*

Sir, ye wote better then I we shuld slo no man.
Cayphas. His dedys I defy! His warkys may we ban;
Therfor shall he by.
Anna.   Nay, on oder wyse than,
And do it lawfully.
Cayphas.   As how?
Anna.   Tel you I can.
275 *Caiphas.* Let se!
Anna. Sir, take tent to my sawes:
Men of temperall lawes,
Thay may deme sich cause;
And so may not we.

280 *Cayphas.* My hart is full cold, nerehand that I swelt.
For talys that ar told I bolne at my belt—
Vnethes may it hold my body, and ye it felt!
Yit wold I gif of my gold yond tratoure to pelt
For euer.
285 *Anna.* Good syr, do as ye hett me.
Caiphas. Whi, shall he ouersett me?
Syr Anna, if ye lett me,
Ye do not youre deuer.

253 I *not in MS.*

Anna. Sir, ye ar a prelate.
Cayphas.   So may I well seme,
290   Myself if I say it.
Anna.   Be not to breme!
        Sich men of astate shuld no men deme,
        Bot send them to Pilate. The temperall law to yeme
        Has he;
        He may best threte hym,
295   And all to-rehete hym.
        It is shame you to bete hym;
        Therfor, syr, let be.
                         [*Caiaphas strikes at Jesus and misses him.*
Cayphas. Fy on hym and war! I am oute of my gate.
        Say, why standys he so far?
Anna.   Sir, he cam bot late.
300 *Cayphas.* No, bot I haue knyghtys that dar rap hym on the pate.
Anna. Ye ar bot to skar. Good syr, abate
        And here:
        What nedys you to chyte?
        What nedys you to flyte?
305   If ye yond man smyte,
        Ye ar irregulere.

Cayphas. He that fyrst made me clerk and taght me my lare
        On bookys for to barke—the dwill gyf hym care!
f. 77a *Anna.* A, good syr, hark! Sich wordys myght ye spare.
310 *Cayphas.* Els myght I haue made vp wark of yond harlot and mare,
        Perdé!
        Bot certys, or he hens yode,
        It wold do me som good
        To se knyghtys knok his hoode
315   With knokys two or thre.

        For sen he has trespast, and broken oure law,
        Let vs make hym agast and set hym in awe.
Anna. Syr, as ye haue hast, it shal be, I traw.
        Com and make redy fast, ye knyghtys on a raw,
320   Youre arament;   [*The torturers come forward.*
        And that kyng to you take,
        And with knokys make hym wake.
Cayphas. Yei, syrs, and for my sake
        Gyf hym good payment.

325   For if I myght go with you, as I wold that I myght,
        I shuld make myn avowe that ons or mydnyght

I shuld make his heede sow, wher that I hyt right.
1 Tortor. Sir, drede you not now of this cursed wight
To-day,
330 For we shall so rok hym,
And with buffettys knok hym.
Cayphas. And I red that ye lok hym,
That he ryn not away;

For I red not we mete, if that lad skap.
335 *2 Tortor.* Sir, on vs be it bot we clowt well his kap.
Cayphas. Wold ye do as ye heytt, it were a fayr hap.
1 Tortor. Sir, sytt ye and see it, how that we hym knap
Oone feste!
Bot, or we go to this thyng,
340 Sayn vs, lord, with thy ryng.
Cayphas. Now he shall haue my blyssyng
That knokys hym the best.
                    [The torturers drag Jesus away.
2 Tortor. Go we now to oure noyte with this fond foyll.
1 Tortor. We shall teche hym, I wote, a new play of Yoyll,
345 And hold hym full hote. Fraward, a stoyll
Go fetch vs!   *[Froward comes forward.*
Froward.   We, dote! Now els were it doyll,
And vnnett.
For the wo that he shall dre,
Let hym knele on his kne.
350 *2 Tortor.* And so shall he for me.
Go fetche vs a light buffit!
                    [Froward fetches the stool.
Froward. Why must he sytt soft—with a mekill myschaunce!—
That has tenyd vs thus oft?
1 Tortor.   Sir, we do it for a skawnce.
If he stode vpon loft, we must hop and dawnse
f. 77b As cokys in a croft.
Froward.   Now a veniance
Com on hym!
Good skill can ye shew
As fell i the dew.
Haue this—bere it, shrew!   *[Hands the stool to Jesus.*
360 For soyn shall we fon hym.

2 Tortor. Com, syr, and syt downe. Must ye be prayde?
Lyke a lord of renowne youre sete is arayde.

337 MS. Sir see ye and sytt.   345 MS. frawrard.

1 Tortor. We shall preue on his crowne the wordys he has sayde.

2 Tortor. Ther is none in this towne, I trow, be ill payde

365   Of his sorow,
  Bot the fader that hym gate.

 1 Tortor. Now, for oght that I wate,
  All his kyn commys to late
  His body to borow.

370 *2 Tortor.* I wold we were onwarde.

 1 Tortor.   Bot his een must be hyd.

 2 Tortor. Yei, bot thay be well spard, we lost that we dyd.
  Step furth thou, Froward!

 Froward.   What is now betyd?

 1 Tortor. Thou art euer awayward.

 Froward.   Haue ye none to byd
  Bot me?

375 I may syng 'ylla-hayll!'

 2 Tortor. Thou must get vs a vayll.

 Froward. Ye ar euer in oone tayll.

 1 Tortor. Now ill myght thou the!

  Well had thou thi name, for thou was euer curst.

380 *Froward.* Sir, I myght say the same to you, if I durst.
  Yit my hyer may I clame; no penny I purst.
  I haue had mekyll shame, hunger, and thrust
  In youre seruyce.

 1 Tortor. Not oone word so bold!

385 *Froward.* Why, it is trew that I told!
  Fayn preue it I wold.

 2 Tortor. Thou shal be cald to peruyce.

     [Froward goes out and comes back with a veil.

 Froward. Here a vayll haue I fon; I trow it will last.

 1 Tortor. Bryng it hyder, good son. That is it that I ast.

390 *Froward.* How shuld it be bon?

 2 Tortor.   Abowte his heade cast.

 1 Tortor. Yei, and when it is well won, knyt a knot fast,
  I red.

 Froward. Is it weyll?

 2 Tortor.   Yei, knaue.

 Froward. What, weyn ye that I rafe?

395 Cryst curs myght he haue
  That last bond his heade!

 1 Tortor. Now sen he is blynfeld, I fall to begyn;

f. 78a   And thus was I counseld the mastry to wyn. *[Striking Jesus.*

2 Tortor. Nay, wrang has thou teld; thus shuld thou com in.
                                                [Striking him.
400 *Froward.* I stode and beheld—thou towchid not the skyn
    Bot fowll.
  1 Tortor. How will thou I do?
  2 Tortor. On this manere, lo!   *[Striking again.*
  Froward. Yei, that was well gone to;
405   Ther start vp a cowll.

  1 Tortor. Thus shall we hym refe all his fonde talys.
                                      [Striking again.
  2 Tortor. Ther is noght in thi nefe, or els thi hart falys.
  Froward. I can my hand vphefe and knop out the skalys.
  1 Tortor. Godys forbot ye lefe, bot set in youre nalys
410   On raw.
    Sit vp and prophecy—   *[To Jesus, as they strike in turn.*
  Froward. Bot make vs no ly—
  2 Tortor. Who smote the last?
  1 Tortor.   Was it I?
  Froward. He wote not, I traw.

                 [They bring Jesus back to Caiaphas and Annas.
415 *1 Tortor.* Fast to Syr Cayphas go we togeder.
  2 Tortor. Ryse vp—with ill grace!—so com thou hyder.
  Froward. It semys by his pase he groches to go thyder.
  1 Tortor. We haue gyfen hym a glase, ye may consyder,
    To kepe.   *[To Caiaphas.*
420 *2 Tortor.* Sir, for his great boost,
    With knokys he is indoost.
  Froward. In fayth, syr, we had almost
    Knokyd hym on slepe.

  Cayphas. Now sen he is well bett, weynd on youre gate,
425   And tell ye the forfett vnto Syr Pylate,
    For he is a iuge sett emang men of state;
    And looke that ye not let.
  1 Tortor.   Com furth, old trate,
    Belyfe!
    We shall lede the a trott.
430 *2 Tortor.* Lyft thy feete, may thou not?
  Froward. Then nedys me do nott
    Bot com after and dryfe.
             [They go out, leading and driving Jesus.

    423 MS. knokyp.   427 MS. crate.
W.P.—I

Cayphas. Alas, now take I hede!
Anna.   Why mowrne ye so?
Cayphas. For I am euer in drede, wandreth, and wo,
435   Lest Pylate for mede let Iesus go;
       Bot had I slayn hym indede with thise handys two
       At onys,
       All had bene qwytt than.
       Bot gyftys marres many man;
440   Bot he deme the sothe than,
       The dwill haue his bonys!

f. 78b Sir Anna, all I wyte you this blame; for had ye not beyn,
        I had mayde hym full tame—yei, stykyd hym, I weyn,
        To the hart full wan with this dagger so keyn.
445 *Anna.* Sir, you must shame sich wordys for to meyn
        Emang men.
       Cayphas. I will not dwell in this stede,
        Bot spy how thay hym lede,
        And persew on his dede.
450   Fare well! we gang, men.   [*Exeunt.*
              Explicit Coliphizacio.

NOTES

1. MACTACIO ABEL

Secunda pagina (footnote). The *Mactacio Abel* is the only numbered pageant in the cycle. For *Glover pac* . . . (i.e. 'Glovers' pageant') see p. xv above.

13. i.e. the devil hang him on the gallows.

25 ff. Cain has a plough-team of eight animals, comprising four oxen and four horses.

37. *Pikeharnes.* Cain's name for his boy seems to be from *pick* 'steal' and *harness* 'armour'. *NED.* (s. Pick-) defines it as 'one who strips the slain of their armour', and gives examples from this pageant and from *Piers Plowman*, B-text, xx. 261, C-text, xxiii. 263. The word no doubt acquired the general meaning 'thief'; see W. Oelrich, *Die Personennamen im mittelalterlichen Drama Englands* (Dissertation, Kiel, 1911), pp. 75–6. Pikeharnes, like his counterpart in the Shepherds' Plays and in the *Coliphizacio* (see notes to 4.145, 6.380–3), has a lot in common with the impudent servant of the mummers' plays; see R. J. E. Tiddy, *The Mummers' Play*, p. 111.

37–45. These lines are arranged as one stanza, as suggested by F. W. Cady (*JEGP.* x. 574), M. G. Frampton (*AB.* xlix. 3), and P. E. Dustoor (*ES.* lxiii. 221).

38. Garcio, in this aside, uses the familiar *thou* in speaking of his master. But when he addresses him openly, he uses the polite *ye*, as in 43.

39. *hold and drife* 'hold the plough and drive the animals'; cf. 62.

42. *Lemyng.* The Surtees glossary gives this as the name of an ox, while the EETS. glossary assumes it to be the name of a horse. The Surtees gloss is supported by the words 'one oxe called lemynge', which occur in a Wakefield will dated 1552–3; see G. D. Lumb, *Testamenta Leodiensia*, p. 332.

44. *Want of mete it gars* 'lack of food causes it', i.e. is why the animals won't pull as hard as they should.

45. 'That's why I lay their fodder behind them.' Garcio's reason for keeping the animals short of food seems to be to immobilize them and so give himself less to do.

46–56. These lines are arranged as one stanza, following Cady, Frampton, and Dustoor.

48. 'Your false cheeks shall pay for that.'

49. 'And have it back right away.' Pikeharnes refers to the buffet that Cain has just given him.

53. '(Do) nothing now but go on shouting quickly (to the team).'

54. 'So that we can get this land ploughed.' A similar construction, with *that* and the present or past subjunctive following an imperative, is found elsewhere, e.g. in 146, 2.317, 3.209, 5.316. Cf. *Canon's Yeoman's Tale (Cant. Tales*, VIII. 1102–3).

56. This line looks like a mischievous aside, but possibly a negative particle has been omitted by the copyist before *let* or *stand*; see *ES.* lxiii. 221. Pikeharnes takes no further part in the action until 385, when he reappears in answer to Cain's summons. In the interval he presumably takes charge of the animals and plough, leaving Cain free to act with Abel the ceremonial burning of the tithes. The plough is again referred to near the end of the pageant (452, 460).

59–60. The meaning seems to be: 'I don't want to curse you; but you'd be as welcome away from here', i.e. your absence would be welcome.

64. Cf. quotation from *Friar Daw's Reply* (1401) in *NED.* s. Grease, *v.*, sense 2: 'Go, grees a shoep undir the taile.'

73. There is no mention of a burnt offering in Gen. iv.

84. 'Let out your geese; the fox wants to preach to them.' This is a variation of the proverb which is more commonly worded 'whanne þe fox prechyth, kepe wel ȝore gees', as in the

Castle of Perseverance 804 (EETS. ES. 91). Cain uses it here to mean that he is not such a fool as to be tricked out of his hard-won possessions by Abel's specious talk. A fox in ecclesiastical attire preaching to a congregation of birds is a favourite subject of the medieval carver and illuminator. See M. D. Anderson, *The Medieval Carver* (Cambridge, 1935), p. 114 and plate XVb; also G. Warner, *Queen Mary's Psalter* (London, 1912), plate 192a, where there is a drawing of a fox, with mitre and pastoral staff, preaching to the birds, one of which is a goose.

88. Apparently another reference to the podex.

94. *and say I bad* 'and tell him I sent you'.

100. *here my hand* 'here's my hand on it'. The scribal substitution of *hend* for *hand* is probably due to the influence of *hend* as a rhyme-word in 102; see ES. lxiii. 222.

103. 'And afterwards (our offering) should be burnt in praise of Him'; see ES. lviii. 168, lxiii. 222.

104. This reference to the priest is a reminder that Cain's unwilling payment of his tithe has a contemporary application. See H. S. Bennett, *Life on the English Manor* (Cambridge, 1948), p. 30: 'The tithe barn was an ever-present reminder of the power and needs of the Church; and many a man must have played the part of Cain in the Towneley play of *The Killing of Abel*.'

110. 'Here's my word that it is not otherwise.' For *Here my trouth* cf. 159, 4.163.

113. *hym*, i.e. God.

114. 'By Him who redeemed me at so dear a price', i.e. by Christ. Such anachronisms are very common in these pageants. A religious oath sounds insincere on the lips of Cain, and it was no doubt meant to. Cain uses the devil's name when he is being natural; a devout oath like this one means that he is telling a lie, and is intent on covering it up. Cf. note to 6.159.

118. 'Does he give *me* anything? May *you* have good fortune in equal measure!'

121. 'It would have appeared otherwise', i.e. things would have been different.

151. Cain seems to be cursing his father in particular; cf. 72–3.

164. 'But I see well enough that I must needs go'; *nede* is adverbial here.

184–5. 'And God forbid you should show me gratitude or courtesy.' Cain has no difficulty in saying 'God forbid' to God Himself.

186. 'So may I enjoy the use of these two legs.' A common type of asseveration in ME.; cf. *Nun's Priest's Tale* (*Cant. Tales*, VII. 3300): 'So moote I brouke wel myne eyen tweye.'

192 ff. The medieval legends of Cain attempted to explain God's dissatisfaction with Cain's offering by making him offer God his worst produce, and not simply 'of the fruit of the ground' (Gen. iv. 3). The repetition of the numbers by Cain in 192 ff. probably means that he is busy selecting the best sheaves for himself as well as miscounting the sheaves in his own favour. Abel's reproof *thou tendys wrang, and of the warst* (224) is no doubt meant to include Cain's shameless arithmetic as well as his dishonesty in keeping the best sheaves for himself.

197. *This hold I thrift* 'I regard this as my earnings' (and therefore due to me).

205. 'If I'm in a hurry to deal out my sheaves in this way, may it be long ere I prosper.'

222. 'Cain, pay correctly the tithe of all your produce together.'

225. *hide myne een*. Cain is contemptuously asking Abel to cover his eyes, so that he cannot see to choose the best sheaves for himself and the worst for God.

229. *is*. The rhyme requires the Northern form *es*; see Introduction, p. xxxii, note 5.

232. 'And so I laid down the sheaves exactly.'

234–5. 'Now if he gets any more—as much as one handful—the devil take me!'

236. *that*. Cain refers to the single sheaf he has already parted with (218–19).

264. 'Aren't you offering yet a tithe of your measly swine?' This question is Cain's way of reminding Abel to look after his own business; cf. 247–8.

265. 'If you pay your tithe correctly, you shall find it out', i.e. it shall be made known to you.

271–2. These two verses form the last line of f. 5a. Below them, in the bottom right-hand corner of the page, the copyist has written 'Bot now syn thou has etc'. These words, which begin f. 6*a*, are the copyist's first indication that he has inadvertently written on f. 6*a* the verses which belong to f. 5*b*, so that f. 6*a* must be taken before f. 5*b*. In the top left-hand corner of f. 5*b* he has written '[M]d that this syde of the leyfe [sh]uld folow the other next syde [ac]cordyng to the tokyns here maide, [an]d then after al stondys in ordre'. Again, in the bottom right-hand corner of f. 5*b* he has written 'Bot hark boy I haue a counsel etc', which are the first words on f. 6*b*. He has reinforced these directions by 'tokyns', so that the reader will know exactly how to correct his error. Wann (*PMLA*. xliii. 142), who describes these tokens in details, suggests that the copyist was 'misled by the coincidence that the first three words of 5b and 6a are identical'. In this edition the copyist's mistake has been corrected in accordance with his instructions, so that 'al stondys in ordre'.

277 ff. The suffocating smoke that rises from Cain's burnt offering of his worst sheaves is a detail of the Cain legend found elsewhere, e.g. in the Cornish *Creation of the World* copied by William Jordan in 1611 (translated by W. Stokes, as appendix to Philological Society Transactions, 1863, p. 87).

288. 'It burns all the worse because of you.'

297. *hob ouer the wall*. For the antics of Hob in Yorkshire folk-lore see E. M. Wright, *Rustic Speech and Folk-Lore* (Oxford, 1913), p. 202; also Bruce Dickins, 'Yorkshire Hobs', Yorkshire Dialect Society Transactions, vii, part xliii (1942), 9–23. The words *ouer the wall* may refer to the balustrade of the balcony on which God made his appearance in the craft-pageants; see *Archaeologia*, xciii. 67–8.

299. *for parels all* 'because of all the dangers (that threaten us)'; cf. 5.136.

306–7. These lines were presumably spoken as an aside; Cain is thinking of a secret place in which to murder his brother.

318. *did bot smoked* 'did but smoke'. The main verb is in the same tense as the auxiliary; cf. 4.414.

324. *cheke-bon. Cursor Mundi* 1073 (Trin. MS.) describes Cain's weapon as 'a cheke boon of an asse'; the pageant of Cain and Abel in the *Ludus Coventriae* makes it a 'chavyl bon' (149); Jordan's *Creation of the World* (in Cornish) has an English stage direction to the effect that Abel is stricken 'with a chawe bone and dyeth'; the Chester pageant does not name the weapon, and the York pageant is defective at this point. The tradition which made Cain's lethal weapon a jaw-bone seems to have originated in England, where it is found as early as the ninth century in the Old English prose *Solomon and Saturn*. It was also a popular motive in English manuscript illuminations from the eleventh to the sixteenth century; see M. Schapiro, *Art Bulletin*, xxiv. 205.

328–35. In accordance with Frampton's suggestion (*AB.*·xlix. 3), these lines have been arranged as one stanza. They may be the last eight lines of what was originally a twelve-line stanza like 25–36.

332. Cain's misuse of *amend* is an ironical way of saying that his amends for the crime will be worse than the crime itself.

339. 'For if I'm caught, I'm as good as dead.'

341. *rayse* has a special connotation here, viz. 'to rouse a beast from its lair'; see *NED*. s. Raise, *v.*¹, sense 4b.

347. 'Whoever was there could see', i.e. anyone already in hell could see for himself.

356–7. 'Deal out your punishment all round (i.e. give it to others), for I don't want any of it, or keep it for yourself when I am gone.'

367. *Gudeboure at the quarell hede*. The origin of *Gudeboure* is uncertain. Walker (*Wakefield, Its History and People*, i. 132–3) gives early spellings like 'Godiboure' (1377) and 'Godithe-boure' (1392); Professor A. H. Smith has come across 'le Godeybowr' in a West Riding Court Roll (1409). Walker assumes, on the basis of the spelling 'Goditheboure', that it must originally have meant 'God i' the bower', with reference to the place where the religious plays of Wakefield were performed. But 'Godithebowre' may very well contain the Christian name *Godith(a)*, and so mean 'Godith's cottage or dwelling'. On the whole it seems safer to identify the first element as OE. *Gōdgȳþ*, ME. *Godith (a)*. There are several references to Goodybower

and its quarry in Wakefield documents, e.g. 'Do. [Henry Grice] for a parcel of land in Goody-bower called Quarrell Pits . . . 2s. od.', in the rental of the Rectory Manor of Wakefield (1556/7); see T. Taylor, *The History of Wakefield*. *The Rectory Manor* (Wakefield, 1886), Appendix, p. x. (During the nineteenth century Goodybower was renamed Brook Street.)

370. *it bese not so*, i.e. no one shall murder you.

372. *sloys the, yong or old*. Dustoor (*ES*. lxiii. 223) suggests the insertion of *the* after *sloys*, thus making this verse correspond more closely to Gen. iv. 15. On the right of vv. 372–3, which are written as one line in the manuscript, a later hand has added the words 'and that shall do thy boddy der'.

389. 'Even if you were my own father.'

392. 'Thus I've come here to get nothing but blows.'

397. *bayn*. EETS. glosses *bayn* by 'quickly', *NED*. (s. Bane, *sb.*[1]) by 'murderer'. But Cain wants Garcio's help in burying Abel's body (382–3), so it does not make sense that he should now be asking Garcio to 'run away with thee quickly' or to 'run away with the murderer'. Holthausen (*ES*. lviii. 170) inserts *body* after *the*; but this emendation is unnecessary if *bayn* is taken to mean 'bones, mortal remains', possibly influenced by ON. *bein* (see *ES*. lxiii. 223).

408. Here *peasse* means the protection granted by the king to a particular person. God's refusal to allow the murderer himself to be murdered in punishment for his crime (371–3) is twisted by Cain into a royal proclamation of pardon of the sort that every man in Wakefield must have heard. (This last statement is made on the authority of Professor J. F. T. Plucknett, who has written to me on the subject in a letter dated 24 Sept. 1951.)

409. In the manuscript these words are written as one line with the preceding verse, but there are two parallel oblique strokes after *peasse* which divide the line into two separate verses. In this edition, therefore, the words *Thrughout this land* are numbered as an independent line; in EETS. they are not thus numbered.

410. 'Yes, at once, I vow to God.'

410–17. These lines fall into three groups—quatrain, couplet, and triplet. It will be noticed that 429–37 also consist of these groups in the same sequence.

411. 'How will you do, long ere you prosper?', i.e. how will you do that, bad luck to you?

413. Garcio is to command silence and attention for his master by shouting *oyes, oyes, oy* (417).

415. 'Then he shall be smooth of fortune', i.e. then he shall find that fortune goes smoothly for him.

418. *Browes, browes*. These words are a sarcastic echo of Cain's *oyes, oyes* in the preceding line. Garcio's thoughts are running on food, here and in the rest of his derisive commentary on Cain's bogus proclamation.

433. 'See that no one says to either of them.' This sentence is left unfinished. Doubtless Cain was put out by Garcio's way of finishing it.

436. 'Badly spun woof comes out badly', i.e. it breaks when it comes out of the shuttle during weaving. The meaning of this proverbial saying (used again in 4.587) is similar to that of another proverb: 'What is bred in the bone will come out in the flesh.' Ray, *English Proverbs* (1670), notes it as a Yorkshire saying.

437. 'May it be long before you get your hose (i.e. before you prosper), if you go about your work in this fashion.' After this angry outburst Cain continues his 'proclamation' in the next line.

438. 'Bid everyone be pleased to pay them.' Cain's optimism is made fun of by Garcio, who thinks it just as likely that Cain will give his horse a wisp of hay (439). This reference to the money that Cain hopes to collect from the audience is reminiscent of the *quête* which ends the performance of a mummers' play; see E. K. Chambers, *The English Folk-Play*, pp. 63 ff.

445. *blissyng withoutten end*. Garcio's general imprecation is a humorous reversal of the solemn benediction which often ends a medieval poem or pageant (see, for example, the ending of Play 2).

450–62. For this Wakefield stanza see Appendix II, p. 127.

459. *bi Codys sydys* is a type of oath characteristic of the violent characters in the Wakefield pageants; cf. note to 5.116.

463–70. These lines have the structure of the Wakefield stanza, except that the cauda lacks a verse to rhyme with 468–9. 463–6 are written as four lines in the manuscript, as they are printed here, with metrical marks after the internal rhymes.

465. An echo of 375. After the rough comedy which follows the murder of Abel the pageant ends solemnly enough with the reminder that Cain is forever damned.

2. PROCESSUS NOE

Wakefeld. This place-name also appears in the title of Play I in the full cycle; see Introduction, p. xiv. Wann (*PMLA*. xliii. 141) observes that under the present title of the pageant in the manuscript 'a heavy black line has been drawn over a very carefully made erasure. The matter erased had evidently a close connexion with the title of the Play of Noah.'

10. *is.* The rhyme requires the Northern form *es*. When a pronoun subject does not immediately precede or follow, *is* (*es*) is used in Northern dialect for all persons of the pres. pl.; see Forsström, *The Verb 'To Be' in Middle English*, p. 192.

14. *Forwhi* is taken here and in 284, 518 as a conjunction meaning 'because', following Adams. But it may also be taken as an interrogative adverb meaning 'why?', as in EETS.

18. 'And seated himself on a level with Him.'

28–9. *maide* not only governs *man*, but is also a causative verb governing the phrase *That place to be restord*. The meaning of these lines is that God made man in order to fill the place left empty by the rebel angels; cf. York VII. 23–4:

Þanne made he manne to his liknes,
That place of price for to restore.

31. *thaym.* The original form was probably *tham*, making an assonantal rhyme with *man began, woman*; see *SP.* xxxiii. 19.

41. *knowe.* The rhyme requires *knawe* or *trowe*; cf. 167, 171.

42. *and sythen.* MS. *in sythen*. The *in* may result from the copyist's confusing the Tironian sign for *and* with *ĩ* (= *in*). But it is also possible that the copyist replaced original *and* by *in* under the influence of *in* preceding and following in the same line.

46. The story of the Oil of Mercy promised by God to Adam, which derives ultimately from the apocryphal Gospel of Nicodemus, is referred to in the Chester play of *Christ's Descent into Hell* 65 ff. (EETS. ES. 115), and is dramatized at some length in the first part of the Cornish trilogy (*Ordinalia*).

49. *syn* is 3 pl. pres., *euery liffyng leyde* 48 being equivalent to a plural subject.

51–3. The seven deadly sins.

56. *alod.* Mätzner glosses this word by 'allowed' (OF. *alouer*); Tolkien gives it as the pp. of ME. *allowe* 'approve' (OF. *alouer*); Onions (*Medium Ævum*, i. 206) and Sisam both identify it with *olod* in a poem attributed to Rolle (see Horstman, *Yorkshire Writers: Richard Rolle of Hampole*, i. 73, line 22). But Sisam glosses it by 'wide-spread (?)', and Onions by 'ruined'. Onions, who compares the Cumberland and Westmorland *aloddin* 'lost, missing' recorded in *EDD.*, derives the meaning of *alod* from Norse *aflóga* (Icel. *aflóga* 'worn out, useless') and its form from ON. *aflóa*. He translates *on vs . . . For syn is now alod* 55–6 by 'on us . . . (who) are now ruined because of sin'. This interpretation, which is adopted here, involves ellipsis of the relative pronoun and Northern syntax of *is* (see note to *is* 10).

66. *my fry shal with me fall.* The relative pronoun is to be understood before *shal*. The word *fall* in this context probably means 'decline morally and physically', and so parallels *widder away* 63. Noah presumably means that he and his family are doomed to moral and physical decay unless God saves them. The use of *fall* links the Noah story to the fall of Lucifer (20 ff.) and the fall of Adam (39 ff.).

85. Sisam emends to *displeates*, but *displeasse* can be 3 pl. pres., agreeing with *syn* used collectively; cf. note to *syn* 49.

97. *vnsoght* 'unexpiated, unatoned' (ON. *úsdttr*). This gloss is given by EETS. and Tolkien. The *NED*. (s. Unsought, sense 1b) has '[found] without being sought for' (OE. *sēcan*, *sōht*).

108. This Northern use of *then* 'nor' is found in local Wakefield documents, e.g. 'And for witnes of the fore seide stuff shuld not be eloigned, enbeiseld, then put away' (1498); see *YAJ*. xv. 93.

109. *Hym to mekill wyn* can mean either 'to his great profit' (OE. *winn*) or 'to his great joy' (OE. *wynn*).

111. *reynand to and fro* 'prevailing on all sides'. Tolkien doubtfully glosses *reynand* by 'running' (ON. *renna*); but 'reign' (OF. *regner*) in the sense of 'prevail, be dominant' is supported by the following passage from Mirk's *Festial* (EETS. ES. 96, p. 72): 'Then, for God segh þis wikednes namly of þes synnys regnyng yn þe world, he sayde þus: "Me forthenkyth þat I made man."'' Cf. York VIII. 14: 'And synne is nowe reynand so ryffe'.

125. *thirté*. The MS. spelling *thrirte* represents a scribal blend of forms like *thritte* and *thirty* (cf. *thyrty* 260).

127. *Anoynt* may have something of its religious meaning here. Anointing with oil has always played an important part in the ceremonies of the Christian Church, and it usually symbolizes the conferring of grace; cf. *Oyle of mercy* 46.

129. *chese*. MS. *chefe*. Long *s* and *f* are more than once confused in the manuscript; cf. 4.617. Emendation of *chefe* to *chese* (made in EETS.) is confirmed by the occurrence of the same phrase—*Thre ches chambre*—in 281, where final *s* in the manuscript has the unambiguous rounded form. It may be noticed that *thre chese chambres* has Vulgate authority: 'deorsum, coenacula, et tristega facies in ea' (Gen. vi. 16). The Vulgate three-tiered ark is shown in the Junian Genesis drawings; see I. Gollancz, *The Caedmon Manuscript* (Oxford, 1927), pp. 66, 68.

143. Emendation to *thame* (cf. 1.421, 5.81) makes better sense, but *hame* 'home' (cf. 1.422) is just possible.

156–8. 'As for beasts, birds, and domestic animals—for you must bear *them* in mind—my advice is that some help be sought for them quickly.'

183. *wife*. This word, required by the context, was first suggested by the Surtees editor.

200. *Stafford blew* is the name of a blue cloth; cf. 'blues of Beverley' and 'blues of Stamford' (see C. M. Waters, *A Short Economic History of England*, Oxford, 1920, p. 121). But the *NED*. quotations s. Stafford make it clear that a humorous pun on 'staff' is intended, and that 'to be clad in Stafford blue' means 'to be beaten black and blue'.

200 ff. Uxor in this pageant, as in the Noah pageants of the York and Chester cycles, is utterly unlike the orthodox theological idea of Noah's wife as a meek and virtuous prototype of Mary (found in the Noah pageant of the *Ludus Coventriae*). The tradition of the perverse and cantankerous Uxor is peculiar to medieval drama in England (see Carey, *The Wakefield Group in the Towneley Cycle*, p. 77), but A. J. Mill (*PMLA*. lxi. 613–26) has shown how widespread it is in European art and folk-lore. Further, it is an old tradition—at least as old as the picture of Noah's ark in the Junius manuscript (A.D. 1000), in which 'one of the women, whom we may assume to be Noah's wife, seems unwilling to mount the ladder, and is expostulating with one of her three sons' (*MLN*. xlix. 88–90). Uxor may have suffered from being associated with Eve, whose very name she has attracted to herself in some versions of the Noah legend; see *Spec*. xvi. 450.

205. Tolkien takes this line to mean 'from morn till eve', with the usual order of words reversed for the sake of rhyme. But it seems better to give the words their literal meaning 'from evening till morning', i.e. all night long. Uxor, in fact, has unquiet nights as well as restless days.

211. *sory*. The rhyme requires *sary*.

214–16. Uxor means that she knows how to pay back her husband by using trickery or force. Her tactics are reminiscent of those used by the Wife of Bath against her first three husbands; see note to 229.

219. *Gill*. This may be Uxor's Christian name, just as it is the name of Mak's wife in Play 4. But in the present context it is more likely to be a contemptuous nickname; cf. *Mawd* 5. 352.

224. *langett.* Frampton (*PMLA.* l. 632) uses this word as one piece of evidence in support of a fifteenth-century date of composition for the pageant. He points out that *NED.* gives no example earlier than 1413 of the original meaning of this word, which was 'the tongue of a balance', and that its first quotation of the derived meaning 'thong used for tying hose' is from the present pageant. Cf. note to 5.357.

229. *byte and whyne.* Cf. *Wife of Bath's Prologue* (*Cant. Tales*, III. 386): 'For as an hors I koude byte and whyne.'

238. *dres me.* Trusler (*SP.* xxxiii. 19) suggests that this was originally *drys me*, to rhyme with *mys* the 237.

247-8. *I may sit downe daw To ken* 'I may have to put up with being known for a fool'; cf. *NED.* s. Sit, *v.*, sense 21d, *EDD.* s. Sit, *v.*, sense II.

261. *strenght.* In the manuscript there is a ligature above the *-gh-*, but no abbreviation mark for *n* is discernible. However, the rhyme with *lenght* shows that *strenght* is the word intended.

271-2. In these lines the Ark is described in terms of a contemporary ship. Noah may well be describing the main features of a large-scale model ship used in the production of the pageant. A. J. Mill (*MLR.* xxxiii. 493) gives evidence that the Plough Ship of the Trinity House Guild at Hull was 'fashioned like a regular masted sailing vessel'.

281. *chambre* (rhyming with *doore, sure, endure*). According to Sisam, this rhyme points to a by-form *chamb(o)ur*; but Zupitza-Schipper insert the words *on flore* after *chambre*.

298. Noah's metaphor, which refers to the instrument on which spun wool was wound, is appropriate here since Uxor is presumably still busy with her spinning.

301. *behete.* Both meaning and metre require some word (taking a heavy stress) after *has.* Manly inserts *spokyn*, Sisam *het*, Zupitza-Schipper *hight*; cf. *As thou me behete hase* 430.

317. *That we be ther or none* 'so that we may be there before noon'; for the construction see note to 1.54.

320. *Brether, sam.* Manly has *Sam* 'Shem' (cf. *Sem* 142); Zupitza-Schipper emend to *Brother Sam*; Sisam leaves these words unchanged and glosses them 'brothers both'. But it is likely that *sam* is the Yorkshire dialect word meaning 'take hold of, collect'; see J. E. Oxley, *TLS.*, 5 July 1934, p. 476. Translate: 'Brothers, collect our things.'

324. *Help.* Uxor uses this word with comic effect, for she is echoing her First Son (318) and Third Son (322). She means: 'While you're busy helping each other, what about helping me?'

344. *Thai.* EETS. *That*, Manly *Thay*; but the MS. reading is clearly *Thai.*

345. *the planettys seuen.* Cf. *the seven starnes* 423. For the astrological significance of the planets, and the misfortunes for which they were held responsible, see W. C. Gurry, *Chaucer and the Mediaeval Sciences* (New York, 1926), ch. vi. Saturn, in particular, was associated with 'flodes . . . foule wederes' (*Piers Plowman*, B-text, vi. 326).

348-9. Cf. Coventry Pageant of the Shearmen and Tailors 455, 457 (EETS. ES. 87):

> Nothur in hallis nor yett in bowris . . .
> Nother in castellis nor yet in towris.

353. i.e. mind your own business, and it will be the better for you. Proverbial; see *NED.* s. Clout, *v.*, sense 1, quotation from Taverner (1539).

355. *And many wynd-blast.* The same elliptic construction, in which the words 'there is' are understood, is used again in 470.

363-4. 'I don't care whether I win or lose your friendship.'

364. *This spyndill will I slip.* Uxor is spinning with a distaff (*rok* 338), a spindle, and a reel (298). The wool fibres on the distaff were twisted into thread by turning the spindle, and the spun wool was later wound into hanks on the reel. Uxor is determined, before she stops work, to strip her spindle, i.e. empty it by using her reel to wind off the yarn.

371. *byr.* The rhyme requires *ber(e)*; see *SP.* xxxiii. 25.

371-2. The audience must have enjoyed the comedy of Uxor's precipitous embarkation after all her delaying tactics.

381. *stynk.* The meaning here is probably 'break wind'; see *EDD.* s. Stink, sense 3, and cf. the following quotation from John Heywood's *John* . . . *Tyb* . . . *and Sir John* (1533), where the context makes it clear that this meaning is intended: 'I shall beate her . . . That she shall stynke lyke a pole kat' (Tudor Facsimile Reprints, 1909, sig. A.ii). Cf. also 'Ise lam thee till thou stinck' in *A York-shire Dialogue* 88 (York, 1683).

382. Uxor ignores her husband's blows, and pretends she has not heard. Her pretence has the infuriating effect on Noah it is intended to have. For nicknames like *Wat Wynk* and *Nicholl Nedy* 405 cf. the comic use of alliterative names in the Prologue of Summoner (*Ludus Coventriae*, EETS. ES. 120, p. 123).

389. *haue a measse of wedows coyll* 'have a dish of widow's pottage', i.e. become a widow.

393. The relative pronoun is to be understood at the beginning of this line. Translate 391–4: 'Other wives that I see here in this place would no doubt like to do the same (i.e. *dele penny doyll* for their husbands), who, for the life they are led, would love to see their husbands dead and buried.'

399. *levyr and long* is an alliterative phrase elaborating *hert.* In medieval physiology the liver was held to be the seat of strong emotions.

417. *weders* is an editorial addition. Manly supplies *strifis*, which is inappropriate here; Sisam inserts *floodis*; Zupitza-Schipper add *wederes*.

cold coth. These words probably relate to *the seven starnes* 423 (see note to 345); cf. 'maladyes colde' in the *Knight's Tale* (*Cant. Tales*, I. 2467), where Saturn is describing his powers for evil.

440–1. 'This labour that I tell of I had in vain.' Noah refers to his sounding of the water.

443. *highter. NED.* (s. Height, *adj.*) records *hight* as a Sc. and North. dialect form of 'high'.

454. *We shuld haue a good feest.* Tolkien (Glossary) suggests that this may be a topical allusion to the feast of Corpus Christi.

457. In Gen. vii. 24, viii. 3 it is a period of 150 days before the flood waters begin to abate.

461. *How.* MS. *Now.* Capital *H* and *N* are not similar enough in the manuscript for confusion between them to be likely. The source of the error may be that a new verse frequently begins with *Now*, e.g. in 449, 451, 467.

466. In Armenia was situated Mount Ararat, where the Ark came to rest; see *Mandeville's Travels*, ch. xvii (EETS. OS. 153, p. 98).

468. *ordand.* MS. *can* before *ordand* is omitted here, following Zupitza-Schipper. Omission of *can*, which improves the rhythm of the line, makes *ordand* the 3 sg. pa.t. of *ordayn*; cf. *ordand* 119.

472. *thi.* Mätzner changes this to *thou*, an emendation since generally accepted. Trusler (*PQ.* xiv. 303) takes *thi* as an adverb meaning 'therefore' (OE. *þȳ*). Her interpretation is adopted here since it makes emendation unnecessary; but it should be noticed that *NED.* (s. Thy, *adv.*) does not give an example of *thi* (as distinct from *forthi*) later than 1275.

499. *Thai tary to thay bryng* 'they tarry till they bring (something)'. Ellipsis of the object after *bryng* is also found in 5.274.

532. *Noy.* MS. *noy* is emended by Mätzner to *noyed* and by Zupitza-Schipper to *now.* But Manly is no doubt right in interpreting it as 'Noah'.

Explicit processus Noe. In the manuscript these words are followed by *sequitur Abraham.*

3. PRIMA PASTORUM

2. 'For they do not feel themselves too cast down.' The word *to* is adverbial and takes a heavy stress; *downe cast* suggests the casting down of Fortune's favourites, as she turns her famous wheel (cf. *kesten downe* 13).

4. *Now in hart, now in heyll* 'now in good spirits, now in health'; *hart* and *heyll* are together opposed to *weytt* and *blast.*

4–9. These lines on the mutability of human affairs are made up of proverbial commonplaces; cf. *A Metrical Proverb* (ed. T. Wright and J. O. Halliwell, *Reliquiae Antiquae*, London, 1841, i. 323):

> After droght commyth rayne,
> After plesur commethe payne;
> But yet it contynyth nyt so,
> For after rayne
> Commyth drought agayne,
> And joye after payne and woo.

7. *in . . . in.* MS. *is . . . is*, emended by Hemingway.

12. *he that most may* 'he who can (do) most', i.e. who is mightiest; cf. note to 485.

17. *Copé.* The rhyme with *he* and *pouerté* shows that MS. *cope* is from OF. *copie* 'plenty, riches'. *Iak Copé* is therefore 'Jack Plenty', typifying a rich man. For the association of riding with wealth and rank see 6.150–1 and cf. *Parson's Tale (Cant. Tales,* X. 435).

19. *I thank it God.* In view of the First Shepherd's misfortunes, the sincerity of this ejaculation is suspect, like that of the beggars in *Piers Plowman* (B-text, vi. 126) who tell Piers they have no limbs to labour with, 'Lorde, ygraced be ȝe'. Cf. *Summoner's Tale (Cant. Tales,* III. 1723).

26. *rott* is a specific disease which attacks the liver of sheep, while *moren* 39 is the generic name for all cattle diseases.

35. 'I am unhappy because of this misfortune!' These words are the object of *I may syng* 32; cf. *I may syng 'ylla-haylll'* 6.375.

36. 'And there's no help for it.'

37–8. The First Shepherd is resolved to make a desperate bid to win back all he has lost. The phrase *cast the warld in seuen* 'stake everything on the throw of a dice, make a desperate venture' is from the game of hazard; cf. note to 5.128.

44. The First Shepherd means that he may still increase the number of his sheep.

48. *ouertwhart.* For the spelling of this word cf. forms like *ortwharte* in *NED.* s. Overthwart.

49. *I say you no wrang* 'I tell you no untruth', i.e. I tell you truly; cf. *sayin' a wrang* 'telling an untruth' in *EDD.* s. Wrong, sense 9.

55. *bosters and bragers.* Cf. 'Bostaris, braggaris, and barganeris' in Dunbar's *Dance of the Sevin Deidly Synnis* 34. The men thus described by the Second Shepherd are probably the retainers maintained by lords; see note to 4.35.

58. *wryers. NED.* (s. Wrayer) defines the sg. of this word as 'accuser, betrayer' (OE. *wrēgere*). But G. V. Smithers (*Archivum Linguisticum*, vi. 78–80) argues strongly in support of the meaning 'quarrelsome person, one who stirs up strife', from OE. *°wrǣgan*, with an *i*-mutated form of the root represented in ME. *wraw* 'angry' (OE. *°wrāh, °wrāg*). This interpretation, which is adopted here, makes the two members of the alliterative phrase *wryers and wragers* roughly synonymous; cf. *bosters and bragers* 55.

60. For the abrupt transition from the plural in 52–9 to the singular *hym* in this line see note to 4.28–45.

62–3. An allusion to 'purveyance', i.e. the seizure or purchase at an arbitrary price of the animals and farm equipment of the husbandman; cf. 4.38 and see note to 4.33.

65. *With a hede lyke a clowde* 'with his head held high in the air like a cloud'.

67 ff. This picture of the upstart retainer aping the dress and behaviour of his lord is reminiscent of Hoccleve's verses in the *Regement of Princes* 442–5 (EETS. ES. 72):

> Some tyme, afer men myghten lordes knowe
> By there array, from oþer folke; but now
> A man schal stody and musen a long throwe
> Whiche is whiche . . .

85. *I say not in skorne* 'I do not speak mockingly', i.e. I ask you cordially (how you are getting on); cf. 'how fare ye, hertely?' in *Summoner's Tale (Cant. Tales,* III. 1801).

89–90. i.e. I thought it was you by the gown you are wearing.

91. *I am euer elyke* 'I am always the same'. The First Shepherd means that his condition, including his *aray*, is always the same and never improves.

92. 'In this kingdom there is none (who is) a shepherd (who) fares worse.'

97–9. A popular saying; cf. *The Papelard Priest* 90 (ed. A. H. Smith, *LMS.* ii. 45): 'I may noust wyue and þriue al in a ȝere.'

97–100. The exchange of proverbs in these lines has an undercurrent of annoyance and is a prelude to the quarrel that follows.

100. The earliest appearance of this proverb, according to the *Oxford Dictionary of English Proverbs*, p. 204; cf. 4.591–2.

101 ff. H. A. Eaton (*MLN.* xiv. 265–8) has shown that the quarrel between Gyb and Iohn Horne about the pasturing of an imaginary flock of sheep, and the intervention of Slawpase in their quarrel, is taken from an old folk-tale of the wise men of Gotham (see 180). There are two slightly different versions of the tale: the one in *Shakespeare's Jest Book. A Hundred Mery Talys*, ed. H. Oesterley from an edition of 1526, pp. 45–6; the other in *Shakespeare Jest Books*, ed. W. C. Hazlitt from an edition of 1630, iii. 4–5. This absurd quarrel has a realistic background in the endless disputes over rights of common that we find recorded in the manor-court rolls of the period.

104. 'Who do you think I am?'

111. *Long ys thou oght-whedir* 'do you want to go anywhere?' For this meaning of *long* see *NED.* s. Long, *v.*[1], sense 7; for *oght-whedir* cf. *NED.* s. Anywhither, Owhither.

116. 'However much you would like to.'

120. *hens I byd flytt* 'I order you to go from here'.

127–33. There are only seven lines in this stanza, which has two instead of the usual four *a*-lines; cf. a similar stanza in 4.262–8. M. G. Frampton (*AB.* xlviii. 366) suggests that these defective stanzas were probably in the exemplar used by the scribe, who has otherwise copied the Wakefield stanza with great accuracy.

136–7. *yit . . . stode* 'I haven't seen any yet, since I stood here'.

139. Proverbial; cf. *The First English Life of King Henry the Fifth* [1513], ed. C. L. Kingsford (Oxford, 1911), p. 52: 'and that night the Frenchmen fishinge before the nett, played the Englishmen at dyce, as if they had þin assured of the victory'; also *The Yorkshire Anthology*, ed. J. O. Halliwell (London, 1851), p. 95: 'He that fishes afore the net, lang fish or he fish get.'

140. *flett*. MS. *bett* is difficult: *NED.* (s. Bet, *sb.*) admits that it 'is quite uncertain in meaning'. Possibly it is a corruption of *flett* 'floor'; cf. *Flyt of this flett* 2. 223.

143. 'It would try a man's wit to learn where you keep yours.' There is a play on *to wyt* and *wytt*.

144. 'Here are old rogues (who) still stand on this ground', i.e. who are still alive.

149. 'For that which comes not quickly (because it does not exist).'

150–1. 'It is far to command an egg to go before it (is ready to) go', i.e. it is absurd to tell an egg to move before it is even hatched. Cf. 'count one's chickens before they are hatched'.

152. 'May you sooner be without sauce than sorrow', i.e. bad luck to you.

153–60. G. H. Gerould (*MLN.* xix. 225–30) has shown that the story of Moll and her broken pitcher is a widespread folk-tale of ancient descent.

154. 'She sheared many sheep (in her imagination), but all the time she had only one (in fact).'

161. 'But since you are devoid of wisdom (needed) for knowing', i.e. since you haven't the wisdom to know what's what. The rhyme requires *knawe*.

169. The names of the First and Second Shepherds. MS. *gyg* (for *Gyb*) may show assimilation of the final consonant to *g*; cf. *Gog* 1. 44, 172.

175. *it* is deliberately ambiguous and may refer to either the meal or the shepherds' wits.

176. Apparently sarcastic. Translate: 'We should be glad, shouldn't we?'

179. *Iak Garcio*. For discussion of the possibility that *Iak Garcio* is another name for the Third Shepherd, and not a new character, see *MLN.* lxviii. 169–72.

182. This line suggests that the playwright already had in mind one of the main items of the comic plot of the *Secunda Pastorum*, namely the trick to pass off the stolen sheep as a new-born baby.

185. Cf. 5.52, where the same phrase is used again as the second *c*-verse.

186. *bere the bell.* Cf. 5.197. This proverbial metaphor is natural to a shepherd, whose bell-wether is the leader of the flock.

188. *pen.* The First Shepherd perhaps calls Iak by this name because of his small size; cf. meanings of *pen* 'short rudimentary feather' and *pen-gun* 'a loquacious person, generally of small stature' in *EDD.* s. Pen, *sb.*[1]. It is also possible, but less likely because of the awkward ellipsis involved, that the First Shepherd means: 'Tell me, are they in a good pen?'

189. For this miracle of midwinter fertility cf. note to 4.718.

199. *I am worthy the wyne*, i.e. I earn my keep; cf. *I am worthy my mete* 4.310 and modern English 'to be worth one's salt'.

203–5. The First Shepherd expresses in legal language his determination not to get involved in argument with the Third Shepherd.

207. 'If I dare say it, you are indeed my brother (i.e. my equal) in this respect.' Cf. a similar retort made by Froward in 6.380.

209. *That thise wordys be purst* 'so that these words may be shut away', i.e. so that we may have done with these angry words. This figurative use of *purst* is appropriate to a shepherd, who would never be without the purse or bag in which he kept his food.

211 ff. In the shepherds' feast which follows, the playwright is burlesquing an aristocratic meat meal for the Christmas season by mixing plebeian and aristocratic dishes incongruously together. Plebeian fare like *a foote of a cowe* 215, *Two blodyngys* 217, and *two swyne-gronys* 229 can never have been ceremoniously carried 'with crakkyng of trumpes' to the dais in the hall. But, in contrast, other dishes like *browne of a bore* 212, *chekyns endorde* 234, *A tart for a lorde* 235, and *A calf-lyuer skorde with the veryose* 236 can all be found in aristocratic menus of the fifteenth century. See *Spec.* xxx. 213–17.

220, 222. A proverb; cf. Cotgrave, *A Dictionarie of the French and English Tongues* (1611) s. Mouton: 'Chair de mouton, manger de glouton: Pro[verb]. Flesh of a Mutton is food for a glutton; (or was held so in old time when Beefe and Bacon were your onely dainties.)' But the proverb has been humorously adapted so that it refers back to the First Shepherd's complaint about losing all his sheep with the rot; cf. 221 and 26.

225. 'An ox-tail that ought not to be wasted.'

226. *I let for no cost* 'I hold back for no cost', i.e. the cost is no hindrance.

227. *A good py or we fayll* 'a good pie (to eat) before we run short (of food)'.

231–2. R. Warner (*Antiquitates Culinariae*, London, 1791, pp. liii–iv) observes that knives were not used at the English table until the reign of James I: 'the disagreeable custom of *feeding with the fingers* prevailed till the middle of the seventeenth century. . . . Perhaps, however, the *spoon* was then more generally used, than it is at present.'

240. *clergé* is emended in EETS. to *clergete*, in order to make a rhyme with *restorite*, *appeté*. But there is no evidence that the form *clergete* ever existed, and it is more probable that *clergé* was pronounced as a trisyllable (*cleregé*, *clerigé*), thus making an assonantal rhyme with *restorité*, *appeté*.

244. *Hely* (MS. *hely*) is no doubt a place-name; cf. 'ale of Halton' in the Chester Shepherds' Play, l. 117 (EETS. ES. 62). It has usually been identified as Ely in Cambridgeshire; but it is more likely to be a 'Healey' in the West Riding of Yorkshire, possibly the township of this name lying between Ossett and Horbury, about four miles south-west of Wakefield. *wynk. NED.* (s. Wink, *v.*[1], sense 7b) suggests that this may mean 'give the tip'.

254. *on my hyppys* is a comic elaboration of *me*, used here partly for convenience in rhyming; cf. *hyppys* 4.558, rhyming with *kyppys, gossyppys, lyppys*.

260. *Be my dam saull, Alyce* 'by the soul of Alice, my mother'. For the Northern uninflected gen. sg. *dam* see Introduction, p. xxxii. *Alyce*, in apposition to *dam*, is uninflected in accordance with regular ME. usage; cf. *Sir Gawain and the Green Knight* 2275: *in kyngeʒ hous Arthor* 'in King Arthur's house'. Alice was a very common name in medieval England and France, and 'Bel Aliz' is the heroine of many *caroles* and romances; see *Oxford Dictionary of English Christian Names* s. Alice.

266. i.e. shall begin the singing.

267. *prays at the partyng* is a proverbial phrase which means 'praise given not too soon, not till the entertainment is over'. The First Shepherd is telling the Second to save up his praise for the best singing until the proper time—that is, when the song has been sung.

270. *I drynke for my parte* 'I'm having a drink for my part in the song'.

271. The First Shepherd, who has had his share of the bottle, is urging the Second to drink with a will: 'God forbid you should spare it (i.e. the ale), even if you drink it all up.' The Second Shepherd does so, judging by the Third Shepherd's angry exclamation in the next line.

278–9. 'No, we're all humble men; and thus, sir, I. think it best you should call us so.' The Third Shepherd has used *knafys* 277 to mean 'rogues', but in his reply the First Shepherd is playing on another and more respectable meaning of the word, such as 'servants' or 'humble men' (see Glossary s. Knafe).

283–4. 'For the good of our souls let us give it to poor men'; *do* 283 functions as an auxiliary of the infinitive *gyf* 284.

286. *begers, frerys* are separated in the manuscript by two parallel oblique strokes. It is possible that *begers* means 'mendicant friars', and is in apposition to *frerys*. As G. R. Owst (*Preaching in Medieval England*, Cambridge, 1926, p. 192) reminds us: 'One type of almsgift . . . is sure to be acceptable [to the mendicant friar], and that is a good dinner, when the work is done.' For another comic allusion to friars see 389–390.

289. For the practice of making the sign of the cross before sleeping cf. lines 24–6 of the Bannatyne MS. of Henryson's *Lion and the Mouse* (ed. G. Gregory Smith, STS., 1906, ii. 305):

> I lenyt doun amangis the flouris sueit,
> Syne maid a corss, and closit baith myne ene.

291. These words are parallel to *For ferde we be fryght* 289.

292–3. Cf. Mark xvi. 6; also the tenth-century St. Gall version of the Easter trope (Young, *The Drama of the Medieval Church*, i. 201):

> Quem quçritis in sepulchro, Christicolç?
> Iesum Nazarenum crucifixum, o caelicolae.

292–5. Cf. the carpenter's 'nyght-spel' in the *Miller's Tale* (*Cant. Tales*, I. 3480–6).

303–4. The sixth-century pseudo-Augustinian sermon *De Symbolo* has 'In medio duum animalium cognosceris' (Young, op. cit., ii. 128), based it is believed on a misunderstanding of Hab. iii. 2; cf. 4.646.

311–12. Possibly an allusion to divine voices that speak out of clouds; see, for example, Exod. xxiv. 16, Luke ix. 35.

321. In this verse, used again as the third *c*-verse in 4.654, *starne* is the subject. The star ultimately derives from the Magi story (Matt. ii).

332 ff. The thirteen prophetic witnesses named here are the same as those of the Arles text of the sermon *De Symbolo* (Young, op. cit., ii. 126–31), except that *Ely* 'Elias, Elijah' (377) replaces Simeon. But although this sermon is the ultimate source of most of the prophetic elements in the pageant, allowance must be made for the intermediate influence of liturgical *Prophetae* plays based on the sermon, for direct biblical influence, and even for the Wakefield author's firsthand knowledge of Virgil's Messianic Eclogue (see note on the two verses quoted from this Eclogue between 387 and 388).

The learning displayed by the Wakefield shepherds is no doubt due to the medieval tradition of scriptural exegesis which made the shepherds that find Christ types of the clergy who by their learning can 'penetrate the letter of Scripture to the underlying meaning' (D. W. Robertson and B. F. Huppé, *Piers Plowman and Scriptural Tradition*, Princeton, 1951, p. 152). The inclusion of the Old Testament prophets and patriarchs in the *Prima Pastorum* reminds us that from earliest times the Christian Church has looked upon the Old Testament as 'the mystical foundation on which the new Gospel was raised' (H. Jenner, *Christian Symbolism*, London, 1910, p. 169). The Old Testament prophets who foretold the birth of Christ and the patriarchs who were his precursors also appear in painted glass and cathedral sculpture; see E. Mâle, *Religious Art from the Twelfth to the Eighteenth Century* (London, 1949), pp. 76–7. In the incomplete Towneley pageant of the Prophets (Play VII) only Moses, David, the Sibyl, and Daniel appear.

348–9. Cf. Isaiah xi. 1 (Vulgate text): 'Et egredietur virga de radice Iesse'; but an intermediate source of this prophecy could have been a *Prophetae* play like that of Limoges (see Young, op. cit., ii. 143). In the Middle Ages Isaiah's prophecy was taken to mean that 'the Virgin Mary shall be born of the stem of David and Christ of her' (B. Smalley, *The Study of the Bible in the Middle Ages*, Oxford, 1941, p. 189).

350. *Sybyll* is the Erythraean Sibyl, of whom St. Augustine says, 'she seems to me to have been a citizen of the city of God'; see *The City of God* in Healey's translation (Everyman's Library 983), xviii. 23.

351–3. The story of Nebuchadnezzar and of the three 'children of Judah' (Dan. i. 6) thrown by him into the fiery furnace, where a fourth person is seen who in form 'is like the Son of God' (Dan. iii. 25). The interpretation of this story as a prophecy of Christ's birth is found in the *De Symbolo*.

358. 'For us to consider.'

359. *Of hym spake Ieromy.* See Jer. xxiii. 5.

359–60. Exod. iii. 2. The burning bush, which was held to prefigure the Virgin Birth, is a type commonly found in medieval literature and iconography. For example, a picture of it, beside one of the Nativity, is given in the *Biblia Pauperum* (ed. J. Ph. Berjeau, London, 1859) with the following text: 'Rubus ardiens qui non consumitur figurat beatam virginem mariam parientem sine corruptione integritatis corporis.'

364. *to se* has the same meaning as *to let se* 'to show'.

368. *sich was neuer sene.* The First Shepherd probably means 'the like of whom was never seen before' (cf. 339–40). But his words might be taken as an expression of scepticism meaning 'such a thing has never been seen'; and this is how the Second Shepherd evidently takes them, for he replies in the next line: 'You're wrong; you'll see him with your own eyes.'

372. 'Very soon'; *so* intensifies the adverb. These words complete the sentence begun in 369.

The Latin verses between 387 and 388. These two lines from Virgil are not word-perfect nor are they in the right order. Lines 6–7 of the Fourth Eclogue read as follows:

> Iam redit et Virgo, redeunt Saturnia regna;
> Iam nova progenies caelo demittitur alto.

The first of the two lines quoted in the pageant may be derived from the *De Symbolo* (see Young, op. cit., ii. 129); but the second is not usually found in this sermon and may therefore be the Wakefield author's own addition.

To Virgil *Virgo* meant the maiden Justicia, who was driven from earth by man's wickedness and enshrined in heaven as the constellation Virgo. According to the Sibylline Oracles, she would return, for the Golden Age (when Saturn was king) was soon to begin again. The Christian interpretation of these Virgilian verses as a prophecy of the advent of Christ was first made by the Emperor Constantine the Great, and later accepted by Augustine and the medieval Church; see J. B. Mayor, W. W. Fowler, and R. S. Conway, *Virgil's Messianic Eclogue* (London, 1907), pp. 16 ff., 123–4.

389–90. *I hold . . . preche* 'I think you must be one of the friars; you preach like one'. For the active part played by the friars as preachers see Owst, *Preaching in Medieval England*, pp. 55 ff. This second comic allusion to the friars (cf. 286) makes it unlikely that the Wakefield author belonged to one of the mendicant orders.

392. *Caton*, i.e. the *Disticha Catonis*, a fourth-century collection of moral maxims in Latin verse attributed to Dionysius Cato. It was used throughout the Middle Ages as a school text-book.

395 ff. The First Shepherd proceeds to translate Virgil's Latin for the benefit of his fellows.

396. *to neuen* 'to name', i.e. as she is called. These words are not in the Latin, and their main function here is to provide a rhyme.

398. *Saturne.* This translates Virgil's *Saturnia regna*; EETS. has *samyne.*

414. According to H. Traver (*MLN.* xx. 4), 'the Second Shepherd shows positive ignorance when he suggests the impossible combination of twenty-four notes to a long'. But N. C. Carpenter (*Spec.* xxvi. 699) accepts the Second Shepherd's statement as meaning twenty-four semiminims to a long. Carpenter points out that the Angel's elaborate style of singing is contrasted with the plainer descant style of the shepherds; cf. note to 4.657.

415. 'I wish that it, the same (notes), might be found by us', i.e. I wish we could hit the same notes.

421. 'Now I want to leap (to it)', i.e. I'll quickly sing the same notes for you; cf. 428.

422. *Breke outt youre voce.* There may be a punning allusion here to 'breaking' in a musical sense; see *NED.* s. Note, *sb.*², sense 2.

Let se as ye yelp 'show us how you sing the high notes'; cf. 4.189, 661.

425. *This sang thou not lose* 'don't you forget this song'.

426. 'For anger', i.e. for getting angry. Cf. 5.239, where the same words are again used as the first *b*-verse.

428. 'He's not in a hurry (to sing) now.' This verse refers back to 421.

430. 'Take up my song.' In using the form *sangre* rather than *sang* the playwright is either forcing a rhyme with *angre*—which is unlikely—or using a genuine dialect form of Scandinavian origin which preserves the nom. sg. ending of ON. *sǫngr* (cf. etymology of Witter, *sb.*¹ in *NED.*).

432. *Fayr fall thi growne* 'may good befall your snout: a grotesque way of saying 'good luck to you'; cf. *So fare fall thare lyppys* 4.560.

434. *mase the.* EETS. *makethe.* The word *mase* has been tampered with by a different hand, which has written *k* over original long *s* (still faintly discernible), and so turned *mase the* into *makethe.*

447–8. 'Even if they once sought him, now their eyes are closed (and so they cannot see him).' EETS. *I-closyd* includes an incomplete and uncancelled letter before *closyd* which could be the first stroke of *p*; possibly the scribe was about to write again the initial *p* of *prophetys* 446, which is placed immediately above in the manuscript.

451. *yond sterne.* The star has already been seen by the Second Shepherd in 321–2.

456. 'You are one of the elders.' In this context *old store* (used literally of live-stock) is humorously applied to the First Shepherd, who is an older man than the Second.

458 ff. Hemingway (p. xi) notes that the shepherds' salutation of the Christ-child is already found in liturgical Shepherds' Plays of the thirteenth century. G. C. Taylor (*MP.* v. 1–38) shows that the form of the shepherds' salutation and even some of the wording of it have been influenced by the popular medieval 'Hail' lyrics.

462 ff. The offering of gifts by the shepherds, like the appearance of the star, is borrowed from the Magi story (Matt. ii), which became closely associated with the story of the shepherds in liturgical Christmas plays.

470. Cf. Heb. xii. 2: 'Jesus the author and finisher of our faith.'

471–2. 'O that you would accept this ball.'

480, 484. Cf. lines 18–19 of the scene inserted between lines 606 and 607 of the Shepherds' Play in certain manuscripts of the Chester cycle (EETS. ES. 62, footnote on p. 157):

> take thie here my well fayer botell,
> for it will hold a good pottell.

485. *He that all myghtys may* 'he who can (do) all mighty deeds', i.e. who is omnipotent. The same phrase occurs in 4.684; cf. 12 and see *English Studies,* viii. 185–6.

4. SECUNDA PASTORUM

1. Cf. York XIV. 71: 'A! lorde, what the wedir is colde!'

10. *husbandys.* MS. *shepardes.* There can be no doubt, in view of the rhyme sequence, that

husbandys (suggested in Manly's edition) is original here. The explanation of the error may be that the copyist had in mind the name of the speaker (*Primus Pastor*).

28. An allusion to the livery worn by maintained men, whose outrageous behaviour is described in this and the following stanza; see note to *mantenance* 35. The mention here of the maintained men and their distinctive costume prepares us for the entry later on of Mak, who pretends at first to be a great man's protégé, and appears suitably dressed for the part; see note to stage direction before 190.

28–45. Most editions transpose these two stanzas, following Kölbing (*ES.* xxi. 165), who points out that this removes the awkward transition from pl. *thay* 25 to sg. *he* 28, and makes *a swane as prowde as a po* 37 an antecedent to *he* 28. But it is not at all certain that such transposition is really necessary, for *he* 28 may function as an indef. pron. meaning 'any man' and refer back to *thay* 25. This use of indefinite *he* with a pl. antecedent is not uncommon in ME.; cf. 3.60.

33. *purveance*. The purveyance or requisitioning of food and vehicles was originally a royal prerogative, the purpose of which was to furnish all that was needed for the king's journeys through his realm. The price paid for the goods requisitioned was an arbitrary one fixed by the purveyor, and sometimes they were not paid for at all. It is not surprising that noblemen found it convenient to follow the king's example, so that purveyance ceased to be exclusively a royal privilege.

35. *mantenance*. The magnates upheld their authority by supporting a host of retainers. There were many enactments against maintenance in the fourteenth and fifteenth centuries, e.g. in 1429 it was ordered that no lord of the Council should 'receive, cheryssh, hold in houshold, ne maynteyne Pillours, Robbours, Oppressours of the people, Mansleers, Felons, Outelawes' (A. Abram, *Social Life in England in the Fifteenth Century*, London, 1909, p. 87).

42–3. 'He must have what he wants, even if I have to go without it.'

49. *balk*, i.e. a strip of rough grass-land between two adjacent furlongs in a common field. These untilled boundary strips were part of the rough pasture on which the peasant grazed his sheep. The First Shepherd's use of this word indicates that the opening scene of the pageant is set in the arable fields of a township, and not (as some commentators have thought) 'on the moors'.

51–4. Coll means that he has arranged to meet his fellow shepherds, and that they should soon be here if they keep their word.

57. *wyndys full kene*. MS. *weders full kene*. It looks as if *weders* has been repeated, in place of another word resembling it, such as *wyndys*; cf. *And wyndes that ar so keyn* XXII. 158.

64. 'As far as I know or as my experience goes.'

64 ff. The Second Shepherd's complaint about his matrimonial miseries belongs to the anti-marital, anti-feminist tradition of the Middle Ages. The Second Shepherd, like Noah in the *Processus Noe*, is a typical henpecked husband of the Middle Ages—and indeed of all ages.

67. *Copyle, oure hen*. A 'copple' is a crest on a bird's head; see *EDD*. s. Copple, where the example 'A copple-crowned hen' is cited. Cf. 'coppull my brode hen' in the *Turnament of Totenham*, ed. W. C. Hazlitt, *Remains of the Early Popular Poetry of England*, London, 1866, iii. 84; also 'Coppe(n)' in *Reynard the Fox*, ed. W. J. Thoms, Percy Society, 1844, pp. 8, 11.

69–70. These lines describe the cackling noise made by Copyle when she lays an egg; Gyll in the throes of childbirth is also said *to crok* 386. The cock and the hen are obviously symbols of man and wife. The idea of 69–72 is that the wife's child-bearing makes domestic life intolerable for the husband; cf. 193–4, 237 ff., 386 ff.

71. Between *is* and *oure* is a word or part of a word which looks like *or*, although a blot on the manuscript makes it difficult to decipher with certainty. It may represent the copyist's wrong first attempt to write *oure* following.

85. There is surely no question here of 'polygamischen Neigungen', as Holthausen (*ES.* lxiii. 218) seems to think. After all, a man can have several wives in succession.

91 ff. These lines are reminiscent of medieval popular songs warning young men against

W.P.—K

marriage. In particular, the proverb in 93 is also found in 'ffor "had y wyst" commeth to late for to lowse yt' in lyric No. 40 of *Secular Lyrics of the XIVth and XVth Centuries*, ed. R. H. Robbins (2nd ed., Oxford, 1955).

91. *of wowyng* 'as to wooing'. Trusler (*PQ*. xiv. 303) suggests emendation to *on wowyng* 'a-wooing'; cf. 172.

93. *that*. MS. *it*, emended by Hemingway. The original probably had the abbreviation β^t for *þat*, a copyist misreading the thorn as *y* and replacing it by *i*.

99. *lyffys*. The rhyme requires *lefys* (OE. *leofian*); see *SP*. xxxiii. 19.

100. *as euer rede I pystyll* 'as I hope to go on reading the Epistle': an asseveration more appropriate to a priest—perhaps the playwright himself—than to a shepherd. The extract from one of the Epistles included in the Mass was read by a subdeacon; see Young, *The Drama of the Medieval Church*, i. 105.

108. Cook observes that the metre would be improved by omitting *I had ryn to*.

109. *God looke ouer the raw* 'may God watch over the company'. This is a benediction addressed by the First Shepherd to the audience; cf. 3.46–7. He then turns to the Second Shepherd and says, in effect, 'You're as deaf as a post.' Evidently he has been trying to attract the attention of the Second Shepherd, who is so busy haranguing the *yong men* in the audience that he has not noticed him.

110. *so tariand* 'for loitering so long'; cf. 6.50.

111. *Sagh thou awre of Daw* 'have you seen Daw anywhere?' *Daw* is sometimes found as a pet-form of *David*, but in this pageant it is doubtless an uncomplimentary nickname derived from *daw* 'fool, simpleton' (which occurs as a common noun in 2.247); cf. *Slawpase*, the unflattering nickname of the Third Shepherd in the *Prima Pastorum*. Daw is much younger than the First and Second Shepherds, and is employed by one of them; see note to 145.

118. Cf. Skelton's *Speke, Parrot* 194: 'Cristecrosse and saynt Nycholas, Parrot, be your good spede!' (A. Dyce, *Poetical Works of John Skelton*, London, 1843, ii. 10). St. Nicholas, as the patron saint of schoolboys and other young people, is rightly invoked by the youthful Third Shepherd.

127. *Noe floode*. The mention of Noah's flood reminds us that there is a definite link between the *Processus Noe* and the Shepherds' Plays, since Noah (as a saviour of sinful mankind) was held to be the type of Christ.

136 ff. These lines may be understood as follows: the Third Shepherd, whose head is full of night fears, is startled for a moment when he comes across the other shepherds unexpectedly (136–7). He is relieved to find that they are a couple of rascals well known to him (138), but impudently decides that they look monstrous enough to warrant his turning the sheep away from them (139–40). It is because he has thought ill of them that he imposes an easy penance on himself (141–4).

138. *shrewys pepe* 'rascals peeping'; cf. *Shrew, pepe* 221. Malone (*MLN*. xl. 35–9) takes *shrewys* to mean 'shrew-mice'.

139. *all-wyghtys*. Manly emends *all* to *tall*. Emendation to *ill wyghtys* is also possible. Malone (op. cit.) takes *all* and *wyghtys* as a compound meaning 'strange creatures, uncanny creatures', from OE *æl-wiht* (recorded only in gen. pl. form *ælwihta* in *Beowulf* 1500). Although Malone's derivation of *all-wyghtys* is adopted here, it is necessary to point out that no other occurrence of this compound is known.

145. It is evident from this line, in which the Third Shepherd greets the other shepherds in turn, that one of them is his master. As the playwright usually thinks in terms of the sequence First Shepherd—Second Shepherd—Third Shepherd, it is likely that *syr* refers to the First Shepherd, and *master myne* to the Second. Daw belongs to the same oppressed class of inferior servants as Pikeharnes in the *Mactacio Abel*, Slawpase in the *Prima Pastorum*, and Froward in the *Coliphizacio*.

149. *mayde* 'eaten'; see *NED*. s. Make, *v*.[1], sense 60.

163–4. 'In return for the food you provide, I shall behave accordingly—work as I'm paid.' For this meaning of *fayre . . . make* see *NED*. s. Fare, *sb*.[1], sense 8.

165. *emang euer lake*. These words as they stand can mean 'betweenwhiles (i.e. between

short spells of work) play all the time'. But *emang euer* may be a transposition of the common phrase *euer emang* 'every now and then', which occurs in 1.391.

169. i.e. I can always run away.

170–1. A proverbial saying; cf. *Proverbs of Hending* (ed. G. Schleich, *Anglia*, li. 265): 'Liʒtte chep luþere forʒeldeþ.'

172. For the custom of taking a companion on a wooing trip see *Othello*, III. iii. 71.

175. *Or I shall make the full rad* 'or I shall very quickly make you (stop your chatter)'. Other editors have derived *rad*, not from OE. *hrade* 'quickly', but from ON. *hræddr* 'afraid'; see next note.

176–7. *With thy gawdys . . . we skorne* 'we scorn your pranks'. For the use of *with* after *skorne* cf. 'they scornyd with me', quoted from the *Paston Letters* in *NED*. s. Scorn, *v.*, sense 1 Previous editors have taken *rad* together with 176 to mean 'afraid of your pranks'; but this leaves *we skorne* hanging in the air. The interpretation given here requires the words *Where ar oure shepe, boy?* 177 to be taken as an interpolation.

186–9. H. Traver (*MLN*. xx. 1) identifies the shepherds' song as a three-part descant. *Stage direction before 190*. J. H. Smith (*PMLA*. lii. 901–2) suggests that Mak's 'chlamys' has 'bagpipe' sleeves—'a variety of the extravagant fashion in sleeves against which the satirists of the late fourteenth and fifteenth centuries were never tired of inveighing'. If Mak's outer garment has sleeves big enough to conceal stolen things, this would explain why the Third Shepherd removes Mak's 'chlamys' (as indicated by the Latin stage direction after 200). Later on, it will be noticed, Mak says to the shepherds *I pray you looke my slefe, that I steyll noght* 396. Smith points out that this extravagant costume is entirely appropriate to Mak's role of 'burlesque maintained man' (201–13).

190. *for thy naymes vij* 'by thy seven names'. Hemingway notes that God has seven names n Rabbinical tradition, but apparently not in Christian literature.

190 ff. Mak's entry starts the action of the play. His theft of a sheep and the trick played to conceal it have been established as a folk-tale motif which is found, with variations of detail, in more than one European literature; see *Spec*. xx. 310–17. The best known of the analogues in English is *Archie Armstrang's Aith*, a ballad by the Rev. John Marriott, printed in the *Minstrelsy of the Scottish Border*; see Kölbing's Appendix to EETS. and also *MLN*. lix. 297–304. But the detection and punishment of the thief are not found in any of the analogues, and this important difference is no doubt due to the Wakefield author's original handling of the traditional tale.

191. *thi will, Lorde, of me tharnys* 'thy will, Lord, concerning me is lacking', i.e. I don't know what you wish to do with me.

199. *Mak*. The origin of this name is uncertain. The names *Mak* and *Gyll* look like a variation of *Iak* and *Gill* (cf. 2.336). *Mak* may possibly be shortened from *Macus*, although A. H. Smith (*Revue Celtique*, xliv. 44) gives no example of this name in Yorkshire later than the twelfth century. The substitution of *Mak* for *Iak* would, however, make more point if *Mak* could be referred to the Gaelic prefix *Mac* or to the Lowland Scottish surname *Mack*; see G. F. Black, *The Surnames of Scotland* (New York, 1946), s. Mac, Mack. It was at Wakefield in 1307 that Robert de Castleford sued Richard son of Brown 'for calling him Robert le Brus, to despite him'; *Wakefield Court Rolls*, ii, YAS. RS. 36, p. 71. The Scots raided as far south as Yorkshire after Bannockburn (1314), and memories of them no doubt persisted. As a name with Scottish associations *Mak* would therefore be particularly appropriate to its sheep-stealing owner. See also W. Oelrich, *Die Personennamen im mittelalterlichen Drama Englands*, pp. 51–2.

201. *a yoman . . . of the kyng*. Cf. 'a yoman of þe crown', whose rank was below that of a 'squyere' and above that of a 'grome', according to the *Boke of Norture* 1117–18, 1121–2 (EETS. OS. 32).

201–13. For Mak's imitation of Southern English in these lines see Appendix IV, p. 131.

208. When the second half of an *a*-line begins with the name of a person addressed, there is no infallible way of knowing whether the name belongs in meaning to the first half of the

line or the second. Thus it is equally possible to punctuate this line with a comma after *qwaynt*, and a question mark after *Mak*; cf. 314, 604 (see note).

216. *sett in a torde* 'put in a turd', i.e. stop your mouth; *sett in* is contrasted with *take outt* 215. Cf. *Bartholomew Fair*, I. iv: 'turd i' your teeth, hold you your tongue.'

221. The meaning may be 'Rascal, pry about!'; cf. *I se shrewys pepe* 138. The word *pepe* 221 is misread as *Iape* in EETS.

224–5. These lines help to prepare us for Mak's sheep-stealing act.

229. Cf. a Scottish version of this proverb quoted by H. H. Wood in *The Poems and Fables of Robert Henryson* (Edinburgh and London, 1933), p. 245: 'Seldome lyes the divel dead by ane dycksyd.' It means that the devil is never to be trusted, even though he should seem quite harmless. The Third Shepherd is saying in effect: 'I don't believe you; you won't get any sympathy from me.'

dewyll. The rhyme requires *deyll*; cf. 3.272.

230. *Therfor.* Mak pays no heed to the Third Shepherd's unkind comment, but continues straight on from 228.

235. *By thi hoode.* Frampton (*AB.* xlviii. 331) is no doubt right in reading the second word as *thi* (EETS. *my*). But 'by my hood' is the more usual wording of this asseveration, e.g. 1.216, 3.136.

she. EETS. *sho.* The manuscript clearly has *she*, although the rhyme requires Northern *sho*; see note to 239.

236. *Lyys* '(she) lies'.

236 ff. These lines draw our attention to Mak's wife, and the emphasis laid on her breeding habits prepares us for the part she is to play later on.

238. 'May any other good she will do fare badly', i.e. bad luck to any other good she's likely to do. The words *othere good* refer back to *drynkys well* 237: she's good at drinking, but that's all she is good at.

239. *sho.* MS. *so*, emended by Hemingway. The Northern form *sho* was evidently unfamiliar to the copyist; cf. *she* 235 and see Introduction, p. xxxii.

246. *dowse* 'sweetheart' (perhaps a euphemism here for 'harlot') is a generic use of the name *Dowse*; see *Oxford Dictionary of English Christian Names* s. Dulcie.

247–8. 'There is no one who thinks (he knows) or (really) knows a worse one than I', i.e. no one, in imagination or in reality, knows a worse one than I do.

251–2. Mak is willing to spend all his money on soul-masses for his dead wife, just as Uxor Noe is for her dead husband (2.390).

262–8. There are only two *a*-lines in this stanza, instead of the usual four; see note to 3.127–33 and *MLN.* lviii. 49–50.

265–8. Cf. the night-spell recited by the Third Shepherd in 3.292–5. A comic effect is intended in making the rascally Mak recite the charm against the evil spirits of the night. This effect is heightened a moment later when Mak proceeds to cast a spell on the sleeping shepherds so' that he can safely steal one of their sheep.

266–7. A corruption of 'in manus tuas commendo spiritum meum' (Luke xxiii. 46). E. M. Clark (*Orate Fratres*, xvi. 73) notes that these words are used in the office of Compline, but that Mak substitutes *Poncio Pilato* for 'Domine' and so commends himself to Pilate's untender mercies.

278. *serkyll*, i.e. the magic circle of necromancy; cf. *Parson's Tale (Cant. Tales*, X. 603).

285–6. 'But yet I must make better efforts if things are to come right.'

289. *nyp nere* 'grab (a sheep) tightly'; cf. *nyp . . . naroo* 437. The meaning 'move rapidly or nimbly', which would fit *nyp* in the present context, is not recorded in *NED.* (s. Nip, *v.*[1], sense 12) earlier than the nineteenth century.

290–2. 'Stop! come this way! Now a fat sheep will cheer us up (lit. improve our mood from sorrow).' *A fatt shepe* is the subject of *mendys . . . sorow*; cf. similar construction in 504.

298. Gyll, like Noah's wife, is busy with her spinning; cf. note to 2. 364.

298–304. 'I don't think I can earn a penny by getting up (i.e. by leaving my work), curse them! Any woman who has been a housewife knows what it means to be got up from her seat continually. I have no work to show because of such small chores.'

307. 'You needn't care about keeping me standing so long.' The interjection *yee* often introduces a sarcastic or derisive statement.

312–14. These lines perhaps show the influence of the parable of the labourers in the vineyard; cf. Matt. xx. 12. Mak's use of the word *grace* also recalls the argument on salvation by grace or by works.

317–19. A popular proverb. Owst (*Literature and Pulpit in Medieval England*, p. 43) shows that it was used by medieval preachers. Whiting (*Proverbs in the Earlier English Drama*, p. 61) quotes a similar proverb in French: 'Tant va le pot a leau quil casse.'

320–1. 'I know what you're prophesying, but leave it unsaid'; cf. *absit omen*.

324. *twelmothe* is probably a phonetic spelling, as Pollard suggests; cf. 'tweluemoᵱe' in *Handlyng Synne* 9089 (MS. Harley 1701) and spellings like *tuelfmoth, tuel-moth* in *NED*. s. Twelvemonth.

330–1. 'Then I may get the devil of a bad time from the whole pack of them'; *by* (OE. *bycgan*) is used here to mean 'get'; *The dewill of* may be taken as a strengthening of *the war* 'the worse'.

339–40. 'Now I'm happy because of the bright day I was born!'

344. *blawes a cold blast* 'a cold blast will blow', i.e. I'll catch my death of cold (figuratively).

350. *Resurrex a mortruus* is a corruption of 'resurrexit a mortuis' in the Creed.

351. *Iudas carnas dominus* is a distortion of 'laudes canas domino', according to Holthausen (*ES*. lxiii. 219). However, the First Shepherd's garbled words are not without meaning of a kind: *Iudas* reminds us of the deceiver Mak; *carnas* is like *carnes*, a word which occurs frequently in the offices for the octave of Corpus Christi, and which may have some connexion in the First Shepherd's mind with the hunger he feels (see 352).

352. *I water fastand* 'I'm tottering with hunger'. *water* looks like a phonetic spelling of *walter* 'totter, move unsteadily'; see *MLN*. xlv. 151 and l. 95–6. For loss of medial *l* before a dental see Appendix III, p. 130.

357–8. For the same alliterative phrase cf. **XXVI**. 623: *I am as light as leyfe on tre*.

359. *So me qwakys* 'I tremble so much'. Other editors have emended MS. *so my qwakys* by inserting *hart* (EETS.) and *body* (Manly) after *my*. But MS. *my* may represent an unstressed form of the pers. pron. *me*, thus making *qwakys* a reflexive verb (see *NED*. s. Quake, *v*.¹, sense 2b), with ellipsis of *I* and with the 1 sg. pres. ending *-ys*.

360. *My hart is outt of skyn*. An equivalent idiomatic phrase in modern English would be 'My heart is in my mouth'; cf. 'to jump out of one's skin (with surprise, fright)'.

362. *To the dowore wyll I wyn*. The Third Shepherd is so scared that he has a blind impulse to rush to the door and make his escape.

369. 'Many are covered like that nowadays, especially on the inside'; cf. Matt. vii. 15.

370–1, 372–4. In the manuscript 370–1 are attributed to the Second Shepherd, and 372–4 to the Third. There can be little doubt that the editorial order of the names (suggested by Manly) is what the playwright intended, for 370–1 are clearly a continuation of the Third Shepherd's words in 368. It has been pointed out (in the note to 145) that the usual order of the shepherds' names is First Shepherd—Second—Third. Probably the playwright (or a copyist) has made the mistake of mechanically preserving this order here.

380. *I trow I be the same* 'I hope I shall be the same'. After his uncomfortable night's rest Mak is wondering whether he will ever be the same again.

380–1. *my nek . . . Enoghe* 'my neck has been lying very crookedly'. Apart from their literal meaning, these words look like a comic allusion to the penalty Mak is afraid of suffering if he is caught with the stolen sheep; cf. 308, 315.

385. The word *sloghe* is 'slough' (i.e. skin), so that the line as a whole is equivalent to *My hart is outt of skyn* 360; cf. Chester play of *Christ's Resurrection* 188–9: 'my hart wholly/ out of Slough is shaken' (EETS. ES. 115). Other editors have taken *of* and *sloghe* together as a compound verb, and have translated: 'That slew my heart' (Adams), 'which smote my heart out(?)' (Cook).

387. *the fyrst cok.* According to Tusser's *Husbandrie* (EDS., 1878, p. 165), the cock crows three times, the first time at midnight.

388. *For to mend oure flok.* Mak's figurative turn of phrase is ironical, since we know that the *yong kid* 387 is the fat sheep he has stolen.

400. '(To see) that we have all our stock.'

403. *the crokyd thorne.* The Surtees editor (p. xv) takes this as an allusion to a remarkable thorn-tree which once grew in Mapplewell (some ten miles from Horbury) and was known locally as the Shepherd's Thorn. But, as Peacock observes (*YAJ.* xv. 100–1), the names 'Thornhill' and 'Thornes' (two parishes adjacent to Horbury) make it safe to localize *the crokyd thorne* somewhere in the immediate neighbourhood of Horbury; see note to 455.

407. *se.* MS. *be,* emended by Manly. In Matt. xii. 29 Jesus speaks of the binding of the strong man, i.e. the devil, in these words: 'Or else how can one enter into a strong man's house, and spoil his goods, except he first bind the strong man?' The meaning of *the dewill in a bande* is obscure, but it may not be too fanciful to suppose that Gyll is thinking of her husband (*Syr Gyle* 408) as the devil whose house, she fears, is about to be entered by the shepherds in search of their lost sheep. On the popular conception of the bound Satan see *Spec.* ii. 187 ff.

414. For the construction cf. note to 1.318. The *NED.* interpretation of *clowse hir toose* as meaning 'flatters, fawns upon' (s. Claw, *v.*, sense 4) does not fit this context. If something more than the literal meaning is intended, the idea may be that Gyll tickles or gratifies her body (see *NED.* s.v., sense 4b); cf. *lakys,* which may refer to playing of an amorous kind.

416. *What.* Adams emends to *Who.* But Gyll means 'What makes me as hoarse as I am?' She is no doubt hoarse with shouting at Mak and the children.

429–30. An allusion to the hue and cry.

435–7. '(Tuck me up well) behind! If Coll and his mate come, they'll nip me hard.' For *vs* meaning 'me' cf. 296.

442. *Syng 'lullay'.* This detail recalls the Nativity theme because Mak is evidently intended to imitate the refrain of a lullaby carol; see R. L. Greene, *The Early English Carols* (Oxford, 1935), pp. 97 ff.

446. 'When you at last hear them coming.'

455. *Horbery shrogys. Horbery* is Horbury, a town some three miles south-west of Wakefield. In the fifteenth century there was a chapelry of Wakefield Parish Church at Horbury; see Peacock, *YAJ.* xv. 100. For the WYks. use of *shrogs* 'bushes, underwood' see Wright, *Rustic Speech and Folk-Lore,* p. 22.

456. 'And among fifteen hogs (i.e. young sheep) I found only a ewe.' The First Shepherd means that he found only a ewe with his hogs because the wether was missing; cf. 451.

458. *by Sant Thomas of Kent.* The same oath is used by Alisoun in the *Miller's Tale (Cant. Tales,* I. 3291).

468. *Shall I neuer ete brede.* This phrase, found again in 6.202, is a common type of asseveration which may be biblical in origin; see Acts xxiii. 14.

wytt. Hemingway emends to *weete;* cf. rhyme-words.

476. *croyne.* The verb 'croon' in Northern dialect could mean 'to roar like a bull' (see *EDD.* s. Croon, sense 1), and something of this meaning may be present both here and in 661.

479–80. 'Who was it that spoke loudly, as though it were broad day?'—instead of being early morning when respectable folk expect to sleep.

482. *were it day* '(as you would see) if it were daylight'.

485. *Ouer a seke womans heede* 'because of a sick woman'; see *EDD.* s. Head, sense 2 (19).

487. *qweasse* 'breathe'. This is recorded in *NED.* as 'Of obscure origin and meaning', but it is probably the same word as *whese* 'wheeze' 5. 472, with the Northern spelling of *wh-*.

488–9. 'Every step you tread goes through my nose so loudly', i.e. goes right through my head.

492. Cf. 3.87.

496. *Thynk ye on yit* 'do you still remember?' Mak, after saying he would like to hire a nurse, asks the shepherds if they still remember his dream about his wife's giving birth to another child (384 ff.).

497–8. 'I've been paid my wages in full for a while—this is my dream come true.' Mak's 'wages' are, of course, his pretended baby.

501. Proverbial; cf. *Song of Lewes* 11 (ed. B. Dickins and R. M. Wilson, *Early Middle English Texts*, p. 11): 'Let him habbe ase he brew, bale to dryng.'

504. 'Nay, neither drink nor food will comfort us.'

505. *alys you oght bot goode* 'does anything but good trouble you?' i.e. is anything wrong with you?

505–6. The Third Shepherd now claims that several sheep have been stolen, although we already know (from 451) that only one sheep is missing. The discrepancy between 505–6 and 451 may perhaps be put down to exaggeration by the Third Shepherd for the purpose of impressing Mak.

516. 'Who took her', i.e. whether we stole her or not. Mak's use of *hir* is puzzling, since it is a wether that has been stolen. Either *hir* is nothing more than a convenient rhyme-word, or possibly Mak is trying to establish his innocence of the theft by deliberately making a mistake about the sex of the sheep.

524. 'He learned early to steal who could not say no (to another's property).' A proverb.

527. 'You come on purpose to rob us.'

533. *farne* is not the same word as *farne* 'fared' 531. It means 'farrowed' literally, and is used humorously here to mean 'laboured (in child-birth)'.

548–9. The comic effect of these lines is obvious if *this* 548 is taken to refer to the 'baby' in the cradle. Translate: 'Apart from this, I've found no live-stock here, tame or wild, that smelled as loud as he (the missing wether) did.'

552. *Syr, don* 'sir, completely'. The Second Shepherd is addressing the First and agreeing with him that they are completely *begyld*.

558. 'A good and happy future to him'; cf. *Kingis Quair*, stanza 185: 'In gude tym and sely to begynne Thair prentisshed.' The words *hys hyppys* are equivalent to 'him' (cf. note to 3.254); *celé* (cf. *Sely* 67) rhymes on its final sound with *se, redé, le*.

559. 'Who were ready so soon to act as his god-parents?' Mak's speed in finding god-parents for his new-born 'baby' becomes credible when it is remembered that baptism in medieval times often took place on the day a child was born.

560. *So fare fall thare lyppys.* Cf. note to 3.432.

562–4. The names *Gybon* (diminutive of *Gyb*) and *Iohn Horne* are those of the First and Second Shepherds in the *Prima Pastorum*. The *garray* made by *Iohn Horne* may therefore refer to the quarrel between the two shepherds when Horne interferes with Gyb's pasturing of his imaginary sheep; see 3.101 ff.

565. 'With the long legs.' These words presumably go together with *Iohn Horne* 563 and indicate that the man who played Horne's part was unusually tall.

567. *I hald for me* 'for my own part, I'm holding back'.

568. *All glad were ye gone* '(I should be) very glad if you were gone'.

577. For *day-starne* cf. 2 Pet. i. 19: 'until the day dawn, and the day star arise in your hearts.' The use of this word later on with reference to the infant Christ (727) is one of the many links between the secular and religious themes of the pageant.

579. Wright (*Rustic Speech and Folk-Lore*, p. 268) observes: 'A custom once common in the northern counties of England—and still extant at the end of last century—was that of presenting a new-born infant with three articles 'for luck', the first time it visited a neighbour or relation. The gifts usually consisted of an egg, a handful of salt, and a new sixpence.' It may be noticed that sixpence was worth a good deal in the fifteenth century when (according to J. E. T. Rogers, *Six Centuries of Work and Wages*, London, 1917, p. 327) the wages of an artisan were 6d. and those of an agricultural labourer about 4d.

582. Mak's anxiety makes him suddenly change the child's waking habits; cf. 557.

586. *We wate ill abowte* 'we pry about wrongfully', i.e. we do wrong to pry about.

587. A proverb; see note to 1.436. The Second Shepherd who does not see and recognize the lost sheep till a moment later, is here attributing the child's deformity to the badness of its parents.

591–2. A proverb; cf. 3.100. The same proverb occurs in *Everyman* 316 with the meaning 'blood is thicker than water'. In the present context the First Shepherd means that nature will show itself in one way or another—if not in a regular, then in an irregular manner. Evidently he still believes that the stolen sheep is a child deformed because of its bad parentage.

596. This line has a proverbial ring. Some editors emend *hang* to *hangys* or *hangs*, but *hang* is kept here because it is a possible Northern pa.t. form.

598–9. Mak and his wife have wrapped a cloth round the sheep's middle, and tucked in its legs so that it cannot struggle or escape.

601. *hornyd lad* 'lad with horns', i.e. devil. The resemblance of the stolen sheep to a devil is strengthened by his *long snowte* 585; Diabolus in the Newcastle play of *Noah* 127 (EETS. ES. 104) swears by his 'crooked snout'.

604. Adams punctuates this line with a question mark after *hatt* and with another after *Mak*, which he encloses in inverted commas. This alters the meaning to: 'What the devil will he be called?—"Mak"?' See note to 208.

605–6. 'Stop that! Now God give him sorrow, I saw (the sheep myself).' The words *Lett be all that* are addressed to the First Shepherd, to reproach him for making light of such *a hee frawde*.

615. *wepyn*. The rhyme requires *wapyn* (ON. *vdpn*); see *SP*. xxxiii. 18.

620. 'You two are well endowed together in one place', i.e. are as clever a pair of rascals as ever lived under one roof.

621, 623–8. In the manuscript 621 belongs to the Third Shepherd, and 623–8 are spoken by the First Shepherd. The editorial order of the names (suggested by Manly) is an improvement, for the First Shepherd has already (in 615) called for the violent punishment of the offenders. For the source of the error see note to 370–1, 372–4.

623. *With you will I be left* 'I will leave myself with you (as the judge)', i.e. I throw myself on your mercy.

628. C. Chidamian (*Spec.* xxii. 186–90) comments: 'The casting in a canvas, an apparently naïve punishment for Mak, had a far richer connotation for the medieval audience than we have ever suspected. For it is just by this method of tossing that primitive and medieval peoples hastened delivery in childbirth. . . . The one receiving the treatment is a man well-versed in obstetric matters who is now fittingly humiliated for staging a pseudo-nativity.'

Stage direction before 638. J. R. Moore (*JEGP.* xxii. 89) observes that angels are not 'clearly accredited with song' in the canonical books of the Bible, and that the *Gloria* became an angelic song only after its introduction into the church service.

639. *that Adam had lorne* 'that which Adam had brought to ruin', i.e. the souls of Adam's descendants.

647. Kölbing (*ES.* xxi. 165) emends *a qwant* to *the qwantest*; Manly suggests changing *that euer* to *as euer*, 'if emendation must be made'. But it is perhaps best to regard this line as a loose colloquial construction, and to leave it unaltered.

648. 'It is a marvellous thing to tell of, to be frightened thus'; cf. construction of 6.10.

649. *he spak vpward*. These words suggest that the Angel spoke to the shepherds from some raised place on the stage; cf. note to 1.297.

654. See note to 3.321.

656. *crakyd*. Cook emends to *crakt*; cf. rhyme-words.

657. According to H. Traver (*MLN.* xx. 4) the Second Shepherd of this pageant, unlike the ignorant Second Shepherd of the *Prima Pastorum* (see note to 3.414), was well versed in music when he perceived in the Angel's song 'the perfect rhythm of *Thre brefes to a long*'.

658. *crochett*. This is the earliest use in English of 'crotchet' as a musical term, apart from its appearance in the *Promptorium Parvulorum* (c. 1440). Traver (op. cit.) shows that the first occurrence of this word in any language can be dated about 1351, and its complete establishment about 1400. Its appearance in the *Secunda Pastorum* may suggest a date not much earlier than about 1400 for the composition of the pageant.

659–60. 'I know how to sing it among us, just as he trilled it.'

662. 'To bark at the moon' was a popular saying which meant 'to clamour in vain'. Here the Second Shepherd uses it to mean that Coll is wasting his efforts in trying to imitate the Angel's style of singing.

666. *fard.* Trusler (*SP.* xxxiii. 18) emends to *rad* 'afraid'; cf. rhyme-words. Rynell (*The Rivalry of Scandinavian and Native Synonyms in Middle English*, p. 157, note 84) points out that *adrad* is a possible alternative.

673. 'We must not forget it.' The Surtees editor reproduces an uncancelled long *s* before *lose* and so creates the ghost-word *slose*.

674–682, 692–700. See note on the prophet element in the *Prima Pastorum* (3.332 ff.). The longwinded discussion of the prophets in the First Shepherds' Play is here reduced to two stanzas, with a consequent gain in dramatic realism. It is also more appropriate that the Third Shepherd, who is the youngest of the three, should not be given any learned prophecies to quote. The mention of the prophets and patriarchs by the older shepherds helps to make an easy transition from the comedy of the Mak episode to the deep religious feeling of the adoration scene.

680–2. Isaiah's prophecy (Isa. vii. 14) is found in Christmas tropes, as for example in the eleventh-century trope from Ivrea; see Young, *The Drama of the Medieval Church*, ii. 6. The early appearance of this prophecy in Christmas tropes and liturgical *Pastores* helps to explain why the other Old Testament prophecies came to be included in the English Shepherds' Plays. For it is reasonable to suppose that Isaiah's prophecy attracted to itself the other prophecies given in the pseudo-Augustinian sermon *De Symbolo* and in the liturgical *Prophetae* based on this sermon. Cf. 5.213–14.

691. *mener* 'lowlier (than he should be)' is emended by Kölbing (ES. xxi. 165) to *meke*, thus making the alliterative phrase *meke and mylde*.

692. 'Patriarchs who once lived, and prophets in the past'; cf. Luke x. 24.

694. *that haue thay lorne* 'they have lost that (chance)'.

696. 'As a sign'; cf. Luke ii. 12.

702. 'Find (us) first of all, and make known (his birth) through his messenger'; cf. Luke ii. 15.

708–9. 'Grant us some joyful means of comforting thy child.'

718. *bob of cherys.* This unseasonable gift, which is a traditional Christmas miracle, can be taken as a symbol of midwinter fertility, a parallel in the world of nature to the miraculous birth of Christ. Like the Christmas cherries in *Sir Cleges* 224–6, the First Shepherd's *bob of cherys* is

> tokenyng
> Off mour godnes þat is comyng;
> We shall haue mour plenté.

There is also a cherry-tree bearing fruit just before Christ's birth in the *Ludus Coventriae* pageant of the *Birth of Christ* 31–42 (EETS. ES. 120). Cf. 3.189.

722. *byrd.* This gift, as well as the ball presented by the Third Shepherd (734), may symbolize attributes of the Trinity. A bird, especially a dove, is a common symbol of the Holy Ghost; a globe, representing the universe, symbolizes God the Father; see Jenner, *Christian Symbolism*, pp. 29, 81.

736. Pollard (p. 190) notes: 'Tennis was a fashionable game in France at the end of the 14th century (cp. the Dauphin's gift of tennis balls to our Henry V.), and was well known in England and Scotland about the same time.'

739. 'My name He named, and alighted in me before He went.'

740. 'I conceived him indeed through God's might, as His purpose was.'

749–50. 'Already the glad tidings of Christ's birth seem to have been told very often.' These lines hark back to *Tell furth as ye go* 744. The Third Shepherd is anticipating the ageless popularity of the Nativity story.

5. MAGNUS HERODES

1. *Nuncius* (speaker's name). The prototype of Herod's messenger is the 'nuntius' or 'internuncius' of the liturgical plays on the Slaughter of the Innocents; see Young, *The Drama of the Medieval Church*, ii. 102 ff.

Mahowne 'Mahomet', represented as a heathen deity scarcely distinguishable from the devil; cf. the Christian practice of giving Lucifer the names of pagan deities like Beelzebub, Baal, and Moloch. Later in this pageant Herod is mentioned several times in association with *Mahowne*, whose cousin he is (54). Cf. York XIX. 15, 19, etc.

2. *Both of burgh and of towne*. This phrase (used again in 462) is opposed to the following *by fellys and by fyrth*, so that the line as a whole means 'both townsfolk and country-folk', i.e. all people; cf. *Both in feyldys and in towne* 4.133.

3–4. *brith, grith*. These metathetic forms have been substituted by the copyist for *birth, girth*; cf. note to 6.382.

4–5. 'Who will promptly speak in a whisper, many a great protection shall befall'; *grith* is the subject and lines 2–3 are the (dative) object of *behapp*. Nuncius promises Herod's protection to all those who speak in a respectful whisper. These opening lines are a variation of the traditional—and no doubt necessary—demand for silence usually found at the beginning of a pageant whose protagonist is a villain (cf. Play 1). Herod's offer of *grith* is the act of a medieval monarch; thus Henry V, after invading Normandy (1417), ordered proclamation to be made that all those who swore allegiance to him would enjoy his peace and protection; see C. L. Kingsford, *Henry V* (London, 1901), p. 217.

9. 'And troubles (shall) entangle you.'

10–11. Cf. 220. Throughout this pageant Herod's kindship is constantly opposed to that of Christ.

10–14. These lines, which echo the opening phrases of a royal letter, were presumably read out as a *sond* (see 7) from King Herod. Nuncius afterwards tells Herod *thi letters haue I layde* 73.

11. *sourmontyng*. MS. *Iourmontyng* is a difficult word. The Surtees glossary identifies it with *se guermenter* 'fret, afflict, vex', recorded by Cotgrave. The EETS. glossary doubtfully interprets it as 'governor'. But *Iourmontyng* is possibly an error for *sourmontyng* 'surmounting, excelling'. A copyist could easily misread initial long *s* as long *i*, or even deliberately substitute long *i* for long *s*, in the belief that the word was meant to alliterate with *Iury* immediately preceding. But *sourmontyng* will, in fact, alliterate satisfactorily with *sternly* in the second half-line, for *s* can alliterate with *st* in these pageants, and the alliterative pattern *xa/ax* is elsewhere found in the long opening lines of the Wakefield stanza (e.g. 3.152). Cf. use of *surmonting* in a poem on Christ's Nativity attributed to Dunbar (ed. J. Small, STS., 1893, ii. 324):

> The potent Prince of joy imperiall,
> The he surmonting Empriour abone.

20. *Tytt teyn shall be told* 'shall quickly be told grief', i.e. know what sorrow is.

23. 'You may trust to that'; cf. 182.

24. *worthy wonderly* 'wonderfully worthy'.

26. *boy*, like *knaue* and *page*, can mean 'rogue' or 'rascal', and something of this meaning is no doubt present here.

29. 'I greatly marvel that it should happen so.' Nuncius is amazed that the new-born child should be hailed as king.

37–8. *kyng of kyngys . . . lord of lordyngys*. These words are used to describe Christ's majesty in Rev. xvii. 14 and xix. 16; cf. note to 291.

39. 'There are at his beck and call those who will boldly boast.' The verb *wate on* usually means 'escort, attend on', as in 6.156. But in the present context *wyngys* suggests that *watys on* has been influenced by its use as a hawking term; cf. the following quotation from Sebright's *Observations on Hawking* (1828) in *NED*. s. Wait, *v*.[1], sense 7d: 'He [the hawk] may thus be made to follow the falconer wherever he pleases; this is called *waiting on*.'

42 ff. Cf. the alliterative listing of names of countries and cities in the *Ludus Coventriae* pageant of the *Temptation* 172-4 (EETS. ES. 120) and in the *Castle of Perseverance* 170 ff. (EETS. ES. 91).

46. *Mownt Flascon* may be Montefiascone, a few miles north-west of Viterbo in Italy. The following description of Montefiascone is given in R. Lassels's *Voyage d'Italie* (Paris, 1671), i. 278: 'Ville située sur une montagne, où il y a un Siege d'Evesché, & qui est renommée à cause de ses excellens vins muscats.'

47. *Kemptowne.* MS. *kemp towne*. The only ancient English place-name resembling this is Kempton in Shropshire. But there is no obvious reason why the Wakefield playwright should have chosen a town in Shropshire to bring about what looks very much like deliberate bathos. It is tempting to identify *Kemptowne* with York, and so credit the dramatist with playing on the name of John Kemp(e), the absentee Archbishop of York from 1426–52.

48. *Susa* is the name of the capital of Prester John's legendary kingdom; see *Mandeville's Travels*, ch. xxxi (EETS. OS. 153, p. 183). It is also the name of the ancient capital of Persia, and of a seaport in the north-east of Tunisia. As Greece is said to be above it (48), its position is roughly that of the Tunisian Susa.

49. *Normondy and Norwa.* Cf. 'Norwaye & Normaundye', which are included among Arthur's domains in the alliterative *Morte Arthure* 44 (ed. E. Björkman, Heidelberg, 1915). *lowtys.* Not only *Normondy* and *Norwa* but all the countries named in 46–8 are presumably to be taken as the subjects of *lowtys*.

58. *we all.* Possibly *we* is a mistake for *ye*.

60. 'Force down your knees'; for the redundant use of *of* after a transitive verb cf. modern dialect usage (*EDD*. s. Of, sense II 5).

62. '(Or) he will be displeased.'

69. *deruly* 'promptly'. But as *u* and *n* are identical in the manuscript this word can also be read as *dernly* 'silently, quietly' (as in EETS.); cf. note to 6.226.

71. Cf. 3.459, where the same words are used by the First Shepherd in addressing the infant Christ.

73. *thi letters haue I layde* 'I have presented your letter'; *letters = sondys* 7.

74. *I haue done I couth do* 'I have done what I could do'.

75. 'Much more besides (have I) shown openly.' Nuncius has done more than merely ask the people to be quiet (74); he has addressed them sternly and at some length about their rebellious talk of a new-born king.

76. *Bot romoure is rasyd so* 'but rumour has been set going so (strongly)'.

80 ff. The medieval tradition of the ranting Herod, which is found in all the English cycles, derives ultimately from Matt. ii. 16: 'Then Herod, when he saw that he was mocked of the wise men, was exceeding wroth.' Herod's raging was later emphasized in patristic commentaries and in the liturgical plays dramatizing the Slaughter of the Innocents; see *Spec.* viii. 63–4. The hatred of tyranny which has gone to the making of the Wakefield author's portrait of Herod is a commonplace of medieval political thought; see, for example, A. P. D'Entrèves and J. G. Dawson, *Aquinas: Selected Political Writings* (Blackwell, Oxford, 1948), pp. 16–19. But his portraiture of Herod has no doubt gained zest from his own observation of contemporary magnates. Typical of these was the Earl of Suffolk, whose choleric behaviour in a court of law is compared with that of Herod, in a letter from J. Whetley to Sir John Paston (1478): 'ther was never no man that playd Herrod in Corpus Crysty play better and more agreable to hys pageaunt than he dud' (*The Paston Letters*, ed. J. Gairdner, v. 321). Cf. note to 98–9.

81. 'And make them go and hang themselves.'

93. *Who that is so bold* 'whoever is impudent enough (to make a noise)'.

96. 'All (the trouble) I will stir up.'

98–9. Herod's bloodthirsty language is reminiscent here of that used by the ruffler in the mummers' plays; see Tiddy, *The Mummers' Play*, pp. 144, 181, 226.

101. *oone*, i.e. Christ.

111. 'What joy it is for me to hear of a rascal who will seize my throne!'

116. *by Gottys dere nalys.* Here *nalys* may mean 'nails of the body' or 'nails of the cross'. Such oaths (cf. *by Cokys dere bonys* 228, 395) are used only by Herod and his soldiers.

128. *set all on sex and seuen* 'play havoc'. This phrase is derived from the game of hazard; cf. 'sette the world on six and sevene' in *Troilus and Criseyde*, iv. 622, and see F. N. Robinson's note on Pandarus's use of the phrase (*Complete Works of Geoffrey Chaucer*, Oxford, 1933, p. 942).

134–5. 'If I don't give him (such) a blow that I shall deprive him of life.'

136. *For parels.* See note to 1.299.

141–4. Two different constructions are run together here. The construction beginning *Sich panys* 141 requires to be completed in 144 by some such words as 'shall make them suffer' or 'shall inflict on them'.

142. 'Most horrible and cruel.' *For-* is an intensive prefix; cf. *For-daunche* 509.

145 ff. The Milites of this pageant correspond to the Armati or Armiger of the liturgical plays on the Slaughter of the Innocents; see Young, *The Drama of the Medieval Church*, ii. 105, 111, 119.

150–1. *Where . . . to-chyde* 'where can I stay without fighting and brawling with rage?'. These words express much the same meaning as 172.

155. According to medieval physiology, the heart was the centre of the vital functions (*gast*).

156–7. *Ther . . . gnast* 'the harm done is not so great that you need gnash your teeth about it'.

162. 'Without other speech (from us)', i.e. without hearing us further.

165. *woth* 'worth' is probably a phonetic spelling; cf. *woth* s. Worth in *EDD.*, and for loss of medial *r* see Appendix III, p. 130. *Woth youre eres* is proverbial; cf. 'worth bothe his eres' in the *Prologue* to *Piers Plowman* (B-text, line 78). Emendation of *eres* to *arse* (*SP.* xxxiii. 18) is unnecessary.

171. *ditizance doutance* is a corruption of 'ditez sans doutance'; cf. Herod's use of *Bewshere* 273 and *adew* 512, and see note to 513. These scraps of French do not indicate that the playwright was following a French source; they were no doubt commonly used by English people, especially those who had little French but great pretensions (cf. the Friar's use of the phrase 'je vous dy sanz doute', *Summoner's Tale*, *Cant. Tales*, III. 1838).

173. *We haue not done all yit*, i.e. we have not yet done everything possible to remedy this dangerous state of affairs.

177. 'If I stay in good health.' The usual phrase is *in quart* (cf. 333). A similar sentiment is expressed by Herod in 262.

183–4. *So bold . . . durst* 'so bold . . . that he dared'; for omission of *that* as a correlative of *so* see *NED.* s. So, sense 25.

186. 'They hadn't the courage to wait.'

202. *Vyrgyll.* Herod had evidently not heard of Virgil's Messianic Eclogue. See note on the two Virgilian verses between lines 387 and 388 of Play 3.

204. *poecé-tayllys.* The word *poecé* is interpreted as 'poet's' in the EETS. glossary and as 'poets'' in *NED.* s. Poet, sense 1. But it more probably means 'poesy', used áttributively before *tayllys* and pronounced as two syllables; cf. 'poysye mater' quoted from Usk's *Testament of Love* (1387–8) in *NED.* s. Poesy.

209 ff. The Primus Consultus and Secundus Consultus are not found in any of the liturgical plays on the Slaughter of the Innocents printed in Young's *The Drama of the Medieval Church*, ii. 102 ff. But two counsellors also appear in Towneley IX (*Cesar Augustus*) and XIV (*Oblacio Magorum*). In the latter pageant (401 ff.) the Primus Consultus and Secundus Consultus, like their counterparts in the *Magnus Herodes*, are commanded by Herod to consult their books, where they also find the prophecies of Isaiah and Micah concerning Christ's birth.

213–14. See note to 4.680–2.

215. ' "Emmanuel" is (he) called'; Matt. i. 23.

219–20. Mic. v. 2.

226. *bot I drynk onys.* At this point Herod refreshes himself, as he may well need to do after all his raging. This intrusive comic touch helps to lighten the monotony of Herod's paranoiac outburst.

229. *Thou can not half thi crede.* The first lesson in the church schools was the learning of the creed, so that these words are equivalent to saying, 'You don't know your A.B.C.'; cf. *Troilus and Criseyde*, v. 89.

244. *a carll in a kafe,* i.e. Christ. This is an allusion to the cave in which Christ was born, according to the Protevangelium xviii ff.; see M. R. James, *The Apocryphal New Testament* (Oxford, 1924), p. 46. Mirk's sermon on the Nativity (EETS. ES. 96, p. 22) describes Christ's birthplace as 'a caue þat was bytwene two howsys'.

249. *We two,* i.e. he and the Second Counsellor.

250. 'With our wits between (us)', i.e. by putting our heads together.

253 ff. In Matt. ii. 16 Herod apparently undertakes the slaughter of the children on his own initiative, but in the liturgical plays dramatizing this episode he acts upon the advice of Archelaus, Internuncius, or Armiger; see Young, *The Drama of the Medieval Church*, ii. 105, 111, 119.

256–7. *of . . . within* 'of two years' growth (i.e. two years old) and under'; Matt. ii. 16.

263. *a pope.* EETS. *Pope.* The erasure of these words was no doubt made after the Reformation; see Introduction, p. xiii.

264. 'My heart is rising now and beating wildly!'

269. *soundys.* MS. *sandys,* emended by Holthausen, *ES.* lviii. 163; cf. rhyme-words. The scribal change of *soundys* to *sandys* was probably due to the influence of the alliterative phrase *see . . . sand* (see 2.75).

270. 'I give you the right of hunting.' Such rights were originally a royal prerogative, but the political dominance of the magnates during the Lancastrian period enabled them to increase their hunting-rights; see A. R. Myers, *England in the Late Middle Ages* (Penguin Books, 1952), p. 138.

273. *byd.* The rhyme requires *bede.*

274. *and bryng* 'and bring (them)'; see note to 2.499.

290. 'Don't stand loitering about before we have been there.'

291. *all-weldand.* This epithet is generally used of God (e.g. in 2.494); cf. note to 37–8.

305–6. 'And I shall make you men of importance, wherever you come, sirs'; cf. 192–3. For *man* in this sense see *NED.* s. Man, *sb.*[1], sense 7.

aywhere. Trusler (*SP.* xxxiii. 19) emends to *aywhore,* thus making a double rhyme on *aywhore, syrs* and *Therfor, syrs* 302.

314. 'If the women (i.e. mothers of the children) behave like madwomen.'

316. 'Now go from here, so that you may get there quickly'; for the construction see note to 1.54.

318. *Al thynk, syrs, I say.* The Third Knight is telling his companions to give thought to their preparations for the coming 'conflict'; he himself will whet his tusks like a boar.

319. The First Knight seems to mean: 'Put me in front, for I'm good enough to fight a score of such people at any time.'

325. *ye* looks like a mistake for *we;* cf. 6.343. But emendation to *we* is not certainly necessary. For all his brave talk about going first (317), the Second Knight may now be telling his companions to go on ahead, while he himself hangs safely behind.

328–9. 'I wager a groat she won't like me very much by the time we part.'

330–1. 'Madam, don't be offended if I kill your boy.' This elaborate politeness is the First Knight's idea of fun.

350–1. Cf. the mothers' vain plea for mercy in liturgical plays (e.g. that from Fleury) on the Slaughter of the Innocents; see Young, *The Drama of the Medieval Church*, ii. 111.

352. *No mercy thou mefe* 'you'll move no mercy (in me)'.

357. *tabard.* Frampton (*PMLA.* l. 632) identifies this as an heraldic tabard, and claims that 'our first knowledge of an armorial tabard dates from . . . 1424'.

380. *I red the not, stry* 'no, I tell you, hag'.

by son and by moyn is an oath used only by pagans in the biblical plays; cf. *by son and moyne* IX. 232.

388–9. *For . . . borow* 'because of the sorrow that God has dearly sent me, who can save me from misery?'

408. 'It is fitting that I should (be the first to) address my lord (Herod).'

427. *I stud and I stard* 'I stood and I glared'. The Third Knight establishes himself as a stern man of action.

439. 'If it please that you would', i.e. if it be your pleasure.

442. 'As sure as I am a crowned king, I think it quite right (that you should be rewarded).'

443. *that has sich a wyght* 'who has such a person (to serve him)'.

445–6. 'Now you can go quickly with plenty of pennies good and round.'

453. *haue.* Here, as often, the present tense has a future meaning—the knights have only the promise of Herod's liberality.

454. 'It (i.e. the gold) will never be used up, truly.'

455–6. This is reminiscent of the 'hail' speeches addressed by the shepherds to the infant Christ in the Shepherds' Plays, e.g. 3.458 ff.

458–9. The place where Mahowne is friendly lord is probably a euphemism for 'hell'; cf. note to line 1.

471. *flode*, i.e. the flood of the children's blood; cf. 313.

492–5. 'After I was dead and rotten, many a tongue would have told how I avenged myself.'

497. 'Who are mad enough to exercise such power.'

501. 'Don't petition any king.'

505. *if I here it spokyn*, i.e. if I hear any more rebellious talk.

507. *Nothyng bese vnlokyn* 'nothing shall be explained', i.e. no explanations will be needed or given.

508. *Begyn I to rokyn.* MS. *rekyn*, but the rhyme requires *rokyn*. These words probably have the same meaning as *begyn I to reyll* 326. Just as *reyll* 'reel' is used in 326 to mean 'run riot, behave violently', so *rokyn* 'rock, stagger, reel' is similarly used in the present context. But see *ES.* lviii. 163 and *PQ.* xiv. 305.

508–9. 'I shall think all indignation (anger, vexation) over-nice', i.e. I shan't spare anyone's feelings. *For-daunche* (see *NED.* s. Daunch) is an adjective with the intensive prefix *for-*; cf. 142.

511. 'Don't be too cruel!' Such advice is not to be taken seriously when Herod is the man who gives it. It is not Herod's cruelty so much as his absurdity and buffoonery which are emphasized at the end of the pageant.

512. *deuyll.* Trusler (*SP.* xxxiii. 19) emends to *deyle*, in view of the rhyme with *counsell* and *cruell.* This emendation is no doubt correct, but *deyll* is a more typical spelling than *deyle*; cf. 3.272.

513. *Franch.* EETS. frau*n*ch, but the manuscript has simply a ligature above final *ch*, and no abbreviation sign for *n*. Herod's parting shot—'I know no more French'—presumably refers to his use of three or four French words; see note to 171.

6. COLIPHIZACIO

At the top of the first page of this pageant (f. 73*b*) are written the following words in an early seventeenth-century hand: *Thomas Hargraues g holy & go holynes and godlynes is the.* For the name *Thomas Hargraues* see Introduction, p. xi.

1. The brutality of the torturers is emphasized in this very first line, where the First Torturer urges Christ forward with language used in driving animals. The same motive is taken up again near the end of the pageant (429–32). The torturers are developed from the 'two false witnesses' of the biblical story (Matt. xxvi. 60) and from the bystanders who buffet Christ (Matt. xxvi. 67, Mark xiv. 65).

4. *trespast*. MS. *trespas* shows omission by haplology of final *t* before the initial *t* of *thou*; cf. *trespast* 316.

10. 'It is a wonderful thing to endure, thus to be going', i.e. this journey is wonderfully hard to endure. For the construction cf. 4.648.

13. This line apparently means: 'By the time you have had two or three promises of a hanging.'

28. Proverbial.

31. *If we dyd neuer yll* 'even though we never did any wrong'.

35–7. *Hisself . . . legeance* 'he shall not excuse himself with any plea, I promise you that'.

46. *syrs*, i.e. Annas and Caiaphas, the high priests. There is no biblical warrant for their joint examination of Christ. Annas is characterized in this pageant as a typical smooth-tongued Pharisee, in contrast to his brutal companion. The violence and bloodthirstiness of Caiaphas go back to the biblical detail that it was he who 'gave counsel to the Jews, that it was expedient that one man should die for the people' (John xviii. 14). But, apart from the influence of the biblical narrative, it is likely that the characterization of Annas and Caiaphas was influenced by the Wakefield author's dislike of the corrupt ecclesiastical lawyers of his own day; see Owst, *Literature and Pulpit in Medieval England*, p. 496.

47. Apparently the First Torturer pauses for a reply from Annas and Caiaphas after line 46, and when none is forthcoming he asks reproachfully, 'Why haven't you asked yet how we've got on?'

48. This line makes better sense with *ye* inserted before *witt*: 'We would like you to know that our bones are all weary.'

50. 'So long delayed', i.e. we've been kept waiting about so long; cf. 4.110.

55. Christ was taken prisoner during the hours of darkness.

64. *Can ye hym oght apeche* 'can you accuse him at all?' i.e. can you bring any charge against him?

65. *He has bene for to preche* 'he has been preaching'.

66. Cf. Luke xxiii. 5; *teche* 'teaches' is an uninflected 3 sg. pres. used here for the sake of the rhyme.

69. *yerde*, i.e. the garden of Gethsemane.

71–2. Matt. xxvi. 56, Mark xiv. 50, etc.

73–4. These words are given to the 'two false witnesses' of the biblical narrative; see Matt. xxvi. 61, Mark xiv. 58.

80–1. The whetstone was an emblem of lying. Brand (*Popular Antiquities*, London, 1849, iii. 389–90) quotes the following passage: 'Lying with us is so loved and allowed, that there are many tymes gamings and prises therefore purposely, to encourage one to outlye another. . . . And what shall he gaine that gets the victorie in lying? . . . He shall have a silver whetstone for his labour.'

82. *wyles*. MS. *lyes*, emended in EETS. The copyist was possibly influenced by the sound of *pryce* 81, which is written just above *lyes* in the manuscript; he may also have had in mind the phrase *fals lyys* used in 226.

82–6. Cf. Nicodemus i. 1: 'We have a law that we should not heal any man on the sabbath: but this man of his evil deeds hath healed the lame and the bent, the withered and the blind . . . on the sabbath day!' (M. R. James, *The Apocryphal New Testament*, p. 96).

90. The Second Torturer offers this information before Caiaphas begins to interrogate Christ; cf. 118.

91. *kyng*. MS. *prophete*, emended by Holthausen (*ES*. lviii. 164). The mistake is due to the scribe's anticipation of *Men call hym a prophete* 110.
Godys son of heuen 'the God of heaven's son'. ME. rarely uses the group genitive; see H. C. Wyld, *A History of Modern Colloquial English* (Blackwell, Oxford, 1936), p. 318.

91–2. Cf. Nicodemus i. 1: 'he saith that he is the Son of God and a king; moreover he . . . would destroy the law of our fathers' (James, op. cit., 96).

94. Cf. Luke xxiii. 2. Caiaphas repeats this accusation in 227.

97–8. John viii. 3–11.

103. *wychcraft.* Cf. Nicodemus i. 1: 'He is a sorcerer, and by Beelzebub the prince of the devils he casteth out devils, and they are all subject unto him' (James, op. cit., 96).

112–13. 'But would you two . . . confirm it (i.e. Christ's condemnation) and at the same time make it certain?'

121–2. i.e. Christ's past words and actions condemn him and prove him to be accursed.

123–4. 'His sour looks remind me that I've forgotten something.'

129. *Of care may thou syng* 'of sorrow may you sing', i.e. may you moan aloud in your misery.

136. *Illa-hayll was thou borne* 'it was bad luck you were born'.

139. 'Now may they outlaw you and raise the hue and cry against you.'

143–4. A Latin proverb; cf. Cotgrave, *A Dictionarie of the French and English Tongues* (1611) s. Consentir: 'Prov. *He consents enough that sayes nothing; (Many, who know not much more Latine, can say,* Qui tacet consentire videtur.)'

148. *in a torde* is an abusive phrase intensifying *Speke on.*

149. *Sir Sybré.* A footnote to *Sybre* in the EETS. glossary comments that the 'surname Sybry, Sibree is common in Yorkshire. Perhaps some malefactor of the name may have rendered it celebrated, so that it may have been half-jocularly put in here'. But the words *Sir Sybré* are pretty certainly a mocking reference to the obscurity of Christ's birth. This being so, it is possible that the dramatist is making derisive use of *sibred* (OE. *sibbrǣden*) meaning 'consanguinity (as an impediment to marriage)' or (especially in E.Angl. dialect) 'marriage banns'; see *NED.* s. Sibred.

159. 'As I hope to go on singing Mass.' Apart from being an obvious anachronism, this asseveration is deliberately and grotesquely out of place in the mouth of a Jewish prelate who is so violently opposed to Christ and all his works, and who in the present context is using the asseveration to affirm his own roguery.

161–2. A proverbial phrase by which Caiaphas means that he makes more by illegal means than he earns as income; cf. *Canterbury Tales, Gen. Prol.* 256. This confession of corrupt practices has a special relevance here if Caiaphas is hoping to get from Christ the *many fees* 83 that he is supposed to have collected for his miraculous cures.

164. 'Neither the blind nor the lame will persecute you.' These words hark back to 82.

166. *Kyng Copyn in oure game. Copyn* is doubtfully explained as 'Empty-skein' in the EETS. glossary; cf. *EDD.* s. Coppin. But it makes more sense to relate the word to *cop* 'a crest on the head of a bird' (*NED.* s. Cop, *sb.*², sense 1d; cf. note to *Copyle* 4.67), and to give it the figurative meaning 'coxcomb' in this context. If such is the meaning, there may be an allusion here to the King of Fools, the *dominus festi* of the Feast of Fools; see Chambers, *The Mediaeval Stage,* i. 321–6. This mockery of Christ's kingship is derived from the biblical account of how the Jews crowned Christ with thorns and hailed him as the King of the Jews (Matt. xxvii. 29, Mark xv. 17–18).

166–7. *thus . . . fatur* 'thus shall I invest you (with the mock-title of *Kyng Copyn*), for being an impostor'.

169. The relative pronoun is to be understood before *the* 'thee'.

175–6. 'Or else I shall be revenged on you before your death becomes known.' In other words, Caiaphas threatens to torture Christ and put him to death in secret.

183. Caiaphas refers to the words spoken by Christ to the people; cf. 173.

184. *Nay, whils I lif, nere* 'no, never while I live'.

190. *fyrst.* The rhyme requires *fryst*; cf. 382.

196. 'I pray you do—and kill him!'

198. 'Without being liable to condemnation.'

200. *wold.* The rhyme requires *wald* (EETS.).

202. *Shall I neuer ete bred.* See note to 4.468.

209. 'You should teach us how to practise meekness'. The rhyme requires *techar* (EETS.).

211. *All soft may men go far.* Proverbial; cf. 'soft and essele men goo far' in the Coventry Weavers' Pageant 551 (EETS. ES. 87).

214–15. A legal proverb.

226. *renyd.* EETS. *reuyd;* but *renyd* 'reigned' is supported by *If he reyne any more* 119 and by the frequent mocking references to Christ's kingship (130, 150, 199, etc.), as well as by the fact that the word meaning 'rob, steal' is elsewhere in these pageants spelt *refe* or *reyfe* not *reue.* For the same reasons *rene* is better than *reue* in 265. Cf. note to 5.69.

241. *thou.* A careful distinction is kept between *thou* and *ye* in this pageant: the torturers and their masters all use *thou* in addressing Christ, while Annas and Caiaphas use *ye* in addressing each other.

244. 'But I shall do what the law requires, even if the people praise you'; cf. 205. Annas's show of fairness contrasts with the behaviour of the Second Torturer, who says that they will accuse Christ even *if other men ruse hym* 33.

246. Cf. Matt. xxvi. 62, Mark xiv. 60.

247-8. 'Listen how they boast that they will condemn thee to hang on a hill.' By 'they' Annas no doubt means Caiaphas and the torturers. The word *ruse* in the sense 'to boast' is usually reflexive; for the infin. construction after *ruse* cf. York XXIX. 271: 'This rebalde he rowses hym it rathely to rayse.'

249-54. Matt. xxvi. 63-4, Mark xiv. 61-2.

253. *I* is added in EETS.

255. 'Bad luck to the feet that brought thee to town!'

258. *redres* 'redress (what is wrong)'.

260. 'He himself says plainly', i.e. he condemns himself out of his own mouth.

265-8. Cf. John xi. 48, 53.

267. 'Therefore, while I still draw breath.' Caiaphas is intent on killing Christ before Christ—as he fears—kills him.

269-70. John xviii. 31: 'Nobis non licet interficere quenquam.'

277-9. According to John xviii. 31, the Jews are free to judge Christ by their own legal processes; but they choose not to do so because it is unlawful for them to put any man to death (cf. 269-70).

281. Caiaphas swells with rage at the thought of Christ's teaching; cf. *talys* 406.

289. *So may I well seme* 'it becomes me well to be one'; *seme* in this sense is usually an impers. verb, as in 3.457.

298-9. These lines are difficult to interpret satisfactorily. They seem to mean: 'Fie on him and worse! I am out of my way (i.e. I'm not within striking distance of Christ). Tell me, why does he stand so far off?' Caiaphas, we may suppose, strikes at Christ and misses him; hence his indignant question *why standys he so far?* Then Annas replies: 'Sir, he has but lately come', i.e. he has only just come—where do you expect him to be standing?

301. *Ye ar bot to skar* 'you are only to frighten him', i.e. you must only frighten him— nothing more.

310. *Els* 'otherwise', i.e. if I weren't a priest. Caiaphas is continuing straight on from 307-8.

334. *For I red not we mete* 'for I don't advise you to meet me', i.e. you had better make yourselves scarce.

335. *on vs be it* 'on our heads be it'.

337. *sytt ye and see it.* MS. *see ye and sytt,* emended by Trusler (*SP.* xxxiii. 19).

338. *Oone feste.* These words may be taken as an adv. phrase here; cf. modern colloquial phrase 'a (fair) treat'.

341-2. Caiaphas cautiously withholds his blessing until after the buffeting.

344. *a new play of Yoyll.* The game which the torturers play at Christ's expense is, in fact, an ancient game known as Hot Cockles, 'in which one player . . . knelt down with his eyes covered, and being struck on the back by the others in turn, guessed who struck him' (*NED*). The identification of this old game with the buffeting of Christ is also found in medieval English sermons, as pointed out by Professor Owst in *Literature and Pulpit in Medieval England,* pp. 510-11.

346-7. *Now . . . vnnett* 'now the other way (i.e. without a stool) it would be painful and difficult (for Christ)'.

W.P.—L

351. *buffit* 'low stool, footstool'. But it seems likely that a pun on 'buffet' (i.e. blow) is also intended; cf. *bofettys to fott* 1.392.

354–5. These lines suggest that a tall man acted the part of Christ: tall enough to make it difficult for the torturers to reach his head easily when he was standing up. The words *hop and dawnse As cokys in a croft* refer to cock-fighting or perhaps to the Shrove-tide amusement of throwing sticks at a cock, which was trained to hop aside in an effort to avoid the fatal blow; see Brand's *Popular Antiquities*, i. 77.

357. 'As good a reason can you show.'

358. 'As fell in the dew.' The meaning is obscure. Froward, who cannot see any sense in fetching a stool for Christ to sit on, apparently means that the reason given by the First Torturer for asking him to bring a stool (353–5) is no more substantial than the dew.

363. There is probably a quibble here on *crowne* 'crown of the head' and *crowne* 'king's crown'; cf. 256.

370. There is biblical authority for the covering of Christ's eyes, e.g. Mark xiv. 65, Luke xxii. 64.

371. 'Yes, unless they are firmly closed (*well spard*), we shall waste our efforts.' The Second Torturer has the game of Hot Cockles in mind (see note to 344); unless Christ's eyes are covered, he will see who hits him and so the guessing game will be spoilt.

379. *curst* 'perverse', with reference to the meaning of the name Froward.

380–3. These lines establish Froward's relationship with Pikeharnes of Play 1, Slawpase of Play 3, and Daw of Play 4. They all have uncomplimentary nicknames, and they all complain bitterly of the treatment they receive from their masters; cf. 1.428, 430, 3.200–1, 4.154 ff.

382. *thrust*. The rhyme requires *thurst*.

387. The *peruyce* was an academic disputation in which students at the Inns of Court had to reply to, and argue on, questions put to them. It was so called from being held originally in the court or porch of a church (OF. *parevis*); cf. *Canterbury Tales*, *Gen. Prol.* 310. The Second Torturer, who is replying sarcastically to Froward's *Fayn preue it I wold* 386, means in effect: 'You shall be called to the bar since you're so good at disputing.'

390. *Abowte his heade cast* '(it should be) put round his head'.

394–6. 'What, do you think I'm mad? He might have Christ's curse who was the last to bind his head.' These words suggest that Froward, after going through the motions of tying the bandage round Christ's head, actually leaves the job to one of his masters to finish because he has a superstitious fear of receiving Christ's curse. It will be remembered that Christ has a reputation for witchcraft (see 103).

397 ff. For the biblical account of the buffeting of Christ see Matt. xxvi. 67, Mark xiv. 65, Luke xxii. 63–4.

398. 'And thus was I advised to gain the mastery', i.e. I was advised to hit the hardest, and this is how it is done; cf. 341–2.

399. *Nay, wrang has thou teld* 'no, you've spoken wrongly'.

400–1. *thou . . . fowll* 'you didn't touch the skin but badly', i.e. you hardly grazed the skin.

406. 'We'll knock all his foolish talk out of him.'

408. *knop out the skalys*. An allusion to the game of ninepins; see *NED*. s. Skayles. In *Queen Mary's Psalter* (ed. G. Warner, plate 196d) there is a drawing of two youths playing at 'club-kayles' with pins and a stick.

409–10. 'God forbid you should leave off, but dig all your nails in together.' For the construction after *Godys forbot* cf. 3.271.

411 ff. This detail of the torturers asking Christ to prophesy who has struck him is found in Matt. xxvi. 68, Luke xxii. 64. But the torturers still have in mind the game of Hot Cockles; see note to 344.

415. *togeder*. The rhyme requires *togyder* (EETS.).

420. 'Sir, for his great boasting (in the past).'

423. *knokyd*. MS. *knokyp*, emended in EETS.

427. *trate*. MS. *crate*. According to *NED*. (s. Crate), the spelling *crate* here is 'a misreading

in some editions of *trate*'. But as *crate* is what is clearly written in the manuscript, the misreading is a scribal, not an editorial, error.

429–32. Cf. note to line 1. The word *lede* 429 is opposed to *dryfe* 432: the torturers lead Christ like a draught-animal, and Froward drives him from behind.

433. *Alas, now take I hede* 'alas, now I see (what may happen)'.

434–41. A. Williams (*The Characterization of Pilate in the Towneley Plays*, pp. 59–60) points out that this reference to Pilate's duplicity and guile links up with the nine-line stanza in the *Conspiracio* (**XX.** 19 ff.) in which Pilate describes his own crookedness.

439. This proverbial saying sounds absurd in the mouth of Caiaphas, who has already admitted his own corruption (see 160–2).

442. 'I blame you for all this, for if it hadn't been for you.'

444. *wan.* Holthausen (*ES.* lviii. 164) emends to *ban* = *bayn* (ON. *beinn*) 'readily, willingly'.

450. *men.* Caiaphas is addressing the audience; cf. 1.463.

APPENDIX I

TWO DOCUMENTS CONCERNING THE WAKEFIELD CORPUS CHRISTI PLAY

There are two documents containing references to the Corpus Christi play of Wakefield. These are: (*a*) the Wakefield Burgess Court Rolls for 1554 and 1556; and (*b*) a York document (dated 27 May 1576) recording the contents of a letter sent by the Ecclesiastical Commissioners to the bailiff and burgesses of Wakefield.

(*a*) *The Wakefield Burgess Court Rolls.* The references to the Corpus Christi play in the Wakefield Burgess Court Rolls for 1554 and 1556 are as follows:

1554

Itm a payñ is layd yt gyles Dolleffe shall brenge In or Causse to be broght ye regenall of Corpus Xty play before ys & wytsonday In pane . . .

Itm a payñ ys layde yt ye mesters of ye Corpus Xti playe shall Come & mayke thayre a Count before ye gentyllmen & burgessus of ye toun before this & may day next In payñ of everye oñ not so doynge, 20s.

1556

Itm a payne is sett that everye crafte and occupacion doo bringe furthe theire pagyaunts of Corpus Christi daye as hathe bene heretofore used and to gyve furthe the speches of the same in after holydayes in payne of everye one not so doynge to forfett xls.

Itm a payne is sett that everye player be redy in his pagyaunt at setled tyme before 5 of ye clocke in ye mornynge in payne of every one not so doynge to forfett vjs. viijd.

Itm a payne is sett yt ye players playe where setled and no where els in payne of no so doynge to forfett xxs.

Itm a payne is sett yt no man goe armed to disturb ye playe or hinder ye procession in payne of everye one so doynge vjs. viijd.

Itm a payne is sett yt everye man shall leave hys weapons att hys home or att hys ynne in payne not so doynge vjs. viijd.

Ye summe of ye expens of ye Cherche mester for ye Corpus Christi playe xvijs. xd.

Item payd to ye preste xijd.

Itm payd to ye mynstrells xxd.

Itm payd to ye mynstrells of Corpus Christi playe iijs. ivd.

Itm payd for ye Corpus Christi playe & ye wrytynge of ye spechys for yt iijs. viijd.

Itm payd for ye Baner for ye mynstrells vjs. viijd.

Itm payd for ye ryngyng ye same day vjd.

Itm payd for garlonds on Corpus Christi day xijd.[1]

In view of the evidence that the Huntington manuscript of the Towneley Plays is an official register of the Wakefield Corpus Christi cycle,[2] the possibility exists that this manuscript is none other than the document referred to as the *regenall* in the Wakefield Burgess Court Roll for 1554.[3] In support of this identification, it may be noticed that the names of crafts in the Huntington manuscript are in a sixteenth-century hand, and that Play XXXII (inscribed *Lysters pag* . . .) has been added to the manuscript in an early sixteenth-century hand. In fact, there is evidence that the manuscript was still being used in the sixteenth century; and the signs of its use at this late date may, like the entries in the Burgess Court Rolls for 1554 and 1556, be connected with an effort to revive the old religious pageants during the reign of Queen Mary

(*b*) *The Commissioners' Instructions concerning the Wakefield Play.* The text of this York document is as follows:

xxvij° die Maii Anno domini 1576 loco Consistoriali ecclesie Eboracensis Coram Magistris Mattheo Hutton Iohanne Gibson et Willelmo Palmer Commissionariis et in presentia mei Willelmi Fothergill notarii publici / This daie vpon intelligence geven to the saide Commissioners that it is meant and purposed that in the towne of Wakefeld shalbe plaied this yere in Whitsonweke next or theraboutes a plaie commonlie called Corpus Christi plaie which hath bene heretofore vsed there / Wherein they ar done tundrestand that there be many thinges vsed which tende to the Derogation of the Maiestie and glorie of god the prophanation of the Sacramentes and the maunteynaunce of superstition and idolatrie / The said Commissioners Decred a lettre to be written and sent to the Balyffe Burgesses and other the inhabitantes of the said towne of Wakefeld that in the said playe no Pageant be vsed or set furthe wherein the Maiestye of god the father god the sonne or god the holie ghoste or the administration of either the Sacramentes of Baptisme or of the lordes Supper be counterfeyted or represented / or any thinge plaied which tende to the maintenaunce of superstition and idolatrie or which be contrarie to the lawes of god or[4] of the Realme / Which lettre was sent accordinglie and was subscribed with the handes of the said Dominus Hutton and of others of the Counsell and commission.[5]

---

[1] These items concerning the Wakefield Corpus Christi play were first edited in full by J. W. Walker in *Miscellanea*, ii, YAS. RS. 74 (1929), pp. 20–2. Walker prints the Wakefield Burgess Court Rolls for 1533, 1554, 1556, and 1579; the present whereabouts of these Rolls cannot be traced, nor are any others known to have survived. For information about the Wakefield Burgess Court see S. H. Waters, *Wakefield in the Seventeenth Century* (Wakefield, 1933), pp. 4–7.

[2] See Introduction, pp. xii ff.

[3] The word 'original' could be used with the same meaning as 'register'; for example, we find the official text of the York Creed play in 1568 termed the 'original or regester' (see A. Raine, *York Civic Records*, vi, YAS. RS. 112, p. 133).

[4] This word is inserted with a caret mark above *and* cancelled.

[5] This transcription has been newly made from a photograph of the document. The original is preserved among the York Diocesan records at St. Anthony's Hall, York. It has been printed by Walker, *Wakefield, Its History and People*, i. 156; by H. C. Gardiner, *Mysteries' End* (New Haven, Yale University Press, 1946), p. 78; and by J. S. Purvis, *Tudor Parish Documents of the Diocese of York* (Cambridge, 1948), pp. 173–4. The transcription given here differs in several details from those previously printed.

H. C. Gardiner has suggested that the corrections in the Huntington manuscript[1] may have been occasioned by the Commissioners' letter (1576) to the
bailiff and burgesses of Wakefield on the subject of their Corpus Christi play.[2]
If this could be proved, we might safely assert not only that the manuscript
contains the Corpus Christi play of Wakefield, but that it is the 'original' or
'register' which was still in use at Wakefield in 1576. It would be as good as
proved if, as Gardiner maintains, 'the corrections which exist in the text of the
Towneley plays today, scanty though they are, touch precisely on the subjects
mentioned in the Commissioners' letter'.[3] But it is not at all certain that this is
so. True, the corrections in the manuscript aim at removing doctrines objectionable to the reformed Church. But an examination of the York document
will show that it is not specifically concerned with the five unrecognized sacra-
ments, the Pope, or the doctrine of transubstantiation—the matters which have
been corrected in the Towneley Plays. The Commissioners object to much
more than this, for they will not allow the representation in any pageant of 'the
Maiestye of god the father god the sonne or god the holie ghoste or the administration of either the Sacramentes of Baptisme or of the lordes Supper . . . or
any thinge plaied which tende to the maintenaunce of superstition and idolatrie
or which be contrarie to the lawes of god or of the Realme'. This compre-
hensive statement amounts practically to a prohibition of the whole Corpus
Christi play. The Commissioners would obviously not have been satisfied with
the tinkering that the text of the Towneley Plays has received. Nevertheless,
the York document undoubtedly lends support to the other evidence that this
text was an official copy of the pageants, used and corrected by the municipal
authorities in general charge of the Corpus Christi play at Wakefield.

[1] For these corrections see Introduction, pp. xii–xiii.   [2] Gardiner, op. cit., 78
[3] Ibid., 121.

APPENDIX II

METRE

The Wakefield Stanza

Plays 2–6, except for two defective stanzas,[1] are written throughout in the same nine-line stanza rhyming *aaaabcccb*,[2] with central rhymes in the lines of the opening quatrain. Play 1 has only one true Wakefield stanza (450–62); the stanza which concludes the pageant is a verse short (463–70). It is possible to regard the Wakefield stanza as one of thirteen verses rhyming *abababab cdddc*, and it is actually found written like this in 1. 450–62. The number of syllables is variable, but there are usually four stresses in each of the first four lines (two before and two after the central rhyme), one in the first *b*-verse, three in each of the *c*-verses, and two in the second *b*-verse.

There is nothing exactly like this stanza to be found anywhere in medieval English literature outside the Wakefield Group; and there can be no doubt that, as it stands, it is the invention of the Wakefield playwright. Nevertheless, a thirteen-line stanza with the same rhyme-scheme, but with heavier stressing and alliteration, is found in other pageants of the Towneley cycle,[3] as well as in poems and plays which have no obvious connexion with this cycle.[4] Again, a nine-line stanza with the same end-rhymes, but without internal rhymes in the first quatrain and with heavier alliteration, is also found outside the cycle.[5] It is probable therefore that the Wakefield playwright has remodelled a stanza close in form to the one we actually find him using in the Wakefield Group.

Whatever his model was, he has created a new stanza with a sound and rhythm all of its own, and with its help he is able to reduce the chaotic movements and swiftly changing moods of everyday life to poetic form and order. In his hands the nine-line stanza becomes a remarkably efficient instrument for rapid monologue or dialogue. It keeps its form even when it is divided among as many as three speakers, and because of the internal rhymes in the opening quatrain the first part of a line can be given to one speaker and the second part to another without metrical anarchy resulting.[6] The same stanza, as the Wakefield Master handles it, is also suitable for graver and more tranquil moments, when the mood expressed is serious, solemn, or tender. On such occasions the stanza is not usually given to more than one or two speakers; a new speaker is

---

[1] See notes to 3.127–33 and 4.262–8.

[2] One stanza (5.46–54) has the end-rhymes *aaaaabbba*.

[3] E.g. XXII, stanzas 1–4.

[4] In the *Anturs of Arther at the Tarnewathelan* (a fourteenth-century metrical romance); in the *Alliterative Poem on Fortune* (printed in *Reliquiae Antiquae*, ii. 7–9); also in the *Castle of Perseverance* (*c.* 1405), the Dublin play of *Abraham and Isaac* (*c.* 1450), and in the Proclamation and some of the pageants of the *Ludus Coventriae* (*c.* 1468).

[5] In the *Tale of the Basyn*, the *Tale of the Lady Prioress and her Three Suitors*, and the *Turnament of Totenham*; see Cargill, *PMLA*. xli. 819.

[6] E.g. 3.262–3.

introduced at the beginning of a line, not in the middle; and the movement of the verse is slowed down by heavier alliteration.

The stanza is more flexibly used in the *Prima Pastorum* than in the *Processus Noe*, and with even greater ease and mastery in the *Secunda Pastorum*.[1] For example, in the *Processus Noe* a change of speaker less frequently breaks the line than it does in the *Prima* and *Secunda Pastorum*; and when a line is thus broken, the break always occurs immediately after the central rhyme.[2] There is nothing in the Noah Play like line 119 of the First Shepherds' Play, which is divided into three, by one break before the central rhyme and by another immediately after it. Nor is there anything in the First Shepherds' Play like lines 114, 328, 402 of the Second Shepherds' Play, where one of the short *c*-verses is divided between two speakers. These differences may be taken as signs of a growing freedom in the Wakefield author's use of his stanza, and may suggest that he wrote these pageants in the order *Processus Noe*, *Prima Pastorum*, *Secunda Pastorum*.[3] On the other hand, his handling of the stanza in rapid dialogue is already extraordinarily expert in the *Processus Noe*, and it is difficult to be sure on metrical grounds alone that this pageant was written much earlier than the *Prima* and *Secunda Pastorum*.

Stanza-linking. It is not usual for one stanza to run on to the next, but examples do occur, e.g. 2.36–7, 3.196–7, 4.520–1, 700–1, 5.432–3, 6.333–4. Occasionally, the linking of two stanzas is contrived by the repetition of a word, e.g. 2.531–2, 549–50, 3.277–8, 5.279–80, 6.27–8, 126–7; but this repetition is not a formal metrical device so much as a dramatic device for showing how one speaker's words can set off a train of thoughts in another.[4]

Alliteration. Sustained alliteration is used but rarely and to gain a special effect: to heighten the dignity of the language (as in Mary's words to the shepherds in the *Prima Pastorum* 485–93), or to add sound and fury to a ranting speech like that of Nuncius at the beginning of the *Magnus Herodes*. Alliterative phrases, on the other hand, are by no means uncommon.[5] These are often to be found in serious contexts, where an archaic poetic diction is appropriate. If a traditional poetic phrase is used in a colloquial context, this may simply mean that the phrase has become established in the speech of the poet's day, e.g. *swete or swynk* 2.195, *still as stone* 2.406. But at times a humorous effect is probably intended, as when the First Shepherd says that the ale offered him by the Second Shepherd is *boyte of oure bayll* 3.247.[6]

Rhymes. Some of the rhymes are ordinary enough, and it is not uncommon for the same rhyme-words to be used in a sequence in different pageants, e.g. *euen, heuen, neuen, seuen* are rhymed together in 2.10–13, 3.37–40, 5.127–30.

---

[1] Carey, *The Wakefield Group in the Towneley Cycle*, pp. 225–8.

[2] E.g. 2.355, 372, 380, 382, etc.

[3] Using the same metrical criteria, Professor Frampton would put the *Magnus Herodes* before the *Processus Noe*, and the *Coliphizacio* between the two Shepherds' Plays; see *PMLA*. liii. 113–15.

[4] Repetition sometimes has the effect of linking lines within the stanza, e.g. 3.100–1, 4.586–7.

[5] Many of these are listed in the Glossary. For the different types of alliteration used in the Wakefield Group see Bunzen, *Ein Beitrag zur Kritik der Wakefielder Mysterien*, pp. 46–7.

[6] See Introduction, p. xxviii.

But, on the whole, the Wakefield playwright varies the thirteen rhyme-words in each of his stanzas with extraordinary skill. Double rhymes are fairly common, both on a dissyllabic word (e.g. *mendyng, endyng, lendyng* 3.78) and on two separate words, e.g. *oppose hym, sloes hym, lose hym* 6.195. Identical rhymes occur, though not normally in consecutive lines, e.g. *borne* in the series *borne, lorne, borne, morne* 4.638. Some of the identical rhymes are on words which are alike in form but not in meaning, e.g. *farne* in the series *barne, farne, warne, farne* 4.530. Assonance sometimes takes the place of rhyme, e.g. *Bedlem* 5.254, rhyming with *reyn, ordeyn, chyldren*. Rhymes showing identity of consonant but difference of vowel are also found, e.g. *togeder* 3.206, rhyming with *broder, oder, foder*. Many of the apparent examples of imperfect rhyme are due to the alteration of one of the rhyme-words by a copyist, e.g. *sory* (for *sary*) 2.211, rhyming with *wary, Mary, tary*.[1] Other 'imperfect' rhymes may in fact have been good rhymes, owing to the convergence of sounds which had earlier been distinct from each other (e.g. *mytyng* 3.477, rhyming with *swetyng, gretyng, metyng*), or owing to the loss of unstressed *-e-*, *-y-* in an inflexional ending.[2]

Metrical Forms of the Mactacio Abel

Apart from the Wakefield stanza near the end of the pageant (450–62), the *Mactacio Abel* shows a great variety of metrical forms. The serious action is mainly developed in regular four-stress couplets, while the antics of Pikeharnes at the beginning and end of the pageant are presented in stanzas or in irregular couplets (monorhymed triplets and quatrains). There are stanzas of eleven, twelve, and thirteen lines at the beginning of the pageant, and interspersed among the regular couplets are shorter stanzas or fragments of stanzas. It seems likely that the Wakefield dramatist thoroughly revised an older pageant, and that in doing so he added the stanzas and probably many of the couplets as well.[3]

[1] For other scribal corruptions of rhymes see notes to 1.229, 2.10, 31, 3.161, 4.235, 615, 5.273, 306, 512, 6.382.

[2] E.g. *crakyd it* 4.656, rhyming with *hakt it, lakt it, knakt it*. For other details concerning the rhymes in the Wakefield Group see Bunzen, op. cit., 44 ff. and Trusler, *SP*. xxxiii. 24 ff.

[3] For further information about the stanza-forms in this pageant see notes to 1.37–45, 46–56, 328–35, 410–17, 450–62, 463–70. The following are also concerned with the metres of the *Mactacio Abel*: Cady, *JEGP*. x. 572–84; Lyle, *The Original Identity of the York and Towneley Cycles*, pp. 94–5; Carey, op. cit., 211–15; Frampton, *AB*. xlix. 3.

APPENDIX III

LINGUISTIC INDICATIONS OF DATE

The following sound-changes, the majority of which are established by rhyme, together suggest a fifteenth-century date for the composition of the Wakefield pageants:[1]

(1) Diphthongization of ME. *a* before *l* and *l* + cons. to *au*: *callys* 3.81, rhyming with *sawlys*; *skawde* 4.596, rhyming with *gawde, frawde, bawde*; *all, call, brall* 5.406, rhyming with *saull*; *gall, shall* 5.475, rhyming with *saull*.

(2) Change of ME. *e* to *a* before *r*: *far* 4.113, *wark* 4.614, *hart* 5.178, *hark* 6.309.

(3) Raising of ME. close *ē* (OE. *ē, ēo*) to [iː]: *mede* 1.294, rhyming with *chyde*; *me* 1.362, rhyming with *hardely*; *be* 2.40, rhyming with *glotony, securly, hastely*; *-tre, we* 2.433, rhyming with *see, wysely*; *se, gle* 3.323, rhyming with *veraly*; *swetyng, gretyng, metyng* 3.476, rhyming with *mytyng* (OF. *mite*); *me* 4.188, rhyming with *tenory, hye*; *fre* 4.644, rhyming with *poorely*.

(4) Raising of ME. open *ē* (OE. *ǣ²*) to [iː]: *see* 2.434, rhyming with *-tre, wysely, we*; cf. *lyefe* 5.310 (within line).

(5) Raising of ME. open *ē* before *r* to [iː]: *to-tyre* (OE. *tōteran*) 5.144, rhyming with *ire*.

(6) Diphthongization of ME. *o* before *ll*: *Mowll* 3.153, rhyming with *sowll, fowll*.

(7) Raising of ME. close *ō* to [uː]: *ado* 3.127, rhyming with *thou*; *doyn, mone* 3.431, rhyming with *growne, ron* (infin.).[2]

(8) Change of *-ght* to *-ft*: *syght* 4.284, rhyming with *lyft, shyft*; cf. *thof* 6.109 (within line).

(9) Loss of *l* before *d*: *skawde* 4.596, rhyming with *gawde, frawde, bawde*; cf. *water* 4.352 (within line).

(10) Loss of *r* before consonants: *warst* 1.224, rhyming with *last*; cf. *woth* 5.165 (within line).

(11) Loss of final *b* after *m*: *lam* 3.182, 501, rhyming with *sam, Gotham, dam* and with *sam, gam*; *dom* 6.88, rhyming with *custom, com*.

(12) Loss of final *-gh*: *plo* 1.460, rhyming with *do, lo*; cf. *plogh* 1.452 (within line). The inverted spelling *sogh* (OE. *sugu, sŭ*) 3.274, rhyming with *enogh, drogh*, also indicates that *-gh* was not pronounced.

---

[1] For these sound-changes see K. Luick, *Historische Grammatik der englischen Sprache* (Leipzig, 1914–21), §§ 479 ff.; R. Jordan, *Handbuch der mittelenglischen Grammatik* (2nd ed., Heidelberg, 1934), §§ 267 ff.; H. C. Wyld, *A History of Modern Colloquial English* (3rd ed., Blackwell, Oxford, 1936), pp. 201 ff.; K. Brunner, *Die englische Sprache*, i (Halle, 1950), pp. 244 ff.

[2] This sound-change is distinguishable from the Northern development of ME. *ōᵢ* to [yː], which made it possible for the Wakefield playwright to rhyme *vntew* 'unto', *lew* 'lo' 2.505 with *trew, new*, and also *floode, stod, good* 4.127 with *rude*. For this Northern development see H. Orton, *ES.* lxiii. 240–1.

APPENDIX IV

MAK'S IMITATION OF SOUTHERN ENGLISH

Mak's *Sothren tothe* in the Second Shepherds' Play (4.201–13) must have had for a Northern audience precisely the same comic appeal that the Northern dialect of John and Aleyn in the *Reeve's Tale* had for a Southern audience. Most of Mak's southernisms are obvious enough. Thus he says *ich be* 201 and *be ich* 207[1] instead of *I am* and *am I*; also *goyth* (imper. pl.) 204 instead of *goys*, and *ye doth* 213 instead of *ye do*. Two of these belong to the 'far South', for a London author like Chaucer normally wrote *I am* not *ich be*, and *ye do(n)* not *ye doth*. The Wakefield dramatist was evidently determined that his southernisms should be as southerly as possible in order to enhance their comic effect.

The words *sond* 202 and *sich* 203 may also be intended as Southern; the characteristic Northern spelling of *sond* is *sand*, and the Northern words for 'such' are *swilk* and *slyke* (the latter found in rhyme in 2.233, 3.94). On the other hand, *sondys* occurs again within the line in 5.7, and *sich* is the form regularly used within the line in all the pageants of the Wakefield Group.[2] If *sond* and *sich* are really intended as southernisms in Mak's speech, they must be scribal elsewhere.

The spelling *some* 202[3] for 'same' may be meant to represent an unfamiliar pronunciation from another dialect.[4] Perhaps *yoman* 201 was originally written *yomon*, thus giving a rhyme on a rounded vowel in *gone, ylkon, yoman, some* 199–202.

It will be noticed that Mak's Southern English is not entirely consistent, for it includes one or two northernisms: *goyth* 204 has a Southern ending, but is written with Northern *oy*; *thwang* 211 (needed as a rhyme-word with the shepherds' *wrang, lang, hang*) is the Northern form corresponding to Southern *thwong, thong*.[5]

---

[1] Mak seems to be using *ich* 201, 207, 211 as a stressed form and *I* 201, 206 as an unstressed form. *NED.* (s. Be) makes the following comment on *be* used as pres. 1 sg.: 'rare and doubtful in ME., but now the regular form in southern and some midland dialects'; cf. Forsström, *The Verb 'To Be' in Middle English*, p. 182.

[2] *Such* appears once in 6.103.   [3] Transcribed as *same* in EETS.

[4] The rounded vowel in *some* is a Western feature, e.g. 'the some sendesman' in the Dublin MS. of the *Wars of Alexander*, the original dialect of which was probably 'extreme N.W. Midl.'; see Oakden, *Alliterative Poetry in Middle English: The Dialectal and Metrical Survey*, p. 95.

[5] Cf. the Southern forms used in rhyme in Chaucer's representation of Northern speech in the *Reeve's Tale*; see J. R. R. Tolkien, 'Chaucer as a Philologist', Philological Society Transactions, 1934, p. 16.

GLOSSARY

This Glossary is intended to include examples of every different word in the six complete pageants of the Wakefield Group, and of its various spellings, forms, and meanings. But no attempt has been made to record all the occurrences of common words; nor are inflexional endings given unless they are liable to cause difficulty. Concerning the alphabetical arrangement it should be noted that (1) consonantal *i* has the same position as vocalic *i*; (2) initial þ, which is rare, is entered under *th-*; (3) initial *v* (= *u*) is entered under *v* (consonant); (4) initial *y* (vowel and consonant) has its usual position, while medial and final *y* are treated as *i*. Where emended readings are included, the MS. readings are given beside them. Expansions of abbreviations are not indicated. This Glossary is designed for use with the Notes, by which it is supplemented.

ABBREVIATIONS

AF.	Anglo-French
allit.	alliterative
Da.	Danish
Du.	Dutch
F.	French
fig.	figurative(ly)
from	is used in etymologies where the word illustrated is a different part of speech from its etymon
G.	German
Icel.	Modern Icelandic
It.	Italian
L.	Latin
LG.	Low German
MDu.	Middle Dutch
ME.	Middle English
MHG.	Middle High German
MLG.	Middle Low German
MSw.	Middle Swedish
Nhb.	Northumbrian dialect of Old English
OE.	Old English, mainly Anglian, but with West Saxon forms of some etymons not recorded in Anglian
OEN.	Old East Norse
OF.	Old French
OHG.	Old High German
ON.	Old Norse, especially Old Icelandic
ONF.	Old Northern French
Sw.	Swedish
WFris.	West Frisian
WS.	West Saxon
WYks.	West Riding of Yorkshire
*	is prefixed to hypothetical forms in etymologies
+	shows that a compound or derivative is first recorded in Middle English
1, 2, 3	indicate persons of pronoun and verb

a, *interj.* ah, oh (in invocation, and to express surprise, pain, or aversion) 2.163, 4.406, 6.255; *a, ye,* oh, really 4.354.

a(n), *indef. art.* a(n) 2.21, 3.151 [OE. *ān*].

abast, *pp.* upset, discomfited 5.27, 156 [OF. *esbaïr,* AF. *abaiss*-].

abate, *v.* humble (oneself) 6.157, grow less 2.445, calm down 6.301 [OF. *abatre*].

aby, *v.* pay dearly for, suffer for 4.272, 5.379 [OE. *abycgan*].

abide, abyde, *v.* await, wait for 2.334, 4.574; *intr.* wait, stay, remain 2.38, 3.119, 4.49, 334, 5.186; 2 *pl.pa.t.* abode, 2.373; *he must abyde,* he must stay as he is 4.81 [OE. *abīdan*].

abite, *v.* pay (dearly) for, suffer for 1.323 [OE. *abītan,* with meaning of ME. *aby*].

abone, aboue, abowne, abuf, *adv.* above 2.146, 6.254; *prep.* above 2.83 (postponed), 442, 5.48 (postponed) [OE. *abufan*].

aboute, abowte, *adv.* round about, on all sides 2.303, 351, 3.172, 4.586, 5.307; *prep.* about, round 4.278 [OE. *abūtan*].

abowne, abuf. See abone.

accord, *sb.* agreement, consent 2.30 [OF. *acord*].

accorde, *v. refl.* agree 4.431 [OF. *acorder*].

accuse, *v.* accuse 6.34, 246 [OF. *acuser*].

adew, *interj.* adieu 5.512, no more, enough (of this topic of conversation) 3.406 [cf. F. *adieu*].

adyld, *pp.* earned 6.199 [ON. *ǫðlask*].

admytte, *v.* admit 2.551 [L. *admittere*].

ado, *sb.* ado, trouble 3.127 [ON. *at* + OE. *dōn*].

adred, *pp.* afraid 2.201, 6.51 [OE. *ondrǣdan*].

aferd, *pp.* afraid 2.316 [OE. *afǣran, afēran*].

afore, *adv.* in front 3.213, 5.65, beforehand 2.164 [OE. *ætforan*].

afrayd, *pp.* afraid 5.478 [AF. *afrayer*].

afright, *pp.* frightened; *not afright,* undeterred 2.541 [OE. *afyrht*].

after, *adv.* afterwards 2.21; *prep.* after 3.11, according to 3.439; *after me,* as I wish 1.414; *cj.* after 2.148 [OE. *æfter*].

agayn, agane, *adv.* again, back 1.49, 2.548, 3.114, 4.343, in reply 6.136; *prep.* against 3.60, 4.29, 5.19 [OE. *ongægn, ongān*].

agaynt, against it 6.19 [OE. *ongægn* + *hit*].

agans, *prep.* against 1.221, 3.54, 5.183 [OE. *ongān* + adv. *-es*].

agast, *pp.* terrified 2.184, 6.317, amazed 2.449 [*a-* + OE. *gǣstan*].

age, *sb.* age; *of oone yere age,* one year old 5.244 [OF. *age*].

aght. See awe.

aght, *sb.* goods, possessions 1.150 [OE. *æht*].

aght, *adj.* eight 1.210 [OE. *ahta, æhte*].

aha, *interj.* aha 1.33 [cf. G. *aha*].

a-hungrye, *adj.* hungry 2.499 [*a-* + OE. *hungrig*].

ay, *adv.* ever, always 3.154, 5.220, 319; *for ay,* for ever 2.26, 4.685, once for all 1.456 [ON. *ei*].

ay, *interj.* ah (expressing surprise or wonder) 4.588 [cf. F. *aï*].

ayll, *sb.*[1] illness, ailment; *in ayll,* ill 3.111 [from OE. *eglan*].

ayll, *sb.*[2] ale 3.244 [OE. *alu*].

ayre, *sb.* heir 4.604 [OF. *(h)eir*].

ayther(e), ather, *cj.* either; *ayther(e)* ... *or* 2.477, 4.459, 518, 6.130; *ather* ... *or* 1.138 [OE. *ægþer*].

aywhere, aywhore, *adv.* everywhere, anywhere 4.632, 5.306, 6.8 [OE. *ǣghwēr, ǣghwār*].

al(l), *adj.* all 2.4, 154; *all we,* all of us 2.456; *all thyng,* everything 1.91, 2.73, 4.126 [OE. *al(l)*].

al(l), *adv.* all, wholly, very 4.4, 192, 568; (strengthening the prefix *to*-) 5.144, 151, 345, 6.295; *all if,* even if 2.231 [OE. *al(l)*].

al(l), *sb.* all, everything 2.1, 145, 3.99, 4.441, 542, 5.92; *at all,* altogether, extremely 6.187 [OE. *al(l)*].

alas, *interj.* alas 5.377, 6.433 [OF. *a las*].

algatys, *adv.* anyhow, in any case 1.166 [cf. ON. *alla gǫtu* + adv. *-es*].

alyene, *adj.* alien 3.351 [OF. *alien*].

alis, alys, 3 *sg.pres.* ails, troubles 2.294, 4.505, 5.114 [OE. *eglan*].

all hayll, *interj.* all hail 1.1 [OE. *all* + ON. *heill*].

allredy, *adv.* already 4.749 [OE. *all* + *rǣde* + *-ig*].

all-weldand, *adj.* almighty 2.494, 5.291 [OE. *all* + *weldan;* cf. OE. *alwaldende*].

all-wyghtys, *sb.pl.* ? monsters, uncanny creatures 4.139 (note) [? OE. *æl-wiht*].

almost, *adv.* almost 1.280, 6.422 [OE. *almǣst, -mǣst*].

alod, *pp.* ruined 2.56 (note) [ON. *aflóa;* cf. Icel. *aflóga*].

alon(e), *adj.* alone 4.334, without equal 2.489, 3.382 [OE. *al + ān*].

alow, *v.* praise, commend 5.405; *pp.* **alowed** 1.296 [OF. *alouer*].

als, also, *adv.* also, as well 1.296, 2.8, 126, 127 [OE. *alswā*].

al(l)way, *adv.* always, all the time 2.59, 120, 500 [OE. *alne weg*].

am, 1 *sg.pres.* am 1.50, 2.65, 6.252 [OE. *am*].

amang, emang, emong, *adv.* meanwhile 2.247, 4.184, betweenwhiles 4.165, together, intermingled 3.306; *euer amang,* continually 1.391; *prep.* among 2.112, 400, 4.378, 5.424, 6.426, by (the joint action of) 3.415 [OE. *onmang*].

amanges, emangys, *prep.* among, amongst 3.403, 5.77, 426 [prec. + adv. *-es*].

amen, *interj.* amen 2.558 [L. *āmēn*].

amend(e), *v.* set right 2.256, make amends for 1.332, 3.396; *intr.* improve 6.262 [OF. *amender*].

amendys, *sb.pl.* amends 3.63 [OF. *amendes*].

amese, *v.* calm 6.185 [OF. *amesir*].

amys, *adv.* amiss, wrongly 1.331, 4.551, 586 [ON. *d miss*].

and, *cj.* and 2.3, if 1.234, 2.297, 3.172, 4.27, 5.137, 6.282 [OE. *and*].

angell, *sb.* angel 2.10, 3.317 [OF. *angel*].

anger, angre, hangere, *sb.* trouble, sorrow 4.40, 6.108, anger 3.426, 5.118, 239 [ON. *angr*].

anger, angre, *v.* anger 1.451, 5.227; *intr.* get angry 5.113 [ON. *angra*].

angré, *adj.* angry 2.187 [ON. *angr +* OE. *-ig*].

any, *adj.* any 2.56, 4.571; *pron.* 4.261, 5.130 [OE. *ānig, ǣnig*].

anoynt, *v.* anoint, smear 2.127 [OF. *enoindre, enoint*].

anone, onone, *adv.* straightway, at once 2.275, 490, 4.440, 5.85 [OE. *on ān*].

anothere, *adj. and pron.* another 4.475, 487, 5.121 [OE. *ān + ōþer*].

answere, *v.* answer 6.181, 232 [OE. *an(d)swerian*].

apase, *adv.* apace, quickly 6.1 [*a-* + OF. *pas*].

apeche, appech, *v.* delay, hinder 1.85, accuse, charge with crime 6.64 [AF. *anpecher,* OF. *empechier*].

apon, *prep.* upon 1.170, 2.526, 4.430 [OE. *uppon*].

appech. See **apeche.**

appere, *v.* appear 2.173, 4.651 [OF. *apareir, aper-*].

appeté, *sb.* appetite 3.239 [OF. *apetit*].

ar, *pl.pres.* 2.199, 5.154, 156 [OE. (Nhb.) *aron*].

aray, *sb.* preparation 6.75, dress, attire 3.90, 5.281; *of aray,* splendid, stately 2.539 [OF. *arei*].

arayd(e), *pp.* made ready 6.362, dressed, clad 4.690 [OF. *areyer*].

arament, *sb.* accoutrement 6.320 [AF. *araiement*].

are, *adv.* before 5.480 [OE. *ǣr,* ON. *ár*].

armowre, *sb.* armour 5.280 [OF. *armeüre, armure*].

ars, *sb.* arse 1.45, 59 [OE. *ærs*].

art, 2 *sg.pres.* art 1.35, 2.163 [OE. *eart*].

as, *cj.* as 2.5, even as 2.427, 3.487, as if (with subj.) 1.27, 4.348, how 3.422, (in asseverations) so, as sure as ever 1.186, 2.191, 4.100, 6.159, (intensive) as . . . as possible 1.49, 2.219, 4.627; *as . . . as* 2.19, (with antecedent omitted) 4.608, 5.99; *as that,* as 2.182; *as com,* may there come 1.118 [OE. *alswā*].

asalis, 3 *sg.pres.* assails, attacks 2.295 [OF. *as(s)aillir*].

ascry, *v.* denounce 6.135 [OF. *escrier*].

aske, hask, *v.* to ask (for) 1.243, 345, 3.73; 1 *sg.pa.t.* ast 6.389 [OE. *āscian*].

aspy, *v.* see, observe, discover 3.361; *pp.* **as(s)pyde** 3.434, 5.400 [OF. *espier*].

assay, *sb.* trial, test; *when it comys on assay,* when it comes to the test 3.13 [OF. *assai*].

as(s)ay, *v.* test, make trial 2.219, 433 [OF. *essayer*].

assent, *sb.* agreement; *was at that assent,* was a party to it 4.459 [OF. *assente*].

ast. See **aske.**

astate, *sb.* condition 4.228, rank 6.291, state (of grandeur) 6.155 [OF. *estat*].

at, *prep.* at 3.201, in 1.346, on 4.641, with 1.421, from 3.162, according to 2.4, 322; (with infin.) *at do,* (things) to do 2.235 [OE. *æt*].

at, *rel. pron.; that at,* that which 3.149 [ON. *at*; but possibly a phonetic reduction of *that*].

ataynt, *pp.* convicted 6.22 [OF. *ateindre, ataint*].

ather. See **ayther(e).**

avayll, *sb.* assistance, aid 5.403; *pl.* avalys, benefits 5.452 [from next].

avayll, *v.* avail, be of use (to) 2.154; 3 *pl.pres.* avalys 5.206; *it avalis you,* is the best thing for you to do 2.296 [a-- + OF. *valoir, vail-*].

avance, *v.* advance 5.273 [OF. *avancer*].

avyse, *sb.* forethought, prudence 4.342 [OF. *avis*].

avyse, *v. refl.* take thought, consider 4.523; *pp.* avisid, determined 1.262 [OF. *aviser*].

avow(e), *sb.* vow, promise 1.410, 3.84, 4.366, 6.326 [from OF. *avouer*].

avowtré, *sb.* adultery 6.98 [OF. *avoutrie*].

aw(e), *sb.* fear, awe 1.31, 6.317; *for his greatt aw,* for great fear of him 5.40 [ON. *agi*].

away, *adv.* away 2.24, 5.484, gone, vanished 2.537; *do away,* enough 6.219 [OE. *on weg, aweg*].

awayward, *adv.* somewhere else 6.373 [OE. *onweg* + *-ward*].

awake, *v.* awake, wake up 3.296 [OE. *awacian*].

awe, 2 *sg.pres.* ought 2.171; 1,2 *sg.p.t.* aght, owed 1.314, ought 4.461; *impers.* in *me aght,* I ought 5.488 [OE. *āgan, āhte*].

awne, *adj.* own 2.74, 5.259, 6.243 [OE. *āgen*].

awre, *adv.* anywhere 4.111, 364 [OE. *āhwēr, āwer*].

bab, *sb.* babe 3.440, 5.388 [shortened from ME. *baban*].

bayle, bayll, *sb.* torment, misery, sorrow 2.26; *pl.* bales 5.389, balys 5.486; *beytter of bayll,* healer of pain, sorrow, i.e. God 2.311; *boyte of oure bayll,* cure for our ills 3.247; *thare balys can not bete,* cannot mend their injuries, i.e. cannot come to life again 5.486 [OE. *balu*].

bayles, *sb.pl.* the sheriff's bailiffs 1.405 [OF. *bailli*].

bayn, bon(e), *sb.* bone 1.324, 2.220, 5.63, 6.48, bones, mortal remains 1.397 [OE. *bān,* ON. *bein*].

bayn, *adj.* obedient 2.308, 5.506 [ON. *beinn*].

bak, *sb.* back 1.242, 2.264, 4.423; *bak and bone,* all over 2.407; *com at thy bak,* come after you 4.329 [OE. *bæc*].

bakys, 3 *sg.pres.* bakes 4.416 [OE. *bacan*].

bales, balys. See bayle.

balk, *sb.* balk 4.49 [OE. *balc(a)*].

ball, *sb.* ball 3.471, 4.734, head (abusively) 1.388 [ON. *bǫllr*].

ban, *v.* curse 2.94, 6.105; *intr.* 1.59, 4.625, 5.360 [OE. *bannan,* ON. *banna*].

bande, *sb.* bond, noose 4.407; *pl.* bandys, Our Lady's bands, confinement at childbirth 2.209 [ON. *band*].

bandys, *sb.*[1] See bande.

bandys, *sb.*[2] swaddling-bands 5.423 [OF. *bande*].

bard, *pp.* barred, shut up 2.328 [OF. *barrer*].

bare. See bere, *v.*

bare, *adj.* bare; *bare of,* devoid of 3.161 [OE. *bær*].

bargan, *sb.* bargain 2.94; *aby the bargan, byes . . . that bargan,* pay (dearly) for it 4.272, 5.21 [OF. *bargaine*].

bark(e), *v.* bark 4.662, (used contemptuously of reading aloud) 6.308 [OE. *beorcan*].

barne, *sb.* child 2.308, 3.319, 4.193 [OE. *barn*].

barons, *sb.pl.* barons 5.3. [OF. *baron*].

bat, *sb.* blow, buffet 5.490 [OF. *batte*].

bawd(e), *sb.* bawd (as a general term of abuse) 4.595, 5.354 [uncertain].

be, bene, *v.* be 2.22, 3.353; 1 *sg.pres.* be 4.201, 207; 2 *pl.* be 3.277; 1 *sg.fut.* be 4.388; 2 *sg.* bese 1.296; 3 *sg.* bees 2.373, beys 5.62, bese 1.250, 3.74, 5.507; 3 *pl.* bese 5.506; 2,3 *sg.pres.subj.* be 2.188, 3.256; 2,3 *pl.* be 2.297, 4.52; 2,3 *sg.imper.* be 2.123, 4.372; 2 *pl.* be 2.524, bese 5.511; *pp.* be 2.192, been 2.456, beyn 1.119, 2.445, bene 3.22 [OE. *bēon, tō bēonne,* dat.infin.].

be, bi, by, *prep.* by 4.244, beside 2.18, by (in oaths) 1.114, 2.386, 3.252, 4.107, by way of, from 2.477, by means of, through 3.39, 4.702, according to 2.452, on, in 2.75, 5.2, in (the words of) 3.335, 5.210; *cj.* by the time that 5.329, 6.13, 126 [OE. *be, bi*].

bed, *sb,* bed 4.76 [OE. *bedd*].

bedeyn, bedene, *adv.* straightway, at once 3.218, 4.263; *all bedeyn,* all together 1.222, 2.442 [uncertain].

beest, *sb.* beast 2.3; *pl.* bestes 3.190, bestys 3.304, 4.646 [OF. *beste*].

befall, *v.* happen, fall out; *fayre myght the befall,* may things turn out well for you, good luck to you 2.514; *ill myght hym befall, fowll myght hym befall,* bad luck to him 1.466, 6.186 [OE. *befallan*].

befe, *sb.* beef 3.220 [OF. *boef*].

before, beforne, *adv.* ahead, in front 1.5, 147, 3.303, 353, 454, 4.401, 5.317, beforehand 6.90, 118, in the past, formerly 4.692; *as sb.* 2.331; *prep.* ahead of, in front of 3.139; (of time) 5.452; *before to,* into the presence of 4.532–3 [OE. *beforan*].

beg, *v.* beg 3.27 [uncertain].

begers, *sb.pl.* beggars, mendicant friars 3.286 [uncertain].

begyles, 3 *sg.pres.* beguiles, deceives 6.83; 1 *sg.pa.t.* **begyld** 4.536; *pp.* **begyld(e)** 3.252, 369, 4.551 [OE. *be-* + OF. *guiler*].

begyn, *v.* begin 1.190, 2.147, 5.84, 6.397; 3 *sg.pres.* **begynnys** 2.463, **begyns** 3.214; 3 *sg.pa.t.* **began,** made (it) in the beginning 2.29; *begyn of,* begin with 2.253; *sb.* **begynnyng** 3.266 [OE. *beginnan*].

begynnar, *sb.* beginner, cause; *begynnar of blunder,* troublemaker 2.406 [from prec.].

behald, behold(e), *v.* behold, see 2.509, 523, 3.253, 4.418; 2 *sg.imper.* behold 4.748; 1 *sg.pa.t.* **beheld** 6.400; *behald on, behold to,* look at 2.343, 534 [OE. *behaldan*].

behapp, *v.* happen, befall 5.5 [from OE. *be-* + ON. *happ*].

beheste, *sb.* promise 3.436 [OE. *behǣs*].

behestys, 3 *sg.pres.* promises 3.300, 4.642 [from prec.]

behete, *pp.* promised 2.301 (not in MS.), 2.430 [OE. *behātan*].

behynd(e), *adv.* behind 1.8, 4.435; *prep.* 1.45; *as sb.* 2.331 [OE. *behindan*].

behold(e). See **behald.**

beyldyng, *sb.* shelter, dwelling 5.35 [from OE. *beldan*].

beytter, *sb.* healer 2.311 [from OE. *bētan*].

beld, *v.* build 6.74 [OE. *byldan*, infl. by OE. *beldan*].

belife, belyfe, *adv.* quickly, at once 1.37, 410, 2.192, 6.428 [OE. **be līfe*].

bell, *sb.* bell; *bere the bell,* take first place, be the best 3.186, 5.197 [OE. *belle*].

belly, *sb.* belly 3.197, 4.228 [OE. *belig*].

bell-weder, *sb.* bell-wether 3.112 [OE. *belle* + *weðer*].

belt, *sb.* belt 6.281 [OE. *belt*].

bemeyne, *v.* mean, signify 4.55 [OE. *be- + mǣnan*].

bend, *v.* bend 2.253, turn, return 3.398 [OE. *bendan*].

bene. See **be,** *v.*

benedicite, bensté, *interj.* bless me (us) 2.163, 4.55; *as sb.* God's blessing 3.46, 4.359 [L. *benedicite*].

benedyght, *adj.* blessed 3.290 [L. *benedictus*].

beneyth, *adv.* underneath 2.137 [OE. *beneoþan*].

benste. See **benedicite.**

bent, *sb.* field, heath 4.142 [OE. *beonet*].

berd, *sb.* beard 6.170; *made thaym a berd,* outwitted them 5.189 [OE. *beard*].

bere, *v.* bear, carry 2.318, 3.186, 5.197, 6.359, wear 5.112, 431, have, possess 2.105, give birth to 5.200, draw (of a ship's displacement) 2.434; *refl.* behave, conduct oneself 1.272; 3 *sg.pa.t.* **bare** 4.603; *pp.* **borne** 3.297, 4.450; *berys . . . downe,* overwhelm 4.134; *bere vp,* maintain 5.477 [OE. *beran*].

bere, *v.* noise (of voice) 3.66, 4.405 [OE. *gebǣre*].

bery, *v.* bury 1.367, 383 [OE. *byrgan*].

beselé, *adv.* diligently 2.240 [OE. *bisig* + *-līce*].

beside, *adv.* close by 4.335 [OE. *be sīdan*].

best, *adj.superl.* best 2.427, 5.281; *adv.* 2.472, 3.265 [OE. *betst*].

bestes, bestys. See **beest.**

betaght, *pp.* devoted; *God betaght,* devoted to God 1.211 [OE. *betǣcan*].

betake, *v.* commit, commend 1.441 [OE. *be- + ON. taka*].

bete, **bent,** *v.* beat 2.407 5.160, 6.219; *pp.* **bet(t)** 2.413, 6.424, **betyn** 2.381 [OE. *bēatan*].

bete, *v.* mend, heal 5.486 [OE. *bētan*].

betyde, *v.* happen; *tyd may betyde,* come what may 5.337; *pp.* **betyd(e),** happened 6.372, fared 5.399 [OE. *be- + tīdan*].

betokyns, 3 *sg.pres.* betokens, signifies 3.321, 4.654 [OE. *betācnian*].

bett. See **bete.**

better, *adj. compar.* better 3.61, 76, 4.44, 285; *as sb.* in *I wote not the better,* I don't know who's the better 3.69; *adv.* 2.175 [OE. *betera*].

betweyn, betwene, *adv.* between 3.217, 4.262, at intervals, continually 4.302; *prep.* between 3.127 [OE. *betwēon(an)*].

betwix(t), betwyx, *prep.* betwixt, between 2.185, 3.304, 4.646 [OE. *betwix* + *-t*].

bewar, 2 *sg.imper.* beware 3.244 [OE. *bēon* + *wǣr*; cf. OE. *bewarian*].

bewshere, *sb.* fair sir 5.273 [cf. F. *beau sire*].

bewty, *sb.* beauty 2.20 [OF. *beauté*].

bi, by. See be, *prep.*

bi, by, *v.* buy 3.43, 101, 130, get 4.330, pay (dearly) for 1.48, 5.21, pay the penalty 6.273; 3 *sg.pa.t.* boght, redeemed 1.114, 3.313, 4.91; *pp.* boght 2.373, 3.74; *it bees boght full dere, full dere bese it boght,* you'll (I'll) pay dearly for it 2.373, 3.74; *som shuld haue boght it full sore,* someone would have paid dearly for it 4.509 [OE. *bycgan*].

by, *adv.* close by, alongside 2.373, 3.168, 4.258 [OE. *bī*].

bid, byd, *v.* order, command, tell with authority 1.380, 2.418, 3.120, 150, 5.273, 6.373; 1,3 *sg.pa.t.* bad 1.3, 2.309, 4.174; *sb.* bydyng, bidding, command 2.375, 5.14 [OE. *biddan*].

byde, *v.* stay, remain 5.150, 169; *pp.* bide 1.61 [OE. *bīdan*].

bylefe, 2 *pl.imper.* leave off 5.354 [OE. *belǣfan*].

bill, *sb.* bill, beak 2.508 [OE. *bile*].

byll-hagers, *sb.pl.* men who hack or hew with bills 3.57 [from OE. *bil* + ON. *hǫggva*].

bynd, *v.* bind, tie up 4.595; 3 *pl.pres.* (as *fut.*) byndys 5.423; 3 *sg.pa.t.* bond 6.396; *pp.* bon, bun, bound, tied 4.80, 6.390, obliged 4.753 [OE. *bindan*].

byr, *sb.* rush 2.371 [ON. *byrr*].

byrd, *sb.* bird 2.514, 4.722 [OE. *brid(d)*].

byrkyn, breke, *v.* break 2.387, 5.63, 84, 108; *pp.* broken 3.156, brokyn 4.612; *breke outt,* force out 3.422 [OE. *brecan*].

byte, *v.* bite, cut; *apon the bone shal it byte,* it shall cut to the bone 2.220 [OE. *bītan*].

byworde, *sb.* proverb 3.481 [OE. *bīword*].

blak, *adj.* black 1.7 [OE. *blæc*].

blakys, 3 *pl.pres.* in *my browes blakys, my brow darkens (with fear)* 4.361 [from prec.].

blame, *sb.* censure, reproof 1.145, 2.299, fault, blame 1.421, 6.442 [OF. *bla(s)me*].

blame, *v.* blame 1.128 [OE. *bla(s)mer*].

blase, *sb.* blaze, brilliant light 3.452 [OE. *blase, blǣse*].

blast, *sb.* blast (of wind) 3.4, strong puff of breath 1.281; *fig.* 4.344 [OE. *blæst*].

W.P.—M

blaw, *sb.* blow 5.134, 6.191 [uncertain].

blaw, *v.* blow 1.7, 275, 4.344, blow a horn 4.112; *pp.* blawen 1.281; *bold bost wyll blaw,* will boldly boast 5.39 [OE. *blāwan*].

blede, *v.* bleed 1.9, 4.730, 5.378 [OE. *blēdan*].

blendyd, *pp.* blended, mingled 3.403 [OE. *blendan*].

blete, *v.* bleat 4.325 [OE. *blētan*].

blew, *sb.* blue cloth 2.200 [OF. *bleu*].

blyn, *v.* cease, leave off 3.429; *of . . . blyn,* cease from 5.344; *or (that) I blyn,* without stopping, straightway 1.324, 2.110 [OE. *blinnan*].

blynd(e), *adj.* blind 5.209; *as sb.* (the) blind 6.82, 164 [OE. *blind*].

blynfeld, *adj.* blindfold 6.397 [OE. *blind* + *fellan*].

blis, blys, *sb.* bliss 1.81, 2.2; *as haue thou blis, as (euer) haue I blys,* as you (I) hope for (eternal) bliss 2.333, 402, 3.261, 4.549 [OE. *bliss*].

blis, blys, *v.* bless 2.174, 4.550; *pp.* blissid 1.169, blist 2.514 [OE. *blētsian,* infl. by OE. *blissian*].

blissyng, blyssyng, *sb.* blessing 1.445, 2.178, 6.341 [OE. *blētsung,* infl. by OE. *blissung*].

blithe, *adj.* blithe, joyful 1.1, 160 [OE. *blīþe*].

blo, *adj.* (black and) blue 2.413 [ON. *blár*].

blode, blood(e), *sb.* blood 1.351, 5.312, 470, one's own flesh and blood 5.363; *my syre of flesh and blode,* my own father 1.389 [OE. *blōd*].

blodyngys, *sb.pl.* blood-puddings 3.217 [from prec.].

blonder, blunder, *sb.* trouble, disturbance 2.406, 4.25, 5.88, 6.18 [unknown].

blott, *sb.* disgrace 4.315, 450 [cf. ON. *blettr*].

bob, *sb.* cluster 4.718 [unknown].

body, *sb.* body 5.390, 6.369 [OE. *bodig*].

bofettys, buffettys, *sb.pl.* blows 1.392, 6.331 [OF. *buffet*].

bogh, *sb.* bough 2.535 [OE. *bōg*].

boght. See bi, *v.*

boy, *sb.* boy, knave 1.39, 5.26, 123; *pl.* boyse 5.336 [cf. AF. *boie*].

boyne, *sb.* prayer 1.183 [ON. *bón*].

boyte, *sb.* remedy, cure 3.247; *it is no boyte,* it is no use 1.376 [OE. *bōt*].

bold, *adj.* presumptuous, impudent 5.21, 93, 6.384, confident 4.271; *and that be ye*

bold, be sure of that 2.524; *adv.* boldly, brazenly 2.50 [OE. *bald*; *balde*].
boldly, *adv.* boldly, impudently 5.76 [OE. *baldlīce*].
bolne, *v.* swell 6.281 [ON. *bólgna*].
bon, bon(e). See **bynd, bayn**, *sb.*
bookys, *sb.pl.* books 5.231, 6.308 [OE. *bōc*].
boost, bost(e), *sb.* boast(ing) 4.34, 5.39, 6.420 [unknown].
bord(e), *sb.* board, plank 2.119, 279, table 3.196; *at bord*, boarding, living 6.146 [OE. *bord*].
bore, *sb.*[1] boar 3.212, 5.318 [OE. *bār*].
bore, *sb.*[2] hole, aperture 1.7 [from OE. *borian*; cf. ON. *bora*].
borne. See **bere**, *v.*
borow, *sb.* surety; *I dar be thi borow*, I'll be bound 2.204 [OE. *borg*].
boro(w), *v.* borrow 1.52, 3.27, 4.38, 295, save, rescue 5.389, 6.369; 1 *sg.pa.t.* **boroed** 1.99 [OE. *borgian*].
bost(e). See **boost**.
bosters, *sb.pl.* boasters 3.55 [unknown].
bot, *adv.* only, no more than 1.272, 288, 2.99, 3.30, 4.173, 374 [OE. *būtan*].
bot, *cj.* but 2.26, except, other than 1.260, 2.97, 4.505, 5.54, 6.366, even, just 3.119, unless 2.44, 4.344, 5.97, 226, 6.191; *bot if*, if not, unless 1.129, 259, 2.247, 3.29, 4.117 [OE. *būtan, būte*].
botell, *sb.* bottle 3.262, 480 [OF. *botel*].
both, *adj. and pron.* both 1.319, 2.185, 6.193; *adv.* in *both . . . and* 2.3 [ON. *bāðir*].
bothom, *sb.* bottom 3.261 [OE. *botm*, **boþm*].
bow, *v.* bow, bend 5.72; *pres.p.* **bowand**, obedient 2.76 [OE. *būgan*].
bowere, *sb.* bower, chamber 2.348, 4.76 [OE. *būr*].
bowne, *adj.* ready 5.13, 463, *bowne to*, going to 3.130 [ON. *búinn, bún-*].
bowrde, *sb.* game, jest 3.482, 4.332 [OF. *bourde*].
bowted, *adj.* booted; *nawder bowted ne spurd*, neither booted nor spurred 6.147 [from OF. *bote*].
brade, *sb.* moment 2.21 [OE. *brægd*].
brade, 3 *pl.pres.* burst into speech 5.76; *brayde of*, take after, resemble 3.153 [OE. *bregdan*].
bragance, *sb.* bragging 4.34 [OF. **bragance*].

bragers, *sb.pl.* braggarts 3.55 [cf. F. *braguer*].
brayde. See **brade**, *v.*
brall, *sb.* row, commotion 6.29 [from next].
brall, *v.* brawl, squabble, make a disturbance 3.280, 5.31, 57, 409 [cf. Du., G. *brallen*].
branch, *sb.* branch 2.511 [OF. *branche*].
brand, *sb.* sword 5.107 [OE. *brand*].
brane, *sb.* brain 4.540, 5.506 [OE. *brægn*].
brane, *v.* brain 5.93 [from prec.].
brast, brist, bryst, *v.* burst 4.629, 5.118, 6.191, break 2.264 [OE. *berstan*, ON. *bresta*].
bred, *pp.* born 4.340 [OE. *brēdan*].
brede, *sb.*[1] breeding, growth 5.256 [from prec.].
brede, *sb.*[2] breadth 2.126 [OE. *brǣdu*].
bred(e), *sb.*[3] bread, 4.155, 394; *as euer ete I brede*, so may I live, on my life 2.395; *shall I neuer ete bred(e)*, not a bite will I eat 4.468, 6.202 [OE. *brēad*].
breder, brether(e). See **broder**.
brefes, *sb.pl.* breves, short notes 4.657 [OF. *bref*].
breke, broken. See **byrkyn**.
brekyll, *adj.* brittle 4.121 [OE. **brycel*].
breme, *adj.* fierce, violent 6.290 [OE. *brēme*].
bren, *v.* burn 1.180, 4.595; 3 *sg.pa.t.* **brend** 1.317, **brened** 1.321; *pp.* **brend** 1.73, 103 [ON. *brenna*].
brere, *sb.* briar 1.202, 4.101 [OE. *brēr*].
breth(e), *sb.* breath 1.280, 3.257, 6.267. [OE. *brǣþ*].
brew, *v.* brew 4.416, 501 [OE. *brēowan*].
brybré, *sb.* theft, larceny 6.153 [OF. *briberie*].
bright, *adj.* bright 2.470, 4.339, 5.280; *as sb.* fair one 4.705; *adv.* brightly 2.9, 3.323 [OE. *byrht, berht*].
brightnes, *sb.* brightness, splendour 2.15, 6.254 [OE. *berhtnes*].
bryng, *v.* bring 2.475, 4.305, 6.117; 3 *sg.pa.t.* **broght**, brought forth 3.414; 3 *pl.* **broght** 5.124; *pp.* **broght** 3.76; *broght on*, put to 1.336; *broght . . . downe*, killed 1.354; *bryng furth*, bring forth 3.343, 4.242; *bryng in blonder*, get into trouble 4.25, 6.18; (with ellipsis of object) 2.499, 5.274 [OE. *bringan*].
brist, bryst. See **brast**.
brystyll, *sb.* bristle (on a hog's back) 4.102 [from OE. *byrst*].

brith, *sb.* good birth, noble lineage 5.3 [OE. (*ge*)*byrd, byrþ-*, ON. *byrð*].

broche, *sb.* brooch 4.28 [OF. *broche*].

brodels, *sb.pl.* scoundrels 5.82 [from OE. *brēoðan, broðen*].

broder, brother(e), *sb.* brother 1.58, comrade 4.471, equal, one of the same kind 3.207; *pl.* **breder, brether(e),** brothers 2.318, brethren, comrades 3.218, 406 [OE. *brōþor*].

brookys, *sb.pl.* brooks 5.232 [OE. *brōc*].

browes, *sb.* broth, pottage 1.418 [OF. *brouetz, broez*].

browes, *sb.pl.* brow, forehead 4.361 [OE. *brū*].

browyd, *pp.* browed; *she is browyd lyke a brystyll,* she has bristly brows 4.102 [from prec.].

browke, *v.* enjoy (use of) 1.186, 448 [OE. *brūcan*].

browne, *sb.* brawn, flesh 3.212 [OF. *brao(u)n*].

brude, *sb.* children 4.237 [OE. *brōd*].

buffettys. See **bofettys.**

buffit, *sb.* footstool, low stool 6.351 [uncertain].

bun. See **bynd.**

burgh, *sb.* borough 5.2 [OE. *burg, burh*].

burn, *v.* burn 2.26; *pres.p.* **burnand** 3.360 [OE. *birnan, byrnan*].

bushe, *sb.* bush 3.360 [OE. *busc,* ON. *buskr*].

busk, *v.* prepare, get ready 5.31, hurry 5.35 [ON. *búask*].

bustus, *adj.* rough, violent 6.213 [cf. OF. *boisteus,* AF. *boistous*].

cach, *v.* get, come by 4.97, 5.57 [ONF. *cachier*].

calf-lyuer, *sb.* calves-liver 3.236 [OE. *calf* + *lifer*].

call, *sb.* summons 5.295 [from next].

call, *v.* call, cry 2.64, summon 3.81, 5.272, address 5.408, name 2.513, 5.28; 3 *sg.pa.t.* **calde** 6.199; *pp.* **cald** 1.61, 2.513, 6.387; *call on,* go on shouting (to the plough-team) 1.53, petition, make supplication to 5.501 [ON. *kalla;* cf. late OE. *ceallian,* from ON. *kalla*].

cam. See **com.**

can, kun, *v.¹* know, know how to, can; 1,2,3 *sg.pres.* **can** 2.229, 250, 256; 3 *pl.* **can** 4.161; 1,3 *sg.pa.t.* **coude** 2.286, **couth(e)** 4.103, 120, **cowth(e)** 2.473,

6.73; 2 *pl.* **cowth** 3.242; *thank . . . kun,* offer thanks, thank 1.185; *can no rede,* (I) am at a loss 1.338; *so as I can,* as well as I can 3.477 [OE. *cunnan, can, cūþe*].

can, *v.²* *auxil.* (used with infin. as equiv. of pa.t.) did 3.154, 6.100; 3 *sg.pa.t.* **couth,** did 4.739 [prec., with meaning of ME. *gan*].

canvas, *sb.* canvas sheet 4.628 [ONF. *canevas*].

carcas, *sb.* carcass 5.85 [AF. *carcas*].

care, *sb.* sorrow, misery 1.33, 2.118, 300, 4.605, 6.129 [OE. *caru*].

care, *v.* be anxious, uneasy 3.163 [OE. *carian*].

caryed, 1 *sg.pa.t.* carried off 4.349 [ONF. *carier*].

caryon, *sb.* carrion 2.502 [ONF. *caroi(g)ne*].

carll, *sb.* churl, base fellow 5.244 [ON. *karl*].

carp, *v.* prate 2.360, 5.78; 2 *pl.imper.* **carpys** 5.33; *sb.* **carpyng,** prattle 1.97 [ON. *karpa*].

cart, *sb.* cart 2.534 [ON. *kartr,* OE. *cræt*].

case, *sb.* happening 3.491, deed, thing 4.315, plight 2.431 [OF. *cas*].

cast, *sb.* trick 4.447 [ON. *kast*].

cast, kast, kest, *v.* cast, throw, put 2.480, 3.281, 4.628, 5.232, cast off 2.262, make 3.289; *pp.* **cast** 3.2, 6.390, devised 5.121, **castyn** 5.478, **kesten** 3.13; *cast the warld in seuen* 3.38 (note) [ON. *kasta*].

castell, *sb.* castle 2.349, 5.268, a tower or embattled platform on a ship 2.272 [late OE. *castel,* ONF. *castel*].

catayll, catall, catell, *sb.* cattle, animals 1.77, 2.156, 326, 4.136, 548 [ONF. *catel*].

cateractes, *sb.pl.* flood-gates 2.343 [Vulgate *cataractae*].

cause, *sb.* cause, reason 2.102, 5.158, legal case or action 6.278 [OF. *cause*].

cause, *v.* cause 4.20 [med. L. *causāre*].

ceyll, seyll, *sb.* happiness, well-being 2.301; *as haue I ceyll,* as I hope for happiness 4.523 [OE. *sǣl*].

celé, sely, *adj.* happy, lucky 4.558, poor, miserable 4.10, 65, silly 4.67 [OE. *sǣlig*].

certayn, certan, *adv.* certainly, for certain 2.176, 3.314 [OF. *certain*].

certys, *adv.* certainly 1.18, 6.128, 312 [OF. *certes*].

cest. See **seasse.**

chace, *sb.* right of hunting 5.270 [OF. *chace*].

chambre, *sb.* chamber, room 2.129, 281 [OF. *chambre*].

chappyd, *pp.* chapped 4.3 [cf. MDu. *cappen*].

chargys, 3 *sg.pres.* charges, orders 5.17 [OF. *charger*].

charys, *sb.pl.* chores 4.304 [OE. *cerr*].

charité, charyté, *sb.* charity, Christian love 3.402; *for charité*, for charity's sake 2.165; *kepe charyté*, be charitable 2.235. [OF. *charité*].

chastice, chastyse, *v.* chastise, curb 2.398, 403; *pp.* **chastysed** 1.327 [OF. *chastiser*].

chateryng, *sb.* chattering 5.79 [onomatopœic].

chaunge, *v.* change, temper 1.263 [OF. *changier*].

chauntt, *v.* sing 4.189 [OF. *chanter*].

chefe, *v.* fare, get on 4.398 [OF. *chever*].

chefe, *adj.* chief, principal 5.38 [OF. *chef*].

cheke-bon, *sb.* cheek-bone, jaw-bone 1.324 [OE. *cēce* + *bān*].

chekyns, *sb.pl.* chickens 3.234 [OE. *cicen*].

chekys, *sb.pl.* cheeks 1.48 [OE. *cēce*].

chepe, *sb.* bargain, purchase 4.170; *as adv.* in *light chepe*, cheaply 1.236 [OE. *cēap*].

chere, *sb.* face 4.102, 730, mood, disposition 4.290; *mery chere*, joy, gladness 2.463; *what chere*, how are you? 4.406 [OF. *chere*].

cherys, *sb.pl.* cherries 4.718 [ONF. *cherise*; cf. OE. *ciris*-].

ches, chese (MS. *chefe*), *sb.* in *thre ches chambre, thre chese chambres*, three tiers of rooms 2.129, 281 [OF. *esches*].

chyde, chyte, *v.* chide, scold, brawl 1.293, 4.626, 5.335, 6.261, 303 [OE. *cīdan*].

chylbed, *sb.* childbed 4.335 [OE. *cild* + *bedd*].

childe, chyld(e), *sb.* child 3.301, 332, 4.537; *pl.* **childer, chylder** 2.327, 527, 3.352, **chyldes** 5.485 [OE. *cild*].

chyte. See **chyde.**

choke, *v.* choke 3.272; *pp.* **choked** 1.282 [OE. *-cēocian*].

chose, *v.* choose 1.196 [OE. *cēosan*].

clame, *v.* claim 6.381 [OF. *clamer, claime*-].

clater, *sb.* noisy talk 6.27 [cf. OE. *clatrung*].

clause, *sb.* close, conclusion 3.241 [OF. *clause*].

clawd. See **clowse.**

cled, *pp.* clad; *cled in Stafford blew*, beaten black and blue 2.200 [OE. *clǣþan*].

clefe, *v.* cleave, split 5.98, 353 [OE. *clēofan*].

clene, *adj.* clean, pure 3.371; *as sb.* 4.710; *adv.* completely 4.694 [OE. *clǣne*].

clens, *v.* cleanse 1.79 [OE. *clǣnsian*].

clere, *adv.* clear(ly) 1.321, 4.103, completely 4.477 [OF. *cler*].

clergé, clergy, *sb.* learning 3.389; *by clergé, by clergy*, with learning, learnedly 3.240, 4.676 [OF. *clergie*].

clerk, *sb.* priest, scholar 4.613, 5.197, 6.307 [OE., OF. *clerc*].

clok, *sb.* clock 4.618 [ONF. *cloke*, MDu. *clocke*].

clok, *v.* cluck 4.70 [OE. *cloccian*].

closyd, *pp.* closed 3.448 [from OF. *clos*].

cloute, clowt, *v.* mend, in *go cloute thi shone*, go and mend your shoes, i.e. mind your own business 2.353, clout, cuff 6.335 [OE. **clūtian*].

clowde, *sb.* cloud 3.65, 311, 6.254 [OE. *clūd*].

clowse, 3 *sg.pres.* scratches 4.414; *pp.* **clawd** 5.353 [OE. *clāwian*].

clowtt, *sb.* swaddling-clothes 4.584 [OE. *clūt*].

cod, *sb.* pillow 3.22 [OE. *codd*, ON. *koddi*].

Codys. See **God.**

cofer, *sb.* coffer, box 3.466, 4.250 [OF. *cofre*].

coyle, coyll, *sb.* cabbage; pottage, cabbage soup 1.426, 2.389 [OE. *cāwl*, ON. *kál*].

cok, *sb.* cock 4.71, 6.355; *the fyrst cok*, the first cockcrow, i.e. about midnight 4.387 [OE. *cocc*].

Cokys. See **God.**

cold(e), *adj.* cold 1.422, 2.61, 4.255, 326, 747; *in hote . . . in colde*, in all circumstances, always 4.419 [OE. *cald*].

colknyfys, *sb.pl.* cabbage-knives, large knives 3.57 [OE. *cāwl*, ON. *kál* + OE. *cnīf*].

com, *v.* come 2.481, 3.11; 2 *pl.imper.* **comys** 5.371; 1 *sg.pa.t.* **cam** 5.424; 3 *sg.* **cam** 1.236, 6.299, **com** 2.519, 6.263; 3 *pl.* **com** 3.173; *pres.p.* **comand** 5.292; **comyng** 3.30; *pp.* **com(m)en** 3.298, 4.200; *comes . . . out* 1.436 (note), 4.587; *com owt with*, bring out, utter 6.174; *com . . . outt*, becomes known 6.175–6; *com in*, begin 6.399 [OE. *cuman*].

comforth, *sb.* comfort 3.6, 5.345 [OF. *confort*].

comforth, *v.* comfort 4.709 [OF. *conforter*].

comly, *adj.* fair, beautiful 2.71; *as sb.* 4.710 [OE. *cȳmlic*, infl. by ME. *com*, *v.*].

commaund, *v.* command 1.419, 2.118, 5.13 [OF. *comander*].

commaundement, *sb.* commandment; *gaf in commaundement*, commanded 2.33 [OF. *comandement*].

commend, 3 *sg.pres.subj.* may commend, commends 1.466 (L. *commendāre*].

commyng, *sb.* coming 3.362 [from OE. *cuman*].

compané, company, *sb.* company 4.53, 220, 5.184 [OF. *compai(g)nie*].

complaynt, *sb.* complaint 4.211 [OF. *complainte*].

conceyue, *v.* conceive 3.397; 3 *sg.pa.t.* **conceyuyd** 4.740 [OF. *concevoir, conceiv-*].

conscience, *sb.* mind, heart 1.263 [OF. *conscience*].

consider, consyder, consydure, *v.* consider 2.291, 3.358, 6.418 [OF. *considerer*].

contynuyng, *pres.p.* continuing, abiding 3.489 [OF. *continuer*].

contrary, *adj.* contrary, opposed to one's interests 4.21 [OF. *contrarie*].

cop, *sb.* cup 3.270, chalice (of the Eucharist) 4.726 [OE. *cuppe*, OF. *cope*].

copé, *sb.* plenty, abundance (personif.) 3.17 [OF. *copie*].

.corn(e), *sb.* corn 1.77, 2.159, 3.83, 4.179, 5.453 [OE. *corn*].

cors, *sb.* corpse 1.378 [OF. *cors*].

cosyn, *sb.* kinsman 5.54 [OF. *cosin*].

cost, *sb.* cost, expenditure 3.226 [OF. *cost*].

cost, *pp.* cost 1.240 [OF. *coster*].

coste, *sb.* region 5.307 [OF. *coste*].

cote, *sb.* coat, tunic (worn under a gown) 2.262; *pay . . . on the cote*, beat 5.326, 421 [OF. *cote*].

coth, *sb.* disease, pestilence 2.417 [OE. *coþu*].

coude. See **can,** *v.*¹.

couer, *v.* cover, hide 1.21 [OF. *covrir*].

couetous, *sb.* covetousness 2.52 [OF. *coveitus*, with meaning of OF. *coveitise*].

counsayll, counsell, *sb.* counsel, advice 2.157, judgment, prudence 4.275, secret

1.394; *preuey counsell*, privy council 5.196 [OF. *conseil*].

counsell, 2 *sg.imper.* counsel, advise 2.472; *pp.* **counseld** 6.398 [OF. *conseiller*].

covntenance, *sb.* composure of face 6.38 [OF. *contenance*].

countré, *sb.* land, region 2.487, district 3.29 [OF. *contrée*].

couth(e). See **can,** *v.*¹ and *v.*².

cow(e), *sb.* cow 3.215, 4.518 [OE. *cū*].

cowche, *v.* bow in reverence 3.478 [OF. *coucher*].

cowll, *sb.* lump, swelling 6.405 [see EDD. s. Cowl, *sb.*³].

cowre, *v.* cower, crouch 4.722, 5.224 [cf. Icel. *kúra*].

cowth(e). See **can,** *v.*¹.

crafe, craue, *v.* crave, beg 1.143, 376, 2.174, 5.468 [OE. *crafian*].

crak, *v.* utter loudly; *how he crakyd it*, how loudly he sang it 4.656; *no langage ye crak*, don't speak loudly (or boastfully) 5.498; *intr.* make a loud noise, bawl 4.477, boast, talk big 3.59, crack, break 6.237 [OE. *cracian*].

craue. See **crafe.**

craw, *sb.* crow; *haue a craw to pull*, have a bone to pick 1.311 [OE. *crāwe*].

creat(o)ure, *sb.* creature 2.4, 78 [OF. *creature*].

crede, *sb.* the Creed 3.470, 4.725, 5.229 [OE. *crēda*].

credyll, *sb.* cradle 4.432, 538 [OE. *cradol*, **crædel*].

crepe, *v.* creep, crawl 1.337, 3.100, 4.591 [OE. *crēopan*].

cry, *sb.* shouting 1.11, proclamation 5.30 [OF. *cri*].

cry, *v.* entreat, beg for (mercy) 1.406, 2.384, 5.350, cry for (vengeance) 1.353, 5.346, call, shout 1.40, proclaim 1.408; *cry on*, go on shouting 1.158; *cry outt apon*, shout at 4.430 [OF. *crier*].

cryb, *sb.* crib, manger 4.645, 689 [OE. *cribb*].

cryb, *v.* feed at a crib; eat (used humorously) 3.208 [from prec.].

cryst-crosse, *sb.* Christ's cross 3.290, 4.268 [OE. *Crīst* + ON. *kross*].

crochett, *sb.* crotchet 4.658 [cf. F. *crochet*].

croft, *sb.* small enclosed field adjoining a house 6.355 [OE. *croft*].

croyne, *v.* croon, sing 4.476, 661 [cf. MDu. *kronen*].

crok, *v.* croak 4.69, 386 [OE. *crācian; cf. OE. *crācettan*].

crokyd, *adj.* crooked 4.403 [from next].

crokys, *sb.pl.* tricks 5.233 [ON. *krókr*].

crop, *sb.* head 3.470, 4.725 [OE. *crop(p)*].

crosse, *sb.* cross 4.118, sign of the cross 3.289 [ON. *kross*].

crownde, *adj.* crowned, with crown 5.442 [AF. *corouner*].

crowne, *sb.* crown 3.337, 5.3, 6.256, crown of the head 6.363; (in asseveration) *by my crowne* 3.88 [AF. *coroune*].

crucyefixus, crucified 3.293 [L. *crucifixus*].

cruell, *adj.* cruel 5.511 [OF. *cruel*].

cubite, *sb.* cubit 2.136; *pl.* **cubettys** 2.124 [L. *cubitus*].

culpabyll, *adj.* guilty 6.109 [OF. *culpable*].

curiose, *adj.* curious, intricate 3.306 [OF. *curius*].

curs, *sb.* curse 4.147, 6.395 [OE. *curs*].

cursed, curst, *adj.* execrable, detestable 6.328, perverse, refractory 3.206, 6.379 [late OE. *cursian*].

custom, *sb.* custom 1.69, 6.87 [OF. *custume*].

dagger, *sb.* dagger 6.444; *pl.* **dagers**, 3.56 [cf. F. *dague*].

day, *sb.* day, daylight 2.3, 3.128, 4.482; *this day*, to-day, now 5.286, 6.220; (in asseveration) *bi this day* 2.386 [OE. *dæg*].

dayde, *pp.* in *may ye be dayde*, you may be summoned to court (to answer for your treatment of Christ) 6.184 [from prec.].

day-starne, *sb.* morning star (used fig.) 4.577, 727 [OE. *dæg* + ON. *stjarna*].

dalys, *sb.pl.* dales 5.451 [OE. *dæl*].

dall, *sb.* hand 4.733 [obscure].

dam, *v.* condemn 6.248 [OF. *damner*].

dam(e), *sb.* lady, mistress 4.159, madam 2.298, 5.330, mother 2.324, 3.181, 6.57, 146; *gen.sg.* **dam**, mother's 3.260; *pl.* **dammys**, mothers 5.422 [OF. *dame*].

dampnabill, *adj.* liable to (judicial) condemnation 6.111, 198 [OF. *dampnable*].

dang. See **dyng.**

dangere, *sb.* power, control; *in thi dangere*, in your power, at your mercy 3.205 [OF. *dang(i)er*].

dar, 1,2,3 *sg.pres.* dare 2.204, 3.414, 4.30, 6.168; 3 *pl.* **dar** 6.300; 1,2,3 *sg.pa.t.* **durst** 2.479, 3.207, 5.184, 6.130; 3 *pl.* **durst** 5.186 [OE. *dearr, dorste*].

dase, *v.* be bewildered 2.314 [ON. *dasask*].

daw, *sb.* jackdaw; fool, simpleton 2.247 [OE. *dawe].

dawnse, *v.* dance 6.354 [OF. *dancer*].

de, dy, *v.* die 5.252, 6.256; 3 *pl.pres.* **dees** 6.84; 3 *sg.pa.t.* **dyed** 4.107 [ON. *deyja*].

declare, *v.* to declare, make known 4.702 [OF. *declarer*].

ded(e), deth, *sb.* death 2.193, 543, 4.621, 5.92, 6.175, 268, 449 [OE. *dēaþ*].

dede, *adj.* dead 1.339, 2.394, 4.229, 486, 5.494 [OE. *dēad*].

dede, *sb.* deed, act 1.12, 2.49, 6.133 [OE. *dēd*].

dedir, *v.* tremble, quake 2.314 [cf. mod.E. *dither, dodder*].

dees. See **de.**

defe, *adj. as sb.* (the) deaf 6.88 [OE. *dēaf*].

defende, *v.* defend 6.115, forbid 5.207 [OF. *defendre*].

defy, *v.* defy 6.227, 272 [OF. *de(s)fier*].

defyles, 3 *sg.pres.* defiles, desecrates 6.85 [OF. *defouler*, infl. by OE. *fŷlan*].

defly, *adv.* in a deaf manner, without hearing 4.109 [OE. *dēaf* + *-līce*].

degrade, 3 *sg.pa.t.* degraded 2.20 [OF. *degrader*].

degré, *sb.* degree, rank, position 2.21, 6.154 [OF. *degré*].

deill, deyll, dele, *sb.* part, quantity 1.450; *neuer a deill*, not at all 1.247; *ich a deyll*, *euery deyll*, every bit, all 2.299, 3.271 [OE. *dǣl*].

deyll, dele, *v.* share, deal out, distribute 1.137, 205, 2.390; *dele aboute the*, deal about you, deal out punishment all round 1.356 [OE. *dǣlan*].

deyll, deuyll, dewill, dewyll, dwill, *sb.* devil 1.4, 3.272, 4.110, 210, 5.512, 6.148; (expressing impatience) *in the dwill(ys) way*, in twenty dwill way, in the devil's name 1.89, 440, 450; *the dewill in youre ee*, confound you 4.217; *the dewill of the war*, the devil of a bad time 4.331; *what dewill*, what the devil 5.114 [OE. *dēofol*].

delay, *sb.* delay 5.283 [OF. *delai*].

dele. See **deill**, *sb.* and **deyll**, *v.*

deme, *v.* to judge 6.278, 291, tell, declare 6.440 [OE. *dēman*].

deny, *v.* deny 5.28 [OF. *deneier*].

departe, *v.* part, divide; *departe . . . fro*, part with, give up 1.217 [OF. *departir*].

depnes, *sb.* deepness, depth 2.434 [OE. *dēopnes*].

dere, *sb.* harm 2.317, 5.372, 6.133 [OE. *daru*, infl. by *derian*].

dere, *adj.* dear, beloved 2.172, 4.728, 5.116; *adv.* dearly 1.114, 2.373, 3.74 [OE. *dēore*].

derly, *adv.* dearly, at great cost 5.389 [OE. *dēorlīce*].

derlyng, *sb.* darling 4.728 [OE. *dēorling*].

deruly, *adv.* promptly 5.69 [ON. *djarfliga*].

des, *sb.* seat, throne 2.17 [OF. *deis*].

desyryd, 3 *sg. and pl. pa.t.* desired 3.441, 445, 4.693 [OF. *desirer*].

destany, *sb.* destiny 4.84 [OF. *destinée*].

det, *sb.* debt 2.222 [OF. *dette*].

deth. See **ded(e)**, *sb.*

deuer, devere, *sb.* duty 2.319, 6.288 [OF. *deveir*].

deuyll. See **deyll**, *sb.*

dew, *sb.* dew 6.358 [OE. *dēaw*].

dewill, dewyll, dy. See **deyll**, *sb.*, de.

dight, dyght, *pp.* prepared 3.288, clad 5.281; *to dede* ... *dyght*, put to death 2.543 [OE. *dihtan*].

dignyté, *sb.* dignity, honour 2.166 [OF. *digneté*].

dyke, *sb.* ditch; *in the dyke*, in dire straits 3.93 [OE. *dīc*].

dyllydowne, *sb.* darling 4.609 [first element may be conn. with ON. *dilla*].

dyn, *sb.* noise, din 1.3, 4.297, 361, 674, 5.82 [OE. *dyne*].

dyne, *v.* eat 4.146; *intr.* 3.197, 4.153; 2 *pl.pa.t.* dynyd 4.503 [OF. *di(s)ner*].

dyners, *sb.pl.* dinners, meals 4.157 [OF. *di(s)ner*].

dyng, *v.* hit, strike 5.170, 6.238; *intr.* fall 5.40; 1 *sg.p.t.* dang 5.425; *downe dyng*, force down, thrust down 5.60 [OE. *dengan*, ON. *dengja*].

dyscypyls, *sb.pl.* disciples 6.71 [OF. *disciple*].

discord, *sb.* discord, strife 2.31 [OF. *discord*].

dysdayn, *sb.* indignation, anger, vexation 5.508 [OF. *desdain*].

dyseasse, *sb.* discomfort, disturbance 4.486 [AF. *disease*].

dyspare, *v.* despair 5.479 [OF. *desperer, despeir*-].

dispyte, *sb.* injury, act of spite 1.314 [OF. *despit*].

dysplayd, *pp.* displayed, shown 5.75 [OF. *despleier*].

displeasse, 3 *pl.pres.* (with sg. subject) displease(s) 2.85; *pp.* **dysplesyd** 5.62 [OF. *desplaisir*].

dysseuer, *v.* depart 2.27 [OF. *dessevrer*].

distance, *sb.* quarrelling; *without distance*, indisputably 2.57 [OF. *distance*].

dystres, *sb.* trouble, misfortune, adversity 3.35 [OF. *destresse*].

dystroew, distroy, *v.* destroy 2.93, 6.73 [OF. *destruire*].

dit, dytt, *pp.* stopped 1.280, 6.178 [OE. *dyttan*].

ditizance doutance. See note to 5.171.

dyuerse, *adj.* diverse, various 6.156 [OF. *divers*].

do, doy, *v.* do, act, make 1.228, 2.103, 235; (as auxil. of pres.) 6.253; (as auxil. of imper.) 2.192, 326; (as auxil. of infin.) 3.283; 2 *sg.pres.* doyst 6.132, **dos**, put 1.360; 3 *sg.* **doys**, answers, serves 3.235, dos 1.277, 4.46; 2 *pl.* doth, 4.213; 3 *pl.* dos 3.56, doth 6.183; 2,3 *sg.pa.t.* did, dyd 2.11, 4.466; 1 *pl.* dyd 6.31; *pp.* doyn(e) 2.139, 3.431, 4.280, done 1.182, 2.148, caused 6.63; *haue done*, get it done, hurry up 2.316, 352, 480, 4.627; *do way, do away*, have done, enough 4.309, 580, 6.219; *do thaym to dede*, put them to death 4.621 [OE. *dōn*].

dogys, *sb.pl.* dogs 4.454 [OE. *docga*].

doy. See **do.**

doyll, *sb.*[1] dole, charitable gift; *penny doyll*, mass-penny, i.e. money paid for a mass for the soul of a dead person 2.390 [OE. *dāl*].

doyll, *sb.*[2] pain, misery 6.346 [OF. *do(e)l*].

dold, *adj.* stupid, inert 2.266, 4.2 [cf. OE. *dol*].

dom, *adj.* dumb 6.173; *as sb.* (the) dumb 6.88 [OE. *dumb*].

dominus, *sb.* Lord; (in asseverations) *Godys dere Dominus* 3.305, *benstē and Dominus* 4.55 [L. *dominus*].

domysday, *sb.* Doomsday 2.25 [OE. *dōmes dæg*].

don, *adv.* completely 4.552 [perhaps adv. use of OE. *dōn*, pp.].

doore, dowore, *sb.* door 4.362, 478; *from doore to mydyng*, from door to midden, i.e. a single step 2.376; *outt of the doore*, homeless, destitute 4.11 [OE. *duru, dor*].

dote, *sb.* dotard, foolish person 2.265, 6.346 [from next].

dote, v. talk foolishly 2.367, 5.327 [cf. MDu. *doten*].

dottypols, *sb.pl.* blockheads 5.231 [prec. + LG. *polle*].

doufe, dowfe, *sb.* dove 2.484, 505, 514 [ON. *dúfa*].

doughty, *adj. as sb.* valiant man 5.16; *superl.* doughtyest 5.109, dughtyest 5.294 [OE. *dohtig*].

downe, *adv.* down 1.354, 2.247, 3.2, 6.253 [OE. *dūne*].

downes, *sb.pl.* hills; *by downes ne by dalys,* on the hills or in the dales, i.e. anywhere 5.451 [OE. *dūn*].

dowore. See doore.

dowse, *sb.* sweetheart (used sarcastically) 4.246 [generic ʋse of *Dowse*, from OF. *douce*].

dowte, *sb.* doubt, uncertainty 3.171, 4.129, 6.55 [OF. *doute*].

dowtys, 3 *pl.pres.* fear 5.45 [OF. *douter*].

draght, *sb.*draught 1.430 [OE. **dræht*, ON. *dráttr*].

dray, draw, *v.* draw, pull 1.29, 2.103, 4.306, disembowel 5.132; *intr.* come, go 2.245, 5.462, 6.116; 3 *sg.pres.* draes, draws 3.287; 2 *pl.imper.* drawes, come 4.290; 1 *sg.pa.t.* drew 6.70; 3 *pl.* drogh, drained, emptied 3.276; *drawes on,* pull away 1.26 [OE. *dragan*].

draw. See dray.

dre, *v.* suffer, endure 4.65, 6.10, 348; *pp.* dreed 2.533 [OE. *drēogan*].

drede, *sb.* dread, fear 1.233, 2.212, 4.121, 5.253, danger 2.425; *no drede,* no doubt 4.264 [from next].

dred(e), *v.* dread, fear 2.47, 55, 5.16, 6.328; 1 *sg.pa.t.* dred 5.480 [OE. *drēdan*].

dreed. See dre.

drely, *adv.* heavily, deeply 3.245 [OE. **drēog* (ON. *drjúgr*) + *-līce*].

dreme, *sb.* dream 4.373, 497 [OE. *drēam*, ON. *draumr*].

dres, *v.* direct; *will I dres me,* I will get ready 2.238 [OF. *dresser*].

dry, *v.* dry 1.13 [OE. *drȳgan*].

dry, *adj.* dry 2.370, 4.155; *as sb.* 4.60 [OE. *drȳge*].

drife, dryfe, *v.* drive 1.39, 2.273, 6.432, compel 4.84; *intr.* rush, hurry 2.193; 1 *sg.pa.t.* drofe 3.131 [OE. *drīfan*].

drynk(e), *sb.* drink 1.430, 2.197, 4.146, 504 [OE. *drinc*].

drynk, *v.* drink 3.191, 4.237, suffer, pay the penalty 2.380, 6.39; *pp.* dronken 3.260 [OE. *drincan*].

drone, drowne, *v.* drown 2.372, flood, inundate 4.132; *pp.* drownde 3.145 [obscure].

drop(e), *sb.* drop, small portion 3.468, 5.265 [OE. *dropa*].

drowne, dughtyest. See drone, doughty.

duke, *sb.* duke 2.74, 3.459, 5.40 [OF. *duc*].

dulfull, *adj.* doleful, dismal 5.322 [OF. *do(e)l*, *dul* + OE. *-ful*].

durst. See dar.

durt, *sb.* dirt, excrement 6.170 [ON. *drit*].

dwell, *v.* dwell 2.43, stay 6.447 [OE. *dwellan*].

dwill. See deyll, *sb.*

easse, ese, *sb.* comfort; *at easse, at ese,* carefree 2.388, 5.469 [OF. *eise*].

ee, *sb.* eye 3.325, 4.217; *pl.* eeyne 4.58, een(e) 1.225, 3.21, 6.58, eyn 5.102; *as long as I haue eyn,* as long as I live 5.174 [OE. *ēge*].

eeyr, eere, *sb.* ear 5.199, 6.134; *pl.* eeres 3.388, eres 5.165, 6.178, erys 3.312 [OE. *ēare*].

eere-marke, *sb.* ear-mark (on a sheep, as a sign of ownership) 4.611 [prec. + OE. *mearc, mærc*].

eest, *adv.* east 3.290, 438; *sb.* 2.453, 4.7 [OE. *ēast*].

eft, *adv.* again 2.241, 4.622 [OE. *eft*].

eft-whyte, *v.* repay, pay back 4.294 [prec. + OF. *quiter*].

eg, *sb.* egg 3.151 [ON. *egg*].

eyll, *sb.* eel 4.356 [OE. *æl*].

eyn. See ee.

elders, *sb.pl.* elders, forefathers 1.101 [OE. *eldra*].

elfe, *sb.* elf 4.616 [OE. *ælf*].

elyke, *adv.* alike, the same 3.91 [OE. *gelīce*, ON. *álíka*].

els, *adv.* otherwise, else 1.4, 2.299, 5.8, 6.310; (pleonastic in apodosis to *bot*) 4.344; *as cj.* in *els that* 3.329 [OE. *elles*].

emang, emong, emangys. See amang, amanges.

emperiall, *adj.* imperial 3.299 [OF. *emperial*].

emperour(e), *sb.* emperor 2.74, 5.223, 6.130 [OF. *emperour*].

encense, *v.* inform, enlighten 5.198 [OF. *ensenser*].

end(e), *sb.* end 1.81, 445; *make end of,* destroy 2.104–5; *make . . . an end,* conclude 3.397; *what ende has thou mayde with the hyrdys,* what happened in the end between you and the shepherds 4.422; *at an end,* finished, done for 6.265 [OE. *ende*].

end, *v.* end, finish 2.131 [OE. *endian*].

endyng, *sb.* ending, death 3.79, 493; *at the endyng,* in the end 4.273 [OE. *endung*].

endlang, *adv.* lengthwise; *ouertwhart and endlang,* wholly, completely 3.48 [from ON. *endlangr*; cf. OE. *andlang*].

endles, *adj.* endless, eternal 2.2 [OE. *endelēas*].

endorde, *pp.* glazed with egg-yolk 3.234 [OF. *endorer*].

endure, induyr, indure, *v.* bear, endure 6.32; *intr.* last 2.148, 283 [OF. *endurer*].

enewe, enogh(e), *adj.* enough 4.500; *adv.* enough 2.532, very 4.381 [OE. *genōg, -nōh*].

enogh(e). See **enewe.**

ensampyll, *sb.* example 5.496 [AF. *ensample,* OF. *essample*].

entent, intent, *sb.* heed, attention 5.6, will, mind 2.113; *in good entent,* with a good will 1.178 [OF. *entent*].

entysyd, 3 *sg.pa.t.* enticed 2.37 [OF. *enticier*].

enuy, *sb.* envy 2.51 [OF. *envie*].

ere, *adv.* before 2.328 [OE. *ǣr*].

eres, erys. See **eeyr.**

erth, *sb.* earth 1.353, 2.42 [OE. *eorþe*].

ese. See **easse.**

esy, *adj.* easy 4.63 [OF. *aisié*].

ete, *v.* eat 2.395, 4.155, 233, 468; 1 *sg.pres.subj.* may eat 4.537; *pp.* **eten** 4.245 [OE. *etan*].

ethe, *adv.* easily 6.141 [OE. *ē(a)þe*].

euen, euyn, evyn, *sb.* evening; *from euen vnto morow,* all night long 2.205; *evyn or at morow,* evening or morning, at any time 3.142; *both euyn and morne, both euen and morow,* both evening and morning, at all times 5.346, 390 [OE. *ēfen*].

euen, *adj.* even; *for euen or for od,* in any event, come what may 3.20 [OE. *efen*].

euen, euyn, evyn, *adv.* even, just, exactly 1.88, 232, 2.29, 3.173, 4.213, evenly, calmly 1.272, to be sure, indeed 3.225, 288; *euen hym by,* on a level with Him 2.18; *ful(l) euen,* in fact, indeed 2.10, 344,

3.39, 397, 488, 4.740, 5.130, 6.94 [OE. *efen, efne*].

euenly, *adv.* exactly 2.258 [OE. *efenlīce*].

euer, *adv.* ever, always 1.466, 2.191, 4.165, 5.110, 6.159; *euer amang,* continually 1.391 [OE. *ǣfre*].

euery, euerich, *adj.* every 2.47; *euerich a,* every 2.544 [OE. *ǣfre + ylc*].

euerichon, euerychon, *pron.* every one 1.22, 5.82 [prec. + OE. *ān*].

euerlastyng, *adj.* everlasting 4.668, 6.4 [from OE. *ǣfre + lǣstan*].

euermore, *adv.* evermore, ever after 1.457, 5.450, always, continually 6.86 [OE. *ǣfre + māre*].

ewe, *sb.* ewe 3.221, 4.457 [OE. *ēowu*].

examyn, *v.* examine 6.190; *sb.* **examynyng** 6.128 [OF. *examiner*].

excuse, *v.* excuse, clear oneself from blame 6.35; 3 *sg.pa.t.* **excusyd** 6.97 [OF. *excuser*].

expownd, 1 *sg.pres.* describe, tell of 2.440 [OF. *espondre*].

expres, *v.* express 2.13 [OF. *expresser*].

expres, *adv.* plainly, clearly 6.260 [OF. *expres*].

face, *sb.* face 2.336 [OF. *face*].

fader, *sb.* father 1.72, 2.415; *pl.* spiritual fathers, religious teachers 3.341 [OE. *fæder*].

fay, *sb.* faith; *in good fay,* in truth 4.563 [OF. *fei*].

fayll, *sb.* in *withoutten fayll, no fayll, saunce fayll,* without fail, for certain 2.149, 3.110, 112, 5.404 [OF. *faille*].

fayll, *v.* fail 2.274, run short 3.227; 3 *sg.pres.* **falys** 6.407; *falys his covntenance,* his face loses its composure, he looks crestfallen 6.38; *fayll of,* fail to reach, fall short of 2.492 [OF. *faillir*].

fayn(e), fane, *adj.* glad 3.8, 176, 4.39, 6.137; *fayn of,* eager for 4.324; *adv.* gladly 1.337, 4.614, 6.386; *fayn I wold (that),* I would be glad (if) 2.526; *wold thou neuer so fane,* however much you would like to 3.116; *as sb.* gladness, joy 3.478 [OE. *fægen*].

fayr, fare, *sb.* fuss, uproar, commotion 4.413, 602; *fayr . . . make,* provide food 4.163 [OE. *fær, faru*].

fayre, fare, *v.* fare, go, behave 1.308, 2.190, 3.180, 4.56, 5.101; 1 *sg.pa.t.* **fard** 5.424, **foore** 4.196; 3 *sg.* **fowre** 4.123;

pp. **farne** 4.531, 576, 6.47; *fayre well, fare well,* farewell 1.463, 2.238, 6.450; *I fare full yll,* I do very badly 3.200 [OE. *faran*].

fayre, fare, *adj.* fair, beautiful, fine 1.122, 169, 4.220, 6.21; *superl.* **farest** 2.79; **faryst** 3.461; *as sb.* **fayre,** fine weather 3.7 [OE. *fæger*].

fayr(e), fare, *adv.* well, favourably 2.514, 3.189, 432, 4.560, 6.127, properly 1.32 [OE. *fægre*].

fayth(e), fath, *sb.* (Christian) faith 3.351; *in fayth, in fath,* in truth, truly 2.228, 330, 4.630 [OF. *feid*].

falys. See **fayll,** *v.*

fall, *v.* fall 2.146, decline morally and spiritually 2.66, fall to one's lot 4.188, happen 4.66, 5.29, hasten 6.397; 3 *sg.pa.t.* **fell** 4.314, 6.358; *pp.* **fallen** 1.27, 2.521; *fare fall the, fare myght you fall,* good luck to you 3.189, 6.127 [OE. *fallan*].

falow, *adj.* fallow, uncultivated 4.13 [from OE. *falh, falg*].

fals, *adj.* false, lying 1.48, 2.35, 4.447, 713, 5.338, 6.9; *adv.* falsely 1.295 [OE. *fals,* OF. *fals*].

fame, *sb.* repute 2.141 [OF. *fame*].

fane. See **fayn(e).**

fang, *v.* take, get 2.245, 4.668 [OE. *fōn, fangen*].

fantom, *sb.* illusion 4.374 [OF. *fantosme*].

far, *adj. and adv.* far 2.439, 3.150, 4.244; *so far can I,* I know this much 4.88 [OE. *feorr*].

far-cast, *sb.* cunning trick 4.341, 593 [prec. + ON. *kast*].

fard, ferd(e), *pp.* afraid 1.145, 2.102, 4.666, 6.71 [OE. *fǣran, fēran*].

fare. See **fayr(e).**

fare, *sb.* fair 3.42 [OF. *feire*].

farenes, *sb.* fairness, impartiality 6.217 [OE. *fægernes*].

farest, faryst. See **fayre,** *adj.*

farne, *pp.* farrowed; laboured (in childbirth) 4.533 [from OE. *fearh, færh*].

farsake, forsake, *v.* leave, forsake 1.403, 3.29, 6.16, neglect 2.273; 3 *pl.pa.t.* **forsoke** 6.72 [OE. *forsacan*].

fart, *sb.* fart 1.369 [cf. OE. *feorting,* ON. *fretr*].

farther, forther, *adv.* further 1.28, 5.334 [OE. *for þor,* infl. by *feorr*].

farthyng, *sb.* farthing 1.99, 4.572 [OE. *fēorðung*].

fast, *adv.* securely 4.595, faithfully 5.120, earnestly 2.488, vigorously 2.232, fast, quickly 2.182, 4.240, 5.65, 6.319; *on fast,* quickly 4.445 [OE. *fæste*].

fastand, *pres.p.* fasting 4.352 [OE. *fæstan*].

fat(t), *adj.* fat 4.292, 371, 451 [OE. *fætt*].

fath. See **fayth(e).**

fathom, *sb.* fathom 2.521 [OE. *fæðm*].

fatur(e), *sb.* impostor 6.140, 167 [OF. *faitour*].

fauoure, favoure, *sb.* favour 5.192, grace, beauty 2.79, 4.721 [OF. *favour*].

fawt(e), *sb.* lack, fault; *for fawte of,* for want of 6.55; *at . . . fynd fawt,* find fault with 1.421 [OF. *faute*].

fe(e), *sb.* goods, possessions 1.76, 2.309, 326, (live) stock 3.105, 188 [OE. *fe(o)h*].

fee, *sb.* fee (as a term of venery), i.e. a share of the game given to a hound or falcon 2.490; *pl.* gifts, payments 6.83 [OF. *fe*].

feest, feste, *sb.* feast, festival, 2.454; *oone feste,* a (fair) treat 6.338 [OF. *feste*].

feft, *pp.* endowed 4.620 [AF. *feoffer*].

feyldys. See **feld.**

feyll, fele, *v.* feel, experience, enjoy 2.121, 4.90, 227; *refl.* 3.2, 4.357 [OE. *fēlan*].

feynd, *sb.* Devil 1.79, 2.35, 4.639 [OE. *fēond*].

fekyll, *adj.* fickle 6.9 [OE. *ficol*].

feld, *sb.* field 1.122; *pl.* **feyldys** 4.133, 167 [OE. *feld*].

fele. See **feyll.**

fellys, *sb.pl.* fells 5.2 [ON. *fjall*].

felow, *sb.* fellow 6.240; *pl.* **felose, felows(e)** 1.10, 4.362, 482, 5.327 [OE. *fēolaga,* from ON. *félagi*].

felowship, *sb.* friendship 2.363 [prec. + OE. *-scipe*].

felterd, *pp.* tangled 3.65 [OF. *feltrer*].

femayll, *adj.* female 2.152 [OF. *femelle*].

fend, *v.* forbid 1.38 [shortened from OF. *defendre*].

ferd(e). See **fard.**

ferd(e), *sb.* fear, in *for ferd(e),* for fear 1.338, 2.315, 5.185, 6.168, for fear (that) 3.289 [from OE. *fǣran, fēran*].

fere, *sb.*[1] in *to my fere,* as my companion 4.100; *pl.* companions 6.64 [OE. *fēra*].

fere, *sb.*[2] company; *in fere,* together 1.383, 4.704 [OE. *gefēre*].

ferly, *sb.* wonder, astonishment; *haue . . . ferly,* be astonished 1.156 [from OE. *fǣrlic;* cf. ON. *ferligr*].

ferme, *adj.* firm 6.112 [OF. *ferme*].

fermes, *sb.pl.* rents (due), taxes 3.30 [OF. *ferme*].

feruent, *adj.* glowing, burning 2.8; *adv.* eagerly 2.77 [OF. *feruent*].

fest, *v.* settle 3.280 [OE. *fæstan*].

feste. See **feest.**

fetch(e), fott, *v.* fetch, bring, get 1.392, 6.346, 351; 1 *sg.pa.t.* **fott,** stole 4.517 [OE. *fetian, feccan*].

fy, *interj.* fie 5.149; *fy on hym, fy on you* 4.204, 6.298; *fy on the dewill* 5.150 [OF. *fi, fy*].

fy, *v.* say fie (to) 6.131 [from prec.].

fyere, fyre, *sb.* fire 4.236, 255, 495, 5.101 [OE. *fȳr*].

fyfe, *adj.* five 1.204 [OE. *fīf*].

fyfty, *adj.* fifty 2.126 [OE. *fīftig*].

fight, fyght, *v.* fight 1.50, 2.138, 4.626, 5.283 [OE. *fe(o)htan*].

fygure, *sb.* emblem, symbol 3.354 [OF. *figure*].

fill, *sb.* one's fill 1.428, 2.207 [OE. *fyllo*].

fill, fyll, *v.* fill 3.197, people 2.180 [OE. *fyllan*].

fynd(e), *v.* find, discover 2.99, 4.702, 5.208, (with infin. phrase as object) find out (how) 3.38; 1 *sg.pa.t.* **fond** 4.457; 1 *pl.* **faunde** 6.69; *pp.* **fon** 2.503, 6.120, **fownde** 3.143, **fun,** learned 4.78, found 4.751 [OE. *fīndan*].

fyngers, *sb.pl.* fingers 4.3 [OE. *finger*].

fyre. See **fyere.**

firmament, *sb.* firmament 2.7 [L. *firmāmentum*].

first, fyrst, *adj.* 2.478, 4.387; *adv.* 1.79, 2.42, 4.702, 5.167 [OE. *fyr(e)st*].

fyrth, *sb.* wood, forest 5.2 [OE. *fyr(h)þ*].

fysh, *sb.* fish 2.3 [OE. *fisc*].

fysh, *v.* to fish 3.139 [OE. *fiscian*].

fyst, *sb.* fist 4.631, 5.184 [OE. *fȳst*].

fytt, *sb.* painful experience 6.49 [OE. *fitt*].

flay, *v.* scare, frighten 2.380; *pp.* **flayd(e)** 4.384, 5.435, 6.182, defeated, routed 5.480 [OE. *-flēgan,* ON. *fleyja*].

flayn, *pp.* flayed, skinned 4.323 [OE. *flēan*].

flat, *sb.* (level) place, plain, field 5.489 [ON. *flǫt*; see A. H. Smith, *English Place-Name Elements,* i. 175].

fle, *v.* flee 1.380, 2.292, 5.371 [OE. *flēon*].

flemyd, *pp.* banished 6.234 [OE. *flēman*].

flese, *sb.* fleece 4.293 [OE. *flēos*].

flesh, *sb.* flesh 1.389, 4.544, 5.99 [OE. *flæsc*].

fleshly, *adj.* natural; *my fleshly get,* my own flesh and blood .5.388 [OE. *flæsclic*].

flett, *sb.* floor, place 2.223, 3.140 (MS. *bett*) [OE. *flett*].

flett, *pp.* floated 2.436 [OE. *flēotan*].

fle-wyng, *sb.* fly's wing 6.94 [OE. *flēge* + ON. *vængr*].

flight, *sb.* flight 2.474 [OE. *flyht*].

flyng, *v.* run, dash 4.573 [cf. ON. *flengja*].

flyt(t), *v.* depart, go away 1.303, 2.223, 3.120, 5.175; 3 *sg.pa.t.* **flyt,** moved 2.17; *pp.* **flyt, flitt,** removed 2.454, 540 [ON. *flytja*].

flyte, *v.* quarrel, wrangle 3.148, 4.625, 6.304 [OE. *flītan*].

flo, floo, *v.* flow 2.101, 115 [OE. *flōwan,* ON. *flóa*].

flode, flood(e), *sb.* flood 2.101, 4.127, 5.471; *on flood(e),* in flood, full to overflowing 5.313, 377 [OE. *flōd*].

flok, *sb.* flock (of sheep) 4.289, (of children) 4.388 [OE. *flocc*].

flone, *pp.* flown 2.487 [OE. *flēgan*].

floore, *sb.* floor 4.13 [OE. *flōr*].

floure, flowre, *sb.* flower (with reference to Christ, as one outstanding in excellence) 3.343, 4.720; *flowre of knyghthede,* flower of chivalry 5.272 [OF. *flour*].

flowyng, *sb.* flood 2.540 [from OE. *flōwan*].

fo, *sb.* foe 1.119; *adj.* in *ichon other fo,* each hostile to the other 2.112 [OE. *fā(h)*].

foder, *v.* feed (used humorously) 3.209 [from OE. *fōdor*].

foyde, *sb.* child 4.720 [OE. *fōda*].

foyll, *sb.* fool 6.343; *pl.* **foles, folys** 3.141, 179 [OF. *fol*].

foyn, *sb.* thrust, jab 5.381 [OF. *foine*].

foyne, fone, *pron.* few 2.99, 4.281 [Northern blend of OE. *fēawe* and *hwōn* (see *MED.* s. Fon, *num.*); cf. ON. *fáeinir*].

foytt, fo(o)te, *sb.* foot 3.215, 4.352, 5.471; *pl.* **fe(e)te** 4.62, 467, **feytt** 4.599; *oone foote,* one step 2.263; *ich fote,* every step 4.488 [OE. *fōt*].

fold, *sb.* sheepfold 4.270 [OE. *fald*].

fold, *suffix as sb.* in *bi foldys seuen,* seven times 2.13 [OE. *-fald*].

fold, *v.* bow, bend, give way 4.3 [OE. *faldan*].

foles, folys. See **foyll.**

folke, *sb.* folk, people 6.225 [OE. *folc*].

folow, *v.* follow, act upon 3.163 [OE. *folgian*].

fon. See fynd(e).

fon, v. make a fool of 6.360; *intr.* be foolish, act the fool 3.393 [obscure; cf. mod.E. *fun*].

fond(e), *adj.* fond, foolish 6.343, 406 [from prec.].

fone, foore, fo(o)te. See foyne, fayre, v., foytt.

for(e), *prep.* for 2.64, 6.7, fit for 3.235, as, for 6.167, (in asseverations) by 4.190, 379, because of, through 1.288, 2.155, 5.26, 6.11, for the sake of 1.254, 400, 2.301, 4.91, 539, for (fear of) 1.31, 2.102, (as precaution) against 3.227, in return for 4.163, in spite of 3.45, 208; *for the (me)*, for all you (I) care 2.193, 6.350; *for me*, for my own part 4.567; *for to* (commonly prefixed to infin.) 1.17, 2.246; *cj.* for, because 1.354, 4.719 [OE. *for(e)*].

forbede, *v.* forbid 1.10; *God forbede* 5.374 [OE. *forbēodan*].

forbot(t), *sb.* forbidding, prohibition; *(ouer) Godys forbot(t)*, God forbid 1.38, 184, 3.271, 4.451, 6.409 [OE. *forbod*].

force, *sb.* strength; *no force*, no matter, it does not matter 1.374 [OF. *force*].

for-daunche, *adj.* very fastidious, over-nice 5.509 [OE. *for-* + *daunche*, poss. rel. to OF. *danger(os)*].

fordo, *v.* ruin, destroy 2.100, 6.30, perish, be destroyed 4.284; *pp.* fordone 2.145 [OE. *fordōn*].

for-fell, *adj.* very cruel, most cruel 5.142 [OE. *for-* + OF. *fel*].

forfett, *sb.* crime, offence 6.425 [OF. *forfet*].

forfett, 3 *sg.pa.t.* sinned, transgressed 6.62 [from prec.].

forgang, forgo, *v.* forgo, go without 1.193, 4.43 [OE. *forgān, -gangan*].

forgoten, forgottyn, *pp.* forgotten 3.263, 6.124 [OE. *forgetan*, with substitution of ON. *geta*].

forlorne, *pp.* ruined, destroyed 5.344 [OE. *forlēosan*].

fornace, *sb.* furnace 3.352 [OF. *fornais(e)*].

forrakyd, *pp.* tired out with walking 4.256 [OE. *for-* + OE. *racian*, ON. *reika*].

forsake. See farsake.

forshapyn, *pp.* transformed 4.619 [OE. *forsceppan*].

forsoth(e), *adv.* indeed, certainly 1.171, 4.749 [OE. *forsōþ*].

forspokyn, *pp.* bewitched 4.613 [OE. *forspecan*].

fortaxed, *pp.* over-taxed 4.16 [OE. *for-* + OF. *taxer*].

forther. See farther.

forthi, forthy, *adv.* therefore 1.45, 4.670 [OE. *forþī*].

forthynkys, 3 *sg.pres.* displeases 4.155, 511 [OE. *forþencan*, infl. by *þyncan*].

for-vgly, *adj.* very horrible, most horrible 5.142 [OE. *for-* + ON. *uggligr*].

forwakyd, *pp.* weary with watching or waking 4.253 [OE. *for-* + *wacian*].

forwhi, forwhy, *cj.* because 2.14, 284, 518 [OE. *for-hwī*].

foryeldys, 3 *sg.pres.* repays 4.171 [OE. *forgeldan*].

fote. See foytt.

fote-hote, *adj.* hot-foot 5.398 [OE. *fōt* + *hāt*].

fott. See fetch(e).

foule, foull, fowll, *adj.* foul, bad, loath-some 4.246, 429; *adv.* badly, evilly 1.436, 3.155, 4.587, 6.186 [OE. *fūl; fūle*].

foull, fowle, fowll, *sb.* bird 2.3, 472; *pl.* 2.156 [OE. *fugol*].

foundyng. See fownd.

four(e), fowre, *adj.* four 1.198, 3.414, 4.363, 5.488 [OE. *fēower*].

fourt, *adj.* fourth 3.353 [OE. *fēorða*].

fourty, *adj.* forty 1.340, 2.148, 5.487 [OE. *fēowertig*].

fownd, *v.* test, try 2.438; *pres.p.* foundyng, hastening 5.457 [OE. *fundian*].

fowre. See fayre, v., four(e).

fox, *sb.* fox 1.84 [OE. *fox*].

fray, *sb.* strife 2.184, attack 5.317 [OF. *effrei*].

fray, *v.* fight 5.282 [AF. *afrayer*].

franch, *sb.* French (language) 5.513 [OE. *frencisc*, infl. by OE. *Francan*].

frast, *v.* ask 2.183 [ON. *freista*].

frawde, *sb.* fraud 4.594; *full of frawde*, deceitful person, impostor 5.355 [OF. *fraude*].

fre, *adj.* free 3.333, 5.56, noble, excellent 2.327, 3.407, free from deductions, net 6.162; *as sb.* noble lord 2.310, 4.644 [OE. *frēo*].

freend, freynd, *sb.* friend 1.120, 2.118, 4.641 [OE. *frēond*].

freyndly, *adj.* friendly 5.324, 459 [OE. *frēondlic*].

freys, 3 *pl. pres.* freeze 4.62 [OE. *frēosan*].

frely, *adj.* noble, excellent 4.720 [QE. *frēolic*].

frendship, frenship, *sb.* friendship 2.121; *on my frenship,* as I love you 2.362 [OE. *frēondscipe*].

freres, frerys, *sb.pl.* friars 3.286, 389 [OF. *frere*].

frese, *sb.* in *no frese,* no doubt 2.391 [cf. MDu. *vrese,* OHG. *freisa*].

fresh, *adj.* fresh 4.546, lively, active 4.356 [OE. *fersc,* OF. *fresche*].

fry, *sb.* offspring, children 2.66, 177 [ON. *fræ, frjó*; cf. F. *frai*].

fryght, *pp.* frightened, scared 3.289 [OE. (Nhb.) *fryhta*].

frightly, *adv.* fearfully 5.478 [prec. + OE. *-līce*].

fro, *adv.* in *to and fro,* to and fro, on all sides 2.111, 3.58 [ON. *frá*].

fro, *prep.* from 2.244, 4.526, 5.85 [as prec.].

from, *prep.* from 2.67 [OE. *from*].

frost, *sb.* frost 3.227; *pl.* 4.58 [OE. *frost*].

full, *adj.* full 1.310, 4.237, 5.355 [OE. *full*].

ful(l), *adv.* very, quite 1.14, 2.8, 10, 6.65 [OE. *full*].

ful(l)fyll, *v.* fulfil, satisfy 5.297, 436 [OE. *fullfyllan*].

fully, *adv.* fully, completely 2.131 [OE. *fullīce*].

fun. See **fynd(e).**

fundlyng, *sb.* foundling, bastard 6.152 [cf. Du. *vondeling*].

furth, *adv.* forth, forward, out, on 1.84, 457, 2.480, 4.398, 6.372; *furth let it rest,* let it rest at that 3.279 [OE. *furþ*].

gad, *v.* gad, wander about 1.149 [obscure].

gaf. See **gif.**

gay, *adj.* bright, fair 6.73 [OF. *gai*].

gayte, gate, *sb.* way, road 4.229, 6.298, 424, journey 3.259; *oure gate let vs go,* let us go on our way 3.452. [ON. *gata*].

gaytt-doore, *sb.* outer door 4.328 [prec. + OE. *duru, dor*].

galy, *adv.* splendidly, showily 3.67 [OF. *gai* + OE. *-līce*].

gall, *sb.* gall 4.106, gall-bladder 5.301 [OE. *galla*].

galon, *sb.* gallon 4.106 [ONF. *galon*].

gam(e), *sb.* mirth, fun, delight 2.529, 3.500, game, diversion 6.166, scheme, intrigue 2.214, 4.427 [OE. *gamen*].

gang, *v.* go 1.74, 4.665, walk 4.379, fare 2.246; 3 *sg.pres.subj.* **gang,** may go 6.229; *pres.p.* **gangyng** 6.10 [OE. *gangan*].

gar, *v.* make, cause (with simple obj.) 1.44, 3.91, (with obj. and active infin.) 2.346, 4.610, 5.179, 6.16; 3 *sg.pa.t.* **gard** 4.650; *pp.* **gart** 6.40 [ON. *gøra*].

garn, *sb.* yarn, spun wool; *ther is garn on the reyll other,* there is other yarn on the reel, i.e. other business on hand 2.298 [ON. *garn*].

garray, *sb.* disturbance, row 4.564 [? from OF. *guerreier*].

gart, make it 3.254 [ON. *gøra* + OE. *hit*].

gast, *sb.* spirit, soul 5.155; *Holy Gast,* Holy Ghost 2.162 [OE. *gāst*].

gate, gatt. See **gayte, get(t).**

gawde, *sb.* trick, prank 4.593; *pl.* 4.176 [cf. OF. *gaudir*].

geder, *v.* gather, pick (up) 3.174, 285 [OE. *gæderian*].

gedlyngys, *sb.pl.* fellows 1.14 [OE. *gædeling*].

geyse. See **goys.**

gentill, gentyll, *adj.* gentle, courteous 4.563, soft, low (of musical notes) 3.418, quiet, docile, 2.505 [OF. *gentil*].

gentlery-men, *sb.pl.* gentry 4.18 [from prec. + OE. *men(n)*].

gere, *sb.* apparel, attire, 3.67, gear, tools 2.245, contrivance 2.274, affair, business 5.370; *not right in his gere,* not in his right mind 6.182 [ON. *gervi*].

ges, *sb.* guess; *bi ges,* by guess-work 1.231; *after my ges,* as I think 3.439 [from next].

gess, *v.* think, suppose 6.160; 1 *sg.pa.t.* **gest** 5.412 [cf. MLG. *gissen*].

get, *sb.* offspring, child 5.388 [from next].

get(t), *v.* get, earn 1.82, 2.326, 3.195; *pres. as fut.* 2.299; 1 *pl.pres.subj.* **get(t),** may get 1.145, 2.184, 4.53; 3 *sg.pa.t.* **gate, gatt,** begot 4.603, 6.366; *gett out of,* leave 5.393 [ON. *geta*].

gett, *v.* watch, tend (sheep) 4.505 [ON. *gæta*].

gif, gyf, *v.* give 1.76, 137, 3.123, 4.139; 1, 3 *sg.pa.t.* **gaf** 1.126, 251, 2.33, 4.183; 2 *pl.* **gaf** 4.571; *pp.* **giffen** 1.140, **gyf(f)en** 1.214, 3.355, 6.418 [ON. *gefa, gifa*].

gyftys, *sb.pl.* gifts 6.439 [ON. *gift*].

gyle, *sb.* guile 2.214; *Syr Gyle* (personif.) 4.408 [OF. *guile*].

gyler, *sb.* beguiler, deceiver, i.e. Devil 4.713 [OF. *guilleor, gileor*].

Gill, Jill (used contemptuously) 2.219; *for Iak nor for Gill*, for nobody 2.336 [petform of *Gillian*, OF. *Juliane*].

gilty, *adj.* guilty 1.329 [OE. *gyltig*].

gyn, *sb.* contrivance 2.128, 276, stratagem 5.261, snare, trap 4.370 [shortened from OF. *engin*].

gyrd, *v.* strike; *gyrd of*, strike off 4.622, 6.200 [obscure].

gyse, *sb.* method, way 4.341 [OF. *guise*].

glad, *v.* gladden 2.491 [OE. *gladian*].

glad, *adj.* glad, happy 1.1, 4.388; *sb.* gladness, joy 4.668 [OE. *glæd*].

gladly, *adv.* gladly; *do gladly* (a polite phrase used in offering food), please take some 3.218 [OE. *glædlīce*].

glas, *sb.* glass 4.121 [OE. *glæs*].

glase, *sb.* blow 4.316, 6.418 [from OF. *glacer*].

gle, *sb.* mirth, joy 4.708, melody, sound 3.326; (allit. phrase) *with gle and with gam*, with joy and delight 2.529 [OE. *glēo*].

glydys, 3 *sg.pres.* glides (along) 3.68 [OE. *glīdan*].

glope, *sb.* palpitation 5.264 [cf. *EDD*. s. Glopping].

glorius, *adj.* glorious 2.166 [AF. *glorious*].

glose, *sb.* false show, pretence 4.413 [OF. *glose*].

glotyny, glotony, *sb.* gluttony 2.37, 52 [OF. *glo(u)tenie, glutonie*].

gloton, *sb.* glutton 3.222 [OF. *gluton*].

gnast, *v.* gnash the teeth (with rage) 5.157 [cf. ON. *gnísta*].

go, *v.* go 2.376, 4.181, walk 3.100, 4.592; 2 *sg.pres.* **goys** 3.82, **gose** 5.334; 3 *sg.* **goyse** 1.221, **gos(e)** 1.255, 4.415; 3 *pl.* **gose** 3.58, 173; 2 *pl.imper.* **goys** 5.194, **goyth** 4.204; *pp.* **gone** 1.24, 2.181, 4.199, dead 2.408, 3.24; *go to*, go to it, get to work 2.236, 3.250, 427; *gone to*, done 6.404; *go slepe*, go and sleep 4.345; *go stalk preuely*, go and make my way stealthily 4.347; *go se*, go and see 4.643; *gone full clene*, clean gone, quite dead 4.694 [OE. *gān*].

God, *sb.* God 1.211, 2.1; (colloquial forms) **Gog** 1.44, 172; *gen.sg.* **Codys** 1.459, **Cokys** 5.228, 395, **Gottys** 5.116 [OE. *god*].

goderhayll, *sb.* good luck; *as interj.* 3.226 [OE. *(tō) gōdre hǣle*, infl. by ON. *heill*].

Godhede, *sb.* Godhead, divinity 4.728; *in Godhede*, (three) in one Godhead 3.470 [OE. *god* + *-hǣdu*].

Gog. See God.

goys, *sb.* goose 3.233; *pl.* **geyse** 1.84 [OE. *gōs*].

gold, *sb.* gold 5.440, 6.283 [OE. *gold*].

good(e), *sb.* good 4.46, 238, something good 3.29; (collective) goods, wealth 1.116, 137, 140; *to good*, kindly 1.172; *for good ne for yll*, for good or evil, for any reason 5.435; *I sett by no good*, I think it of no importance 5.469 [OE. *gōd*].

good(e), *adj.* good 2.102, 4.181, 449; *good skyll*, very reasonable 3.199; *goode spede*, quickly 4.462; *as sb.* good sir(s) 3.135, 4.484; *adv.* in *as good*, as well 3.120, 6.26; *good right*, quite right 5.442 [OE. *gōd*].

gossyppys, *sb.pl.* god-parents 4.559 [OE. *godsibb*].

Gottys. See God.

gowne, *sb.* gown 2.262, 3.89 [OF. *goune*].

gowrde, *sb.* gourd 3.483 [cf. F. *gourde*].

grace, *sb.* (divine) grace, favour, goodwill 2.551, 3.124, 468, 4.751, 5.266, mercy 6.3, luck 4.314; *with ill grace*, bad luck to you 6.416 [OF. *grace*].

gracyous, gracius, gracyus, *adj.* gracious 2.28, 165, 5.219, fortunate, prosperous 4.244; *adv.* graciously 5.13 [OF. *gracious*].

grales, *sb.pl.* graduals, i.e. antiphons sung as part of the Mass 5.205 [OF. *grael*].

grame, *sb.* anger, wrath 2.89 [OE. *grama*].

grameré, gramery, *sb.* learning 3.242; *by grameré*, in Latin 3.387 [OF. *gramarye*].

grath, *sb.* readiness; *with grath*, without delay 2.482 [ON. *greiði*].

graue, *sb.* grave 6.101 [OE. *græf*].

graunt(t), *v.* grant 2.178; 2 *sg.imper.* 4.708; *intr.* agree, consent 4.39, 185 [AF. *graunter*].

greatt, gret(t)e, *adj.* great 1.14, 2.58, 3.370, 4.105, 506, 5.4; *compar.* **gretter** 3.70, 4.36, 433; *grete ne small*, nothing 1.237; *grete and small*, all 2.90, 344 [OE. *grēat*].

grefe, *sb.* hardship, suffering 4.95, hurt, injury 1.67, 3.53, 5.363; *take it to no grefe*, don't take offence 4.575 [OF. *gref*].

grefe, greue, *v.* trouble, vex, hurt 1.458, 4.29, 397, 577, 5.155 [OF. *grever*].

greyn, grene, *adj.* green; *as sb.* greensward 2.534, 4.634 [OE. *grēne*].

grese, *v.* grease, apply a salve (to sheep) 1.64 [from OF. *gresse*].

gret(t)e, gretter. See **greatt.**

grete, *v.*[1] greet 4.470; *pres.p.* **gretyng** 5.13 [OE. *grētan*].

grete, *v.*[2] weep 3.21; *pres.p.* **gretyng** 3.478 [OE. *grētan, grēotan*].

greuance, grevance, *sb.* injury 1.402, 6.39, offence, wrong 2.58 [OF. *grevance*].

greue. See **grefe,** *v.*

grym, *adj.* grim, fearsome 3.66 [OE. *grim(m)*].

grynde, *v.* afflict, torment 3.40 [OE. *grindan*].

gryssed, *pp.* sunk in grass 3.189 [from OE. *græs, gærs*].

grith, *sb.* peace, protection 5.4 [OE. *griþ*].

groches, 3 *sg.pres.* is unwilling 6.417 [OF. *gro(u)cher*].

groyn, growne, *sb.* snout; nose (used contemptuously) 5.382; *fayr fall thi growne,* good luck to you 3.432; *pl.* **gronys,** see **swyne-gronys** [OF. *groign*].

groyne, grone, *v.* groan 2.409, 4.70, 335, 442 [OE. *grānian*].

grote, *sb.* groat 5.328 [MDu. *groot*].

groved. See **grufe.**

grownd(e), *sb.* ground, earth 3.144, bottom (of the sea) 2.439, land 2.465, 5.268; *on grownde,* on earth 5.443 [OE. *grund*].

growne. See **groyn.**

grufe, *v.* grow; *begynnys to grufe to vs,* will soon begin for us 2.463; 3 *sg.pa.t.* **groved,** grew 1.199 [OE. *grōwan*].

guttys, *sb.pl.* guts 5.240 [OE. *guttas*].

ha, *interj.* (expressing surprise) in *hay, ha* 3.86 [cf. OF. *ha*].

ha, ha, *interj.* (representing laughter) 3.226 [OE. *ha ha*].

had-I-wyst, if I had known; *as sb.* a vain regret 4.93.

hafe, haif, hayfe, haue, *v.* have, possess 1.430, 2.11, 175, (as auxil.) 2.286; 1 *sg.pres.* **haue** 2.46, (not prec. by pron.) **has** 5.406; 2 *sg.* **has(e)** 2.430, 6.8; 3 *sg.* **has** 2.301; *pl.* **haue** 3.392, 6.11, (not prec. by pron.) **has** 2.95, 397, 4.87, 692; 1 *sg.pa.t.* **haide** 1.36; 3 *sg.* **had(e)** 3.158, 4.516; *pl.* **hade** 4.424; *pp.* **had** 6.29; *haue at the,* let me get at

you 2.219, 5.381; *haue . . . on thy hode,* here's one for your hood 5.339 [OE. *habban*].

hafles, *adj.* helpless, destitute 5.484 [OE. *hafenlēas*].

hay, *sb.* hay 1.88, 439, 2.159 [OE. *hēg*].

hay, *interj.* (expressing surprise) in *hay, ha* 3.86 [cf. G. *hei*].

haif, hayfe. See **hafe.**

haill, hayll, *interj.* hail 3.458, 4.710, 5.71, 6.46 [ON. *heill*].

haytt, hote, *adv.* violently, severely; *haldys me full haytt,* is giving me an uncomfortable time 4.227; *held thaym full hote,* made it hot for them 5.420; *hold hym full hote,* make it hot for him 6.345 [OE. *hāte*].

hak, *v.* break long notes into short ones, trill (used sarcastically) 4.476; 3 *sg.pa.t.* **hakt,** trilled (used seriously) 4.657 [OE. *-haccian*].

hald, hold, *v.* hold, keep, guard 1.39, 2.217, 3.436, 4.227, 6.201, think, consider 1.148, 197, 230, 2.233, 3.389, 437, 4.551, 6.20, bet, wager 5.328; *refl.* think oneself 5.436; *intr.* hold back, refrain 4.567; 1 *sg.pa.t.* **held** 5.420; *pp.* **halden** 6.27, **holden** 4.410, 717 [OE. *haldan*].

half, *adj.* half 1.428, 5.229 [OE. *half*].

hall, *sb.* hall, dwelling 2.67 [OE. *hall*].

halt, *adj.as sb.* (the) lame 6.82 [OE. *halt*].

hame, home, *sb.* home 1.422; *adv.* 4.94, 319 [OE. *hām*].

hamyd, *pp.* hamstrung 4.15 [from OE. *ham(m)*].

hand, *sb.* hand 2.74, 4.283; *pl.* **handys** 2.211, **hend** 1.102, 2.34, 255, 6.264; *at hand,* near, close by 4.112; *in hand,* in charge 5.105, afoot 5.289 [OE. *hand*, ON. *pl. hendr*].

handyll, *v.* handle 5.325 [OE. *handlian*].

handlang, *adj.* little 4.412 [OE. *hand* + *lang*; cf. OE. *handleng(u)*].

handtamyd, *adj.* tame, submissive 4.17 [OE. *hand* + *tam, temian*].

hang, hyng, *v.* hang 1.13, 4.210, 308, 5.132, 241; 3 *sg.pa.t.* **hang,** was crucified 3.49, was hanged 4.596; *pp.* **hanged** 4.315, **hangyd** 4.44; *sb.* **hangyng** 6.13 [OE. *hangian*, ON. *hengja*].

hangere. See **anger,** *sb.*

hap, *sb.* chance, luck, fortune 3.40, a chance, happening 6.336 [ON. *happ*].

hap, *v.* cover 4.434; *pp.* **happyd, hapt** 4.1, 369 [unknown].

happyn, happen 2.481; 3 *sg.pa.t.* **happynyd,** fared 3.155 [from ON. *happ*].

har, *sb.* hinge; *out of har,* out of joint 6.210 [OE. *heorr(a)*].

harbar, *sb.* shelter, lodging; *outt of howse and of harbar,* out of house and home 4.245 [OE. *herebeorg*].

hard. See **her(e).**

hard, *adj.* hard 4.316, 545; *adv.* hard 2.199, 4.74, harshly, cruelly 4.75, soundly 4.287 [OE. *heard; hearde*].

hardely, *adv.* certainly, by all means 1.128, 363, 366, 2.522 [next + OE. *-līce*].

hardy, *adj.* bold, presumptuous 1.12, 3.108, 5.90 [OF. *hardi*].

hare, *sb.* hare 3.182 230 [OE. *hara*].

hark(e), harkyn, herk, herkyn, *v.* listen (to) 3.19, 296, 393, 4.362, 612, 5.83; *hark after,* listen 4.664 [OE. *hercnian*].

harlot(t), *sb.* rascal 1.22, 5.358, 6.129, 310 [OF. *harlot*].

harmeles, *adj.* unhurt, unharmed 5.483 [OE. *hearm + -lēas*].

harmes, *sb.pl.* injuries 5.8 [OE. *hearm*].

harnes, *sb.pl.* brains 4.192 [ON. *hjarni*].

haro(o), horow, *interj.* a cry for help 1.275, 4.438, 5.391 [OF. *haro(u)*].

harrer, *interj.* gee up 1.55.

harstow. See **her(e).**

hart, hert, *sb.* heart 2.399, 3.8, 4.360, 6.183, intent, purpose 5.178; *in hart,* in good spirits 3.4; *thy hart is in thy hose,* your heart's in your boots 3.424 [OE. *heorte*].

hart-blood, *sb.* heart's blood 5.373 [OE. *heorte + blōd*].

hart-langyng, *sb.* heart-longing, heart-yearning 6.12 [OE. *heorte + langung*].

hart-stangyng, *sb.* agony of heart, heartache 6.11 [from OE. *heorte + ON. stanga*].

has, hask. See **hafe, aske.**

hast, *sb.* violence 2.411, haste 5.280; *haue hast,* be in a hurry 1.135, 6.318; *in hast,* quickly 2.158 [OF. *haste*].

hast, *v.* hasten 2.182, 5.279 [OF. *haster*].

hast(e)ly, *adv.* quickly, promptly 2.39, 109 [from OF. *haste;* cf. OE. *hǣstlīce*].

hat(t). See **hight.**

hatters, *interj.* confound it 4.543 [? OE. *hæteru,* perhaps in sense of 'Christ's or holy garments'; see *NED.*].

haue. See **hafe.**

he, *pron.* 3 *sg.masc.* he 2.17; (pleonastic, repeating subject) 1.7, 5.458; *indef.* any man 4.28; *acc.dat.* **hym** 2.21; *refl.* **hym(self)** 2.18 (first), 19; **hisself, hysself,** he himself 6.35, 260; *gen.* **his, hys** 1.9, 4.558; *pron.* his folk 2.553, 5.301 [OE. *he, him, his*].

he(e), hye, *adj.* high, noble, exalted 2.469, 553, 3.442, serious 4.594; *on he,* (from) on high 6.254; *adv.* loudly, shrilly, 4.489 [OE. *hēh*].

heade, he(e)de, *sb.* head 1.367, 2.387, 4.390, 469, 5.93, 6.327, 390, 396; *ouer . . . heede,* because of 4.485; *pl.* **heedys** 5.36, **heydys** 4.283 [OE. *hēafod*].

hede, *sb.* heed, notice; *take hede,* take heed 2.424, 3.162, 6.433; *take hede to,* look to 4.200 [from OE. *hēdan*].

heder, hedir, hedyr, hyder, *adv.* hither, here 1.37, 2.290, 3.109, 4.262, 6.117, 389, to me 2.291 [OE. *hider*].

hederward, *adv.* hither, this way 4.290, 5.371 [OE. *hiderweard*].

hed-maspenny, *sb.* mass-penny, i.e. money paid for a mass for the soul of a dead person 4.252 [OE. *hēafod + mæsse + penig*].

he(e)de, heedys. See **heade.**

heght, hight, *sb.* height 2.260; *of heght,* in height 2.125; *on hight,* in height 2.136, on high 1.246, 4.282, loudly 3.498, 4.299 [OE. *hēhþu*].

heydys. See **heade.**

heyll, *sb.* health 3.4 [OE. *hǣlu,* ON. *heill*].

heyll, *v.* heal 6.88 [OE. *hǣlan*].

heynd, *adj.* gracious, courteous, gentle 4.638, 5.10; *as sb.* **heyndly,** gracious lord 5.320, 455; *adv.* **heyndly,** courteously, graciously 5.208 [OE. *gehende*].

heytt. See **hight.**

hek, *sb.* inner door 4.305; *pl.* racks for fodder 1.47 [OE. *hecc*].

hell, *sb.* hell 2.42, 3.185, 5.52 [OE. *hell*].

helme, *sb.* helm, tiller 2.272 [OE. *helma*].

help, *sb.* help 3.423 [OE. *help*].

help, *v.* help 2.322, 4.322; 3 *sg.pres.subj.* 2.247 [OE. *helpan*].

helpars, *sb.pl.* helpers 3.94 [from prec.].

helpyng, *sb.* help, assistance 3.36 [from OE. *helpan*].

hen, *sb.* hen 4.67 [OE. *hen(n)*].

hence, hens, *adv.* from now 2.25, from here 1.299, 2.292, 3.120, 4.204, 5.316 [OE. *heonan + adv. -es*].

hend. See **hand.**

hent, v. catch, get 5.8; hent to, lay hold of 2.420 [OE. hentan].

heppe, sb. heap 3.417 [OE. hēap].

her, hir, hyr, pron. 3 sg. fem. acc. dat. gen. her 2.505, 3.155, 181, 4.103; refl. herself 4.413 [OE. hire].

her(e), v. hear, listen (to) 1.40, 2.72, 4.325, 5.111, 137; 2 sg.pres.subj. here, may hear 1.175; 2 sg.imper. here 1.68, 183; 2 pl. here 6.302, herys 3.282; 1, 3 sg.pa.t. hard 1.34, 3.326, 4.112, 5.141; 2 pl. hard 4.656; pp. hard 2.46; harstow, do you hear 1.386; harstow . . . of all, do you hear everything 6.129 [OE. hēran].

here, sb. hair 3.65 [OE. hēr].

here, adv. here 2.174, here is 1.100, 110, 159, 2.257, 3.212, 215, 4.163; hereaboute, hereabouts 1.66; hereafter 6.189; herby, close by 5.26; herein 4.359; heretyll, concerning this matter 5.260 [OE. hēr].

herk, herkyn, hert. See hark(e), hart.

hertely, adv. in heart 2.388 [OE. heortlīce].

hete, hett. See hight.

hetyng, sb. promise 4.717 [from OE. hātan, hēt].

hetys, sb.pl. promises 6.13 [OE. hāt, infl. by hātan, hēt].

heuen, sb. heaven 1.353, 2.11, 3.185, 5.52 [OE. heofon].

heuy, adj. heavy 3.21 [OE. hefig].

heuynes, sb. heaviness of heart, sorrow 3.34 [OE. hefignes].

hewed, 3 pl.pa.t. hewed 6.76, 78 [OE. hēawan].

hy, v. hasten, hurry 1.43, 2.371, 4.670, 5.65; refl. 2.289, (1 pl.imper.) 2.312; 1 pl.pa.t.subj. hyde, would hurry 5.398; pp. hyde, sped 3.432 [OE. hīgian].

hy, sb. haste; in hy, in haste, swiftly 5.128, 147 [from prec.].

hide, hyde, v. to hide 1.225, 470, 4.333, 5.36; pp. hid, hyd 1.378, 6.370 [OE. hȳdan].

hyder. See heder.

hid(o)us, hydus, adj. hideous, terrible 2.101, 417, 4.58 [AF. hidous].

hye. See he(e).

hyer(e), hyre, sb. hire, pay 4.161, 254, 497, 6.381; I shall gyf hym his hyre, I shall pay him out 5.102 [OE. hȳr].

hight. See heght.

hight, hyght, v. promise 4.472; pass.infin.

W.P.—N

hatt, be called, named 4.604; 3 sg. hat, is called 1.15; 2,3 sg.pa.t. hight, hyght, promised 2.46, 4.431; 2 pl. heytt, hett, promised 6.285, 336; pp. hete, called 5.215 [OE. hātan].

highter, adj.compar. higher 2.443 (note) [OE. hēh, infl. by hēhþu].

hill, hyll, sb. hill 1.170, 2.337, 466, 6.247 [OE. hyll].

hym, hymself. See he.

hyne, sb. servant 4.147 [OE. hīna, gen.pl. of hīgan].

hyng. See hang.

hyppys, sb.pl. hips 3.254, 4.558 [OE. hype].

hir, hyr. See her.

hyrdes, sb.pl. herdsmen, shepherds 3.296 [OE. heorde, hirde].

hyrd-men, sb.pl. herdsmen, shepherds 4.638 [OE. (WS.) hierdeman].

hyre. See hyer(e).

hyre, v. hire 4.496 [OE. hȳrian].

his, hisself, hysself. See he.

hit, it(t), pron. 3 sg.neut. it 1.241, 315, 2.174, 4.497; (pleonastic, repeating subject) 5.209; (anticipating subject) it is, there is 3.481; (with pl. verb. ref. to prec. pl. noun) they 3.173; (coalescing with prec. word) 2.517 3.254, 271, 4.594, 6.19 [OE. hit].

hyte, interj. gee up, go on 1.55, 3.150 [cf. G. hott].

hytt, v. hit 3.121; 1 sg.pa.t. hyt 6.327 [late OE. hittan, from ON. hitta].

ho, interj. ho, stop 2.229, 3.103, oh 3.157 [cf. OF. ho].

ho, v. stop 2.411 [from prec.].

hob, sb. Hob, hobgoblin 1.297 [a familiar by-form of Rob].

hode, hoode, sb. hood 1.388, (used to mean 'head') 5.339, 6.314; (in asseveration) bi my hode 1.216, 3.136, by thi hoode 4.235 [OE. hōd].

hogys, sb.pl. young sheep 4.456 [OE. hogg].

hoill, hole, adj. hollow 1.7; sb. hole 1.337 [OE. hol].

hoylle, hole, adj. whole, sound 2.388, 6.174 [OE. hāl].

hoyne, hone, v. delay 1.133, 2.319 [obscure].

hoyse, hose, sb.pl. stockings, hose 1.153, 437, 2.225, 3.424 [OE. hosa, hose].

holard, sb. fornicator, libertine 5.358 [from OF. holeur].

hold. See hald.

hold, *sb.* in *haue hold*, take hold of 4.350 [OE. *hald*].

hole. See hoill, hoylle.

holgh, *adj.* hollow, empty 1.310 [from OE. *holh*].

holy, *adj.* holy 2.162, 4.378, 6.208 [OE. *hālig*].

holsom, *adj.* wholesome 3.248 [OE. **hālsum*].

home. See hame.

homward, *adv.* homewards 2.182 [OE. *hāmweard*].

hone. See hoyne.

honest, *adj.* honest 5.413 [OF. *honeste*].

honoure, *sb.* honour 5.190 [OF. *honour*].

honoure, *v.* honour 5.222 [OF. *honourer*].

hoode. See hode.

hoore, *sb.* whore 5.340 [OE. *hōre*].

hop, *v.* hop, leap 6.354 [OE. *hoppian*].

hope, *v.* think, suppose, expect, hope 1.424, 4.115, 298, 425, 5.262, 6.200 [OE. *hopian*].

hore, *sb.* hair; jot or tittle 3.132; (in asseveration) *by my hore* 3.455 [ON. *hдr*].

hornyd, *adj.* horned, with horns 4.601 [from OE. *horn*].

horow. See haro(o).

hors, *sb.* horse 1.439 [OE. *hors*].

horsman, *sb.* horseman 3.17 [OE. *hors* + *man(n)*].

hose. See hoyse.

hose, *adj.* hoarse 4.416 [OE. *hās*].

hote. See haytt.

hote, *adj.* hot; *in hote ... in colde*, at all times, in all circumstances 4.419 [OE. *hāt*].

house, howse, *sb.* house 4.237, 245, 391; *houses of offyce*, stables 2.134 [OE. *hūs*].

householde, *sb.* household 4.420 [prec. + OE. *hald*].

how, *adv.* how 4.189, how much 2.250; howso, howsoeuer, however 2.210, 4.427; *as how*, how 6.274 [OE. *hū*].

how, *interj.* ho 1.37, 384, 3.82, 83, 4.290 [cf. ME. *ho*].

howre, owre, *sb.* hour 4.97, 5.191 [OF. *(h)ure*, AF. *houre*].

howse, howso, howsoeuer. See house, how, *adv.*

hufe, *v.* linger, wait 2.461 [obscure].

hunder. See vnder.

hundreth, *adj. and sb.* hundred 2.57, 3.110, 5.444, 487 [ON. *hundrað*].

hunger, hungre, *sb.* hunger 2.155, 6.382 [OE. *hungor*].

hungré, *adj.* hungry 3.286 [OE. *hungrig*].

hus. See we.

husbande, *sb.* husband 4.406; *pl.* husbands 2.208, husbandmen, farmers 4.10 (MS. *shepardes*), 4.22 [late OE. *hūsbonda*, from ON. *húsbóndi*].

huswyff, *sb.* housewife 4.301 [OE. *hūs* + *wīf*].

I, ich, *pron.* 1 *sg.* I 2.13, 4.201, 207, 211; omitted before *me qwakys* 4.359, *syttys* 6.155; *acc.dat.* me 2.66, 82; *refl.* myself 1.361, 2.238, 5.274; *gen.* my 2.66, myn(e) 1.59, 221, 2.74, 5.388; *pron.* myne 1.123, 2.226; myself 4.617, 6.128 [OE. *ic, mē, mīn*].

Iak, Jack, used generically in *for Iak nor for Gill*, for neither man nor woman, for nobody 2.336 [pet-name for *John*, shortened from *Jankin, Jackin*].

iangyls, 2 *sg.pres.* chatter, babble 1.134; 3 *sg.* ianglis 1.6; *sb.* ianglyng, babbling, wrangling 1.270, 4.174 [OF. *jangler*].

ich. See I.

ich, *adj.* each, every 1.109, 2.151, 4.488; *ich a*, each, every 1.290, 2.273; *ich a deyll*, every bit, all 2.299 [OE. *ylc*].

ichon, *pron.* each one, every one 2.112, 279 [prec. + *ān*].

if, *cj.* if 2.188, even if 4.43, 232, 254 [OE. *gif*].

ilk, ylk, *adj.* every 3.10, 4.241, 5.191 [OE. *ylc*].

ilka, *adj.* every 5.84, 6.78 [prec. + OE. *ān*].

ilkon, ylkon, *pron.* each one, every one 4.200, 5.139 [as prec.].

ill, yll, *adj.* bad, wicked 2.208, 3.425, 4.172, painful, disagreeable 6.49, unlucky, unfortunate 4.150, 6.255, ill, unwell, 4.231; *as sb.* evil 2.95, 5.435, 6.31; *adv.* badly, wickedly, unluckily, hardly 1.165, 3.200, 4.1, 5.145, 186 [ON. *illr; illa*].

illa-hayll, ylla-hayll, *sb.* bad luck; *as interj.* 6.375; *as adv.* 6.136 [ON. *illr* + *heill*].

ill-spon, *adj.* ill-spun, badly spun 1.436, 4.587 [ON. *illa* + OE. *spinnan*].

i(n), *prep.* in, into 2.2, 3.245, 6.358, on 2.42 (first), 145 [OE. *in*].

in, *adv.* in 2.326, 3.173 [OE. *inne*].

indede, *adv.* indeed 5.227, 6.436 [OE. *in* + *dēde*].

indew, *v.* invest, endow 6.166 [OF. *enduire*].

indoost, *pp.* indorsed, i.e. beaten on the back 6.421 [OF. *endosser*].

induyr, indure. See **endure.**

innocent, *sb.* innocent 5.388 [OF. *innocent*].

inpossybyll, *adj.* impossible 3.373 [OF. *impossible*].

inquere, *v.* inquire 5.201, 6.224 [OF. *enquerre*].

inrold, *pp.* enrolled, recorded 3.334 [OF. *enroller*].

inspyryd, *adj.* inspired 3.446 [OF. *inspirer*].

insure, *v.* guarantee, warrant 6.36 [AF. *enseurer*].

intent. See **entent.**

into, *prep.* into 2.327, 335, 5.100 [OE. *intō*].

inwardly, *adv.* at heart, heartily 6.182 [OE. *inweardlīce*].

io, io furth, *interj.* gee up, go on 1.25, 42, 55; (intensified by *do*) 6.1 [? rel. to ME. *yode*].

ioy, *sb.* joy 4.550, 5.111 [OF. *joie*].

ioy, *v.* gladden 3.499 [OF. *joir*].

ire, *sb.* anger 2.51, 5.100; *in ire,* angry 1.316 [OF. *ire*].

irregulere, *adj.* irregular, disobeying the rule of the Church 6.306 [OF. *irreguler*].

is, 3 *sg. and pl.pres.* is, are; 3 *sg.pres.* is 1.229 (rhyme requires *es*), 2.1; 3 *pl.* (not prec. by pron.) are 2.10 (rhyme requires *es*), 2.56, 3.95; (with ellipsis of *it*) 4.195, 479, 5.111 [OE. *is,* ON. *es*].

ist, is it 2.517 [OE. *is* + *hit*].

it(t). See **hit.**

iuge, *sb.* judge 6.426 [OF. *juge*].

iwis, iwys, *adv.* indeed, certainly 2.550, 3.457, 4.587 [OE. *gewiss, mid gewisse*].

kafe, *sb.* cave 5.244 [OF. *cave*].

kakyls, 3 *sg.pres.* cackles 4.68 [cf. Du. *kakelen*].

kap, *sb.* cap (used to mean 'head') 6.335 [OE. *cæppe*].

kast. See **cast,** *v.*

keyle, keill, *v.* cool; *from cares the to keyle,* to preserve you from sorrows 2.118; *cares ... keill,* assuage sorrows 2.300 [OE. *cēlan*].

keyn, kene, *adj.* sharp 6.444, keen, piercing 4.57, 128, bitter 5.409 [OE. *cēne*].

ken, *v.* know 1.16, 4.14, 248; 3 *sg.pa.t.* **kend,** taught 1.72; 2 *pl.* 6.263; *pp.* **kend,** taught 1.101; *daw to ken,* to be known for a fool 2.247–8 [OE. *cennan*].

kene. See **keyn.**

kepe, *v.* keep, guard, preserve 2.235, 3.55, 4.742, 5.337, look after, have charge of 3.103, 4.136, 6.160, be going on with 6.419, care for, desire 5.146; *sb.* **kepyng,** keeping, custody 1.349 [OE. *cēpan*].

kest(en). See **cast,** *v.*

kyll, *v.* kill 6.206; *kyll ... downe,* kill off 5.237 [obscure].

kyn, *sb.* kindred 5.345, 6.368; *no kyns,* of no kind, no kind of 5.312; (with loss of inflexion) *all kyn,* every kind of 1.203; *no kyn,* any (kind of) 2.138, 6.229 [OE. *cynn*].

kynd(e), *sb.* nature 4.591, race 4.679, progeny, offspring 3.395; *ich kynd,* every kind of 2.151 [OE. *(ge)cynd*].

kynde, *pp.* conceived 5.210 [OE. *cennan*].

kyndly, *adv.* duly, properly, thoroughly 5.37 [OE. *(ge)cyndelīce*].

kyng, *sb.* king 2.71, 3.337, 4.201, 5.3, 6.130 [OE. *cyn(in)g*].

kyppys, 3 *sg.pres.* snatches 3.253, 4.557 [ON. *kippa*].

kyrk, *sb.* church 6.208 [ON. *kirkja*].

kis, kys, *v.* kiss 1.59, 3.263, 4.584 [OE. *cyssan*].

knafe, knaue, *sb.* boy 4.554, lad, boy (employed as a servant) 1.382, 4.147, 6.393, servant 6.102, person of humble birth 2.173, 3.278, rogue, rascal 3.120, 144, 277, 5.164 [OE. *cnafa*].

knakt, 3 *sg.pa.t.* sang, trilled (with breaking of long into short notes) 4.659 [cf. MHG. *knacken,* Du. *knakken*].

knap, knop, *v.* strike, knock 6.337, 408 [echoic].

knaue. See **knafe.**

knaue-childe, *sb.* male child 4.338; *pl* 5.256 [prec. + OE. *cild*].

knaw, knowe, *v.* know, get to know 2.167, 4.247, 5.133, 6.192, experience, endure 2.41, tell, confess 2.246; *intr.* know, have understanding 3.161; 1 *sg.pa.t.* **knew(e)** 1.443, 6.76; 2 *pl.* **knew** 4.499; *knew ... of,* had some knowledge of 3.407 [OE. *cnāwan*].

kne, *sb.* knee 2.488, 3.189, 4.608, 6.157 [OE. *cnēo*].

kneyll, knele, *v.* kneel 4.686, 722, 5.67, 6.157; *pres.p.* kneland 2.488 [OE. *cnēowlian*].

knyght, *sb.* knight 3.459, 5.20 [OE. *cniht*].

knyghthede, *sb.* knighthood, chivalry 5.272 [prec. + **-hǣdu*].

knyt, 2 *sg.imper.* tie 6.391; *pp.* closed, shut up 2.451 [OE. *cnyttan*].

knok, *sb.* knock, blow 2.342, 6.207, 315 [from next].

knok, *v.* knock 4.392, 6.314; *pp.* knokyd (MS. *knokyp*) 6.423 [OE. *cnocian*].

knop. See knap.

knot, *sb.* knot 6.391 [OE. *cnotta*].

knowe, kun. See knaw, can, *v.*[1]

lad, *sb.* servant 3.71, low-born fellow, rascal 5.105, 111, 6.154, 334, lad, boy 1.2, 4.387; *gen.sg.* lad 5.304 [obscure].

lady, *sb.* lady, mistress 5.432, the Virgin Mary 4.672; *oure Lady*, the Virgin Mary 4.19, 553 [OE. *hlǣfdige*].

lagh(e), *v.* laugh 4.610, 715, 5.472; *pres.p.* laghyng 5.66 [OE. *hlǣhhan*].

lay. See ly, *v.*[1]

lay, *v.* lay 1.45, 2.34, wager 2.479, 4.293; *refl.* lie down 4.353, be brought to bed (of a child) 4.520; 1 *sg.pa.t.* lade 5.425, laide 1.232; 3 *sg.* lade 4.520; 1 *pl.* layd 4.353; *pp.* laide 2.282, layd(e), laid (low) 3.159, laid (close) 5.433, presented 5.73; *lay furth*, bring out 3.211; *lade on*, attacked 5.425 [OE. *lecgan*].

layn, *sb.* concealment; *I kepe not layn*, I have no wish to conceal anything 5.146 [from ON. *leyna*].

lak, *v.* lack 4.269, miss 4.425; 3 *sg.pres.* lakkys 4.269; 3 *sg.pa.t.* lakt 4.658 [cf. MLG. *lak*].

lakan, *sb.* baby 4.242 [cf. ON. *leika*].

lake, *sb.* sport, game 5.322, glee 5.66 [ON. *leikr*].

lake, *v.* sport, play 3.465, 4.165, (? in amorous sense) 4.414 [ON. *leika*].

lam, *sb.* lamb 3.182, (fig.) 3.501 [OE. *lamb*].

lame, *adj. as sb.* (the) lame 6.164 [OE. *lama*].

land(e), *sb.* land 1.54, 2.492, 4.13, 5.461; *in (on) land*, in the land, on earth 2.145, 5.262, far away 1.303 [OE. *land*].

land-lepars, *sb.pl.* vagabonds 5.166 [cf. Du. *landlooper*].

lang, *v.* long, wish (to) 4.209; 2 *sg.pres.* longys, want to go 3.111; 3 *sg.pa.t.* langyd, longed (for something) 4.42 [OE. *langian, longian*].

lang, long, *adv.* long, a long while 1.75, 113, 2.192, 244, 4.2, 317, 377; *compar.* langer(e) 5.117, 6.104, longer 1.284, 2.531 [OE. *lange, longe*].

langage, *sb.* language 5.246; *no langage ye crak*, don't speak loudly (or boastfully) 5.498 [OF. *langage*].

langer(e). See lang, *adv.*

langett, *sb.* thong used for tying hose 2.224 [OF. *languette*].

langyd. See lang, *v.*

lap, *v.* enfold, entangle 5.9; *pp.* lappyd, entangled 4.4, lapt, wrapped 4.368 [from OE. *lappa, læppa*].

lare, lore, *sb.* (religious) lore, learning 6.307, rule of behaviour 1.455 [OE. *lār*].

last, *v.* last, endure 2.265; *pp.* last 3.3; *be lastyng*, endure 3.385 [OE. *lǣstan*].

last, *adj.superl.* last 4.423; *as sb.* in *at last*, *at the last*, at last, in the end 4.318, 342; *adv.* 5.146 [OE. *latost, lætest*].

late, *adv.* late 4.82, 222, 6.368, lately, recently 2.442, 6.299 [OE. *late*].

lately, *adv.* slowly, sparingly 4.157, 162 [OE. *lætlīce*].

laton, *sb.* Latin 3.391 [OF. *latin*].

law(e), *sb.* law 1.69, 5.38, 6.17, practice, ways 3.162 [OE. *lagu*, from ON.].

lawde, *sb.* praise 3.501; *ᵣ*. lawdys, lauds (constituting with matins the first of the canonical hours) 4.180 [OF. *laude*].

lawfully, *adv.* lawfully 6.258, 274 [OE. *lagu + -fullīce*].

lawse, *v.* loosen, undo 3.167; 3 *sg.pa.t.* lowsyd, delivered 2.209 [from ON. *lauss*].

le, ly, *sb.* lie 4.59, 116, 560; *pl.* lyys 6.226; *no ly*, truly 4.59; *make . . . a ly*, tell a lie 4.116, 6.412 [OE. *lyge*].

leche, *sb.* physician 1.83 [OE. *lēce*].

lechery, *sb.* lechery 2.53 [OF. *lecherie*].

led. See leyd.

leder, *sb.* leader; *leder of law*, ruler 5.38 [from OE. *lēdan + -ere*].

leder, ledyr, *adj.* lazy, sluggish 2.289, 4.147 [OE. *lȳþre*].

lee, *sb.* lea, pasture-land, meadow 3.316 [OE. *lēh*].

leest. See les.

lefe, leyfe, *sb.* permission, leave 4.395, 578, 584, 5.97 [OE. *lēaf*].

lefe, leif(e), leyfe, leyff, lyefe, *v.*[1] leave 1.91, 252, 3.251, 5.205, 310; *intr.* stop, leave off 5.354, 6.109, 409, stay, remain 1.195; *pp.* **left** 2.524, 4.179, 623 [OE. *lǣfan*].

lefe, *v.*[2] believe 4.31; 2 *pl.imper.* **leyfe,** believe (me) 5.131 [OE. *lēfan*].

lefe, leif, *adj.* dear 1.65, 68, 5.362; *compar.* **leuer** in *I am leuer,* I would rather 3.193, *I had leuer* . . . *or,* I would rather . . . than 4.486 [OE. *lēof*].

left. See **lefe,** *v.*[1]

leg, *sb.* leg 3.233, 4.3 [ON. *leggr*].

lege, *v.* cite, bring forward 6.21 [AF. *aleg(i)er*].

legeance, *sb.*[1] plea, statement made in excuse 6.37 [OF. *alégance*].

legeance, *sb.*[2] allegiance, (performance of) feudal duties binding a liegeman to his lord 5.272 [OF. *ligeance*].

legende, *sb.* a lesson read at matins from Scripture or from the lives of the saints 5.203 [OF. *legende*].

leyd, *v.* lead (life) 2.393; *pp.* **led,** treated 2.202, 4.75, 6.52 [OE. *lǣdan*].

leyde, *sb.* man, person 2.48 [OE. *lēod*].

leif(e), leyfe, leyff. See **lefe.**

leyfe, *sb.* leaf 4.358 [OE. *lēaf*].

ley-land, fallow land, pasture-land 4.111 [OE. *lǣge + land*].

leyn, *adj.* lean 1.112 [OE. *hlǣne*].

leyn(e), *v.* give 1.115, 4.217; 3 *sg.pres.* **lenys** 1.118 [OE. *lǣnan*].

leke, *sb.* leek 1.285 [OE. *lēc*].

lele, *adj.* honest 4.521; *adv.* truly, faithfully 2.446 [OF. *leël*].

lemyd, 3 *sg.pa.t.* shone 3.316 [OE. *lēomian,* ON. *ljóma*].

lendyng, *pres.p.* dwelling 3.80 [OE. *lendan*].

lenght, lennthe, *sb.* length 2.123, 257 [OE. *lengþu*].

lenyd, 1 *sg.pa.t.* leaned 3.325 [OE. *hleonian*].

lenys, lennthe. See **leyn(e), lenght.**

lepe, *v.* leap, run 3.421, 4.169 [OE. *hlēapan*].

lere, *v.* teach 5.216, 6.67, 169, learn 3.392, 4.288; 3 *sg.pa.t.* **lerd** 6.169; *pp.* **lerd** 3.392 [OE. *lǣran*].

lernyd, 3 *sg.pa.t.* learned 4.524 [OE. *leornian*].

les, *adj.compar. as sb.* less 4.254; *les* . . . *more, les and more,* all 1. 468, 2.94; *superl.* **leest** 2.452 [OE. *lǣssa, lǣst*].

lese, *sb.* lying, falsehood; *without lese,* truly 2.390 [OE. *lēas*].

lesson, *sb.* lesson 3.357, 4.79 [OF. *lecon*].

lest, *cj.* lest 2.55 [OE. *þē lǣs þe*].

let(t), *v.*[1] let, allow 1.84, 3.118, 4.120, cause to, make 5.81; (forming imper.) 1.21, 2.411, 3.208, 4.595, 621, 754, 5.238; *let(t) se,* show (us, me) 3.422, 4.189, 6.275; *let(t) be,* stop, leave off 4.602, 674, 6.297 [OE. *lǣtan*].

let(t), *v.*[2] hinder, prevent 2.341, 470, 6.287; *intr.* hold back, refrain 3.226, delay, tarry 6.427; *lett* . . . *of,* keep . . . from 4.263 [OE. *lettan*].

letherly, *adv.* badly 4.171 [OE. *lȳþre + -līce*].

letht, *sb.* ease, rest 6.142 [obscure].

letter, *sb.* letter (of a word); *a letter,* a small part, a little 3.124; *no letter,* not the least part, not a jot 4.32; *pl.* letter, writ 5.73 [OF. *lettre*].

leuer. See **lefe,** *adj.*

leueryng, *sb.* liver-pudding in the form of a sausage 3.217 [from OE. *lifer*].

leuyn, levyn, *sb.* lightning 2.346 flash of, lightning, bright light 4.650 [obscure].

levyr, *sb.* liver; *levyr and long,* liver and lung 2.399 [OE. *lifer*].

lew, lo, *interj.* lo, see 1.34, 2.453, 507, 4.197; *we lo, we* . . . *lo,* ah well 1.223, 2.238 [OE. *lā*].

lewde, *adj.* simple, ignorant 4.707, 5.103 [OE. *lǣwede*].

lewté, *sb.* loyalty, fidelity 5.15 [OF. *le(a)uté*].

ly. See **le.**

ly, lig, lyg, *v.*[1] lie 1.330, 2.409, 4.335, 677; 3 *sg.pres.* **ligys** 1.220, 2.84, **lyys** 1.239, 4.13; 3 *sg.pa.t.* **lay** 4.166; *pp.* **lygen** 4.380, **lyne** 6.101 [OE. *licgan,* ON. *liggja*].

ly, *v.*[2] tell lies 5.31; 2 *sg.pres.* **lyys** 5.225; 3 *sg.* **lyes** 6.80 [OE. *lēgan*].

lyars, *sb.pl.* liars 5.163 [OE. *lēgere*].

lyefe, lyes. See **lefe,** *v.*[1], **ly,** *v.*[2].

lif(e), lyfe, *sb.* life 1.325, 2.34, 193, 4.82, 5.92; *on lyfe,* alive 5.310, in this life 4.23, on earth 5.12; *bi God on life,* by the living God 1.19 [OE. *līf*].

lif, lyf, *v.* live 1.136, 2.145, 5.262; *pres.p.* **liffand** 2.73, **lif(f)yng** 2.47, 48,

lyfyng 5.12; *pp*. **liffyd** 2.58; *sb*. **lifyng,** livelihood 1.98 [OE. *lifian*].

lyft, *v*. lift, raise 4.283, 584 [ON. *lyfta*].

lig(ys), lyg(en). See **ly,** *v*.¹

light, lyght, *sb*. light 3.434, 4.296, 6.55, radiance 2.557 [OE. *lēht, līht*].

lyght, *v*. alight, come down (describing the Incarnation) 4.677; 3 *sg.pa.t*. **lyght** 4.739; *pp*. delivered (of a child) 4.337 [OE. *līhtan*].

light, lyght, *adj*. light 4.357, 6.351, cheap 4.170; *light chepe*, cheaply 1.236; *adv*. quickly 5.445 [OE. *lēht, līht; lēhte*].

lyghtys, 3 *sg.pres*. lightens, grows cheerful 4.138 [OE. *līhtan*].

lightly, lyghtly, *adv*. easily, readily 1.217, 4.143, 5.225, quickly 5.392 [OE. *lēhtlīce*].

lightnes, *sb*. brightness, radiance 2.16 [OE. *līhtnes*].

lyys. See **le, ly.**

lik, *v*. lick; *lik on*, have a taste of 2.378 [OE. *liccian*].

like, lyke, *v.impers*. please, in *lykys me*, it pleases me 3.106; *if it lyke*, if it please 5.439; *pers*. like 2.361, 5.31; *and shal he like full ill*, and he shall be very displeased 1.256 [OE. *līcian*].

like, lyke, *adj. and adv*. like 3.65, 4.102, 5.236, 6.362; (foll. by *to, vnto*) 2.83, 506; (foll. by infin.) likely to 3.353, 4.308 [OE. *gelīc; (ge)līce*].

likyng, lykyng, *sb*. pleasure 5.18; *for to haue thare likyng*, to have what pleases them 2.75 [OE. *līcung*].

liknes, *sb*. likeness 2.28 [OE. *līcnes*].

lyne. See **ly,** *v*.¹.

lyne, *sb*. plumb-line 2.461 [OE. *līne*, OF. *ligne*].

lippis, lyppis, lyppys, *sb.pl*. lips 1.21, 3.251, 6.172; *so fare fall thare lyppys*, good luck to them 4.560 [OE. *lippa*].

lyst, *sb*. desire, inclination 5.183; *do thyn awne lyst*, do as you please 6.243 [ON. *lyst*].

list, lyst, *v.impers*. wish, desire, in *me list*, I wish 1.59; *pers*. 1.149, 3.204, 421, 428, 4.148, 209, 476, 5.353 [OE. *lystan*].

litill, lytyll, *adj*. little 3.466; *as sb*. 2.187, 507, 3.473, 4.165 [OE. *lȳtel*].

lo. See **lew.**

lofyng, louyng, *sb*. praise 1.103, 3.296 [OE. *lofung*].

loft, *sb*. air; *(vp)on loft*, high up 5.339, 6.354, loudly 4.480, 754 [ON. *(ā) lopt*].

lok, *v*. lock up 6.332 [from OE. *loc*; cf. ON. *loka*].

loke, look(e), *v*. inspect, examine 4.396, watch over, take care of 4.219; *intr*. see, make sure (that) 1.310, 433, 2.129, 4.424, 5.281, 6.427; *look well abowte*, look well about (you) 3.172; *looke ouer*, watch over 4.109 [OE. *lōcian*].

lone, *sb*. gift 1.117 [OE. *lān*, ON. *lán*].

long. See **lang,** *adv*.

long, *sb*. lung 2.399 [OE. *lungen*].

long, *adj*. long 2.377, 4.182; *as sb*. long note 3.414, 4.657 [OE. *lang, long*].

longer, longys. See **lang,** *adv. and v*.

longys, 3 *sg.pres*. belongs 5.461 [from OE. *gelong*].

lonys, *sb.pl*. loins 3.230 [OF. *lo(i)gne*].

look(e). See **loke.**

lord, *sb*. the Lord, lord 2.28, 3.64; *as interj*. 3.1, 4.1, 57, 355 [OE. *hlāford*].

lord-fest, *adj*. bound to a lord 4.20 [OE. *hlāford + fæst*].

lordyng, *sb*. lord 4.202, 5.34 [OE. *hlāfording*].

lore, lorne. See **lare, lose.**

los, *sb*. loss 4.506 [OE. *los*].

lose, *v*. destroy 6.197, lose 2.363, forget 3.425, 4.673, waste 1.152; *pp*. **lorne,** lost 4.451, ruined, brought to ruin 4.639, 5.58, **lost,** lost 4.108, wasted 3.225 [OE. *losian, -lēosan*].

losell, *sb*. rogue, scoundrel 5.133, 154, 6.117 [app. from ME. *lose(n)*, pp. of prec.].

lote, *sb*. noise 4.409 [ON. *lát*].

loth(e), *adj*. hateful 1.161, unwilling 4.397 [OE. *lāþ*].

lothes, *sb.pl*. troubles, injuries 5.9 [OE. *lāþ*].

lott, *sb*. lot, fortune, 4.314, 5.399 [OE. *hlott*].

louyng. See **lofyng.**

low, *adj*. low 2.21; *adv*. 2.84, 5.68 [ON. *lágr*].

lowde, *adv*. strongly (of smell) 4.549; *on lowde*, loudly 3.66 [OE. *hlūde*].

lowked, *pp*. closed 6.58 [OE. *lūcan*].

lowly, *adv*. humbly 5.18 [ON. *lágr + OE. -līce*].

lowsyd. See **lawse.**

lowt, *v*. bow down to, reverence 1.435; 3 *pl.pres*. **lowtys** 5.41, 49 [OE. *lūtan*].

luf, *sb*. love 2.82, 3.402, 4.569, loved one 5.363 [OE. *lufu*].

luf, *v*.¹ love 2.47; 2 *pl.imper*. **luf** 5.15 [OE. *lufian*].

luf, *v.*[2] praise 1.435 [OE. *lofian*].

luf, *adj.* dear, beloved 5.73 [OE. *lēof*].

lufe, *sb.* palm of hand 2.462 [ON. *lófi*].

lufly, *sb.* lovely child 4.684 [from OE. *luflic*].

lullay, *interj.* lullaby 4.442, 445 [*onomatopœic*].

lurdan, *sb.* (lazy) lout 5.163, 490 [OF. *lourdin*].

lust, *sb.* wish, desire 5.297, 436 [OE. *lust*].

mad, *adj.* mad 1.93 [OE. *gemǣdd*].

madyn, *sb.* maiden, virgin 3.370, 4.711, 5.200 [OE. *mægden*].

may, 1,2,3 *sg.pres.* may, can 1.57, 2.480, 3.28; (with ellipsis of *do*) 3.12, 485, 4.630, 684, 6.42; 1,2,3 *pl.* **may** 2.4, 175, 361; 1,2,3 *sg.pa.t.* **myght** 2.5, 38, 191; 1 *pl.* **myght** 3.440 [OE. *mæg*].

maide, mayde. See **make,** *v.*

mayll, *sb.* bag, wallet 3.224; *pl.* **malys** 5.453 [OF. *male*].

mayll, *adj.* male 2.152 [OF. *ma(s)le*].

maylleasse, *sb.* sickness; *at maylleasse,* sick, unwell 4.485 [OF. *malaise*].

mayn, *sb.* strength, might 2.310 [OE. *mægen*].

mays. See **make,** *v.*

make, *sb.* one's equal 1.443, mate, consort 2.139 [OE. *gemaca*].

make, *v.* make 2.104, 263, cause (foll. by infin., with or without *to*) 2.28–9, 82, 3.145, 4.211, 5.255; 3 *sg.pres.* **mays** 4.30, **makys** 1.192, **mase** 3.434, 6.103; 1 *sg.pa.t.* **made** 2.82, **maide** 2.91; 2 *sg.* **maide** 2.3; 3 *sg.* **made** 2.19; *pp.* **maide** 2.73, **mayde,** eaten 4.149 [OE. *macian*].

maker(e), *sb.* Creator 2.1, 3.485, 4.711 [prec. + -*ere*].

malys. See **mayll,** *sb.*

malison, *sb.* curse 1.355 [OF. *maleison*].

man, *sb.* man 2.28, 3.369, servant 1.58; *gen.sg.* **mans,** in *mans wonder,* prodigy of mankind, monster 2.408, *mans mordere,* murderer 5.387; *pl.* **men** 3.93, men of note 5.305, liegemen 1.20; *gen.pl.* **mens** 1.122, 3.53 [OE. *man(n)*].

maner(e), *sb.* manner, way 4.47, 6.403 [OF. *manere*].

mangere, *sb.* manger (used humorously to mean 'table') 3.201 [OF. *mangeure*].

mangyng, *sb.* eating, meal 3.232 [from OF. *mangier*].

many, *adj. and pron.* many 1.47, 4.89, 5.57; *many a* 2.130, 4.96; (without indef. art.) 2.355, 436, 3.445, 5.4; *many other mo,* many others as well 3.378 [OE. *manig*].

manyfold, *adj.* manifold, in *other wise manyfold,* in many other ways 2.54; *adv.* in *trew full manyfold,* honest as can be 1.425 [OE. *manigfald*].

mankyn, *sb.* mankind 2.71 [OE. *mancyn(n)*].

manteyn, *v.* maintain, uphold 4.621 [OF. *maintenir*].

mantenance, *sb.* maintenance 4.35 [OF. *maintenance*].

mar, *v.* hinder, stop 2.129, spoil, ruin 6.439; 3 *pl.pres.(intr.)* **mars,** perish 3.93; *pp.* **maryd,** in *as myght I be maryd,* bad luck befall me (if it isn't so) 6.118 [OE. *merran*].

mare, *sb.*[1] mare 1.28, 3.164 [OE. *mere*].

mare, *sb.*[2] nightmare, goblin 6.310 [OE. *mare*].

maryd. See **mar.**

markys, *sb.pl.* marks (each about ⅔ of a pound, 13*s.* 4*d.*) 5.267, 463 [OE. *marc*].

maroo, *sb.* mate 4.436 [obscure].

mase. See **make,** *v.*

masons, *sb.pl.* masons 6.76 [OF. *masson, maçon*].

mast, *sb.* mast 2.263 [OE. *mæst*].

master, *sb.* master 1.3, 3.71, 4.145, 6.102 [OE. *mægester,* OF. *maistre*].

master-men, *sb.pl.* masters, employers 4.156 [prec. + OE. *men(n)*].

mastré, mastry, *sb.* mastery, authority 5.130, 6.398; *what mastry he mays,* no matter what force he uses 4.30; *sich mastré to make,* to exercise such power 5.497 [OF. *maistrie*].

mater, *sb.* matter, affair 5.157, 6.23 [OF. *matere*].

matyns, *sb.pl.* matins (constituting with lauds the first of the canonical hours) 5.206 [OF. *matines*].

maw, *sb.* belly 4.110 [OE. *maga*].

mawd, Maud (used contemptuously to mean 'hag') 5.352 [OF. *Maud*].

me. See **I.**

measse, *sb.* mess, dish (of food) 2.389 [OF. *mes*].

mede, *sb.* reward 1.294, bribe 6.435, merit 3.467; *to mede,* as a reward 2.122, 4.668 [OE. *mēd*].

medyll, *sb.* middle, waist 4.534 [OE. *middel*].

medill-erd, *sb.* the world 2.100 [prec. + OE. *eard;* cf. OE. *middangeard*].

mefe, move, *v.* move, affect, excite 4.192, 5.125, 352, 472, stir up (strife, trouble) 5.96; *pp.* **mevid,** swept away 2.542 [OF. *moveir, moev-*].

meyll, *sb.* meal, ground grain 3.170 [OE. *melo*].

meyn, *adj.* mean, poor 1.111; *compar.* **mener** 4.691 [OE. *(ge)mǣne*].

meyn, *v.* complain; *refl.* 1.113; 3 *sg.pres.* **menys** 5.19 [OE. *mǣnan*].

meyn(e), mene, *v.* mean, intend, think, have in mind 3.19, 128, 370, 4.130, 711, 5.103, 251, speak 6.445; *refl.* remember 4.220; 3 *sg.pa.t.* **ment** 4.740; *pp.* **ment** 4.141; *on . . . mene,* think of 4.635 [OE. *mǣnan*].

meyne, *sb.* the middle part in a harmonized three-part song 4.188 [OF. *meen, meien*].

meyte, mete, *v.* meet 1.364, 4.402, 5.184; 1 *sg.pa.t.* **mett** 3.141; 1 *pl.* **met** 3.206; *pp.* **mett** 5.182 [OE. *mētan*].

mekenes, *sb.* meekness, gentleness 5.100, 6.209 [ON. *mjúkr* + OE. *-nes*].

mekill, mekyll, *adj.* great, much 1.237, 2.109, 4.65, 6.40; *mekill thank,* thanks very much 4.382; *adv.* greatly 6.5 [OE. *micel,* ON. *mikill*].

mele, *sb.* meal 4.522 [OE. *mēl*].

mell, *v.* speak of 5.195; 3 *sg.pres.subj.* declare 2.44 [OE. *meðlan*].

melt, *v.* melt 4.529 [OE. *meltan*].

mend, *v.* avail, profit 5.352, make good, increase 4.388; *mendys oure chere (mode),* will cheer, comfort us 4.290, 504; *sb.* **mendyng,** improvement (in behaviour) 3.78 [OF. *amender*].

mendys, *sb.pl.* amends 4.567 [OF. *amendes*].

mene. See **meyn(e),** *v.*

menee, meneye, menye, *sb.* household 2.22, 290, retinue, servants 3.401, company 4.346 [OF. *mai(s)nee*].

mener. See **meyn,** *adj.*

meng, *v.* stir up; *meng you with myrth,* make you merry 5.1 [OE. *mengan*].

menye, menys, ment. See **menee, meyn,** *v.,* **meyn(e),** *v.*

mercy, *sb.* mercy 2.44, 5.352 [OF. *merci*].

mery, *adj.* merry, joyous 1.2, 2.463, 3.243, 4.667 [OE. *myrge*].

merys, 3 *sg.pres.* is merry 4.714 [OE. *myrgan*].

merkyd, *pp.* aimed; *we haue merkyd amys,* we have aimed wrongly, i.e. have made a mistake 4.551; *he is merkyd amys,* he is wrongly formed, i.e. deformed 4.586 [OE. *me(a)rcian*].

meruell, *sb.* (a) marvel, miracle 3.323, 370, 4.82, 648; *(greatt) meruell haue I,* I marvel (greatly) 5.29, 6.242 [OF. *merveille*].

mervelus, *adj.* marvellous 2.12 [OF. *merveillos*].

mes, *sb.* Mass 5.206, 6.159 [OE. *mæsse, messe,* OF. *messe*].

mesel, *adj.* measly 1.264 [OF. *mesel*].

messyngere, *sb.* messenger 4.702 [OF. *messagier*].

mesure, *sb.* measure, size 1.51 [OF. *mesure*].

met(t), mete. See **meyte.**

met(t)e, *sb.* food 1.44, 2.160, 4.310, 504, meal 3.214 [OE. *mete*].

metyng, *sb.* meeting 3.479, 4.716 [OE. *mēting*].

mett, *adj.* measured 3.484 [from OE. *metan*].

mevid, my. See **mefe, I.**

mych, *adj.* much 1.235, 5.453 [OE. *micel*].

mydday, *sb.* midday; *mydday nor morow,* midday nor morning, i.e. at any time 4.9 [OE. *middæg*].

mydyng, *sb.* midden; *from doore to mydyng,* from door to midden, i.e. a single step 2.376 [cf. Da. *mødding*].

mydnyght, *sb.* midnight 6.326 [OE. *midniht*].

myght. See **may.**

myght, *sb.* might, strength 2.542, 4.740, 5.279; *pl.* mighty deeds, works 3.485, 4.684; *at my myght,* if I can help it 1.208, as far as I can 2.322 [OE. *miht*].

myghtfull, *adj.* mighty 2.1 [prec. + *-ful*].

myghty, *adj.* mighty 2.168, 5.1 [OE. *mihtig*].

myghtyus, *adj.* mighty 5.220 [prec. + OF. *-os*].

myld(e), *adj.* mild, gentle 3.370, 4.535, 711 [OE. *mild*].

myles, *sb.pl.* miles; *be myles,* for miles 6.84 [OE. *mīl*].

mylk-pycher, *sb.* milk-jug 3.159 [OE. *milc* + OF. *pich(i)er*].

mylksop, *sb.* an affectionate term for a baby 3.469 [OE. *milc* + *sopp*].

myln-whele, *sb.* mill-wheel 3.126 [OE. *mylen* + *hwēol*].

myn(e). See I.

myn, *v.* remember 4.675; *myn of, myn on,* bear in mind 2.551, 4.745 [ON. *minna, minnask*].

myn, *adj.compar.* smaller, in *more and myn,* all 2.112, 278; *nawther more nor myn,* neither more nor less 3.172 [ON. *minni*].

mynde, *sb.* mind 3.37 [OE. *(ge)mynd*].

myre, *sb.* mire, bog 4.160, 256, 494 [ON. *mýrr*].

myrk, *adj.* unenlightened 6.211 [OE. *mirce*].

myrth, *sb.* mirth, joy 3.500, 4.667, 5.1, 100 [OE. *myrgþ*].

myrth, *v.* gladden, entertain 4.184 [from prec.].

mys, *sb.* loss, privation 2.551, wrongdoing 3.396, 6.6 [OE. *miss*].

mys, *v.* fail 2.404, do without 1.219, 2.237 [OE. *missan*].

myscary, *v.* go astray, come to harm, perish 4.22; *pass.* 6.54, 119; *pp.* **myscaryd** 6.54, 119 [OF. *meskarier*].

myschaunce, myschaunsce, *sb.* misfortune, disaster 1.404, 6.40; *with a mekill myschaunce,* bad luck (to him) 6.352 [OF. *meschaunce*].

myschefys, *sb.pl.* misfortunes, injuries 3.51, 5.156 [OF. *mesch(i)ef*].

myself. See I.

myster, *v.* need 3.231 [from OF. *mest(i)er*].

mytyng,*sb.* tiny child 3.477 [from OF. *mite*].

mo, *adj.compar.* more (in number) 2.134, 4.124; *many other mo,* many others as well 3.378; *as pron.* more, others 2.152, 391, 3.136, 4.675 [OE. *mā*].

mode, *sb.* mood, feelings 4.504, 5.472 [OE. *mōd*].

moder, *sb.* mother 2.354 [OE. *mōdor*].

moyn(e), mone, *sb.* moon 2.6, 355, 3.434, 4.190, 5.380, month 2.478 [OE. *mōna*].

mold, *sb.* earth; *apon mold,* on earth, alive 2.62, 5.19 [OE. *molde*].

mom, *sb.* a muttered sound; *yit myght thou say 'mom',* yet you could mumble something 6.172 [echoic].

mompyns, *sb.pl.* teeth 3.210 [ON. *munnr* + OE. *pinn*].

mon, *v.auxil.* shall, must 1.18, 265, 375, 3.496, 5.318 [ON. *monu, munu*].

mone. See **moyn(e).**

mone, *sb.* complaint, lamentation 4.47 [OE. *mān].

moneth, *sb.* month 4.234 [OE. *mōnaþ*].

moore, *sb.* moor 4.10, 197 [OE. *mōr*].

mop, *sb.* moppet (an affectionate term for a baby) 3.467, 4.724 [obscure].

morder, *sb.* murder 5.489 [OE. *morþor,* AF. *murdre*].

morderd. See **murder.**

mordere, *sb.* murderer 5.387 [OE. *myrþra,* AF. *mordreour*].

morder-man, *sb.* murderer 5.361 [OE. *morþor* + *man(n)*].

more, *adj.compar.* more, greater 2.13, 317; *as sb.* 3.219; *more and les, more and myn,* all 2.11, 112, 278; *superl.* **most**, most, greatest 2.16; *as sb.* 3.12; *both the most and the leest,* all 2.452 [OE. *māra, mǣst* (late Nhb. *māst*)].

more, *adv.compar.* more 2.505, 3.243; longer, in *any more* 1.6, *no more* 2.418; *superl.* **moste**, most 1.65, 5.1 [as prec.].

moren, *sb.* murrain, plague, pestilence 3.39 [OF. *morine*].

morne, *sb.* dawn, daybreak 4.695, morning 3.82, 4.449, 5.346; *at morne,* in the morning 4.178 [OE. *morgen*].

mornyng, *sb.* morning 2.498 [prec. + *-ing*].

morow(e), *sb.* dawn, daybreak 6.59, morrow, morning 2.205 [OE. *morgen*].

most(e). See **more.**

mot, 3 *sg.pres.* must 1.254; 1,2,3 *sg.pa.t.* **must** 2.80, 130, 210; 1,3 *pl.* **must** 2.135, 6.354; *impers.* in *must vs,* we must 2.292, 334, 3.100 [OE. *mōt, mōste*].

moton, *sb.* mutton 3.220 [OF. *moton*].

move. See **mefe.**

mowrne, *v.* mourn, grieve 6.433 [OE. *murnan*].

mowrnyng, *sb.* mourning, lament 3.28, 4.94 [OE. *murnung*].

muk, *sb.* muck, dung 2.62 [cf. ON. *myki*].

multyplé, multiply, multiplie, *v.* multiply, increase 3.44; *intr.* 2.31, 179 [OF. *multiplier*].

murder, *v.* murder 6.207; *pp.* **morderd** 5.418 [OE. *-myrþr(i)an,* OF. *murdrir*].

must. See **mot.**

mustard, *sb.* mustard 3.213 [OF. *mo(u)starde*].

na, no *adv.* no 1.158, 252, 311, 2.550, not any 1.199 [OE. *nā*].

nay, *adv.* nay 2.385, 3.101, 4.45; *as sb.* in *withoutten nay,* undeniably 2.2 [ON. *nei*].

nayle, nayll, *sb.* nail 2.119, 273; *pl.* **nalys,** nails 5.116, finger-nails 6.409 [OE. *nægel*].

nayme, name, *sb.* name 1.144, 147, 2.162, 4.190, 378, renown 5.109, 6.147 [OE. *nama*].

nakyd, *adj.* naked 4.255, 308, 682 [OE. *nacod*].

nalys, name. See **nayle, nayme.**

name, *v.* name 6.165 [OE. *namian*].

namely, *adv.* especially 4.369 [OE. *nama* + *-līce*].

nap, *v.* nap, take a nap 3.22; *pp.* **nappyd, napt** 4.2, 370 [OE. *hnappian, hnæppian*].

nar, nere, *adv.*(*compar.*) near(er) 1.62, 2.370, 3.168, 4.246, 6.134, nearly 2.412, 5.376, closely, tightly 4.289; *as prep.* near (to) 3.287, 4.353, 703; *superl.* **next,** in *at next,* immediately following 4.251 [ON. *nær,* OE. *nēr;* OE. *nēxt*].

naroo, *adv.* closely, hard 4.437 [OE. *nearwe*].

nately, *adv.* thoroughly, to some purpose 4.158 [ON. *neytr* + OE. *-līce*].

nather, nawder, nawther, nother, nowder, nowther, *adj.*(*pron.*) neither 1.193; *adv.*(*cj.*) neither (foll. by *ne, nor, then*) 1.11, 293, 423, 2.534, 535, 3.172, 4.625, 6.147, 164 [OE. *nā(w)þer, nō(w)þer*].

nawre, *adv.* nowhere 4.367 [OE. *nāhwǣr, nāwer*].

ne, *adv.* not (preceding verb) 3.455; *cj.* nor 2.536, 5.435 [OE. *ne*].

nede, neyde, *sb.* need 1.125, 152, 2.426, 4.119, 729; *at my nede,* in my time of need 3.468 [OE. *nēd*].

nede, *v.* need 3.163, 4.275, 5.371; *impers.* in *what nedys the, what nede (nedys) you,* why should you 5.156, 409, 6.303 [OE. *nēodian, nēdan*].

nede, nedys, *adv.* needs, of necessity 1.164, 191, 463 [OE. *nēde, nēdes*].

nedyll, neld, *sb.* needle (as something valueless) 1.123, bit, scrap 4.233 [OE. *nēdl*].

nedys. See **nede,** *adv.*

neemly, *adv.* nimbly 4.271 [OE. *nǣmel* + *-līce*].

nefe, *sb.* fist 6.407 [ON. *hnefi, nefi*].

negh, nygh, *v.* approach, come near 2.370, 4.530 [from OE. *nēh*].

neyde. See **nede,** *sb.*

neyn, *adj.* nine 1.218 [OE. *nigon*].

nek, *sb.* neck 1.46, 4.308, 380, 5.126, 6.237 [OE. *hnecca*].

neld, nere. See **nedyll, nar, neuer.**

nerehand(e), nerehandys, *adv.* near, nearly 4.2, 11, 5.462, 6.280 [OE. *nēr* + *hand*].

nese, noyse, nose, *sb.* nose 4.488, 612, 5.337, 471 [OE. *nosu, næs-*].

nesh, *adj.* soft 4.545 [OE. *hnesce*].

nett, *sb.* net 3.139 [OE. *nett*].

neuen, neuyn, *v.* name 3.396, 4.191, appoint 5.129, mention, speak of 2.12, 3.398, 486, 4.648, 6.93, tell (truth) 3.411, (with cognate obj.) utter, pronounce 4.739; *intr.* say, speak 3.37, 6.250 [ON. *nefna*].

neuer, nere, *adv.* never 1.18, 2.24, 4.166, 6.184, not at all 2.313, 3.91, 4.343 [OE. *nǣfre*].

neuertheles, *adv.* nevertheless 3.435 [OE. *nǣfre* + *þe* + *lǣs;* cf. *nā þe lǣs*].

new, *adj.* new 2.199, 5.277, 6.344; *as sb.* 6.74; *adv.* newly 3.405 [OE. *nēowe*].

newys, 3 *sg.pres.* in *newys me,* is renewed for me, newly grows for me 1.189 [OE. *nīwian*].

next, nygh. See **nar, negh.**

nyght, *sb.* night 2.3, 3.287, 4.41; *on the nyghtys,* by night 4.136 [OE. *niht*].

nyll, 1 *sg.pres.* will not 3.198 [OE. **nyllan*].

nyp, *v.* nip, pinch 4.437, seize, grab 4.289; *nyp at,* reduce, whittle away 4.161 [cf. Du. *nijpen*].

no. See **na.**

no, *adj.* no 2.34; (before a vowel) **none** 1.31, 110 [OE. *nān*].

nobyll, noble, nobull, *adj.* noble 2.128, 276, 5.261 [OF. *noble*].

noght, not(t), *adv.* not 2.117, 155, 4.425 [OE. *nāht, nōht*].

noght, nott, *sb.* nothing, nought 2.96, 4.76, 93, 6.431 [as prec.].

noyn(e), none, *sb.* noon, midday 2.317, 481, 4.54, 279, 479 [OE. *nōn*].

noyse. See **nese.**

noys(e), nose, *sb.* noise 1.11, 4.429, 5.335, reputation 4.224; *withoutt noyse,* in a quiet manner, without any fuss 4.669 [OF. *no(i)se*].

noyte, noytt, note, *sb.* affair, work, business 2.264, 4.303, 411, 5.325, 400, 6.343, ado 2.368 [OE. *notu*].

noytys, *sb.pl.* (musical) notes 3.306 [OF. *note*].

noman, *sb.* nobody 4.30 [OE. *nān* + *man(n)*].

none. See no, noyn(e).

none, *pron.* none, no one 1.126, 2.524, 4.253, 477, 5.53, 6.373 [OE. *nān*].

nonys, in *for the nonys*, on purpose 4.527, 5.227, for the time being, while it lasted 6.49 [OE. **for þām ānum* + adv. *-es*].

nor, *cj.* nor 2.138, 4.247, 5.31 [OE. *nōþer*].

nores, *sb.* nurse 4.496 [OF. *nor(r)ice*].

north, *sb.* north 2.477 [OE. *norþ*].

nose, not(t), note, nother. See nese, noys(e), noght, noyte, nather.

nothyng, *sb.* nothing 1.53, 2.470, 3.31; *as adv.* not at all 2.289, 5.472 [OE. *nān* + *þing*].

novels, *sb.pl.* tidings, news 2.508 [OF. *novel(l)e*].

now, *adv.* now 2.48 [OE. *nū*].

nowder, nowther. See nather.

now-on-dayes, *adv.* nowadays 4.28 [OE. *nū* + *on* + *dæges*].

obediand, *adj.* obedient 2.121 [OF. *obedient*].

obey, *v.* obey 5.58 [OF. *obeir*].

od, *adj.* odd 2.57, 3.20 [ON. *odda-*].

oder, other(e), *adj.* other, another 2.160, 3.208, 4.137; *pron.* another, the other 1.371, 5.218; *none othere*, not otherwise 1.110; *ichon other*, each to the other 2.112 [OE. *ōþer*].

of, *adv.* off 4.622 [OE. *of*].

of, *prep.* of 2.1, from, out of 2.119, 209, 3.342, 483, 5.219, 6.57, (born) of 4.711, about, concerning 2.110, 3.491, as to, as for 2.156, 4.91, for 4.225, against 2.90, in respect of, in 2.79, 543, 3.458, (of height, breadth, etc.) in 2.123, 520, (introd. a measurement) 2.126, out of, among 4.456, some of, a portion of, one of 1.139, 3.211, 223, 389, 6.283 [OE. *of*].

offend, *v.* offend 2.108 [OF. *offendre*].

offer, offre, *v.* offer to God, offer a gift as an act of worship 1.177, 3.462, offer money for a mass 4.251; 3 *sg.pa.t.* offyrd 1.105 [OE. *offrian*, OF. *offrir*].

offeryng, *sb.* gift made as an act of worship 5.124 [OE. *offrung, offring-*].

offyce, *sb.* in *houses of offyce*, stables 2.134 [OF. *office*].

offre, offyrd. See offer.

oft, *adv.* oft, often 1.162, 2.187, 4.56 [OE. *oft*].

oft-tyme, *adv.* often 3.93 [prec. + OE. *tīma*].

oght, *pron.* anything 3.73, 4.397, 5.247, 6.367; *adv.* at all 6.51, 52, 245 [OE. *ā(wi)ht, ōwiht*].

oght-whedir, *adv.* anywhere 3.111 [prec. + OE. *hwider*].

oy, oyes, *interj.* oyez, hear ye 1.417 [OF. *oyez*].

oyle, *sb.* oil 2.46 [OF. *oile*].

old, *adj.* old 1.330, 372, 2.60, 5.91 [OE. *ald*].

olif-tre, *sb.* olive-tree 2.510 [OF. *olive* + OE. *trēo*].

omnypotent, *adj.* omnipotent 4.737 [OF. *omnipotent*].

on. See oone, *pron.*

on, *adv.* on, away 1.26, 30, 53, 158 [OE. *on*].

on, *prep.* on, upon 2.34, at 2.137, in 2.422, 4.726, 6.273, 308, 403, a- 4.172 [OE. *on*].

onys, onone, ons. See anone, o(o)nes.

on-slant, *adv.* aslant; *he shall on-slant*, he shall come to grief 5.237 [uncertain].

onwarde, *adv.* onward, forward; *I wold we were onwarde*, I wish we were getting on with it 6.370 [OE. *on* + *-weard*].

oone, *adj.* one, a single 1.192, 2.2, 4.324, 457; *all oone*, at one, agreed 4.566 [OE. *ān*].

oone, on, *pron.* one (person or thing) 2.209, 4.472, 5.101, some one 3.310, 4.183, 5.199; *on nor other*, one or the other, either 1.433 [as prec.].

oone, *adj.* alone 6.79; *by myn (thyn) oone*, by myself (yourself) 4.46, 441 [OE. *āna*].

oon(e)ly, *adv.* only 2.288, 307 [from OE. *ānlic*].

o(o)nes, onys, ons, *adv.* once 4.29, 103, 5.59, 6.326, one day, sometime 2.207; *for ones and for ay*, now and forever 4.685; *this onys*, this once, this time 6.47 [OE. *ānes*].

oostré, *sb.* inn, hostelry 2.329 [OF. *host(e)rie*].

open, *v.* open 4.305 [OE. *openian*].

open, *adj.* open 2.344 [OE. *open*].

opynly, *adv.* openly, plainly 5.75 [OE. *openlīce*].

oppose, *v.* examine, interrogate 6.195; *pp.* opposed 6.120 [OF. *opposer*].

opprest, *pp.* oppressed 4.22 [OF. *oppresser*].

or, *cj.*[1] or 2.133 [OE. *ōþer*].

or, *cj.*[2] before (often with *subj.*) 1.80, 241, 2.110, 130, 3.151, 4.39, 183, 5.94, than (after *leuer*) 4.486 [ON. *ār*].

or, *prep.* before, ere 2.228, 317, 481, 5.120, 6.137 [as prec.].

ordayn, ordan, ordeyn, *v.* make, build 2.309, give 3.479; *intr.* prepare, make preparations 5.255; 3 *sg.pa.t.* **ordand,** decreed 2.468; 2 *sg.pa.t.subj.* **ordand,** should build 2.119; *pp.* **ordand,** decreed 1.465 [OF. *ordener, -aine*].

orders, *sb.pl.* orders (of angels) 2.10 [OF. *ordre*].

other(e). See **oder.**

other, *adv.* or; *other . . . or,* either . . . or 1.62 [OE. *ōþer*].

othergatys, *adv.* otherwise, differently 1.121 [OE. *ōþer* + ON. *gata* + adv. *-es*].

otherwhile, *adv.* at other times 2.213 [OE. *ōþer* + *hwīl*].

ouer, *prep.* over, above 1.297, 2.65, 4.283 [OE. *ofer*].

ouerall, *adv.* everywhere 5.30 [OE. *ofer all*].

ouercast, *pp.* overcast 2.354 [OE. *ofer* + ON. *kasta*].

ouerlaide, *pp.* covered 2.306 [OE. *oferlecgan*].

ouersett, *v.* overcome, get the better of 6.286 [OE. *ofersettan*].

ouertwhart, *adv.* athwart, crosswise; *ouertwhart and endlang,* wholly, completely 3.48 [OE. *ofer* + ON. *þvert*].

oure. See **we.**

out(e), outt, owte, *adv.* out 2.128, 3.170, 422; *outt . . . fro,* away from 4.526, 530; *interj.* (expressing dismay, anger, indignation) 1.275, 2.408, 4.438, 5.148; *out(e) apon the, out on the,* fie on thee 1.398, 2.229, 408, 5.382 [OE. *ūt, ūte*].

outhorne, *sb.* a horn sounded to raise the hue and cry against a criminal, hue and cry 6.139 [OE. *ūt* + *horn*].

outrage, *sb.* passion, fury, violence of language 5.245 [OF. *outrage*].

out-thrist, *v.* thrust out 6.192 [OE. *ūt* + ON. *þrýsta*].

owre, *sb.* See **howre.**

ox-tayll, *sb.* ox-tail 3.225 [OE. *oxa* + *tægl*].

page, *sb.* boy, lad 5.247 [OF. *page*].

pagina, *sb.* pageant or scene in a Corpus Christi cycle (title of Play 1) [Anglo-Latin *pagina*].

pay, *sb.* satisfaction, liking; *oght that he wold to his pay,* anything he takes a fancy to 3.73 [OF. *paie*].

pay, *v.* pay 1.438, 3.31, 4.162; 1 *sg.pa.t.* **payd** 5.421; *pp.* **paide, payde,** pleased, content 1.230, 4.425, 5.436, 6.25; *therof am I paide,* I am pleased with it 2.283; *pay . . . on the cote,* beat 5.326, 421; *yll payde (of)* displeased (with) 6.181, 364 [OF. *payer*].

payment, *sb.* payment 6.324 [OF. *paiement*].

payn(e), *sb.* pain, torment, suffering 2.40, 4.40; *pl.* **panys** 5.141; *for Godys payn,* for (the sake of) God's (Christ's) passion 1.400, 4.539; *put vnto payn,* put to torment 2.547; *in payn of,* on pain of 3.424 [OF. *peine*].

paynt, *v.* make specious use of (words) 6.21; *intr.* talk speciously 4.210 [OF. *peindre, peint*].

paynt, *adj.* painted, decorated 4.28 [from prec.].

pak, *sb.* pack, gang 4.330, flock 4.424 [cf. MDu. *pak*].

panyere, *sb.* pannier, large basket 3.281 [OF. *paniere*].

panys. See **payn(e).**

pant, *v.* pant, breathe hard 5.238 [cf. OF. *pantoisier, -iser*].

paradise, paradyse, *sb.* Paradise 2.31, 5.46 [OF. *paradis*].

paramoure, *adv.* with passionate devotion, passionately 2.80 [OF. *par amour*].

parels, *sb.pl.* perils, dangers 1.299, 5.136 [OF. *peril*].

parloures, *sb.pl.* private rooms 2.133 [OF. *parlour*].

parte, *sb.* part, share 1.76, 3.251, 269, 270; *my parte haue I fun,* I've found out what I have to do 4.78 [OF. *part*].

parte, *v.* part company 5.329 [OF. *partir*].

party, *sb.* part; *most party,* most part (of) 2.49 [OF. *parti*].

partyng, *sb.* parting, leave-taking 3.267 [OF. *partir* + OE. *-ing*].

partryk, *sb.* partridge 3.234 [cf. OF. *pertrix*].

pas, *v.* pass 1.368; *intr.* pass, go 3.133, go by, wag 4.120; *pp.* **past** 3.1, 5.119; *pas of,* come out of 3.342 [OF. *passer*].

pase, *sb.* pace, rate of walking 6.417, going, way 3.492 [OF. *pas*].

past. See pas.

pasture, *sb.* pasture 4.181 [OF. *pasture*].

pasture, *v.* pasture, graze 3.105, 188 [OF. *pasturer*].

pate, *sb.* pate, head 3.121, 4.150, 6.300 [obscure].

paternoster, *sb.* Paternoster, Lord's Prayer 4.104 [L. *pater noster*].

patryarkes, *sb.pl.* patriarchs 4.692 [OF. *patriarche*].

peasse, *sb.* peace 3.400, silence 1.269, 5.74; *cry my peasse*, proclaim that I am under the king's protection 1.408 [OF. *pais, pes*].

peas(se), pes(e), *v.* calm, quell 5.245, quieten 1.413; *intr.* be silent, keep quiet 5.117; (as an exclamation) silence! 1.393, 3.369, 4.174, 5.91, 470, 6.43 [OF. *paiser*].

peasse, *adj.* quiet, silent; *be peasse youre dyn,* hush your row 1.3 [from OF. *pais, pes*].

pelt, *v.* go on striking 6.283 [uncertain].

pen, *sb.* ? a nickname for a small person 3.188 (note) [? OF. *pen(n)e*].

penneles, *adj.* penniless 3.33 [OE. *pennig* + -*lēas*].

penny, *sb.* penny 4.299, 732, 6.381; *penny doyll,* mass-penny 2.390 [OE. *pennig*].

people, *sb.* people 6.16 [AF. *people*].

pepe, *v.* peep, peer, pry 4.138, 221, 581, 590 [obscure].

perauentur, peraventure, *adv.* perhaps 2.503, 6.188 [OF. *par aventure*].

perchaunce, *adv.* perhaps 5.274 [AF. *par chance*].

perdé, perdy, *interj.* by God, indeed 2.512, 4.51, 426, 5.86, 182, 6.150 [OF. *par dé*].

perish, *v.* perish 2.94 [OF. *perir, periss-*].

perlous, *adj.* perilous 2.431 [OF. *perillous*].

perpetuall, *adj.* everlasting 3.297 [OF. *perpetuel*].

persaue, *v.* perceive 6.100 [OF. *perceivre*].

persew, *v.* persecute, torment 6.164; *persew on,* proceed with, press forward with 6.22-3, 449 [AF. *pursuer*].

persons, *sb.pl.* persons (of the Godhead) 2.2 [OF. *persone*].

peruyce, *sb.* a legal disputation among students at the Inns of Court 6.387 [OF. *parevis*].

pes(e). See peas(se).

pestell, *sb.* leg, haunch 3.216 [OF. *pestel*].

py, *sb.* pie 3.227 [cf. OF. *pie*].

pycher, *sb.* pitcher 3.155 [OF. *pich(i)er*].

pik, pyk, *sb.* pitch 2.127, 282 [OE. *pic*].

pyn, *sb.* pin (as something of little value) 2.364 [OE. *pinn*].

pynd, *pp.* penned, shut up 2.332 [OE. *pyndan*].

pyne, *sb.* suffering 2.437; *bi Godys pyne,* by God's (Christ's) Passion 2.227 [OE. *pīn*].

pypys, 3 *sg.pres.* squeaks, peeps 4.195; 3 *sg.pa.t.* piped 1.298 [OE. *pīpian,* OF. *piper*].

pystyll, *sb.* apostolic Epistle, or extract from it, read as part of the Mass 4.100, 5.205 [OE. *pistol,* L. *epistola*].

pyté, *sb.* pity 5.427 [OF. *pité*].

place, *sb.* place 2.29, 4.703 [OF. *place*].

play, *sb.* mirth, joy 3.11, 5.363, game, sport 6.344 [OE. *plega*].

play, *v.* play 4.447; *refl.* in *play the withall,* amuse yourself with (it) 3.475, 4.735 [OE. *p eg(i)an*].

playn, plane, *adj.* plain, clear 5.507; *adv.* plainly 3.177 [OF. *plain*].

plane, *sb.* plain, (level) ground 3.115 [OF. *plain*].

planettys, *sb.pl.* planets 2.345 [L. *planēta*].

platers, *sb.pl.* platters, wooden plates 4.547 [AF. *plater*].

pleas(se), *v.* please 6.189; *intr.* be pleased 1.438 [OF. *plaisir*].

plenté, *sb.* plenty, abundance 1.202, 3.400, 5.441; *as adv.* (in) plenty 2.146 [OF. *plenté*].

plete, *v.* plead 3.204 [OF. *plaitier*].

plo, plogh(e), *sb.* plough 1.36, 460, 2.534, 3.62 [OE. *plōg, plōh,* ON. *plógr*].

ployde, *pp.* ploughed 1.54 [from prec.].

plom, *adj.* perpendicular, straight down 2.520 [from OF. *plomme*].

po, *sb.* peacock 4.37 [OE. *pāwa,* ON. *pá*].

podyng, *sb.* pudding; *ther is a podyng in the pot,* there's business to attend to 1.386 [uncertain].

poecé-tayllys, *sb.pl.* stories in verse 5.204 [OF. *poesie* + OE. *talu*].

poetré, *sb.* poetry 3.386 [OF. *poetrie*].

poynt, ponte, *sb.* point; *in poynt for to, in ponte to,* on the point of 4.22, 629 [OF. *point(e)*].

poll, *sb.* head 3.245 [cf. MDu. *polle*].

poll, *v.* shear 3.154 [from prec.].

ponder, *v.* ponder, think 3.367, 4.131 [OF. *ponderer*].

ponte. See **poynt**.

poore, *adj.* poor 3.93, 4.12, 701: *adv.* piteously 4.195 [OF. *povre, poure*].

poor(e)ly, *adv.* humbly, meanly 4.645, 690 [prec. + OE. -*līce*].

pope, *sb.* Pope 5.263 [OE. *pāpa*].

pork, *sb.* pork 3.234 [cf. F. *porc*].

pose, *sb.* a cold in the head 3.423 [OE. *pos*].

pot(t), *sb.* pot 1.386, 4.317, 5.99 [OE. *pott*].

potell, *sb.* pottle, two quarts 3.484 [OF. *potel*].

pouerté, *sb.* poverty 3.16 [OF. *poverté, pouerté*].

powderd, *pp.* seasoned 3.216 [OF. *poudrer*].

pownde, *sb.* pound 3.146, 5.267 [OE. *pund*].

pray, *v.* pray, beg (for) 2.72, 242, 4.396; *pp.* **prayd(e)** 5.74, 6.361 [OF. *preier*].

prays, *sb.* praise; *prays at the partyng* 3.267 (note) [from next].

prase, *v.* praise 6.102 [OF. *preis(i)er*].

prat(t)y, *adj.* pretty 3.477, 4.607 [OE. *prættig*].

preche, *v.* preach 1.84, 3.390, 6.65 [OF *prech(i)er*].

preest, *sb.* priest; *gen.sg.* **preest** 1.104 [OE. *prēost*].

prelate, *sb.* prelate 6.154 [OF. *prélat*].

presence, *sb.* presence 4.205 [OF. *presence*].

present, *sb.* presence 6.158 [OF. *present*].

preue, prufe, *v.* prove 6.386, test, try (out) 2.460, 6.363 [OF. *prover, preuv-*, OE. *prōfian*].

preuey, *adj.* private; *preuey counsell*, privy council 5.196 [OF. *privé*].

preuely, *adv.* stealthily 4.270, 347 [prec. + OE. -*līce*].

pryce, *sb.* prize 6.81 [OF. *pris*].

pride, pryde, *sb.* pride 2.37, 543, 6.224, mother's pride, i.e. baby 5.336 [OE. *prȳdo*].

pryk, *sb.* point 6.263 [OE. *prica*].

prynce, *sb.* prince 3.335 [OF. *prince*].

procede, *v.* proceed 5.271 [OF. *proceder*].

processus, *sb.* story, pageant, (title of Play 2) [L. *prōcessus*].

profer, *v.* offer 4.249; *pp.* **profyrd** 1.107 [OF. *proffrir, proferer*].

promysed, 3 *pl.pa.t.* promised 5.120 [from sb. derived from L. *prōmissum*].

prophecy, *sb.* prophecy 4.674 [OF. *profecie*].

prophecy, *v.* prophesy 6.411; 3 *pl.pa.t.* **prophecyed** 4.676 **prophesyde** 3.377 [OF. *prophecier*].

prophetys, *sb.pl.* prophets 3.441, 4.692 [OF. *prophete*].

prouand, *sb.* fodder 1.45 [OF. *provende*].

prow, *sb.* profit, advantage 1.163 [OF. *prou*].

prowde, *adj.* proud 4.37; *make it as prowde*, behave as proudly 3.64; *superl.* **prowdist**, in *prowdist of pryde*, greatest in pride 2.543; *adv.* **prowdly** 2.17 [OE. *prūt, prūd; prūtlīce*].

prufe. See **preue**.

puf, *interj.* a representation of the sound of blowing 1.277 [echoic; cf. MDu. *puf*].

pull, *v.* pull 2.153, 5.85, pluck 1.311; *pull on*, pull away 1.30 [OE. *pullian*].

punyshid, *pp.* punished 1.373 [OF. *puniss-*, extended stem of *punir*].

purches, *sb.* illegal gains 6.161 [OF. *purchas*].

purpose, *sb.* purpose, intention 6.192 [OF. *purpos*].

purs, *sb.* purse, bag 3.30 [OE. *purs*].

purst, 1 *sg.pa.t.* put in my purse 6.381; *pp.* **purst**, shut up, put away (as in a purse) 3.209 [from prec.].

purvaye, *v.* provide 2.553 [AF. *purveier*].

purveance, *sb.* purveyance 4.33 [OF. *purveance*].

put, *v.* put 5.157; 3 *sg.pa.t.* **put** 2.21; *pp.* **put** 2.39, 547 [late OE. **pūtian*].

quarell, *sb.* quarry 1.367 [cf. OF. *quarrier*].

quart, *sb.* quart 3.272 [OF. *quarte*].

quart(e), qwarte, *sb.* good health 5.177; *in quarte*, in good health, safe and sound 1.368, 5.333 [from ON. *kyrt*, earlier **kwert*, neut. of *kyrr*]. .

quetstone, *sb.* whetstone 6.80 [OE. *hwetstān*].

qwaynt, qwant(t), *adj.* crafty, cunning 4.593, elegant, refined 4.647; *why make ye it so qwaynt*, why are you behaving so proudly 4.208 [OF. *queinte*].

qwake, *v.* tremble 1.338; *refl.* in *so me* (MS. *my*) *qwakys* 4.359 (note) [OE. *cwacian*].

qwant(t), qwarte. See qwaynt, quart(e).

qweasse, whese, v. wheeze 5.472, breathe 4.487 [ON. *hvæsa*].

qwelp, sb. whelp 3.425 [OE. *hwelp*].

qwhy, whi, why, adv.interrog. why 2.294, 4.56, 114; interj. (expressing surprise) why 6.179, 286 [OE. *hwī*].

qwite, qwyte, v. pay (back) 1.52, 315, 2.228; pp. qwytt 3.146, 4.497, 6.438; *qwite hym his mede*, pay him back 2.216 [OF. *quiter*].

rad, adv. quickly, soon 4.175 [OE. *hrade*].

radly, adv. quickly, promptly 5.4, 65 [OE. *hrædlīce*].

rafe, v. rave, talk wildly 3.273, 5.245, 6.394; 3 pl.pres. rauys, in *in thare wyttys that rauys*, who are mad enough 5.497; 3 sg.pres.subj. rafe, raves 1.424; *my wytt away rafys*, I'm going off my head 5.234 [OF. *raver*].

rayn, sb. rain 2.445; pl. ranys 4.128 [OE. *regn*].

rayn, v. rain 2.147; 3 pl.pres. renys, are raining down 2.351 [OE. *regnian*].

rayse, rase, v. raise 6.84, 100; 3 sg.pres. subj. rayse, raises, rouses 1.341; pp. rasyd, made to rise from one's seat 4.302, set going 5.76 [ON. *reisa*].

rake, sb. way, path; *on a rake*, at a run 5.65 [OE. *racu*].

ramyd, pp. beaten down, oppressed 4.16 [from OE. *ram(m)*].

ram-skyt, sb. ram-diarrhœa 2.217 [prec. + ON. *skita*].

ran. See ryn.

rang, 3 pl.pa.t. rang 4.180 [OE. *hringan*].

ranys. See rayn, sb.

rap, v. hit, strike 6.300 [cf. Sw. *rappa*].

rase, sb. rush (of water) 2.429; *on a rase*, rushing 3.451 [ON. *rás*].

rase, rauys. See rayse, rafe.

ravyn, sb. raven 2.479 [OE. *hræfn*].

raw, sb. company, audience 4.109; *on (a) raw*, in turn, all together 6.193, 319, 410 [OE. *rāw*].

rawnson, v. ransom, redeem 3.298 [OF. *ransonner*].

rebell, adj. rebellious 1.291 [OF. *rebelle*].

receyfe, resaue, v. receive, accept 1.432, 3.472 [ONF. *receivre*].

reche, v. reach, hand 3.242; 3 sg.pres.subj. reche, reaches 6.67 [OE. *ræcan*].

recorde, v. record, tell of 3.233, 495, testify 3.327 [OF. *recorder*].

red, 2 sg.imper. in *thou red*, get ready, put things in order 4.336 [OE. *(ge)rædan*].

red(e), reede, sb. advice, counsel; *can no rede*, (I) am at a loss 1.338; *do my reede*, take my advice 4.623, 6.201 [OE. *rēd*].

red(e), reede, reyde, v. advise 1.133, 257, 2.341, 4.467, 5.83, 6.332, 334, read 4.100, think 2.427, tell 5.380; *hard red* (infin.), heard tell 2.46 [OE. *rēdan*].

redé, redy, adj. ready 4.441, 559, 5.191, 6.319; (for emphasis before a past participle) *redy dyght*, ready and prepared, all ready 3.288 [OE. *rǣde + -ig*].

redres, v. redress, amend 6.258 [OF. *redrecier*].

reede. See red(e).

reepe, sb. handful 1.235 [OE. *reopa*].

refe, reyfe, v. rob of, deprive of (with double object) 4.19, 5.135, 236, 6.406 [OE. *rēafian*].

reherse, v. repeat 3.387 [OF. *rehercer*].

rehett, v. rate, rebuke 5.161 [obscure].

reyde, reyfe. See red(e), v., refe.

reyll, sb. reel, instrument on which yarn is wound 2.298 [OE. *hrēol*].

reyll, v. go round, circulate (of a drinking-cup) 3.270, reel, stagger 3.122, move quickly, behave recklessly, run riot 4.274, 5.326 [from prec.].

reyn(e), rene, v. reign, exercise power (said of Christ) 5.253, 6.119, 265; pres.p. reynand, prevailing, dominant 2.111; pp. renyd, reigned 6.226 [OF. *regner*].

rek, v. care 3.455; refl. trouble oneself 1.247; *rek of*, care about 4.307 [OE. *reccan*].

releasse, sb. discharge (from punishment), pardon 1.407 [OF. *reles*].

renabyll, adj. eloquent 6.110 [OF. *renable*].

rene, renyd, renys. See reyn(e), rayn, v.

renk, sb. man, knight 5.70 [OE. *rinc*].

renowne, sb. renown 5.50, 6.362; *good of renowne*, of good renown 5.430 [AF. *renoun*].

rent, sb. revenue, income 5.267, 6.162 [OF. *rente*].

repent, v. repent 2.81, 4.143 [OF. *repentir*].

repentance, *sb.* repentance 2.56 [OF. *repentance*].

reprefe, reprufe, *sb.* shame, disgrace 2.84, 4.576, reproof, rebuke 5.157; *for reprefe,* for shame 5.342, 355 [OF. *repro(u)ve,* AF. *repreove*].

reprefe, *v.* reprove, rebuke 4.30 [OF. *reprover,* AF. *repreov-*].

reprufe. See **repre ɔ,** *sb.*

requyryd, 3 *pl.pa.t.* sought, inquired after 3.447 [OF. *requerre, requier-*].

rerd, *sb.* roar 2.101 [OE. *reord*].

resaue. See **receyfe.**

reson, *sb.* reason 2.501, 4.502; *by reson* (cf. F. *par raison*), therefore 2.81 [OF. *reson*].

rest, *sb.* rest 1.326, 3.287, 4.8, 19 [OE. *rest*].

rest, ryst, *v.* rest 4.470, 630; *furth let it rest,* let it rest at that 3.279 [OE. *restan*].

restord(e), *pp.* restored, renewed 2.29, restored to a state of grace 3.496 [OF. *restorer*].

restorité, *sb.* restorative 3.238 [variant of OF. **restoratif, restauratif*].

reualacyon, *sb.* (divine) revelation 3.355 [OF. *revelacion*].

reuerence, *sb.* deference, respect 4.206 [OF. *reverence*].

rew, *v.* regret 2.202, 6.20; *impers.* grieve 6.165 [OE. *hrēowan*].

rewarde, *sb.* reward 5.426 [ONF. *reward*].

rewarde, *v.* reward 3.487 [ONF. *rewarder*].

rewarder, *sb.* rewarder 3.467 [prec. + OE. *-ere*].

rewle, 2 *sg.imper.* rule, guide 2.429 [OF. *reuler*].

rewthe, *sb.* (a) pity 4.418 [OE. *hrēow* + *-þ*].

ryall, *adj.* royal 5.70, 502 [OF. *rial*].

rychere, *adj.compar.* richer 4.244; *superl.* **rychest** (MS. *ryches*) 3.15 [OE. *rīce,* OF. *riche*].

ryches. See **ryke.**

ryches, *sb.* wealth 3.401 [OF. *richesse*].

rychest. See **rychere.**

ryde, *v.* ride 4.172; *pres.p.* **ridyng** 6.151; *sb.* **rydyng,** expedition on horseback 5.417 [OE. *rīdan*].

ryfe, *v.* tear 1.153, 5.89, break 2.399, 4.83; *pp. as adj.* **ryffen,** torn 1.141 [ON. *rīfa*].

ryfe, *adv.* often 3.96 [OE. *rȳfe*].

ryffen. See **ryfe,** *v.*

right, *sb.* right(s) 3.460, 5.236 [OE. *riht*].

right, *adj.* right 4.182, true 2.471; *good*

right, quite right 5.442; *not right in his gere,* not in his right mind 6.182 [OE. *riht*].

right, *adv.* correctly 1.222, 2.139, just, right, exactly 1.319, 2.513, 4.432, 6.58, very 3.269, 4.377, (with neg.) at all 2.96, 524, 5.125; *as right,* right away 1.49 [OE. *rihte*].

ryke, *sb.* kingdom 3.92; *pl.* **ryches** 5.470 [ON. *ríki,* OE. *rīce*].

ryn, ron, *v.* run 1.147, 390, 2.101, 277, 3.428, 433, 4.467, 5.313, 6.82; 3 *sg.pa.t.* **ran** 5.110; *pp.* **ryn** 4.108, 160, **run** 4.256; *ran with spere,* rode or jousted with spear 5.110 [OE. *rinnan*].

ryng, *sb.* ring 6.340 [OE. *hring*].

rype, *v.* ransack 4.515 [OE. *rȳpan*].

ryse, *v.* rise, get up 1.182, 4.299, 377, be elated 5.264, result 1.163; 3 *sg.pa.t.* **rose** 4.519; *pres.p.* **rysand** 5.264; *pp.* **rysen** 2.442; *ryse vp,* stand up 6.416 [OE. *rīsan*].

ryst. See **rest,** *v.*

ro, *sb.* rest, peace; (in asseveration) *as euer haue I ro,* as I hope to have peace 2.237 [OE. *rōw,* ON. *ró*].

rob, *v.* rob 4.527 [OF. *rob(b)er*].

robers, *sb.pl.* robbers 3.52 [OF. *rob(b)ere*].

roys, *sb.* rose, ruse, *v.* boast 6.247, praise 1.95, 3.234, 6.33, 244 [ON. *hrósa*].

rok, *sb.* distaff 2.338, 4.389 [cf. ON. *rokkr*].

rok, rokyn (MS. *rekyn*), *v.* rock, shake 6.330; *intr.* behave violently, run riot 5.508 [late OE. *roccian*].

romoure, *sb.* rumour, talk 5.76 [OF. *rumour*].

ron. See **ryn.**

roode, *sb.* cross; (in asseveration) *by the roode* 4.182, 236, 374 [OE. *rōd*].

rope. *sb.* rope 1.461 [OE. *rāp*].

rore, *v.* roar, cry loudly 5.386 [OE. *rārian*].

rose. See **ryse, roys.**

rost, *sb.* roast meat 1.422, 3.224 [OF. *rost*].

rott, *sb.* (the) rot, a liver disease in sheep 3.26 [cf. Icel. *rot*].

rot(t)yn, roton, *adj.* rotten 3.221, 5.494; *as sb.* 6.125 [ON. *rotinn*].

route, rowte, *sb.* company, crowd 5.309; *on a route,* in a body, in a mass 2.305 [OF. *route*].

rownde, *adj.* round 4.278, 5.445 [OF. *round*].

rowne, *v.* whisper, speak in a whisper 4.263, 5.4, 6.134 [OE. *rūnian*].

rowte. See **route.**

rude, *adj.* rough, violent 4.128 [OF. *rude*].
rugh, *adj.* rough 4.101 [OE. *rūh*].
run, ruse. See **ryn, roys.**

sabate-day, *sb.* Sabbath day 6.85 [L. *sabbatum,* OF. *sabbat* + OE. *dæg*].
sacrifice, *sb.* sacrifice 1.71 [OF. *sacrifice*].
sad, *adj.* sad 4.667; *adv.* heavily, hard 4.386 [OE. *sæd*].
sadly, *adv.* deeply 3.260 [OE. *sæd* + *-līce*].
safe, saue, *v.* save, keep safe 2.309, 3.307, 5.190; *pp.* **sauyd** 2.517; *youre worship to safe,* saving your reverence (apologetic phrase) 5.247 [OF. *sa(u)ver*].
safe, *adj.* safe 1.429; *vowche . . . safe,* vouchsafe, grant 1.449 [OF. *sauf*].
sagh. See **se(e), v.**
say, *v.* say 1.32, 2.183, 3.60, 4.29; 1 *sg.pres.* **sayn** 5.22, 466; 1,3 *sg.pa.t.* **saide** 1.34, 2.280, **sayd(e)** 3.157, 4.680; 3 *pl.* **sayd(e)** 4.423, 5.123; *pres.p.* **sayng** 3.381; *pp.* **sayd(e)** 2.302, 3.96; *say . . . nay,* refuse 2.385, 4.45; *says . . . agane, agane says,* gainsays 3.60, 4.29; *say agaynt,* deny it 6.19; *says he oght agane,* does he say anything in reply 6.136 [OE. *secgan*].
sayf, saue, *prep.* save, except 2.106, 5.412 [OF. *sauf*].
sayll, *sb.* sail 2.153; *on sayll,* a-sailing 3.258 [OE. *segl; seglian*].
sayn. See **say.**
sayn, sane, *v.* bless 6.340; *sane . . . from,* protect from 3.50-1 [OE. *segnian*].
saynt, *v.* play the saint 4.209 [from OF. *saint*].
sake, *sb.* in *for . . . sake,* for (one's) sake 3.297, 5.67; *for thi sake,* for you 1.250; *for syn sake,* because of sin 2.88; *for that lad sake,* because of that lad 5.304 [OE. *sacu*; cf. ON. *fyrir sakir*].
salt, *adj.* salt 4.546 [OE. *salt*].
sam, *v.* take hold of, collect (things) 2.320 [OE. *samnian*].
sam, *adv.* together 4.620; *all sam (togeder),* all together 1.446, 2.292, 530, 3.179, 499 [OE. *æt samne*; cf. ON. *allir saman*].
same, some, *adj.* same 1.51, 4.178; *pron.* in *of the same,* in the same way 1.129; *that same,* that same (song) 3.415; *the self and the some,* the selfsame, the very same 4.202 [ON. *samr*].
sand, *sb.* sand; shore, land 2.75 [OE. *sand*].
sane. See **sayn.**

W.P.—O

sang, sangre, song, *sb.* song 3.305, 413, 430, 4.183, 667 [OE. *sang, song,* ON. *sǫngr*].
sant, *sb.* saint 2.555, 3.445, 4.118, 5.236 [OF. *saint*].
sare, sore, *adj.* in pain 4.231, grieved, distressed 3.9, 4.531; *sb.* pain 4.444; *adv.* sorely, severely, bitterly 1.187, 2.91, 4.509, 5.155 [OE. *sār; sāre*].
saue, sauyd. See **safe, v., sayf.**
sauyoure, *sb.* Saviour 4.719 [OF. *sauveour*].
saull, *sb.* soul 1.254, 2.390, 3.260, 5.407; *gen.sg.* **saulis** 1.83; *pl.* **saules** 3.283, **sawlys** 3.77 [OE. *sāwol*].
saunce, *prep.* without; *saunce fayll,* without fail, for certain 3.112, 5.404 [OF. *sans*].
saw. See **se(e), v.**
saw, *v.* sow (seed) 1.124; 1 *sg.pa.t.* **sew** 1.200 [OE. *sāwan*].
sawe, *sb.* speech, words 1.68, 3.163, 5.162 [OE. *sagu*].
sawlys. See **saull.**
sawse, *sb.* sauce 3.237 [OF. *sausse*].
sawsed, *pp.* sauced 3.215 [from prec.].
scapethryft, *sb.* spendthrift 1.384 [ONF. *escaper* + ON. *þrift*].
scremyd, 3 *sg.pa.t.* screamed, gave a shrill cry 3.310 [OE. **scræman*].
se(e), *sb.* sea 2.434; *bi see and bi sand, on se and bi side, thrugh all sees and soundys* (MS. *sandys*), everywhere 2.75, 542, 5.269 [OE. *sǣ*].
se(e), *v.* see 1.307, 7.96, 191, 5.168; *pass.* in *be seyn,* appear 1.121, 5.120, 175; 2 *sg.pres.* **seys** 4.305; 3 *sg.* **sees** 6.82; 2 *pl.* **seys** 5.61; 1, 2 *sg.pa.t.* **sagh** 3.180, 4.111, 606, **saw** 4.617; *pp.* **seyn,** watched over, protected 5.291, **sene** 3.368, 4.693; *sagh thou awre of Daw,* have you seen Daw anywhere 4.111; *se ye awre of Mak,* do you see Mak anywhere 4.364; (pleonastic) *se . . . in sight, se . . . with ee (eyn),* see 3.340, 4.473, 5.102 [OE. *sēon*].
seasse, sesse, *v.* cease, stop 1.406, 5.79, 87, 6.222; *pp.* **cest** 2.451; *of . . . seasse,* cease from, stop 1.270 [OF. *cesser*].
securly, *adv.* certainly, assuredly 2.38, 372 [OE. *sicorlīce*].
sede, seyde, *sb.* seed 1.124, offspring 3.469 [OE. *sēd*].
sees, seyll. See **se(e), ceyll.**

seymland, *sb.* looks, demeanour 2.211
[OF. *semblant*].

seyn. See **se(e),** *v.*

seyn, *adj.* seen, plain, evident 3.14, 6.121
[OE. *gesēne*].

seyr, *adj.* different, various; *into seyr
countré,* to different lands 2.487 [ON. *sér*].

seys. See **se(e),** *v.*

sek, *sb.* sack 3.164 [ON. *sekkr*].

sek-band, *sb.* string for tying round the
neck of a sack 3.167 [prec. + ON. *band*].

seke, *v.*[1] seek (out), look for 3.320, 4.655,
6.84; 2 *pl.imper.* **sekys** 5.204; 1,3 *pl.pa.t.*
soght 4.398, 5.123; *pp.* **soght** 2.157,
3.415, 4.719 [OE. *sēcan*].

seke, *v.*[2] sack 3.175 [from ON. *sekkr*].

seke, *adj.* sick 2.61, 4.485 [OE. *sē(o)c*].

sekenes, *sb.* sickness 4.227 [OE. *sē(o)cnes*].

sekir, *adj.* sure 1.295 [OE. *sicor*].

selcouthly, *adv.* strangely, wonderfully
5.25 [OE. *seldcūþ* + *-līce*].

seldom, *adv.* seldom 4.229 [OE. *seldan*].

self, *adj.* self; *as sb.* in *hisself,* he himself
6.35, 260; *the self and the some,* the selfsame, the very same 4.202 [OE. *self*].

sely. See **celé.**

seme, *v.impers.* befits, becomes 3.457,
seems, appears 3.391; *pers.* 6.289 (note)
[ON. *sóma, sœmdi*].

sen, syn, *cj.* since 1.182, 2.73, 3.161,
4.621, 5.146, 6.57; *sen that, syn that*
1.166, 6.236; *prep.* since 1.105, 4.382,
6.59 [OE. *siþþan*].

send, *v.* send 2.207; *pp.* **send** 2.254, 3.395,
sent 4.738 [OE. *sendan*].

sene. See **se(e),** *v.*

serkyll, *sb.* circle 4.278 [OF. *cercle*].

sermonyng, *sb.* preaching, sermonizing
1.86 [from OF. *sermoner*].

seruand, seruant, *sb.* servant 2.65, 110,
4.154 [OF. *servant*].

serue, *v.* serve 1.129; *seruys of noght,* is of
no use, no avail 4.93 [OF. *servir*].

seruyce, seruyse, *sb.* service 1.82, 3.200,
6.383 [late OE. *serfise,* from OF. *servise*].

seson, *sb.* season; *a seson,* for a while 4.498
[OF. *se(i)son*].

sesse. See **seasse.**

sesse, *v.* seize 5.111 [OF. *seisir*].

set(t), *v.* set, put, place 3.213, 4.216, 5.319,
6.317, 409, lay (table) 3.196; *refl.* seat
oneself, sit 2.18, 340; *pp.* **sett,** seated
4.298, settled 6.60; *set(t) ... on,* set ...
to 1.274, 3.268; *bi all men set I not a fart,*

I shan't care a damn for any man 1.369;
sett I my mynde, I make up my mind, re-
solve 3.37; *sett the on sayll,* set you a-sailing, i.e. start you off 3.258; *sett all on
seuen,* made all the world in seven days
3.487, 4.738; *set all on sex and seuen,* play
havoc 5.128; *I sett by no good,* I think it of
no importance 5.469; *settys not a fle-wyng
bi,* doesn't care a hang for 6.94 [OE. *settan*].

sete, *sb.* seat, throne 3.384, 6.362 [ON.
sæti].

seuen, seven, sevyn, *adj.* seven 1.206,
2.13, 423, 3.38, 5.128, seven days 3.487,
4.738 [OE. *seofon*].

sevenfold, *adv.* sevenfold 1.373 [OE.
seofonfald].

sew. See **saw.**

sewrly, sure, *adv.* surely 2.282, certainly,
indeed 3.380 [OF. *s(e)ur* + OE. *-līce*].

sex, *adj.* six 1.206, 2.57, 5.128 [OE. *sex*].

shak, *v.* shake 5.499; 3 *sg.pa.t.* **shakyd,**
quaked 3.316; *pp.* **shakyn** 3.170 [OE.
scacan].

shakyls, *sb.pl.* shackles 4.72 [OE. *sceacel*].

shal(l), *v.auxil.* shall, will, must; 1,2,3
sg.pres. **shal** 2.103, 121, 138; 1,2,3 *pl.*
shall 2.24, 179, 332; 1,3 *sg.pa.t.*
shuld 2.76, 390; 1,2 *pl.* **shuld** 2.325,
416; with ellipsis of foll. verb, as 'go'
1.374, 5.237, 'have' 2.227 [OE. *scal,
scolde*].

shame, *sb.* shame 4.377, disgrace, ignominy,
harm 2.301, 6.148, 163, shameful conduct, wicked behaviour 5.343 [OE.
scamu].

shame, *v.* be ashamed 6.445 [OE. *scamian*].

shank, *sb.* leg 1.186, 4.565 [OE. *scanca*].

sharp, *adj.* sharp, violent 2.350, 356 [OE.
scearp].

she, *pron.* 3 *sg.fem.* she 2.186, 4.235, 240;
sho (MS. *so*) 4.239 [see *NED.*].

shedys, 2 *sg.pres.* shed, spill 5.375;
1 *sg.pa.t.* **shed** 5.470 [OE. *scēadan*].

shefe, sheyfe, *sb.* sheaf 1.192, 251 [OE.
scēaf].

sheyn, *adj.* bright, shining 5.292 [OE.
scēne].

sheynd, *v.* destroy 4.640 [OE. *scendan*].

sheld, *v.* shield 2.301 [OE. *sceoldan*].

shepard, *sb.* shepherd 3.92, 4.288 [OE.
scēpherde].

shepe, *sb.* sheep 3.24, 4.292 [OE. *scēp*].

shepe-mete, *sb.* a meal of mutton 4.324
[prec. + OE. *mete*].

shepe-tayll, *sb.* sheep's tail, i.e. sheep 3.109 [OE. *scēp* + *tægl*].
shew, *v.* show 3.443, 6.357; 1 *sg.pa.t.* **shewed** 2.82 [OE. *scēawian*].
shyft, *sb.* means, effort; *make better shyft,* make better efforts 4.285 [cf. ON. *skipti*].
shyne, *v.* shine 2.9, 453; 3 *sg.pa.t.* **shone** 3.323 [OE. *scīnan*].
ship, shyp, *sb.* ship 2.119, 3.145 [OE. *scip*].
shyre, *sb.* shire 4.253 [OE. *scīr*].
shyre, *adv.* brightly, clearly 1.317 [OE. *scīre*].
sho. See **she.**
shoyn, shone, *sb.pl.* shoes 1.153, 2.353, 4.62 [OE. *scō(h)*].
shope, 3 *sg.pa.t.* shaped, made 1.174 [OE. *sceppan*].
shorne, *pp.* cut, reaped 1.201, 241 [OE. *sceran*].
short, *adj.* short, brief 3.79 [OE. *scort*].
showre, *sb.* attack (of pain), pang 4.96; *pl.* showers 2.350 [OE. *scūr*].
showte, *v.* shout 6.180 [cf. ON. *skúta,* sb.].
shrew(e), *sb.* rascal, villain 1.30, 380, 4.151, 210, 221, 453, 6.359; *pl.* 1.327, 4.138 [OE. *scrēawa, scrǣwa*].
shrew, *v.* curse 1.341, 388, 3.251, 276, 6.169 [from prec.].
shrogys, *sb.pl.* bushes, underwood 4.455 [obscure].
shuld. See **shal(l).**
sich, such, *adj. and pron.* such 1.201, 2.400, 4.83, 5.79, 6.15, 103, such as 3.368; *sich . . . none* none such 3.326, 339; *and sich,* and suchlike, and the like 4.203 [OE. *swilc*].
side, syde, *sb.* side 2.137, seaside, shore 2.542; *on syde,* aside 6.223; (in asseveration) *bi Codys sydys,* by God's sides 1.459 [OE. *sīde*].
sygh, *v.* sigh 4.74 [OE. *sīcan, sīhte*].
sight, syght, *sb.* sight 1.209, 4.284, 473, glance 2.469; *pl.* sights, apparitions 4.137; *before his sight, in sight,* before his eyes, in his presence 2.48, 555, 3.502 [OE. *gesiht, sihþ*].
syluer, *sb.* silver 5.440 [OE. *silfor*].
symple, *adj.* simple 2.173 [OF. *simple*].
syn(e). See **sen, sithen.**
syn, *sb.* sin 2.38, 5.343; *gen.sg.* **syn** 2.88 [OE. *synn*].
syn, *v.* sin 2.37; 3 *pl.pres.* **syn** (with sg.

subject) 2.49; 3 *sg.pa.t.* **synde** 5.211 [from prec.].
syng, *v.* sing 4.103, 186, sing ruefully, bewail, lament 3.32, 6.129, 375; *pp.* **songyn** 3.269 [OE. *singan*].
synk, *v.* sink 3.245; *pp.* **sonken** 3.261 [OE. *sincan*].
syppys, 3 *sg.pres.* sips 3.252 [obscure].
sir, syr(e), *sb.* lord, master 2.396, 4.159, 5.103, father 3.181; *my syre of flesh and blode,* my own father 1.389; (as polite form of address) sir 2.294, 336; (pref. to names) 6.2, 94 [OF. *sire*].
sit, sytt, *v.* sit 3.191, 4.49, 495, 6.352; 1 *sg.pres.* **syttys,** (I) sit 6.155; *impers.* in *it syttys,* it is fitting 5.408; *sit downe,* rest content, put up (with) 2.247 [OE. *sittan*].
sithen, sythen, syne, *adv.* afterwards 1.103, 2.32, 3.100, 4.613, 6.74; *or syne,* ere long 2.228; *vnto syne,* till later 3.198, 4.148 [OE. *siþþan*].
skabbid, *adj.* scabby 1.248 [from ON. **skabbr*].
skayll, *sb.* drinking-cup 3.249 [ON. *skál*].
skalys, *sb.pl.* skittles, ninepins 6.408 [variant of ME. *kayles*; cf. MDu. *kegel, keyl-*].
skalp, *sb.* head, skull 5.353 [cf. ON. *skálpr*].
skant, *sb.* scarcity 2.198 [from ON. *skamt*].
skap(e), *v.* escape 1.313, 5.484, 6.334; *pp.* **skapyd** 4.316 [ONF. *escaper*].
skar, *v.* scare, frighten 6.301; *pp.* **skard** 4.289, 648 [ON. *skirra*].
skarthis, *sb.pl.* shards, fragments 3.160 [ON. *skarð*].
skaunce, skawnce, *sb.* joke, jest 1.401, 6.353 [from ME. *ascaunce, askaunse*].
skawde, *sb.* scold 4.596 [ON. *skáld*].
skelp, *sb.* slap, blow, 2.323, 3.424 [obscure].
skill, skyll, *sb.* what is right or reasonable 1.260, 272, cause, reason 6.357; *as it is skill,* as is reasonable 2.334; *good skyll,* very reasonable 3.199 [ON. *skil*].
skyn, *sb.* skin 5.85, 6.400; *outt of skyn* 4.360 (note) [ON. *skinn*].
skyp, *v.* skip 3.115 [cf. MSw. *skuppa*].
sklanders, 2 *sg.pres.* slander 4.461 [OF. *esclandrer*].
skorde, *pp.* scored, cut 3.236 [ON. *skora*].
skore, *sb.* score, twenty 5.319, twenty pounds 4.631 [ON. *skor*].

skorne, *sb.* scorn, derision 3.85, 5.57, insult 4.452, 6.138 [OF. *escarn*].

skorne, *v.* scorn, despise; *with thy gawdys ... we skorne*, we scorn your pranks 4.176–7 [OF. *escarnir*].

skreme, *sb.* scream, high-pitched cry 3.328 [from OE. **scrǣman*].

skryke, *v.* shriek 2.232 [ON. *skrækja*].

slayn. See **slo.**

slake, *v.* assuage 3.299; *slake ... from*, relieve from 4.678–9 [OE. *slacian*].

siane. See **slo.**

slape, *adj.* smooth, in *slape of thrift* 1.415 (note) [ON. *sleipr*].

slefe, *sb.* sleeve 4.28, 396 [OE. *slēfe*].

sleght, slyght, *sb.* skill 2.137, trick, ruse, stratagem 4.433, 5.121 [ON. *slœgð*].

sleght, *adj.* mean, base 5.235 [ON. *sléttr*, earlier **sleht-*].

slepe, *sb.* sleep; *on slepe*, asleep 6.423 [OE. *slēp*].

slepe, *v.* sleep 3.102, 4.254; *go slepe*, go and sleep 4.345; *sb.* **slepyng**, in *on slepyng*, asleep 1.348 [OE. *slēpan*].

slete, *sb.* sleet 4.61 [OE. **slēt*].

slyght. See **sleght**, *sb.*

slyke, *adj.* such 3.94; *none slyke*, (there is) none such (as she is) 2.233 [ON. *slíkr*].

slip, *v.* strip, empty (a spindle) 2.364 [cf. MLG. *slippen*; *NED.* s. Slip, *v.*[1], Slipe, *v.*[2]].

slythys, 3 *sg.pres.* slips, slides away 4.122 [OE. *slīdan*].

slo, *v.* slay 1.363, 6.271; 3 *sg.pres.* **sloys** 1.372; 3 *sg.pres.subj.* **slo** 1.371; 2 *pl. imper.* **slo** 5.308, **sloes** 6.196; 1 *sg.pa.t.* **slogh** 1.395; 3 *sg.* **slo** 1.434; *pp.* **slayn** 2.307, 6.436, **slane** 3.61, **slone** 3.26 [OE. *slēan*, ON. *slá*].

slogh. See **slo.**

sloghe, *sb.* slough, skin; *my hart out of sloghe* 4.385 (note) [cf. LG. *sluwe*, *slu*].

sloys. See **slo.**

slokyn, *v.* suppress, do away with 4.677 [ON. *slokna*].

slone. See **slo.**

sloth, *sb.* sloth 2.53 [OE. *slēwþ*, infl. by *slāw*].

small, *adj.* small, humble, 2.90, fine (of musical notes) 3.306, 418; *adv.* in a small voice, feebly 1.298, fine 5.99 [OE. *smæl*; *smale*].

smart, *adv.* sharply, severely 3.253 [from OE. *smeart*].

smeke, *sb.* smoke 1.286 [OE. *smēc*].

smylde, 3 *sg.pa.t.* smelled 4.549 [early ME. *smellen*, *smüllen*].

smyle, *v.* smile 2.215 [OE. **smīlan*; cf. OHG. *smīlan*, Sw. *smila*].

smyte, *v.* smite 2.215, 6.305; 3 *sg.pa.t.* **smote** 6.413 [OE. *smītan*].

smoke, *sb.* smoke 1.277 [OE. *smoca*].

smoked, 3 *sg.pa.t.* smoked 1.318 [OE. *smocian*].

smote. See **smyte.**

snaw, *sb.* snow 4.61 [OE. *snāw*].

snek, *sb.* latch 4.306 [obscure].

snowte, *sb.* snout (used derisively to mean 'nose') 4.585 [cf. MDu. *snūte*, *snuut*].

so, *adv.* so, thus 2.391, 396, and so, then 6.416, (that being) so 6.180; (intensifying a verb) 2.277, 357; (intensifying an adj. or adv.) 2.165, 3.67, 253; (before an adj.) such (a) 1.358; (in adjurations) so 4.550, 560, 561; (as an exclamation of surprise) 3.246, 4.588; *so ... as* 3.67–8, 323, 4.701; *so as*, as well as 3.477 [OE. *swā*].

soceres, socour(e), *sb.* help, aid 2.157, 254, 6.85 [OF. *socours*].

sod, *sb.* sod, clod 2.58 [MLG., MDu. *sode*].

sodan, *adj.* sudden, unexpected 4.137; *adv.* **sodanly** 5.181 [OF. *soudain*].

soferan, sufferan, *sb.* sovereign 2.92, 5.499; *adj.* 4.719 [OF. *soverain*].

soft, *adv.* softly 4.484, 6.204, at a leisurely pace 6.211; *compar. adj.* **softer**, gentler 1.162 [OE. *sōfte*].

sogh, sowe, *sb.* sow 3.216, 274 [OE. *sugu*, *sū*].

soght. See **seke**, *v.*[1].

soyn(e), sone, *adv.* soon, quickly 1.132, 2.21, 479, 4.478, 6.72; *full sone*, straightway, very quickly 2.147, 4.50 [OE. *sōna*].

sold, *pp.* sold 3.146, 333 [OE. *sellan*].

sole, *sb.* (level) place 2.391 [OF. *sole*].

som, *adj.* some 2.157, 6.218; *pron.sg.* someone 4.509, something 6.174; *pl.* some 1.20 [OE. *sum*].

some. See **same.**

somkyns, *adj.* some kind of 4.708 [OE. *sum + cynn*].

somwhat, *sb.* something 3.308, 4.146, 5.289, 6.124 [OE. *sum + hwæt*].

somwhere, *adv.* somewhere 1.348 [OE. *sum + hwēr*].

son, *sb.*[1] son 3.356, 4.260, lad 6.389; *pl.* **sonnes**, sons 2.141 [OE. *sunu*].

son, *sb.*[2] sun 2.6, 5.380 [OE. *sunne*].

sond, *sb.* messenger, envoy 4.202; *pl.* messages 5.7 [OE. *sand*, *sond*].

sonder, *adv.* in in *sonder*, asunder, apart 2.407, 5.89, separately 1.155 [OE. *onsundran*; cf. ON. *í sundr*].

sone, song, songyn, sonken, sonnes. See **soyn(e), sang, syng, synk, son,** *sb.*[1].

soper, *sb.* supper 4.166 [OF. *soper*].

sore. See **sare.**

sory, *adj.* sad, wretched 2.61, 264, 5.25 [OE. *sārig*].

soro(w), *sb.* sorrow, pain 1.33, 2.206, 4.66, 5.388, 6.63 [OE. *sorg*].

sotelté, *sb.* craftiness, cunning 6.97 [OF. *s(o)utilté*].

soth(e), *adj.* true 2.512, 4.214; *sb.* truth 2.246, 4.468, 6.440 [OE. *sōþ*].

sothely, sothlé, sothly, *adv.* truly 2.496, 3.374, 5.211 [OE. *sōþlīce*].

sothen, *pp. as sb.* boiled meat 3.224 [OE. *sēoðan*].

sothren, *adj.* Southern 4.215 [OE. *sūþerne*].

soundys (MS. *sandys*), *sb.* sounds, straits 5.269 [OE., ON. *sund*].

sourmontyng (MS. *Iourmontyng*), *pres.p.* surmounting, excelling 5.11 [OF. *sourmonter*].

southe, *sb.* south 2.477 [OE. *sūþ*].

sow, *v.* pain, grieve 4.98; *intr.* tingle with pain 6.327 [obscure].

sowde, 3 *sg.pa.t.* soughed, made a rushing sound 3.312 [OE. *swōgan*].

sowe. See **sogh.**

sowked, 1 *sg.pa.t.* sucked, had suck (from) 6.57 [OE. *sūcan*].

sowll, *sb.* sauce, relish 3.152 [OE. *sufel*].

sowre, *adv.* bitterly, severely 4.98 [from OE. *sūr*].

sowre-loten, sowre-lottyn, *adj.* sour-looking 4.102, 6.123 [OE. *sūr*, ON. *súrr* + ON. *láta*].

space, *sb.* space, room 3.123, space of time, while 2.337; *in this space*, now 2.552 [OF. *espace*].

spak(e). See **speke.**

spar, *sb.* spar, piece of timber 2.130 [MLG., MDu. *spar(re)*].

spar, *v.* fasten, secure 4.327; *pp.* **spard** 6.371; *out to spar*, to shut out 2.128 [OE. *gesparrian*].

spare, *v.* spare 2.379, 5.312, refrain from

using 6.309; *pp.* **sparde** 5.359 [OE. *sparian*].

spart, spare it, in *Godys forbot thou spart*, God forbid you should spare it, 3.271 [prec. + OE. *hit*].

spede, *sb.* help(er) 3.295; *goode spede*, quickly 4.462 [OE. *spēd*].

spede, *v.* speed, help 1.58, 4.118; (used sarcastically of the Devil) 1.4, 151, 5.226; *God spede*, God speed (you) 2.190; *He spede youre pase*, may He speed your going, speed you on your way 3.492; *intr.* fare, prosper, in *ill myght thou spede*, bad luck to you 1.165; *yll spede othere good that she wyll do* 4.238 (note); *refl.* go quickly, get a move on 5.274, 315 [OE. *spēdan*].

speke, *v.* speak 2.383, 3.66; 3 *sg.pa.t.* **spak(e)** 3.315, 4.479; *pp.* **spoken** 3.262, 4.321, **spokyn** 4.700; *speke on*, go on and speak 6.145, 148 [OE. *sp(r)ecan*].

spell, *v.* speak 3.412, 5.53 [OE. *spellian*].

spend, *v.* use 2.130; *pp.* **spent**, shed 5.391 [OE. *spendan*].

spendyng, *sb.* money 4.173, 277 [OE. *spendung*].

spent. See **spend.**

spere, *sb.* spear 5.110, 252 [OE. *spere*].

spy, *v.* watch, observe, 6.448; *intr.* 4.343; *pp.* **spied**, **spyde**, discovered 4.332, 5.188, kept watch 5.152; **spyde with**, detected in 2.544–5 [OF. *espier*].

spill, spyll, *v.* destroy, kill 5.258, 6.30, injure 4.540 [OE. *spillan*].

spyn, *v.* spin 2.238, 4.298; *pp.* **spon** 2.337 [OE. *spinnan*].

spyndill, *sb.* spindle (used in spinning) 2.364 [OE. *spinel*].

spyrd, 2 *pl.pa.t.* asked 6.47 [OE. *spyrian*].

spitus, spytus, *adj.* spiteful, 2.416, cruel 2.455, 4.57 [shortened from AF. *despitous*].

spoken, spokyn, spon. See **speke, spyn.**

sponys, *sb.pl.* spoons 3.231 [OE. *spōn*].

spott, *sb.* disgrace 4.452 [cf. LG. *spot*].

spouse, *sb.* spouse, wife 4.513 [OF. *spuse*]

spray, *v.* spring, take rise 5.219 [obscure].

spryng, *v.* spring up, begin 3.29, spread, extend 5.109 [OE. *springan*].

sprote, *sb.* shoot, sprout 1.290 [OE. *sprota*].

spruse, *sb.* spruce fir; *spruse cofer*, coffer made of spruce fir 3.466 [alteration of AF. *Prus*].

spurd, *adj.* spurred; *nawder bowted ne spurd*, neither booted nor spurred 6.147 [from OE. *spura*].

spurne, *v.* spurn, strike (the toes) against something 4.144 [OE. *spurnan*].

sqwyere, *sb.* squire 5.20 [OF. *esquier*].

stabyll, *adj.* stable, secure 3.375, 6.112 [OF. *stable*].

staf, *sb.* staff 2.381, shepherd's crook 4.169 [OE. *stæf*].

stak, *sb.* stack; *broght in stak*, stacked 1.241 [ON. *stakkr*].

stald, stold, *pp.* stuck 2.525, 6.202 [OF. *estaller*; cf. OE. *forþsteallian*].

stalk, *v.* stride 4.48, walk softly, cautiously 4.270, 347 [cf. OE. *bestealcian, stealcung*].

stall, *sb.* place, station 1.375, 465, 2.345, throne 5.111 [OE. *stall*].

stamerd, 3 *pl.pa.t.* staggered 4.129 [OE. *stamerian*].

stand(e), *v.* stand 1.27, 4.232, stand still 1.56, be 3.205, 5.92; 1 *sg.pa.t.* **stode** 2.425, **stud** 5.427; 3 *pl.* **stod** 4.129; *pres.p.* **standyng**, being 2.416; *for me ye stand none aw*, you do not stand in awe of me 1.31; *howsoeuer it standys*, however matters stand 2.210; *by stand*, stand by, assist 3.168; *standys . . . owte*, stands out, shines out 3.322; *as it standys*, as matters stand 4.12; *sb.* **standyng** 4.307 [OE. *standan*].

stanys, stank. See **stone, stynk.**

stard, 1 *sg.pa.t.* glared, looked fiercely 5.427 [OE. *starian*].

stark, *adj.* stiff 2.268 [OE. *stearc*].

starne, sterne, *sb.* star 2.8, 3.321, 4.654; *the seven starnes*, the seven planets 2.423 [ON. *stjarna*].

start, *v.* start, flinch 5.179; 3 *sg.pa.t.* in *start vp*, started up, came suddenly into view 6.405 [OE. *styrtan*, *stertan*].

state, *sb.* state, position 2.443; rank 6.426; *in state*, ready 4.152 [OF. *estat*, L. *status*].

sted, *pp.* placed 6.53; *hard sted*, hard put to it 2.199, 4.74 [ON. *steðja, staddr*].

stede, *sb.* place 4.620, 5.254; *in no stede*, nowhere 4.470; *to anothere stede*, somewhere else 4.487; *in this stede*, here 5.94 [OE. *stede*].

stedfast, *adj.* steadfast 1.180 [OE. *stedefæst*].

steyll, stele, *sb.* steel; *trew as stele* 2.120, 4.226, 699; *as adj.* 5.107 [OE. *stēle*].

steyll, *v.* steal 4.396, 524; *pp.* **stollyn**, stolen 4.506; *sb.* **stelyng** 4.225 [OE. *stelan*].

step, *v.* step 6.372 [OE. *steppan*].

stere, *v.* steer 2.175 [OE. *stēoran*].

stere-man, *sb.* steersman 2.427 [OE. *stēor-man(n)*].

stere-tre, *sb.* tiller 2.433 [OE. *stēor* + *trēo*].

sterne. See **starne.**

sternly, *adv.* sternly 5.11 [OE. *styrnlīce*, *steornlīce*].

steuen, steven, stevyn, *sb.* voice 1.175, 2.72, 3.409, 6.92 [OE. *stefn*].

sty, *sb.* path, in allit. phrase *bi sty . . . bi strete* 1.365 [OE. *stīg*].

styk, *v.* stab 6.264; *pp.* **stykyd** 6.443 [OE. *stician*].

still, *v.* silence 2.217 [OE. *stillan*].

still, styll, *adj.* still, motionless 4.114, 6.28, quiet, silent 4.94, 372; *still as (a) stone*, perfectly quiet, still 2.406, 2.525; *adv.* softly, gently 4.74, 6.204, incessantly 4.194 [OE. *stille*].

stynk, *v.* stink; 3 *sg.pa.t.* **stank** 1.283; *to thou stynk*, till you stink, i.e. break wind 2.381 (note) [OE. *stincan*].

stynt, *v.* stop 5.82 [OE. *styntan*].

styr, *v.* stir, move 2.366, 5.97; 3 *sg.pa.t.* **styrd**, incited 2.37 [OE. *styrian*].

stod(e). See **stand(e).**

stoyll, *sb.* stool 6.345 [OE. *stōl*].

stokyn, *pp.* fastened, shut 6.172 [OE. *stecan*].

stokys, *sb.pl.* stocks 6.203 [OE. *stocc*].

stold, stollyn. See **stald, steyll**, *v.*

stomak(e), *sb.* stomach 1.432, 4.166 [OF. *estomac, stomaque*].

stone, *sb.* stone 2.406, 525, 4.49; *pl.* **stanys** 1.47, **stonys** 5.170 [OE. *stān*].

stone-styll, *adj.* perfectly still 4.232, 280 [prec. + OE. *stille*].

store, *sb.* store, provisions 3.211, 223, livestock 3.130, 4.400, plenty, abundance 5.446; *bi me he settys no store*, he sets no store by me 2.92; *old store*, old ones, elders ('live-stock' used fig.) 3.456; *in store*, in (their) keeping 4.86, in reserve 5.384 [OF. *estor*].

stormes, *sb.pl.* storms 4.6, 128 [OE. *storm*].

stott, *sb.* heifer 4.518 [OE. *stot*].

stout(e), *adj.* fierce 2.304, valiant 5.308; *adv.* fiercely 2.347; *adv.* **stowtly**, haughtily, arrogantly 3.72 [OF. *estout*].

strayd, *pp.* strewn 5.481 [OE. *strēgan*].

strang, *adj.* gross, flagrant 5.361 [OE. *strang*].

strate, *sb.* evil or difficult plight 4.311, 6.53 [OF. *estreit*].

strenght (MS. *streght*), *sb.* strength; *full strenght*, fully, in full measure 2.261 [OE. *strengþ*].

strete, *sb.* street 1.365, 5.482 [OE. *strēt*].

stry, *sb.* hag 5.348, 380 [OF. *estrie*].

strydys, 3 *sg.pres.* strides 3.72 [OE. *strīdan*].

stryfe, *v.* strive, quarrel 1.17, 2.107 [OF. *estriver*].

stryfys, *sb.pl.* quarrels, disputes 2.400 [OF. *estrif*].

stright, **stryght**, *adv.* straightway, at once 4.434, 5.237 [from OE. *streccan*, *streht*].

stryke, *v.* strike 2.231 (*subj.*); 3 *sg.pa.t.* **stroke** 4.618; *pres.p.* **strykeand** 1.391 [OE. *strīcan*].

stroke, *sb.* blow 2.382, 4.217 [OE. **strāc*].

strokid, 3 *sg.pa.t.* stroked, rubbed 1.88 [OE. *strācian*].

stud. See **stand(e)**.

stuf, *v.* stuff, fill 2.155; *hymself to stuf*, glutting himself 2.85 [OF. *estoffer*].

such, sufferan. See **sich, soferan**.

suffre, *v.* allow 5.129 [OF. *suffrir*].

sugar, *sb.* sugar 5.475 [OF. *çucre*].

sup, *v.* sup, taste 1.426, 3.178 [OE. *sūpan*].

suppos(e), *v.* suppose, imagine 2.221, 3.311, 4.223; *to me thay wyll suppose*, they will suspect me 4.428 [OF. *supposer*].

sure. See **sewrly**.

suspowse, *sb.* suspicion 4.514 [from OF. *supposer*, infl. by AF. *suspecioun*].

swayn, swane, *sb.* serving-man 4.37, 5.20 [ON. *sveinn*].

swedyll, *v.* swaddle 4.432, 598 [from OE. *sweþel*].

swedyll-clowte, *sb.* swaddling-clothes 5.310 [prec. + OE. *clūt*].

swelt, *v.* die 4.525, 6.280 [OE. *sweltan*].

swerd(e), *sb.* sword 2.103, 6.70 [OE. *sweord*].

swere, *v.* swear 2.227, 5.373 [OE. *swerian*].

swete, *adj.* sweet 4.730 [OE. *swēte*].

swetyng, *sb.* sweet one, sweetheart 3.476, 4.306, 715 [prec. + -*ing*].

swette, *sb.* sweat; *a cold swette*, a sweating-fit accompanied by a feeling of cold; (fig.)

a terrifying predicament 4.326 [OE. *swāt*, infl. by next].

swet(t)e, *v.* sweat 4.503; (allit. phrase) *swete or swynk, swettys and swynkys*, sweat or (and) toil 2.195, 4.154 [OE. *swǣtan*].

swevyn, *sb.* dream 4.384 [OE. *swefn*].

swyme, *sb.* swoon 1.27 [OE. *swīma*].

swyne, *sb.pl.* swine 1.264 [OE. *swīn*].

swyne-gronys, *sb.pl.* snouts of swine 3.229 [prec. + OF. *groign*].

swynke, *v.* toil 6.40; (allit. phrase) *swynke and swette*, toil and sweat 4.312 [OE. *swincan*].

tabard, *sb.* tabard 5.357 [OF. *tabart*].

taght. See **tech(e)**.

tayll, *sb.* tale, talk, words 2.315, 5.402; *pl.* **talys** 5.115, 6.281; *withoutt any talys*, truly 5.454; *in oone tayll*, in agreement 6.377 [OE. *talu*].

tak(e), *v.* take 1.387, 2.55, catch, capture 1.405, 4.326, 6.68, get, receive in payment 3.31, 4.164, make 2.137, 272, take up, begin (a song) 4.754; 1 *sg.pa.t.* **takyd** 4.254; 3 *sg.* **toke** 6.75; 1 *pl.* **toke** 6.68; *pp.* **takyn** 4.616, **tane** 4.326, 6.139; *take the that*, take that 1.387; *take at*, take up, begin 3.430 [ON. *taka*].

talys. See **tayll**.

talk, *v.* talk 4.47; *pp.* **talkyd** 6.126; *sb.* **talkyng**, talk(ing), speech 5.80, 199, 6.45, 127 [OE. **talcian*].

tame, *v.* tame 5.80 [OE. *temian*, infl. by next].

tame, *adj.* tame 4.548, 6.443 [OE. *tam*].

tane. See **tak(e)**.

tar, *sb.* tar 2.127 [OE. *teru*].

tar(r)y, *v.* hinder, delay, keep waiting 2.236; *intr.* linger, loiter, wait about 2.210, 4.666, 5.290; *pres.p.* **tariand** 4.110, **taryyng** 2.497; *pp.* **tarid** 6.50, 121; *sb.* **taryyng**, delay 2.377 [obscure].

tart, *sb.* a baked pie, sweet or savoury 3.235 [OF. *tarte*].

tast, *v.* make trial of, sound (water) 2.448 [OF. *taster*].

tech(e), *v.* teach 1.455, 3.394, 5.496, 6.344; 3 *sg.pres.* **teche**, teaches 6.66; 3 *sg.pa.t.* **taght** 1.151, 6.307 [OE. *tǣcan*].

techere, *sb.* teacher 6.209 [prec. + -*ere*].

teyn, ten(e), *sb.* anger, wrath, rage 1.21, 5.148, 151, affliction, suffering, grief

2.533, 3.20, 5.20, 100, 118; *of teyn*, malicious, malevolent 4.713 [OE. *tēona*].

teyn, tene, *v.* annoy, anger 5.115, harm, hurt 4.218 (MS. *teyle*), 5.249; *pp.* **tenyd** 6.353; *intr.* be grieved, vexed 2.210, 4.636 [OE. *tēonian, tēnan*].

teynd, tend, *sb.* tithe 1.73, 107, 177, 188; *to teynd*, as a tithe 1.214 [OE. *tēn + -d*; cf. ON. *tíundi*].

teynd, tend, *v.* pay tithe 1.102, 108, 222; 1 *sg.pa.t.* **teyndyd** 1.231; *pp.* **teyndid** 1.273 [from prec.].

teynfully, *adv.* shamefully, grievously 5.56 [from OE. *tēonful*].

teld. See **tell.**

tell, *v.* mention 3.184, tell, relate 2.164, 3.317, 5.51; 3 *pl.pa.t.* **told**, in *of told*, told of 3.332; *pp.* **teld**, spoken 6.399, **told** 3.177, 5.20, reckoned up 4.272; *tell furth*, make known 3.491, 4.744 [OE. *tellan*].

temperall, *adj.* civil, in *temperall law(es)* 6.277, 292 [L. *temporālis*].

tempest, *sb.* tempest 4.6 [OF. *tempeste*].

tempyll, *sb.* temple 6.73 [OE. *tempel*].

ten(e). See **teyn.**

ten, *adj.* ten 1.218 [OE. *tēn*].

tend. See **teynd.**

tenderly, *adv.* carefully 5.6 [OF. *tendre* + OE. *-līce*].

tenyd. See **teyn**, *v.*

tenys, *sb.* tennis 4.736 [AF. *tenetz*].

tenory, *sb.* tenor (part) 4.186 [OF. *tenor*; cf. It. *tenore*].

tent, *sb.* notice, attention; *take tent*, pay attention 1.249, 3.334, 6.276 [OF. *atente*].

tent, *v.* look after, mind 2.433; *intr.* pay attention 2.421; *tent hedir*, pay attention (to me) 2.291 [from prec.].

tent, *adj.* tenth 2.478 [OE. *tēn + -t*].

tethe. See **tothe.**

tethee, *adj.* peevish, bad-tempered 2.186 [obscure; see *EDD.* s. Teethy].

thai, thay, *pron.* 3 *pl.* they 2.24, 549; *acc.dat.* **thaym** 2.31, **tham(e)** 1.421, 431, 2.143 (MS. *hame*), 5.81, **them** 3.333, 5.424, **thym** 6.83; *refl.* themselves 3.2, 5.81 (second), 187; *gen.* thare 1.45, 2.75, 4.349 [ON. *þeir, þeim, þeira*].

thaym, tham(e). See **thai.**

than, then, *adv.* then 3.18, 478, 4.270, 388, 664, 6.273, 438, 440; *then and then*, time and again 4.66 [OE. *þanne, þænne*].

than, then, *cj.* than 1.109, 2.13, 4.248, 6.271, nor 2.108, 535 [as prec.].

thank, *sb.* thanks 4.382; *in thank*, graciously 1.176; *thank . . . kun*, offer thanks, thank 1.185 [OE. *þanc*].

thank, *v.* thank 2.172, 4.561; *I thank it God*, I thank God for it 3.19 [OE. *þancian*].

thar, 1,2 *sg.pres.* need 1.293, 4.307, 5.479 [OE. *þearf*].

thare. See **thai.**

tharmes, *sb.pl.* bellies; (fig.) children 4.391 [OE. *þarm*].

tharnys, 3 *sg.pres.* is lacking 4.191 [ON. *þarfna, þarnask*].

that, *cj.* that 2.91, 5.470, so that 2.155, 4.83, 5.251, 472, lest 2.184, 372; (after imperative) so that, in order that 1.54, 146, 3.209, 5.316; (omitted as correlative of *so*) 5.184 [OE. *þæt, þætte*].

that, þat, *demonstr. adj.* the, that 2.28, 39 [OE. *þæt*].

that, þat, *pron.* that, it 1.387, 2.146, 3.171, 4.694 [OE. *þæt*].

that, *rel.pron.* that, which, who 2.1, 4, 4.173, 5.61, that which 2.164, 3.445, 4.21, 98, 639 (second), those who 5.12, 39; (omission of rel.) 2.56, 66, 170, 393, 3.92, 144, 146, 4.8, 393, 6.169 [OE. *þæt*, for *þe*].

the, þe. See **thou.**

the, *v.* thrive, prosper; (in asseveration) *as euer myght I the*, so may I prosper, as I hope to prosper, 2.328, 4.463; *ill myght thou the*, bad luck to you 6.378 [OE. *þēon*].

the, *def.art.* the 2.6, 6.16 [OE. *se* (late *þe*)].

the, *adv. with compar.* the; *the wars I the see*, the worse for seeing you 2.191 [OE. *þy̆, þē*].

theder, thedir, thyder, *adv.* thither, there 1.466, 2.312, 4.467, 6.417 [OE. *þider*].

thederward, *adv.* thither 2.245 [OE. *þiderweard*].

thefe, theyf, *sb.* scoundrel, villain 1.317, 398, 5.338, 6.256; *pl.* thieves 3.52, 4.526, scoundrels 5.152, 154 [OE. *þēof*].

theft, *sb.* theft 4.621 [OE. *þēofð*].

them, then. See **thai, than.**

thens, *adv.* thence 2.548 [OE. *þeonan + adv. -es*].

ther(e), *adv. demonstr.* there 2.317; *indef.* 2.298, 3.404, 4.37; *ther(e) as*, where 1.307, 2.325; *rel.* where 1.88, 163, 4.475,

644; **therafter**, accordingly 1.296,
4.164; **therapon**, on it 2.282; **therat**,
at that 5.488; **therfor**, for that
reason 2.20, 4.230; **therin**, in it 3.170;
therof, of it 4.119, with it 2.283;
theroute, therowte, away from here
1.60, outside, out of doors 6.56; **thertyll**,
to it, to that 4.76, 431, about it 5.434,
for that purpose 4.281; **therto**, to it, to
that 2.385, 3.497, for it, for them 2.102,
4.394 [OE. *þēr*].
these. See **this**.
thew, *sb.* courteous action, courtesy 1.185
[OE. *þēaw*].
thi, thy. See **thou**.
thi, *adv.* therefore 2.472 (note) [OE. *þȳ*].
thyder. See **theder**.
thyk, *adv.* thick, in abundance 3.30 [OE.
þicce].
thym, thyn(e). See **thai, thou**.
thyn, *adj.* thin, scanty 3.171 [OE. *þynne*].
thyng, *sb.* thing; *all thyng*, everything 1.91,
2.73, 4.126; *al this thyng*, all this 2.154;
for oone thyng or oder, in spite of everything
3.208; *all other thyng*, every other thing
5.202; *pl.* **thyng**, things 4.200 [OE. *þing*].
thynk(e). See **thynkys**.
thynk, *v.* think, consider 3.235, 243, 4.83,
bear in mind, remember 6.208, intend
1.216, 4.395, 5.175, 238; 1,3 *sg.pa.t.*
thoght 2.19, 3.89, 4.184; *pp.* **thoght**,
thought of, imagined 2.286; *thynk ye on*,
do you remember 4.496 [OE. *þencan*,
þōhte].
thynkys, 3 *sg.pres.impers.* (with dat. pron.)
it seems 2.511; (without inflexion)
thynk(e) 1.158, 233, 2.255, 399, 5.437;
(with nom.pron.) *what thou thynk*, whatever seems good to you 2.196; *bot euen as
thou thynk*, but (do) just as you think fit
2.379; 3 *sg.pa.t.* **thoght** 2.425, 3.309
[OE. *þyncan, þūhte*].
thirté (MS. *thrirte*), **thyrty**, *adj.* thirty
2.125, 260 [OE. *þrītig*].
this, thys, *demonstr. adj. sg.* this 2.70,
4.234; *pl.* **these** 4.20, **this(e)** 2.181,
445, **thyse** 4.18; *pron.sg.* this 2.11; *pl.*
these 3.145, **thise** 2.471 [OE. *þis*].
thystyll, *sb.* thistle 1.202, 4.101 [OE.
þistel].
tho, *demonstr.pron.pl.* those 2.228, 5.310
[OE. *þā*].
thof, though, *cj.* though 6.109, 172 [ON.
þó(h)].

W.P.—O*

thoght. See **thynk, thynkys**.
thoght, *sb.* thought, mind 1.180, 2.156,
4.92 [OE. *þōht*].
thole, *v.* allow 4.306, 6.157 [OE. *þolian*].
thoner-flone, *sb.* thunder-dart, lightning
3.324 [OE. *þunor + flān*].
thoners, *sb.pl.* thunderstrokes, thunder-
bolts 2.346 [OE. *þunor*].
thor(e), *adv.* there, then 1.146, 282, 4.508,
530, 5.316, 6.43 [OE. *þār(a)*].
thorne, *sb.* thorn, thorn-tree 4.403 [OE.
þorn].
thoro(w), thrugh, *prep.* through 2.278,
4.488, 5.93, throughout 5.269, because of
4.35, by means of 4.740, 6.82 [OE. *þurh,
þorh*].
those, *adj.pl.* those 3.53; *pron.* 2.45 [OE.
þās].
thou, *pron.* 2 *sg.* thou, you 2.3; *acc.dat.* **the,
þe**, thee, you 1.65, 2.72, 406; *refl.* (to,
for) thyself, yourself 1.357 387, 2.224;
gen. **thi, thy** 2.4, 461, **thyn(e)** 6.17,
178 [OE. *þū, þē, þīn*].
though. See **thof**.
thowsand(e), *sb.* thousand 5.419, 444,
463 [OE. *þūsend*].
thowsandfold, *adj.* thousandfold 5.22
[OE. *þūsendfald*].
thrafe, *sb.* a measure of corn (often consist-
ing of two stooks of twelve sheaves each)
1.197 [cf. Icel. *þrefi*].
thrall, *sb.* slave 1.464, 5.56 [late OE. *þrǣl*,
from ON. *þrǽll*].
thrang, *sb.* throng, audience 3.47 [OE.
geþrang].
thraw, *sb.* while, moment; *a thraw*, for a
while 1.30 [OE. *þrāg, þrāh*].
thrawe, *v.* throw 3.164 [OE. *þrāwan*].
thre, *adj.* three 1.194, 2.2, 3.191, 4.707,
6.13 [OE. *þrēo*].
threpe, *v.* wrangle, haggle 4.168 [OE.
þrēapian].
threte, thrett, *v.* threaten 5.159, 6.220,
294 [OE. *þrēatian*].
thrid, thryd, *adj.* third 2.460, 6.74 [OE.
þridda].
thrife, thryfe, *v.* thrive, prosper 1.18,
4.27; (in asseveration) *long or I (thou)
thrife*, bad luck to me (you) 1.205, 411; *as
euer myght I thryfe*, as I hope to prosper
2.191, 243 [ON. *þrífask*].
thrift, thryft, *sb.* earnings, profit, sub-
stance 1.197; (good) fortune, prosperity,
in *as com thrift apon the so* 1.118 (note),

slape of thrift 1.415 (note); (in asseveration) *by my thryft*, as I hope to prosper
2.218, 3.263; *yll thryft*, bad luck 4.150
[ON. *þrift*].

thryng, *v.* in *thryng out*, drive out, knock
out 6.125, burst out 5.240 (*intr.*);
3 *sg.pa.t.* **throng**, pressed together 3.416
[OE. *þringan*].

throte, *sb.* throat 1.289, 4.410 [OE. *þrote*].

thrugh. See **thoro(w).**

thrughout(t), thrugoutt, *prep.* throughout 1.409, 5.254, 417 [OE. *þurhūt*].

thrust, *sb.* thirst 6.382 [OE. *þurst*].

thus, *adv.* thus, so 2.89, 192, 5.159, 6.246
[OE. *þus*].

thwang, *v.* be flogged 4.211 [from OE.
þwang].

tyd, *v.* happen; *tyd may betyde*, come what
may 5.337 [OE. *tīdan*].

tyde, *sb.* time; *this tyde*, now 1.467, 3.431,
4.77, 5.32; *in þat tyde*, then 2.39 [OE,
tīd].

tydely, *adv.* quickly 2.291 [ON. *tīðliga*].

tye, *v.* tie 2.225; 1 *sg.pres.* **tyes** 1.46 [OE.
tēgan].

til(l), tyll, *prep.* to 1.113; *as adv.* towards
(it) 4.433; *cj.* till, until, 1.9, 61, 2.337;
(foll. by *that*) 4.279 [OE. (Nhb.) *til*, ON.
til].

tylthe, *sb.* tilth, arable land 4.13 [OE. *tilþ*].

tyme, *sb.* time 1.105, 2.460, 4.269 [OE.
tīma].

tyme, *v.* fare; *God gif you ill to tyme*, God
grant that you fare ill 1.26 [from prec.; cf.
OE. *getīmian*].

tymely, *adv.* early, soon 4.524 [OE.
tīmlīce].

tyn(e), *adj.* tiny 3.467, 4.724 [unknown].

tyne, *v.* waste, spend in vain 2.441, 3.200;
pp. **tynde**, lost 3.39 [ON. *týna*].

tyr, *interj.* a shepherd's call used in driving
sheep 3.113, 114.

tyte, tytt, *adv.* quickly, soon 1.53, 3.149,
5.20; *as tyte*, as quickly as possible 2.219,
4.627; *compar.* **tytter** 3.152 [ON. *tītt*].

tythand, tythyng, *sb.* tidings, news
2.199, 4.199, 5.265 [OE. *tīdung*, ON.
tīðindi].

tytt, tytter. See **tyte.**

to, *adv.* too 4.237, 666, 5.511, 6.368, too
much, too far 3.2 [OE. *tō*].

to, *cj.* till 2.241, 381, 4.108, 279, 333, 5.83,
6.192; (foll. by *that*) 4.280 [OE. *tō*].

to, *prep.* to 2.9, towards, with regard to

1.316, 4.428, 514, against 3.325, at
2.343, in 2.255, in, according to 2.28, for
5.99, 449, for, as a 1.214, 2.109, 122,
4.254; *adv.* in *go to*, go to it, get to
work 2.236, 3.250, 427; *to and fro* 2.111,
3.58 [OE. *tō*].

to-chyde, *v.* brawl violently 5.151 [OE.
tō- + *cīdan*].

to-day, *adv.* to-day 2.481 [OE. *tō dæg*].

togeder, togedyr, *adv.* together 2.292,
3.110, 6.58, at the same time 6.113 [OE.
tōgædere].

toyne, *sb.* tone (of a musical note); *out of
toyne*, out of tune 4.477 [OF. *ton*, L.
tonus].

toke. See **tak(e).**

token, tokyn, *sb.* sign, omen 2.471, 4.320,
696, proof, evidence 3.160, 4.611 [OE.
tācen].

tokynyng, *sb.* token, sign 2.476 [OE.
tācnung].

told. See **tell.**

tome, *adj.* empty 4.547 [OE. *tōm*].

to-morne, *adv.* to-morrow 4.251, 6.137
[OE. *tō morgen*].

tong, *sb.* tongue 2.217, 4.663, 5.51 [OE.
tunge].

tonyd, *adj.* in *well tonyd*, sung with a good
tone 3.419 [from OF. *ton*].

too, *sb.* toe 4.265; *pl.* **toes** 4.144, **toose**
4.414 [OE. *tā*].

top, *sb.* top 2.469, head, crown 4.265,
fighting-top (platform for archers at the
mast-head of a ship) 2.271 [OE. *top*].

tord(e), *sb.* turd 4.216; (as an abusive exclamation) 3.192, 388, 6.148 [OE. *tord*].

to-rehete, *v.* rebuke severely 6.295
[obscure].

to-rent, *pp.* torn to pieces 5.390 [OE.
tō-rendan].

torne, *pp.* torn, injured 5.56 [OE. *teran*].

tothe, *sb.* tooth (used fig. to mean 'accent')
4.215; *pl.* **tethe** 1.9 [OE. *tōþ*].

to-tyre, *v.* tear to pieces 5.144; *pp.* **to-
torne** 5.345 [OE. *tō-teran*].

to-torne. See **to-tyre.**

toute, *sb.* behind, backside 1.63, 64
[obscure].

tow, *sb.* fibre of flax or hemp prepared for
spinning; *haue tow on my rok*, have tow on
my distaff, i.e. have work on hand 4.389
[cf. ON. *tō*].

towch, *v.* touch 2.462; 2 *sg.pa.t.* **towchid**
6.400 [OF. *toucher*].

towne, *sb.* town 3.87, 4.133, 492, 5.2, 6.364; (allit. phrase) *in towre and in towne* 5.12, 193 [OE. *tūn*].

towre, *sb.* tower 2.349, 5.12, 193 [late OE. *tūr*, from OF. *tour*].

tray, *sb.* misery; (allit. phrase) *with tray and with teyn,* in misery and suffering 2.533 [OE. *trega*].

trane, *sb.* trick 6.138 [OF. *traïne*].

trant, *sb.* trick 5.235 [cf. MDu. *trant*].

trapt, 3 *sg.pa.t.* trapped 4.371 [OE. *-træppan*].

trast, *v.intr.* rest assured 5.23 [ON. *treysta*].

trate (MS. *crate*), *sb.* old woman (used contemptuously of Christ) 6.427; *pl.* **trattys,** old women, hags 5.394 [AF. *trote*].

tratoure, tratur, *sb.* traitor 5.164, 6.171, 283 [OF. *traitre, traitour*].

trattys. See **trate.**

trauell, *sb.* labour, toil 1.152, 2.440 [OF. *travail*].

trauell, *v.* be in labour (of a woman in child-birth); *trauell . . . of,* be in labour with 4.386-7 [OF. *travailler*].

traw(e), trow(e), *v.* believe (in), be sure, think 1.19, 2.45, 244, 3.416, 4.51, 210, 6.414, hope 4.380; 3 *sg.pres.* **trowse** 4.247; 1 *sg.pa.t.* **trowed** 1.163; *pp.* **trowde,** believed (possible) 3.67, **trowyd** 3.324 [OE. *trēow(i)an, trūwian*].

tre(e), *sb.* tree 2.34, 4.358, piece of timber 2.253, cross 3.49 [OE. *trēo*].

trede, *v.* tread 4.488 [OE. *tredan*].

trespas, *sb.* offence, sin, wrong 4.624 [OF. *trespas*].

trespas, *v.* trespass, sin 4.622; *pp.* **trespast** 6.4 (MS. *trespas*), 316 [OF. *trespasser*].

tresure, *sb.* treasure 5.438 [OF. *tresor*].

trete, *v.* treat, deal with 6.217; *intr.* come to terms 3.203 [OF. *tretier*].

trew, true, *adj.* true, truthful, honest 1.425, 2.201, 4.52. 521, 6.75; *trew as stele* 2.120, 4.226, 699; *trew for to trist,* true and trustworthy 2.515 [OE. *trēowe*].

tryble, *sb.* treble (part) 4.187 [OF. *treble*].

trinité, trynyté, trynyty, *sb.* Trinity 2.30, 169, 254 [OF. *trinité*].

trist, tryst, trust, *v.* trust 2.505, 515, 4.448, 5.180, 182, 6.193 [OE. **trẏstan*].

trone, *sb.* throne 3.384, 5.138 [OF. *trone*].

trott, *sb.* in *lede the a trott,* lead you at a trot 6.429 [OF. *trot*].

trott, *v.* trot, go quickly 1.390; *trott on,* trot along 6.1 [OF. *troter*].

trouth, trowth, *sb.* truth 3.411, (plèdged) word, promise 1.110, 159, 4.163 [OE. *trēowþ*].

trow(e), trowde, trowed, trowyd, trowse, trowth, true. See **traw(e), trouth, trew.**

truly, *adv.* truly 3.37, 4.259, 5.146 [OE. *trēowlīce*].

trus, *v.* in *trus sam,* pack up 2.316; *trus,* come on 3.202, 287 [OF. *tr(o)usser*].

trussell, *sb.* bundle 1.170 [OF. *troussel*].

trust. See **trist.**

tup, *sb.* tup, male sheep 3.117 [obscure].

turne, *sb.* in *I wyll gyf my shepe a turne,* I will turn my sheep round 4.139-40 [AF. *t(o)urn*].

turne, *v.* turn 2.336, 4.130, 1 *sg.pa.t.* **turnyd** 4.423; *pp.* **turned** 5.100, misled 6.106; *turne the vntill,* turn on you 2.218 [OE. *turnian,* OF. *t(o)urner*].

turtill, *sb.* turtle-dove, 2.506 [OE. *turtle*].

twelf, *adj.* twelve 4.618, 5.22 [OE. *twelf*].

twelmothe, *sb.* twelvemonth 4.324 [OE. *twelf mōnaþ*].

twenty, *adj.* twenty 1.440, 3.414 [OE. *twentig*].

twyys, *adv.* for the second time 2.362 [OE. *twiga* + adv. *-es*].

twyn, *v.* sever, separate 1.325 [cf. OE. *(ge)twinn*].

two, *adj.* two 1.192, 2.151, 3.147; *in two,* (broken) in two 2.412 [OE. *twā*].

vayll, *sb.* veil, bandage for the eyes 6.376, 388 [AF. and ONF. *veile*].

vayn, *adj.* worthless, useless 1.90; *in vayn,* in vain 2.360, 4.542 [OF. *vain*].

velany, *sb.* evil, wrongdoing 2.67 [OF. *vilanie*].

vengeabyll, *adj.* vengeful, cruel 6.194 [AF. *vengable*].

vengeance, veniance, venyance, *sb.* vengeance 1.353, 2.55, 5.167, 6.355 [OF. *vengeance,* AF. *veniance*].

vengyng, *sb.* vengeance 5.242 [from OF. *venger*].

veniance, venyance. See **vengeance.**

veray, *adj.* true 2.1, real 2.198 [OF. *verai*].

veralee, veraly, *adv.* verily, truly 3.324, 441 [prec. + OE. *-līce*].

verament, *adv.* truly 2.6 [OF. *veraiment*].

veryose, *sb.* verjuice, juice of crab-apples or unripe grapes 3.236 [OF. *verjus*].

verse, *sb.* verse 3.386 [OE. *fers*, OF. *vers*].

vessell, *sb.* vessel, ship 2.327 [OF. *vessel*].

vexed, *pp.* vexed, annoyed 6.187 [OF. *vexer*].

vile, vyle, *adj.* vile, worthless 6.140, 171 [OF. *vil*].

virgyn, vyrgyn, *sb.* virgin 3.342, 371. 4.676 [OF. *virgine*].

vyrgynyté, *sb.* virginity 3.365 [OF *virginité*].

vitayll, *sb.* victuals, food 2.155 [OF. *vitaille*].

vnburnyd, *adj.* unburnt 3.362 [OE. *un-* + *birnan, byrnan*].

vnceyll, *sb.* unhappiness, misery, misfortune 3.3, 187, 5.327 [OE. *unsǽl*].

vncessantlé, *adv.* incessantly 2.147 [OF. *incessant* + OE. *-līce*].

vndemyd, *pp.* unjudged, uncensured 6.230 [OE. *un-* + *dēman*].

vnder, hunder, *prep.* under 1.64; *adv.* underneath 2.409, under 4.24 [OE. *under*].

vndertake, *v.* promise, affirm 2.274 [OE. *under* + ON. *taka*].

vndo, *v.* undo 4.404, 478 [OE. *undōn*].

vnethes, vnneth, *adv.* with difficulty, hardly 6.42, 282 [OE. *unēaþe* + adv. *-es*].

vneuen, *adj.* at odds, at sixes and sevens 4.192 [OE. *unefen*].

vnfyld, vnfylyd, *adj.* undefiled 3.366, 371 [OE. *un-* + *fȳlan*].

vngayn, *adj.* inconvenient; *at vngayn*, inconveniently 1.379; *adv.* **vngaynly**, improperly 5.160 [cf. ON. *úgegn*].

vnglad, *adj.* wretched, miserable 2.22 [OE. *unglæd*].

vnkyndnes, *sb.* unnatural behaviour 2.12 [OE. *uncynde* + *-nes*].

vnlokyn, *pp.* revealed, explained 5.507 [OE. *unlūcan*].

vnneth. See **vnethes**.

vnnett, *adj.* difficult, troublesome 6.347 [OE. *unēaþe*].

vnrid, vnryde, *adj.* hard, severe 2.40, 3.11 [OE. *ungerȳde*].

vnsoght, *adj.* unexpiated, unatoned 2.97 [ON. *úsdttr*, earlier **unsaht-*].

vntew. See **vnto**.

vnthankys, *sb.* in *myne vnthankys*, against my will 1.187 [OE. *unþanc*].

vntill, *prep.* to 1.427, on 2.218 [ON. **und* (?) + *til*].

vnto, vntew, *prep.* to 2.241, 4.270, until 2.25, 3.198, 4.148, in 2.505 [OE. **untō*].

vntold, *adj.* untold, immense 5.438 [OE. *untald*].

voce, voyce, *sb.* voice 1.351, 3.422 [OF. *vois*].

vowchesaue, vowchsayf, *v.* vouchsafe, deign 2.172, give 3.474; (with vb. and adj. separated) *he vowche it full well safe*, may He very kindly grant it 1.449 [OF. *voucher sauf*].

vp, *adv.* up 2.153, risen 4.365 [OE. *ūp, upp(e)*].

vphefe, *v.* raise up, lift up 6.408 [OE. *ūphebban*].

vphold, *pp.* upheld, fulfilled 3.344 [OE. *up(p)* + *haldan*].

vpryse, *v.* rise to one's feet 6.228 [OE. *up(p)* + *rīsan*].

vpward, *adv.* on high, from above 4.649 [OE. *ūpweard*].

vs. See **we**.

vse, *sb.* practice 6.87 [OF. *us*].

vse, *v.* practise 1.393 [OF. *user*].

wached, 2 *pl.pa.t.* kept watch, kept vigil 6.56 [OE. *wæccan*].

wafe, waue, *v.* put away 5.246; *intr.* wander 1.431, 6.103 [ON. *veifa*].

wafys, 2 *pl.imper.* give up, abandon 5.498 [AF. *weyver*].

wage, *sb.* wage 5.444 [ONF. *wage*].

way, *sb.* way 1.89, 2.435, 5.316, way of life 3.76; *adv.* away, in *do way*, enough 4.309 [OE. *weg*].

wayte, waytt. See **witt**, *v.*

wake, *v.* awaken, arouse 2.89; *intr.* stay awake 4.415; 2 *sg.imper.* **wake**, in *wake thou*, you stay awake 4.257; 2 *pl.* **wakys**, wake up 4.362 [OE. *wacian*].

wake, *adj.* weak 6.322, slender 3.30 [ON. *veikr*].

wakyns, 3 *sg.pres.* wakens 4.557, 582 [OE. *wæcnan*].

wald. See **will**, *v.*

walk, *v.* walk 3.18, 4.10; *pres.p.* **walkand** 1.106; *pp.* **walkyd** 6.122; *sb.* **walkyng** 6.41 [OE. *walc(i)an*].

wall, *sb.* wall 1.297, 2.515, 4.443 [OE. *wall*].

waloway, *interj.* alas 5.362 [OE. *wā lā wei*].

walteryng. See **water**, *v.*[2].

wamans, wan. See **woman, wyn**, *v.*

wan, *adj.* black, evil 6.444 [OE. *wann*].

wanders, 3 *sg.pres.* goes here and there 4.415 [OE. *wandrian*].

wandreth, *sb.* distress, misery; (allit. phrase) *wandreth, and wo* 2.40, 6.434 [ON. *vandræði*].

wane, *sb.* wain, wagon 3.62, 4.38 [OE. *wægn, wæn*].

wanys, 3 *sg.pres.* wanes, grows less 2.458; *pres.p.* **wanand** 2.493; *pp.* **wanyd** 2.450 [OE. *wanian*].

want, *sb.* want, lack (of food) 1.44, 2.194 [from ON. *vant*, neut. adj.].

want, *v.* want, lack 3.152, 4.421; 1 *sg.pa.t.* **wantyd** 1.124 [ON. *vanta*].

wantones, *sb.* insolence, arrogance 5.498 [OE. *wan-* + *togen* + *-nes*].

war, *v.imper.* look out 5.238, 6.200; (as a call used in driving animals) *war (oute)* 1.25, 29 [OE. *warian*].

war, *adj.* in *be war (of)*, beware (of), take care 4.92, 117, 6.241 [OE. *wær*].

war, *adj. compar.* worse 6.298; *as sb.* 4.247, 331 [ON. *verri*].

warand, *v.* warrant, promise 5.263 [ONF. *warandir*].

ware. See **was**.

wary, *v.* curse 2.208; *pp.* **waryd**, cursed 4.712, accursed 6.120 [OE. *wærgan*].

wark(e), *sb.* work 2.130, 244, action, deed 4.614; *made vp wark of*, made short work of 6.310; *pl.* deeds, doings 6.105 [OE. *werc*].

wark, *v.* ache 2.269 [OE. *wærcan*].

warld, *sb.* world 2.70, 303, 4.56, everything, one's all 3.38; *gen.sg.* worldly, earthly 1.150, 5.369 [OE. *weorld*].

warlo(o), *sb.* warlock, the Devil 4.640, 712 [OE. *wærloga*].

warn(e), *v.* warn, tell 1.456, 2.110, 3.320 4.532, 653 [OE. *warnian*].

wars, *adj.compar.* worse 1.109, 4.119, 5.164; *adv.* in *the wars I the see*, the worse for seeing you 2.191; *adj.superl.* **warst**, worst 1.35; *as sb.* 1.224 [OE. *wyrsa, wyrsta*].

was, *sg. and pl.pa.t.* was; were; 1,2,3 *sg.* **was** 1.350, 2.12, 4.260; 1 *pl.* (prec. by pron.) **were** 4.363, 5.191; 3 *pl.* (prec. by pron.) **wore** 3.352, (not prec. by pron.) **was** 3.160, 4.127, 559; 1,2,3 *sg.pa.t.subj.* **were** 1.154, 2.200, 388; 3 *sg.* **ware** 5.481, **wore** 6.120; 1,2,3 *pl.* **were** 1.27, 2.394, 526; 2 *pl.* **wore** 4.510 [OE. *wæs wæron*, ON. *várum*].

wast, was it 4.594 [OE. *wæs* + *hit*].

waste, *adv.* in vain, to no purpose 1.134 [ONF. *wast*].

wat, *sb.* person 1.14 [obscure].

wate. See **witt**.

wate, *v.* watch for 5.467; *wate . . . abowte*, look about, pry about 4.586; *ther watys on his wyngys* 5.39 (note); *on . . . wate*, attend on 6.156 [ONF. *wait(i)er*].

water, *sb.* water 2.128 [OE. *wæter*].

water, *v.*[1] in *thay water myn eeyne*, they make my eyes water 4.58 [OE. *wæterian*].

water, *v.*[2] totter, move unsteadily 4.352 (note); *pres.p.* **walteryng**, sprawling 4.236 [frequentative of OE. *wæltan*].

watt, waue. See **witt, wafe**.

wawghes, *sb.pl.* waves 2.426 [ON. *vágr*].

wax, *v.* grow, become 2.60, 5.314; 3 *pl.pa.t.* **wex** 6.71 [OE. *waxan*].

we, *pron.* 1 *pl.* we 2.184; *acc.dat.* **hus, vs**, us 2.46, 55, me 4.296, 437; *refl.* ourselves 1.79; *gen.* **oure** 2.301, **oures** 5.447 [OE. *wē, ūs, ūre*].

we, *interj.* (for emphasis, or to express surprise, grief) 1.53, 212, 2.217, 5.148, 6.217; *we lo, we . . . lo*, ah well 1.223, 2.238 [OE. *wā (lā)*].

wed, *pp.* wedded, married 4.73, 5.433 [OE. *weddian*].

wede, *sb.* garments 4.731 [OE. *wēd*].

weder, wedir, *sb.* weather 1.169, 2.470; *pl.* **weders**, foul weather, storms 2.451, 4.1, 57 [OE. *weder*].

wedyng, *sb.* marriage 4.92, 94 [OE. *weddung*].

wedir, *sb.* wether 4.451 [OE. *weðer*].

wedys, *sb.pl.* weeds 1.203 [OE. *wēod*].

wedmen, *sb.pl.* married people 2.400, married men 4.65 [OE *weddian* + *man(n)*].

wedows, *gen.sg.* widow's 2.389 [OE. *widewe*].

weft, *sb.* weft, woof 1.436, 4.587 [OE. *weft*].

weght, *sb.* weight 1.51 [OE. *wiht*, ON. *vætt*].

weyd, 3 *sg.pa.t.* weighed 4.631 [OE. *wegan*].

weyll, *sb.* happiness 4.125 [OE. *wela*].

weyll, wel(e), well, *adv.* well 2.119, very 4.716, (with compar.) much 4.191, 5.164, kindly, generously 1.449, easily 2.5; *predic.* well off, lucky 3.1, 183, satisfactory 6.393; *well were he*, he'd be lucky (who) 2.339; *well is vs*, we are fortunate 2.459; *well is me day bright* 4.339 (note); *well were me*, I would be happy 4.685 [OE. *wel*].

weyn(e), wene, *v.* think, expect 1.149, 381, 2.444, 3.215, 4.129, 712, 5.101, 6.212 [OE. *wēnan*].

weynd, *v.* go 1.78, 301, 444, 6.424; *refl.* 1.453; 3 *sg.pa.t.* went 3.153, 4.460; 3 *pl.* went 5.153 [OE. *wendan*].

weytt, wete, *sb.* wet 3.4, 4.60 [OE. *wǣta*].

weytt, wete, *adj.* wet 4.156, 494, 671 [OE. *wǣt, wēt*].

welcom, *v.* welcome 1.23, 5.66 [OE. *wilcumian*, infl. by *wel*].

welcom, *adj.* welcome 1.60 [OE. *wilcuma*, infl. by *wel*; cf. ON. *velkominn*].

wel(e), well. See **weyll**, *adv.*

well-wirkand, *adj.* well-doing 2.120 [OE. *welwyrcende*].

well-wroght, *adj.* well-planned, well-contrived 5.370 [OE. *wel* + *wroht*].

wel-ner, *adv.* well-nigh 4.387 [OE. *wel* + *nēr*].

wemay, weme, wemo, *interj.* (expressing impatience) 1.148, 198, 3.388, 6.170 [cf. ME. *we*, interj.].

wene. See **weyn(e).**

wenyand, *sb.* the time of the waning moon, considered an unlucky time; *in the wenyand*, confound you 1.226; *walk in the wenyand*, bad luck to you 4.405 [from OE. *wanian*].

went. See **weynd.**

wepe, *v.* weep 4.193, 582; *sb.* **wepyng** 5.344 [OE. *wēpan*].

wepyn, *sb.* weapon 4.615 [OE. *wēpn*].

were. See **was.**

were, *v.* wear 1.153; *pp.* **worne**, spent, used up 5.454 [OE. *werian*].

wery, *adj.* weary 1.242, 4.156, 256, 671, 6.48 [OE. *wērig*].

west, *adv.* west 3.290; *sb.* 4.7 [OE. *west*].

wete. See **weytt.**

wett, *pp.* wet 4.103 [OE. *wǣtan, wētan*].

wex. See **wax.**

whall, *sb.* whale 4.105 [OE. *hwæl*].

what, *pron.interrog.* what 2.163, 4.55; *indir.* 1.34, 2.183, 4.305; *exclam.* 1.28, 3.102, 4.148, 602; *indef.* whatever 2.196, (foll. by *that*) 4.84; **whatso**, whatever 4.360; **whateuer** 5.289; *adj.* 5.111; *indef.* whatever 4.30, 5.19; *adv.* why 1.345, 6.303, 304, to what an extent, how

3.1, 4.1, 287, 355, 629 [OE. *hwæt*; *swā-hwæt-swā*; *hwæt* + *ǣfre*].

wheder, *pron.* which (of the two) 3.70; *cj.* *wheder . . . or*, whether . . . or 1.77, 2.363 [OE. *hwæþer*].

wheder, whedir, *adv.* whither, where 1.374, 2.313, 3.82 [OE. *hwider*].

when, *adv.* when 3.405, 4.74, 5.424 [OE. *hwænne, hwanne*].

wher(e), *adv.interrog. and rel.* where, whither 2.22, 192, 4.177, 5.150; *wher that*, where 6.327; **whereas**, wherever 3.495; **whereso**, wherever 1.364; **wheresoeuer**, wherever 3.106, 6.89; **wherof**, with what 1.108; **wherto**, to what end, why 4.168, 636 [OE. *hwǣr, hwēr; swā-hwǣr-swā*].

whese. See **qweasse.**

whett, *v.* whet the tusks, i.e. prepare for an attack 5.318 [OE. *hwettan*].

whi, why. See **qwhy.**

which, *pron.* which 2.331 [OE. *hwilc*].

whik, whyk, *adj.* living, live 4.548, 6.265 [OE. *cwic*].

while, *sb.* while, time; *a handlang while*, a little while, a moment 4.412 [OE. *hwīl*].

whils, whyls, *cj.* while 1.158, 2.397, 6.184 [OE. *hwīle* + adv. -*s*].

whylst, *cj.* whilst 3.166 [prec. + -*t*].

whyne, *v.* whine 2.229 [OE. *hwīnan*].

whyp, *sb.* whip 2.378 [obscure].

whyr, *interj.* a shepherd's call used in driving sheep 3.117.

whystyll, *sb.* whistle, used humorously to mean 'throat' in *wett hyr whystyll* 4.103 [OE. *hwistle*].

who, *pron.interrog.* who; *who is*, who is it 2.295, 4.195, 479; *indef.* in *who that*, whoever 1.6, 5.93; **whoso**, whoever 1.12, 3.60, 6.160; *rel.* **whom** 3.396 [OE. *hwā; swā-hwā-swā*].

whop, *interj.* a shepherd's call used in turning sheep 3.119 [cf. WYks. dial. *whap*].

whore, *adv.interrog.* where 4.402 [OE. *hwār(a)*].

whoso. See **who.**

wychcraft, *sb.* witchcraft 6.103 [OE. *wiccecræft*].

widder, *v.* wither 2.63 [OE. **widr(i)an*].

wide, wyde, *adj.* wide, spacious 2.541; *adv.* a long way, far 3.13 [OE. *wīd; wīde*].

wife, wyff, *sb.* woman 1.413, wife 2.106, 4.305; *pl.* **wyfys**, wives 4.85 [OE. *wīf*].

wyfe, *v.* take a wife, marry 3.97 [OE. *wīfian*].

wight, wyght, *sb.* creature, person 2.47, 544, 5.443, 6.328, child 4.709 [OE. *wiht*].

wyghtly, *adv.* nimbly, quickly 5.396 [ON. *vīgt* + OE. *-līce*].

wyk, *adj.* wicked 6.262 [obscure].

wylde, *adj.* wild 4.548, 712 [OE. *wilde*].

wyles, wylys, *sb.* wiles, ruses 5.233, 6.15 [OE. *wil*].

will, wyll, *sb.* wish, desire 1.244, 4.376, that which one desires 4.73, 198; *thi will . . of me tharnys* 4.191 (note); *if thi wylles be,* if it be thy will 4.706; *at youre (awne) will,* at your pleasure, as you wish 5.259, 293 [OE. *gewill, willa*].

will, wyll, *v.* desire, will, wish, and as *fut.auxil.* 1,2,3 *sg.pres.* **will** 2.55, 64, 3.119; 2 *sg.* **wilt** 1.50, 2.226; 1,2,3 *pl.* **will** 2.45, 369, 418; 1 *sg.pa.t.* **wald** 4.108, **wold** 2.396; 2,3 *sg.* **wold** 2.47, 516; 3 *pl.* **wold** 2.107; *wilt thou so, will thou bot so,* you will, will you? 2.226, 3.119; (with ellipsis of verb of motion) 1.28, 2.504, 3.42 [OE. *willan, wolde, walde*].

wyn, *sb.* profit, advantage; *hym to mekill wyn,* to his great profit 2.109 [OE. *win(n)*].

wyn, *v.* win, gain, earn 2.363, 4.299, 6.398; *intr.* win one's way, get (to) 4.362, get away, escape 2.24, 549; 1 *sg.pa.t.* **wan,** gained 1.139; *pp.* **won,** redeemed, saved 4.752; *wyn to end,* manage to finish 2.130-1 [OE. *winnan*].

wynd-blast, *sb.* blast of wind 2.355 [OE. *wind* + *blæst*].

wyndys, *sb.pl.* winds 4.57 (MS. *weders*), 128 [OE. *wind*].

wyndo(w), *sb.* window 2.136, 280 [ON. *vindauga*].

wyne, *sb.* wine 3.199 [OE. *wīn*].

wyng, *sb.* wing 2.474, 5.39 [ON. *vœngr*].

wynk, *v.* close one's eyes 1.227, doze, sleep 4.156, 6.37, 'give the tip' 3.244 (note) [OE. *wincian*].

wynnyngys, *sb.pl.* winnings, earnings 1.111 [from OE. *winnan*].

wipe, *v.* wipe 1.238 [OE. *wīpian*].

wirk, wyrk, *v.* do 4.542, practise 6.209; *intr.* work 2.262, 4.164, act, behave 1.70; 2 *sg.pa.t.* **wroght,** made 2.4; *pp.* **wroght** 1.181, 2.98, 154, 4.720; *wirk . . . thaym wo,* bring sorrow upon those 2.116 [OE. *wyrcan, worhte, wrohte*].

wyrship, worship, *v.* worship 1.71, 3.331 [from OE. *w(e)orþscipe*].

wysdom, *sb.* wisdom, sense 3.161 [OE. *wīsdōm*].

wise, wyse, *sb.* manner, way; *other wise manyfold,* in many other ways 2.54; *on no kyn wyse,* not in any way, not at all 6.229; *on oder wyse,* in some other way 6.273 [OE. *wīse*].

wyse, *adj. as sb.* (the) wise 1.70; *adv.* wisely 6.77 [OE. *wīs; wīse*].

wysely, *adv.* carefully 2.435 [OE. *wīslīce*].

wish, *sb.* wish, desire 2.4 [from OE. *wȳscan*].

wisp, *sb.* wisp 1.439 [cf. WFris. *wisp*].

wist, wyst. See witt.

wist, 2 *pl.imper.* in *wist ye,* be quiet, whisht 1.226 [see *NED.* s. Whist, *v.*[1]].

wyst, *v.* know 5.136 [OE. *witan,* infl. by *wiste,* pa.t.].

wite, wyte, *v.* blame 1.322; *all I wyte you this blame* 6.442 (note) [OE. *wītan*].

with, *prep.* (together) with 3.446, by 2.199, 4.18, 384, 616, by means of 2.101, towards 2.36, with, against 2.138 [OE. *wiþ*].

withall, *adv.* besides, as well 3.419; *prep.* therewith, with (it) 1.238, 3.475, 4.735 [OE. *mid alle,* OE. *wiþ* subst. for *mid*].

within, *adv.* within, inside 2.127, 4.369, 5.101, less 5.257; *prep.* in 2.70 (postponed) [OE. *wiþinnan*].

without(e), withoutt(en), *adv.* outside 2.127; *prep.* without 2.2, 31, 3.194, besides, in addition to 3.383; *cj.* unless 5.242 [OE. *wiþūtan*].

witnes, wytnes, *sb.* witness 3.379, 6.259 [OE. *witnes*].

wit(t), wytt, *sb.* mind, reason 1.300, 5.234, intelligence, understanding 3.143, 6.67; *pl.* wits 3.171, 173, 5.250; *bi my wit,* as I think, in my opinion 2.452, 6.111, by (means of) my wits 3.38 [OE. *witt*].

witt, wyt(t), *v.* know, learn 3.143, 5.418, 6.48; 1 *sg.pres.* **wate** 2.444, 6.367, **watt** 5.487, **wote** 3.69, 6.344; 3 *sg.* **wayte** 4.75; 2 *pl.* **wote** 1.5, 3.243; 3 *pl.* **waytt** 4.226; 1 *sg.pres.subj.* **wytt** 4.468; 1,3 *sg.pa.t.* **wist, wyst** 2.516, 5.181; 2 *pl.* **wyst** 4.196; *pp.* **wyst** 4.93; *wyst ye,* if you knew 4.531; *well wyt ye,* rest assured (of) 5.418, 6.3 [OE. *witan*].

wo, *sb.* woe, misery 2.40; *wo is me this dystres* 3.35 (note); *wo is hir,* unhappy is she 3.181; *wo is hym has*, unhappy is he (who) has 4.8, 393; *wo is hym is oure cok*, unhappy is he (who) is our cock 4.71; *adj.* woeful, miserable 4.87, 540 [OE. *wā*].

wod, *sb.* wood 4.650 [OE. *wudu*].

wode, wood(e), *adj.* mad, furious 1.159, 2.426, 4.373, 5.314; *if thou were wood, and he were wood*, even if you are (he is) furious about it 1.173, 3.134 [OE. *wōd*].

wofull, *adj.* woeful 4.420 [OE. *wā* + *-full*].

wogh, *sb.* evil, harm 2.533 [OE. *wōh*].

wold. See **will**, *v.*

wold, *sb.* command, control; *haue all in wold*, have control of everything 5.92 [OE. *gewald*].

wolfe-skyn, *sb.* wolfskin 4.368 [OE. *wulf* + ON. *skinn*].

wols-hede, *sb.* wolf's-head, i.e. a summons to hunt down an outlaw like a wolf, sentence of outlawry 6.139 [OE. *wulfes-hēafod*].

woman, *sb.* woman 2.30, 4.539; *gen.sg.* **wamans** 4.608, **woman** 4.342, **womans** 4.485; *pl.* **women** 2.208 [OE. *wīfmann, wimman*].

won. See **wyn**, *v.*

won, *pp.* wound, twisted 6.391 [OE. *windan*].

wonder, *sb.* (a) wonder, marvel 2.265, 3.143, 4.83, 6.10, wondering 5.87, distress, grief 5.369; *mans wonder*, prodigy of mankind, monster 2.408; *adj.* wondrous, marvellous 2.496; *adv.* wonderfully 1.231, 3.306 [OE. *wundor*].

wonder, *v.* wonder, marvel; *wonder ... apon*, marvel at 5.504 [OE. *wundrian*].

wonderfull, *adj.* wonderful 5.199 [OE. *wundorful*].

wonderly, *adv.* wonderfully, to a wonderful degree 5.24 [OE. *wundorlīce*].

wone, *sb.* abundance; *in wone*, in plenty 1.116 [ON. *vān*].

wonys, *sb.pl.* (with sg. sense) dwelling 4.526, 5.169, 229, 393; *in wonys*, everywhere, anywhere 5.104; *worthi in wonys*, distinguished among men 6.46 [? as prec.].

wonte, *pp.* wont, accustomed 6.250 [OE. *gewunod*].

wood(e). See **wode**.

word(e), *sb.* word 2.49, 380, something said 3.497; *at a worde*, without more ado, at once 4.212 [OE. *word*].

wore, worne, worship. See **was, were, wyrship**.

worship, *sb.* worship, honour 1.181, 6.201, reverence 5.247 [OE. *w(e)orþscipe*].

worshipfully, *adv.* with honour 5.66 [prec. + OE. *-fullīce*].

worth, woth, *adj.* worth 1.123, 5.165, 6.13 [OE. *w(e)orþ*].

worthi, worthy, *adj.* worthy, noble, distinguished 2.19, 5.24, 6.46, deserving, worthy (of) 3.199 (note), 4.310, 5.426; *were worthi, art worthy to*, deserve to 2.200, 6.256; *superl.* **worthiest, worthyest** 2.489, 5.55, **worthyst** 3.459 [OE. *wyrþig, *w(e)orþig*].

wote, woth. See **witt, worth**.

woth, *sb.* danger 2.416 [ON. *vāði*].

wowyng, *sb.* wooing 4.91; *on wowyng*, a-wooing 4.172 [OE. *wōgung*].

wragers, *sb.pl.* wranglers 3.58 [cf. ME. *wrag*, v.].

wrake, *sb.* harm, injury 2.138 [OE. *wracu*].

wrake, *v.* avenge 5.323; *pp.* **wrokyn** 4.614, 5.493, 6.175 [OE. *wrecan*, infl. by prec.].

wrang, wrong, *adj.* wrong 2.188, 4.658; *sb.* wrong 1.228, 4.208, 6.227, untruth 3.49; *adv.* astray 4.181, 6.52, crookedly 4.380, wrongly, incorrectly 1.224, 6.399 [late OE. *wrang*, from ON. *wrangr*].

wryers, *sb.pl.* quarrelsome people 3.58 (note) [from OE. *wrǣgan*].

wrightry, *sb.* carpentry 2.250 [OE. *wryhta* + OF. *-(e)rie*].

wryng, *v.* wring 3.28; *pres.p.* **wryngand** 2.211; *sb.* 6.237 [OE. *wringan*].

wrythys, 3 *sg.pres.* twists about, changes 4.126 [OE. *wrīþan*].

wrytyng, *sb.* writings, literature 5.201 [OE. *writing*].

wrytys, 3 *sg.pres.* writes 1.427 [OE. *wrītan*].

wroght, wrokyn, wrong. See **wirk, wrake**, *v.*, **wrang**.

wroth, *adj.* wrathful, angry 1.160, 2.36 [OE. *wrāþ*].

yai, ye(e), yei, yey, *adv.* yes, indeed 1.51, 2.370, 3.88, 371, 4.594; (introducing a contemptuous or sarcastic reply) 1.134, 266, 356; *a, ye*, oh, really 4.354 [OE. *gē(a)*].

yare, *adj.* ready, prepared 4.704 [OE. *gearu*].

ye(e). See **yai**.

ye(e), *pron.* 2 *pl.* you 2.155, 397; *acc.dat.*

you 1.406, 2.296; *refl.* yourself 5.436, yourselves 5.449; *gen.* **youre** 3.173, **youres** 5.449; **youreself**, you yourself 6.263 [OE. *gē, ēow, ēower*].

yede, yode, 3 *sg.pa.t.* and 1,2,3 *pl.* went 4.183, 367, 503, 506, 6.312 [OE. *ge-gān, ge-ēode*].

yei, yey. See **yai.**

yelde, *v.* yield up, give up 5.155 [OE. *geldan*].

yelp, *sb.* boast(ing) 2.321 [OE. *gelp*].

yelp, *v.* sing loudly, sing on a high note 3.422 [OE. *gelpan*].

yeme, *v.* have charge of 6.292 [OE. *gēman*].

yerde, *sb.* garden 6.69 [OE. *geard*].

yere, *sb.* year 2.57, 3.99, 4.241; *at yere tyme,* at the proper season of the year 1.200; *none þis yere,* none at all 4.569–70; *of oone yere age,* one year old 5.244 [OE. *gēr*].

yis, *adv.* yes 1.116, 4.328 [OE. *gīse*].

yister-euen, *sb.* yesterday evening 4.382 [OE. *gestrenǣfen*].

yit, *adv.* still 2.359, 3.144, as yet, till now 3.136, also, moreover 5.452, 6.93, again 1.30, all the same, none the less 2.12; *or yit,* or else 1.138, 4.64; *cj.* and yet, but 2.17, 197, 4.138 [OE. *gēt, gīt*].

yode. See **yede.**

yoyll, *sb.* Yule 6.344 [OE. *gēol,* ON. *jól*].

yoman, *sb.* yeoman 1.15; *yoman . . . of the kyng,* royal official 4.201 [? OE. *geongman(n)*].

yond, *adj.* yonder 1.452, 3.321, 4.603, 654, 6.283; *as pron.* that 2.453 [OE. *geond*].

yonder, *adv.* yonder 1.343, 3.322, 5.327 [cf. prec.].

yong, *adj.* young 1.444, 2.397, 4.91, 387, 5.91; *yong or old,* any one, whoever it is 1.372 [OE. *geong, gung*].

you, youre(s), youreself. See **ye(e).**

yrk, *v.* loathe 6.210 [uncertain].

INDEX OF NAMES

For the generic use of personal names see the Glossary.